I would like to dedicate this book to
my grandparents, Elena and Alberto Arellano
and the memory of Maria Luisa Campos and Pedro Villoldo
for their unbounded love and nurturing.

ALBERTO VILLOLDO

I would like to dedicate this book to
Clara Sidermen,
Pearl Dychtwald,
and Jessica Brackman—
three generations of wonderful, supportive,
and loving women.

KEN DYCHTWALD

CONTENTS

ACKNOWLEDGMENTS   ix

INTRODUCTION   xi

I. The Self   1

AGING by Ken Dychtwald   5

SEXUALITY by Lonnie Barbach   25

HUMAN INTELLIGENCE by Jonas Salk   43

HEALING by Alberto Villoldo   59

THE BODY by Michael Murphy   77

THE BRAIN by Karl Pribram   91

PARAPSYCHOLOGY
by Stanley Krippner and Arthur Hastings   105

RELATIONSHIPS by Marilyn Ferguson   121

COMMUNITIES by Carl R. Rogers   135

II. The Culture and Beyond   147

EDUCATION by Jean Houston   151

WORK by Willis Harman   171

LEISURE by Don Mankin   189

POLITICS by Frederik Pohl   207

HEALTH CARE by Rick Carlson   225

ART by Livio Vinardi   241

RELIGION by Harvey Cox   251

CONSCIOUS EVOLUTION
by Barbara Marx Hubbard and Barry McWaters   265

SCIENCE by Timothy Leary   277

NOTES   299

INDEX   309

MILLENNIUM

MILLENNIUM

Glimpses into the 21st Century

Edited by
ALBERTO VILLOLDO
and KEN DYCHTWALD

J. P. Tarcher, Inc.
Los Angeles
Distributed by Houghton Mifflin Company
Boston

Library of Congress Cataloging in Publication Data

Main entry under title.

Millennium: glimpses into the 21st century.

Bibliography: p. 299
Includes index.
1. Twenty-first century—Forecasts—Addresses, essays,
lectures. I. Dychtwald, Ken, 1950–   . II. Villoldo, Alberto.
CB158.M54   303.4   80-53147
ISBN 0-87477-145-5   AACR2

J. P. Tarcher, Inc.
9110 Sunset Blvd.
Los Angeles, CA 90069
Library of Congress Catalog Card No.: 80–53147

Design by Barbara Monahan

MANUFACTURED IN THE UNITED STATES OF AMERICA

D 10 9 8 7 6 5 4 3 2 1

First Edition

ACKNOWLEDGEMENTS

There are many people without whose help this book would never have been conceived or written. First, and most of all, we'd like to thank our editor, Kirsten Grimstad, for her untiring support, commentary, and wise counsel; Jeremy Tarcher, our publisher, for his innovative publishing style and his deep commitment to a more humane vision of the future; Connie Moss for her excellent editorial help; Dick Gunther for his assistance in helping to clarify the initial vision and focus of this project; Lonnie Barbach for her patience and encouragement; Nesta Lowenberg for her continual support, kindness, and love; and finally our thanks to Jean Price and Mickie Denig for their laborious typing and retyping of the manuscript.

The whole universe, after all, is out there waiting to be explored. All of space and time beckons to us. For the moment, voyages of the imagination are the only kind most of us can take; all the more reason, then, to make those voyages as rewarding as possible. Outworn action-plot formulas, clumsy prose, themes that merely recapitulate the themes of older stories not much good in their own rights, stale editorial comments on the sad state of contemporary affairs, and other such unnecessary baggage we try to avoid in these pages. Our goal here is expansion of consciousness: we want the reader to come forth larger than he was before, having seen visions new to his experience.

(**Robert Silverberg,**
New Dimensions III, 1973.)

INTRODUCTION

Frankly, I'm tired of reading the same old stories. My library is filled with thousands of books, most of which express only the most timid and conservative (and often dreary) aspect of each author's ideas. Publicly and in print, our intellectual heroes and heroines will only go so far, never pushing too hard against the imagined boundaries of intellectual credibility. After neatly and cleverly explaining how we got to where we are and how we could have done it differently, time is up. The chapter ends, the lecture is over, the book concludes.

Damn! I say to myself. We were just getting started. I want to know where we go from here. I want more from these people than just their public posture, their "stock," time-tested information. I want to hear more of the uncertain, unproven, risky ideas. I want to hear their dreams and private intuitions. These may turn out to be more accurate than their public projections.

At these moments, my inner urge has been to grab these visionary individuals, lock them in a secluded room, and hijack their hearts and minds off to the future, keeping them there for as long as it takes to learn their deepest fears, passions, and excitements regarding the future evolution of our species.

My questions would be many: Just what is the next step? What comes after automation? Will there be any changes in the human body or mind in our lifetimes? Is it possible that as a species we have not yet come close to realizing our true evolutionary potentials? Might we be standing at the brink of a major leap in human consciousness that could radically change the face of life on earth forever? And if, like the creeping caterpillar, we are only at the larval stage of a more magnificent new life form, what are we becoming? What will we look and feel like in the future? Will our minds have additional capacities in the twenty-first century? Will we still have sex drives? Will aging be abolished? If so, what will become of death? What kind of human relationships will the future bring and how will we get from here to there? What kind of political system could possibly govern the future human? What role will religion, love, and beauty play in our lives? Might we even separate from our "womb," planet Earth, and travel to other solar systems throughout the universe where we would breed entirely new civilizations?

In a sense, *Millennium: Glimpses Into the 21st Century* is the fulfillment of this fantasy. With this volume, we wanted to gather some of the most visionary scientists, philosophers, and futurists of our time to let their private intuitions run free in addressing these questions.

Yet, for all of my future-related zealousness, I'm not naive enough to expect that anyone can actually predict the future. I do believe, however, that there are people among us whose level of wisdom and insight move them just a bit farther out along the frontier of knowledge than the rest of us. When these people pursue their ideas out as far as possible, squinting their eyes and straining to see what lies on the farthest horizon, their views and visions may not only bring a bright focus on the normal problems and issues of today but may also illuminate the unknown, uncharted territories of tomorrow.

Throughout history, human development has consistently been inspired and propelled by those people who have the insight to perceive some aspect of the future world, as well as the courage to communicate these visions to others. These evolutionary adventurers are not unlike the early frontiersmen and explorers who ventured out past the bounds of normal behavior and the known physical world to risk a glimpse of unknown realms. Some of these explorers met success, others discovered nothing new, some met with failure, while others never lived to communicate what they found. Yet human development in part does seem to depend on this continual process of growth, expansion, discovery, and therefore on the spirits and actions of those willing to throw grappling hooks high over the wall of tomorrow.

Of course, the history of future forecasts contains a fair measure of ultimately inaccurate stabs in the dark . . .

> In the early 1950's, when the first pioneering Univac 1 computer was delivered to the U.S. Bureau of the Census, the experts in the new field of computing machines sat down and predicted a market for computers of all types soon reaching several dozen. They added that by 1970, there would be no less than 100 computers in the United States. In 1970, the American computer population fell just short of 200,000 units. . . . Similarly, a Midwest utility offered Henry Ford a good job if he would stop working with his gasoline engine and devote himself to something useful. . . . Lord Rutherford, who was once the

world's leading expert on nuclear physics, maintained until his death in 1937, that the concept of releasing atomic energy was "pure moonshine." (Paul Dickson, *The Future File*, 1977.)

. . . we are also witness to those rare moments when true visionary insight, such as that displayed by Jules Verne, H. G. Wells, Aldous Huxley, and Arthur Clarke, reaches deep inside us, grabs hold of our spirits, and shakes us to the core of our being. While we can't be certain in advance that any forecast or speculation will prove true and accurate, we can allow the imaginative thinkers among us an opportunity to finish their lectures, write the next chapters, complete the imaginative epilog to their books, and answer some of the less certain, riskier questions so many of us are asking.

In 1978, when it first occurred to me to put together such a collection of illuminating glimpses into the coming century, I felt that I was lacking one thing—a copilot. Frankly, the project seemed too large and unruly for just one person. In addition, I had this crazy feeling that if my mind were to be venturing off into the third millennium for a while, I wanted someone to be with me, someone whose interest, intelligence, and enthusiasm would inspire and support my own. Coincidentally, while lecturing at a conference in Washington, D.C., I happened to share my interest with a fellow psychologist and author, Alberto Villoldo. As soon as we began to talk about our fascination with the unknown and the farthest reaches of human experience, it was clear to both of us that we were as one mind on this theme. For the first time, in fact, I felt I had met someone whose life experience, style of behavior, and areas of curiosity so paralleled my own that I began to wonder if he were joining me in my venture or I in his. And, peculiarly, he was thinking the same thing. Needless to say, we agreed that this project was now "ours."

As we talked, we realized we shared a disappointment with the gizmo and gadget orientation of traditional futuristics and were troubled by the fact that few people in the human development fields were willing to share their private feelings about the future of our species. And perhaps most importantly, we both felt an unquenchable urge to deepen our understanding of the possibilities for human growth and evolution that we may encounter as we become citizens of the twenty-first century, especially in view of the gloomy forecasts that have begun to inundate the media.

After agreeing on the basic concept, we set out to locate the contributors, talking and arguing over which people and viewpoints should share this journey with us, as though we were carefully staffing a star ship. We were sure of one thing: this book would focus on the person, individually and collectively. Without denying the absolute relevance and importance of themes related to technological development and the utilization of world resources, we wanted this book to look at the other, less considered aspect of planetary growth: true human potential. And so we looked for future-minded scientists and philosophers with a decidedly human-centered orientation. In addition, since we felt that so many of the books and studies about the future have projected a negative bias, we were eager to staff our crew with adventurers who smiled a lot . . . and whose perspectives were positive and constructive.

In *Millennium: Glimpses Into the 21st Century*, we have attempted to present an exciting alternative view of the future. In this volume, eighteen of the world's most imaginative and visionary scientists and philosophers have set out to uncover and explore the key human qualities that have given birth to life as we know it today and may very well generate an array of transformational possibilities in the near and distant future. It is a book about *human evolution*. If there is a common theme that runs through all the chapters, it is that we as a species are far from having completed our evolutionary development. We do not believe that the human race has reached an evolutionary dead end. Rather, we all share a deep feeling that, whatever the human adventure is really about, instead of winding down, it is perhaps just truly beginning. Just as the first water-dwelling creature poking his nose up through the liquid surface to get a good sniff of fresh air was a prelude to evolutionary transformation, so too are a growing number of us pushing beyond our limits and reaching deeper within ourselves, and in so doing, perhaps moving a bit closer to fulfilling our ultimate human destinies. While we are all aware that the present preoccupation with material development will probably continue to yield more and more extraordinary technologies, we feel that we are also on the verge of a profound awakening of our inner selves. For the farther we reach into outer space, the closer we are brought to the realization that the realms of the human body, mind, and spirit are at least as vast, unexplored, and untamed as the deepest reaches of the universe.

Ken Dychtwald
October 1980

Part I

THE SELF

THE PACE OF CHANGE IN TODAY'S WORLD HAS ALL BUT BAN-
ished traditional notions of the self and its purpose and meaning. The
currently vast market for personal growth literature alone attests to a burgeoning preoccupation with the quest for individual identity. The options
that await us are broad, spanning the spectrum from returning to our
ancestral roots to changing our self-image with the seasons of our lives. Out
of the creative fusion of personal history with personal growth a new self is
already emerging that embraces change as its challenge and its strength.

We begin with the many aspects of the self projected into the next
millennium. Ken Dychtwald opens the volume with a new look at aging.
By the end of the twentieth century one of every two Americans will be
over 50 years old. And, by the year 2020, Ken points out, 50 percent of our
population will be "senior citizens." America is coming of age, he claims,
and with it a new scenario incorporating life extension and meaningful
adulthood is unfolding. Next, Lonnie Barbach sketches out the widening
horizons of human sexuality and sexual relationships that are now already a
significant part of our lives. As women and men come to rely less on socially
defined sexual roles, many of the old assumptions and restrictions will fall
away, opening up relationships to a greater range of possibility. Same-sex
relationships, serial monogamy, and old/young coupling (among others)
will begin to be seen in the same light as more conventional relationships.
The forecast is nothing short of a new and far more encompassing notion of
pleasure, communication, and closeness.

Jonas Salk takes on the hefty topic of the future intelligence of our
species. The criterion for successful evolution has changed, he points out,

from the survival of the fittest to the survival of the wisest. Although best known for the discovery of the polio vaccine, Jonas has been a catalyst of leading-edge ideas in biology, philosophy, psychology, and a dozen other fields in the behavioral and applied sciences. Alberto Villoldo focuses on the evolving art of healing. The future of the art lies in discovering our capacities for *self*-regulation and *self*-regeneration. The time is at hand when we can train our brains to produce the chemicals it needs to heal the body, as well as developing states of optimal health, of well-being, and of ecstasy.

Is the body capable of continually surpassing its previous achievements? Michael Murphy's chapter indicates that indeed runners may break the three-minute-mile barrier sometime in the next century, and that human capabilities are virtually unbounded. Karl Pribram charts the three major breakthroughs that have revolutionized our understanding of the brain and its function from a hierarchically organized system to a unified system in which each part reflects the whole. Pribram's holographic theory of memory has played a leading role in furthering this dimension of understanding. Stanley Krippner and Arthur Hastings confront us with the possibility that in the future parapsychology may be used as a military weapon, as well as for fascinating applications in the area of public health. Casting a visionary eye on love relationships, Marilyn Ferguson discerns an emerging pattern in which rigid and fearful clutching to the status quo is giving way to relationships that support each individual's growth and change—however terrifying that may be. Carl Rogers provides the bridge from the individual standing alone to the forming of community and raises the question of whether a true planetary community is feasible in the future.

Regardless of whether the scenarios by the authors come true in the next two years or in the next two hundred, there can be no doubt that we are in the throes of change. What we refer to as The Self is being redefined today, and will be undergoing drastic change in the next decade. For some the transition will be smooth and graceful, perhaps like the way a caterpillar becomes a butterfly or a snake sloughs off dead skin that is no longer needed. For others, perhaps, the change will be harder, like the story told to us by the late Alan Watts, of a kind of monkey traps used in Asia:

> A coconut is hollowed out and attached by a rope to a tree. At the bottom of the coconut a small slit is made and some sweet food is placed inside. The hole at the bottom is just big enough for the monkey to slide in his open hand, but does not allow for a closed fist to pass out. The monkey smells the sweets, reaches in with his hand to grasp the food and is then unable to withdraw it. The clenched fist won't pass through the opening. When the hunters come, the mon-

key becomes frantic but cannot get away. There is no one keeping that monkey captive. But so strong is the force of greed in the mind that it is a rare monkey which can let go. All we need do is open our hands, let go of our self, our attachments, and be free.

Ken Dychtwald is a psychologist, author, and pioneer in the fields of human development, health promotion, and gerontology. Born in 1950, Dychtwald has been labeled the "wunderkind of the human potential movement" by the San Francisco Examiner and has been actively involved in designing and implementing programs for human development for over a decade. Early in his career he served as a seminar leader at the Esalen Institute and as a special consultant on human development to the Change in Liberal Education Project, a division of the Association for American Colleges and Universities. He went on to become a codirector of the newly formed SAGE Project, a position he held for five years during which time SAGE developed an international reputation as a highly successful preventive health and longevity program for the elderly, funded by the National Institute of Mental Health in Washington, D.C. As part of his responsibilities at SAGE, Dr. Dychtwald helped design and develop nearly one hundred similar age-related programs and courses at health centers, hospitals, and universities throughout the United States and Canada. In 1977, Dychtwald became the founding president of the Association for Humanistic Gerontology which serves as an international network of people and programs dedicated to positive approaches to aging and programs for the elderly.

In addition to lecturing and conducting seminars nationwide on aging, longevity, optimal performance, health promotion, and life-design, he is currently president of a consulting company, Ken Dychtwald and Associates, and serves as an advisor and consultant to government, industry, and media. Dr. Dychtwald is also an adjunct instructor in the areas of psychology, gerontology, and health-related sciences at several colleges and universities.

His publications include Bodymind *(translated into several foreign languages),* The Aging of America *(forthcoming), and numerous articles in professional journals and popular magazines.*

Ken Dychtwald's deep involvement for nearly a decade in the field of aging, coupled with his major contributions to the area of human development, mark him as a young gerontologist with one foot in the present and one foot in the twenty-first century. In the following chapter he explains the age-related social and biological contexts in which we are presently involved and lays out a variety of scenarios for the way in which life, aging, and death may become transformed by the dawn of the third millennium.

KEN DYCHTWALD
AGING

Aging . . . All too frequently when we think or hear about aging, we assume that the less said or thought, the better. In this day and age, with our culture's extreme youth orientation, many of us would prefer to assume that aging doesn't exist . . . and that we will all remain twenty-three forever. Yet, a deeper examination of age-related issues reveals a fascinating, many-sided picture of this natural and, at least until now, inevitable process. For while most people only associate aging with wrinkles and graying hair, there are actually six different aspects of aging.

THE MANY FACES OF AGING

Chronological aging is the most obvious form of aging and the one that remains indifferent to our whims, desires and discoveries. This form of aging is dependent only on the passing of time. Inexorably, we become a little older each day. This is not to say that we become more or less healthy, more or less beautiful or more or less aware . . . simply one day older. For in chronological time there is no absolute relationship between age and health, beauty, or knowledge; there is only the steady ticking of the clock and the continual accumulation of minutes, days, and years. So, twenty-five years after our birth, we become twenty-five years old . . . fifty years and we celebrate our fiftieth birthday . . . and so on. While many people have come to associate particular psycho-social, physical, or social import to various stages in life, none of these characteristics are relevant within the purely chronological framework.

Spiritual aging is usually considered the process wherein the deepest aspects of one's self develop, mature, ripen, and blossom. While spiritual age is not necessarily equal to chronological age, it is frequently the case that the more years and experiences one has and the more lessons learned from these experiences, the more opportunities for spiritual development. Spiritual aging is usually thought of as an extremely positive form of aging and it comes as a great compliment when one is told that he or she is an enlightened "old soul."

Emotional aging is the normal developmental process of moving through the various experiences and transitions of our lives. Throughout this slow and sometimes painful process we continually redefine and renegotiate our beliefs, priorities, and motivating passions. Emotional aging frequently runs concurrent with chronological aging and is usually thought of in terms of various life stages. Hence, the baby becomes a child, who then becomes a teenager, who then becomes a young adult . . . and on and on until he or she eventually becomes an elder. In regard to the overall context of aging, emotional aging is thought of as a very positive experience and those people who are most emotionally mature are frequently thought of as being "wise," "sage-like" and "worldly." Yet, not everyone ages emotionally at the same rate and some people live a great many years without ever fully developing and cultivating the emotional self. This is a bit like the employee who, after ten years of below-adequate work with a company, feels that he has now accumulated ten years of experience; while in reality, he may have only had one year of experience, repeated ten times.

Mental or intellectual aging occurs as an individual accumulates knowledge or information. This process can be facilitated through classroom learning, on-the-job experience or simply through day to day involvements. Intellectual aging can be aided by the passing of years but is not necessarily dependent on clock time for its cultivation. In fact, there are many ten- and fifteen-year-olds walking around today who have more mental development and sophistication than either their parents or grandparents. In this sense, they are more mentally "aged" than those who are chronologically, emotionally or even spiritually older. Like the previous two forms of aging, mental aging is usually regarded positively.

Social aging refers to our age-related roles as defined by society's beliefs, priorities and expectations. Since this form of aging is socially rather than individually oriented, it tends to change as cultural demographics and lifestyles alter. For example, in pre-industrial America, before the concept of retirement at sixty-five became popular, people acquired greater authority as they grew older. By age seventy, for example, an individual might feel as though he or she had arrived at a wonderful stage in life . . . a time to assume the role of family head, take charge of community decisions and enjoy the fruits of a long, full life. However, as

America became more industrial and urban, the importance of the elderly family member declined significantly and soon, the older one became, the less he or she was able to fully and meaningfully participate in familial, work and community activities.

In contrast, in many contemporary Asian countries the older people get, the more social status they accrue. In India it is believed that life begins at fifty-three and we see that people yearn to live to ripe old ages so that they can arrive at the noble elder position in their life. This is a far cry from the system in America where the older people get, the more they're disregarded and the more they wish they were still young. In addition, it is important to note that while at present the social context of aging is fraught with negativity, this particular aspect of aging is nevertheless still capable of changing and redefining itself.

The last aspect of aging is the one that usually comes to mind when we think of growing older. *Physical aging* is probably the one dimension of the aging process that nobody looks forward to and that is almost always thought of in negative terms. And for good reason. When we think of growing older we usually think of loss . . . loss of health, loss of sexual potency, loss of beauty, loss of coordination, loss of strength, and loss of vitality. And since these are exactly the qualities that most of us treasure and enjoy, it stands to reason that the idea of losing these attributes would frighten and trouble us.

The concern over physical aging is certainly not just a modern phenomenon and in many ways the entire history of civilization has been a continual struggle against the forces of physical aging and toward the ever-elusive "fountain of youth." In fact, the various attempts throughout history to prolong youth and health seem more like a sampling from "Ripley's Believe It or Not" than a testimony to human intelligence and reason.

According to Joel Kurtzman and Phillip Gordon in *No More Dying*,

> The search for a way to restore youth and vigor and extend life goes back long before Isabella and Ferdinand dispatched Ponce de Leon to find the Fountain of Youth. In an attempt to lengthen life and increase strength, the Egyptians and Romans ate garlic in massive quantities. The emperors of China during the time of Confucius hired alchemists, who prescribed precise doses of gold and mercury—considered everlasting because they appeared not to tarnish, although mercury is in fact highly poisonous—to extend their lives. Alchemy spread to Europe, and during the Middle Ages such men as Francis Bacon, the British philosopher and author, and Paracelsus, the Swiss-born "father of modern medicine," practiced it, seeking the magical Philoso-

pher's Stone that would transmute lead into gold and mortals into immortals. Many Europeans also tried plant remedies such as the root of the mandrake plant . . . a narcotic (and also a poison), the mandrake root was thought to restore sexual potency. Insects were also popular anti-aging remedies; Spanish Fly, made from the Blister Beetle, was not only considered an aphrodisiac but also a sexual rejuvenator, although in fact it did nothing but produce tremendous irritation and itching in urethra and bladders.[1]

The enthusiastic and sometimes bizarre degree to which humankind has continually searched for ways of preserving youth and health certainly has not diminished in fervor or imagination during the twentieth century. For even in this "civilized" time, zealous gerontologists and health "experts" throughout the world have laid youth-sustaining claims to such methods and procedures as: the transplantation of monkey and goat testicles, cell therapy involving the swallowing of whole chicken embryos, bloodletting, blistering, and castration to name just a few.

For the purposes of this article and in order to examine the most profound and dramatic aspects of the present and future of aging, I will be limiting my discussion to the social and physical characteristics of aging. Of all the various categories of aging, these are the only two that really stand to change considerably during the coming years. Whereas the chronological, spiritual, emotional, and intellectual characteristics of aging will, in all likelihood, maintain their descriptive identities, the future does seem to hold unimagined discoveries and revisions regarding the length of time that humans will be living as well as the social context in which this mass longevity may occur.

In addition, in order that this discussion maintain a sense of focus and proportion, I will deal primarily with aging as it exists now and may develop in the future of the United States.

THE AGING OF AMERICA: A PERIOD OF TRANSITION

As a culture we are presently aging very rapidly. Because of such recent, radical lifestyle changes as limited population growth, redefined male/female roles, the breakdown of the nuclear family, and significant advances in sanitation, food distribution and health care, America is quickly shifting from being a youth oriented culture to one in which the fastest growing segments of the population are adults and elders. In the past one hundred years, the total U.S. population has increased by a factor of five, but the over-sixty-five segment has multiplied an astounding eighteen times.[2] The extraordinary rate of increase in our older population is matched in intensity only by the striking decline in the number of citizens who are under twenty-five years of age, a group which has already begun to shrink by more than 630,000 each year.[3] There are presently 50,000,000 Americans over the age of fifty, and 23,000,000 of these have already celebrated their sixty-fifth birthday.[4] If current trends continue we can expect that by the end of the twentieth century one of every two Americans will be over fifty and nearly one-fourth of the population will be over sixty-five. By the year 2020, every other American may well be a senior citizen.[5]

As a result of this dramatic population shift, in the coming years we will witness major social changes related to aging and old age. Just as a suit of clothing begins to tear and stretch as its wearer grows and gets bigger, so will all of our cultural values and institutions be forced to alter and shift to accommodate the aging of America. The early signs of this transformation are already popping up around us: the laying off of thousands of grade and high school teachers; the closing down of hundreds of colleges and universities due to decreasing enrollment; heightened interest in lifelong learning; raised public consciousness about midlife crises; older models and movie stars in the media; a shifting of health care systems away from childhood-related sickness to age-related disease, with preventive health an increasingly popular theme; enhanced interest in leisure and recreational activities for the mature consumer; a rash of new television shows, movies, and magazines focused on the needs, interests, and potentials of adults and elders such as "Over Easy," "Going in Style," and *Prime Time Magazine.*

As more people are realizing that they will themselves grow older, we are beginning to see an aggressive movement to uncover and uproot many of the current ageist images and attitudes. Certainly the emergence of the Gray Panthers as a powerful national coalition, and the swelling of the American Association of Retired Persons to over twelve million members mark the beginning of this irreversible trend toward a new image of aging in America. And we can be sure that when Ralph Nader and Jane Fonda approach their fiftieth birthdays, they will be outspoken campaigners for the right to a healthy, long life!

In addition, all of the institutions that exist to support the psychological, social, political, economic, educational, health, and spiritual needs of our culture will be forced to shift their focus away from a narrow youth orientation to one in which the entire age spectrum is respected, considered, and nourished appropriately. Although hard to imagine, it may soon be an honor and a privilege to be older.

IMAGES OF AGING

Until recently, of course, few people paid substantial attention to the needs, potentials, and concerns of the adult and elder years. Prior to the twentieth century, life expectancy was less than fifty years, so most people saw no reason to plan for old age—just as American society in general has done little to prepare for its present and future demographic conditions. American lifestyle had always been characterized by a continual burgeoning of youth and the predictable death of its adults around their fiftieth birthdays. Little did our parents and grandparents expect that advances in health care might one day allow them to live twenty or thirty years longer than they anticipated...nor did they assume that factors such as zero population growth, depleted natural resources, and altered lifestyles would shrink the youthful segment of society to the point where adults and elders will soon no longer be in the minority, but will solidly plant themselves as a growing national majority comprising both sexes, all races, and all socioeconomic orientations.

Average life expectancy now stands at 74 years—70 for men and 77 for women—and may very well be elevated to 100-plus years by the turn of this century.

Historically, attitudes toward aging and the elderly, toward age-related social roles, have emerged and been developed through direct intergenerational contact. Until recently, families and towns were set up so that each person had ample opportunity to interact with his or her parents, grandparents, aunts, uncles, neighbors, and older relatives of friends. Older community members were often well known and usually the most knowledgeable about all aspects of life—from child rearing to cow-milking. In addition, since there were very few elders in proportion to the general population, growing older was frequently associated with a rise in importance, stature, and potential for significant social contribution. However, recent changes in work, family and social patterns have radically altered this format. Many people get married later in life and thus some children never get to meet their grandparents. Many younger people move away from home—to attend college, to get married, or to strike out on their own—and thus disengage themselves from active involvement in the lives of their parents and grandparents.

With the advent of retirement communities, some elders choose to isolate themselves from young people; similarly, young and middle aged people select appropriate age ghettos in which to live. Mandatory retirement, assembly line factories, and large, impersonal stores and businesses have also eliminated many of the small shops, working teams, and apprenticeship models that once provided a great deal of intergenerational involvement and support.

With the growing absence of meaningful involvement of older people in all aspects of American lifestyles, the shaping of most attitudes toward the elderly has fallen increasingly into the hands of government agencies, commercial media and profit-making corporations, none of which have proven themselves effective at enhancing the quality of life for this segment of the population. And since few older people are involved in the important social policy decisions made on their behalf, they are repeatedly neglected in exactly those situations where they might benefit the most from humane and fair representation. This sad point is exemplified by the fact that although this country grosses almost a trillion dollars a year, we spend only 4.2 percent of it toward aiding the old, compared to England and France which spend 6.7 percent and 7 percent of their gross national products respectively.[6] And although the elderly comprise 12 percent of the total population, only 3 percent of the faces we see on our television screens belong to older people.

In addition, most of America's elderly suffer from dangerously low levels of mental and physical health. Throughout life we are told that "when you have your health you have everything!" Yet as we grow older it seems increasingly difficult to maintain the basic vitality, fortitude, and independence that are essential to health and long life.

This situation is compounded by the embarrassing fact that few doctors, nurses, or counselors in America know very much about the physical, mental, or emotional needs of the adult and elder populations. Nearly all of our present institutions and methods for health care are almost exclusively directed toward the acute sicknesses of youth and must now refocus to the special concerns and chronic degenerative diseases of middle and old age.

According to Dr. Robert Butler, Director of the National Institute of Aging:

> The majority of older people can't afford proper medical care; doctors and health personnel are not trained to deal with their unique problems; their medical conditions are not considered interesting to teaching institutions; and they are stereotyped as bothersome, cantankerous and complaining patients. Direct prejudices exist. . . . Professionally, physicians are uninterested in the aspect of medicine most crucial to the old; the care of chronic conditions. . . . American medicine takes an extremely narrow view of acute illnesses. . . . Since chronic conditions are by nature irreversible (though nonetheless treatable) doctors tend to view them with despair and even nihilism.[7]

Many contemporary critics of our present health care system suggest that a majority of diseases and problems related to aging could be prevented if only our health care providers were better acquainted with the unique nature of age-related disease.[8] For now that we have replaced infant mortality, infectious disease, and the plagues as the primary causes of death with lifestyle-related disorders such as heart disease, cancer, arthritis, and diabetes, it is becoming strikingly obvious that very few people actually die from old age. Instead, most of our adult and elder populations are being slowly drained of health, vitality, and life by stress, chemical pollutants and contaminants, lack of proper nutrition and exercise, and the loneliness, anomie, and frustration that comes from being ostracized from the mainstream of cultural life.

Discerning the true relationship between health, lifestyle, and aging is a profound issue, for in the final analysis, most people don't really seem to be bothered by the simple fact of growing older. Instead, what is most frightening is the loss of social status that has come to be associated with the passing of years, and the sad decline in health which has historically been considered an inevitable aspect of aging.

TOWARD A NEW IMAGE OF AGING

But, what if we were able to eliminate disease and age-related deterioration of the body and mind? What if people could grow older and maintain their youthful vigor and beauty? Since disease is the primary cause of premature death (most gerontological researchers tell us that the natural human life-span is 120–150 years),[9] what if there were some extraordinary advances in the various sciences of the body and mind that could extend human life-span? Instead of living only sixty or seventy short years, what if we each could have one or two hundred full years of vigorous life? What if our belief in the impossibility of life extension is just an example of human skepticism and nearsightedness?

A story about R. Buckminster Fuller—now in his eighties—illustrates this idea. Apparently when Fuller was thirty-six he decided to commit suicide. By his own standards, his life had not turned out much of a success. His marriage was on the rocks, but most important, by his calculations, he only had a few more years to live. For men born in his era, life expectancy was only forty-two. So, seeing himself in the twilight of his life, Bucky decided to end it all. Needless to say, his attempt at suicide was unsuccessful and he has lived to see countless extraordinary developments in the world . . . a primary one being the continual elevation of life expectancy. Although many of us are too young to appreciate what Bucky has learned, his story is a fresh reminder that the future may hold unimaginable discoveries that could profoundly affect each of our lives in ways we haven't even begun to consider.

While most futurists turn their sights and research attention to faster ships and smaller micro-chips, a growing legion of gerontological researchers have made their goal the eliminating of aging. And, because of numerous recent discoveries, we are closer than ever before to truly understanding the secrets of aging. As the pace of research accelerates, we may soon find that our new understanding of the aging process will allow us access to a variety of methods for controlling disease, perhaps even reversing the aging process forever. If this occurs, we may be the first generation of "Homo Longevus," or "long-lived humans." Whereas our ancestors could only dream of an extended life-span, we may soon be able to live a great many years in the absence of disease and deterioration. The eternal quest for a long, healthy life characterized by an active, productive, socially meaningful, and sexually potent lifestyle may soon be within reach.

THEORIES OF AGING

Although the field of gerontology is still in its infancy and our understanding of the aging process is far from complete, seven general viewpoints have emerged that collectively represent the current state of knowledge.

One theory that has gained great popularity in recent years is the *stress* theory of human aging. Pioneered by Dr. Hans Selye, who is internationally renowned for his work on the relationship between stress and disease, this theory holds that the body's replaceable cells, constantly abused by stress, improper nutrition, lack of fresh air, insufficient exercise, and excessive toxins are forced to use up their longevity potential decades before nature has intended.[10] As was shown by Dr. Leonard Hayflick in his classic experiments in the 1950s, most human cells can duplicate and replace themselves only a finite number of times before they lose this capacity and die. Not unlike the metaphorical nine lives of a cat, each human cell has fifty lives, that is, approximately fifty duplications before the cell automatically shuts down and dies.[11]

How we choose to stretch these lives out over time is largely related to the way we live and how we care for our health. As Selye points out, the combination of stressful living with unhealthy lifestyles can serve to speed up the cellular aging process considerably, leading to disease and death long before the true biological potential has been realized.

The *DNA*, or the *error catastrophe*, theory has been proposed by a variety of researchers, among them Dr. Leslie Orgel of the Salk Institute in

San Diego and Dr. F. Marott Sinex of Boston University School of Medicine.[12] This theory holds that the cause of aging lies in the DNA molecule, the long twisted double chain of atoms found in the nucleus of every cell believed to contain the blueprints for all biological processes. It is the DNA molecule that manufactures RNA molecules, which in turn are responsible for manufacturing the protein enzymes necessary for bodily growth and health. As a result of a variety of factors such as pollution, radiation, cigarette smoking, or just plain biological "errors," DNA molecules gradually lose their ability to reproduce themselves accurately, thereby malforming the RNA, which in turn confuses the manufacture of protein enzymes. Cell deterioration and disease are the outcomes, a process destined to accelerate until the body has lost its capacity to operate with a necessary level of organismic law and order.

A third important theory of aging, called the *free radical* theory, has been proposed by Dr. Denham Harman of the University of Nebraska College of Medicine.[13] Free radicals are parts of molecules that have broken loose from their parent molecule home due to radiation, chemical pollutants, and undigested fats. Likened to biological "rapists," these highly unstable units race throughout the molecule ecosystem and wreak havoc on anything that gets in their path. Eating and smashing their way through the body, they tear, split, and mutate every kind of cellular tissue. They are particularly dangerous if they join with DNA or RNA molecules, for as I previously explained, damage to these key biological ingredients can disrupt the body's essential mechanisms for health and revitalization.

The *crosslinkage* theory of aging was developed by Dr. John Bjorksten while he was working as a biochemist for Ditto copying machines. While studying the unavoidable deterioration of the copier's gelatin film, he noticed that the wearing out of this film was a process very similar to that of the stiffening and aging of human joints and muscles. He discovered that the wearing out of these tissues was due to the formation of chemical bridges, called crosslinkages, between proteins. These bridges occur when an amino acid of one molecule combines with an amino acid in another, forming one large and extremely awkward molecule. The new molecule isn't as efficient as either of the former molecules, and the fragile bridge that exists between its two parts seriously interferes with the production of RNA by DNA, in turn preventing the production of vitally needed proteins. Bjorksten believes that crosslinkages are caused by a variety of common pollutants, such as lead and tobacco smoke.[14]

The *neurotransmitter* theory places the source of aging deep within the brain. This theory is based on a recognition of the body's need continually to achieve and maintain a natural level of homeostasis.[15]

According to researcher Dr. Caleb Finch of the Andrus Gerontology Center at the University of Southern California, the most important elements in attaining homeostasis are the two major regulatory systems—the endocrine and nervous. Paying particular attention to the functioning of the hypothalamus which controls many of our basic functions—including sleep, thirst, hunger, sexual drive, body water and salts balance, body temperature, blood pressure, and hormone release—this view of aging assumes that physical decline is due to the body's inability to maintain homeostasis, normally regulated through endocrine and brain control. Because of the essential role that the hypothalamus plays in this process, its breakdown or degeneration can cause a complete disruption of the body's natural regeneration processes, eventually leading to disease, aging, and death.

Another theory of aging is the *immunologic* theory.[16] According to Dr. Roy Walford of UCLA, its principal proponent, the major components of the body's natural immune system are two types of white blood cells, "B" cells and "T" cells. B cells are primarily concerned with fighting bacteria and viruses by releasing appropriate antibodies into the bloodstream, while the main job of T cells is to attack and destroy cells foreign to the body such as transplant and cancer cells. For reasons not presently understood, the body's immunological system sometimes breaks down and becomes less able to rid the body of harmful agents and therefore less able to deter aging. In addition, when the immunological system degenerates in this fashion, its capacity for discrimination is diminished, creating a situation in which the body's own disease fighting system turns against itself and kills healthy cell tissue. According to Walford, the gradual deterioration and degeneration of the body's immune system is at the root of most age-related sickness and breakdown.

The last major theory of aging, and one which has become increasingly popular in recent years, is the *psychogenic* theory. According to two of its most outspoken proponents, myself[17] and the late Wilhelm Reich,[18] there are many instances where premature aging, disease, and even death occur when there is no purely biological basis for bodily breakdown. In these instances, it appears that the mind has actually influenced the body in such a way as to create or generate real states of illness, bodily malfunction, and biological degeneration. Although the scientific evidence to support this theory is just beginning to accumulate, the notion that the mind can affect physical states has been observed in such phenomena as hypnosis, Voodoo, and the unusual forms of sorcery practiced by Australian aboriginal magicians. In these contexts, it is believed that deep within the unconscious mind lives an awareness and control of all biological processes. In normal states of consciousness, this control is utilized in a productive fashion, wherein the mind maintains and coordinates basic bodily functions such as breathing, respiration, and nerve and glandular activity. However, when the unconscious mind alters its usual program, either as a result of some profound suggestion (as in hypnosis or voodoo) or deep distress (such as the loss of a loved one, or a traumatic failure), these biological processes which insure the health and liveliness of the individual can become disrupted, leading to instant pain, disease, or even death.

While we are accustomed to thinking of these kinds of events in supernatural terms, they are actually quite common and can frequently be seen in everyday activities. For example, observe how school children become mildly sick the day before a test and then well again when friends come over to play. One need only examine the psychosocial information underlying most age-related diseases such as cancer, arthritis, and cardio-vascular disease to notice how they most frequently manifest during periods of severe depression, emotional negativity, and social alienation. [19]

Although these seven theories of aging may seem disparate, they collectively suggest several basic notions regarding physical aging. First, the process of aging is at work throughout one's life and the effect of aging appears to be cumulative rather than being an isolated event. Second, it seems, at present, that although few—if any—people actually live past 120 or 130 years, the human organism does have the genetic capacity to do so. At this time, chronic degenerative diseases are the major form of death-related illness. Since such diseases are lifestyle related, the individual has a profound capacity to influence his health, and therefore his longevity potential. In addition to being related to individual lifestyle choices, health and aging can be negatively affected by environmental stimulation such as pollutants, contaminants, noise, and artificial lighting. Third, although the genetic information that predisposes the human organism to certain diseases and a specific life span has historically been fixed, it may be possible to alter the course of aging by adjusting the genetic code. Finally, the rate a person ages and the disease patterns he or she will experience are not purely biological events. Instead, they are deeply connected to his or her psychological, social, and spiritual position and context.

THE FUTURE OF AGING: PROLONGEVITY

While we can only speculate about what the near and distant future may hold in the way of anti-aging miracles, my own research and observations lead me to believe that by the dawn of the 21st century each or all of the following areas could present the information and/or technology that could change the face of aging forever.

Traditional Medicine

Dr. Robert Butler, the director of the National Institute of Aging in Washington, D.C., feels that as much as 80 percent of the degenerative disease that older people suffer, such as arthritis, diabetes, respiratory ailments, and cardiovascular disease, could be prevented or eliminated if our medical and health care systems were more effectively attuned to age-related disease.

At present, the aging individual is all too frequently poorly or improperly diagnosed and then left to wade through a continually thickening mire of drugs, hospital visits, and humiliating treatment. Even today, when elders make up more than 12 percent of the American population, the health care system is still embarrassingly ill-equipped to study, diagnose, and treat the mental and physical needs of this growing segment of our population. However, with expected improvement and advances in this system, the average life expectancy could very well be elevated by as much as twenty years, accompanied of course by a radical decline in age-related morbidity.[20] Or, according to Dr. Ernest L. Wynder, President of the American Health Foundation, "It should be the function of medicine to have people die young as late as possible."

Energy Medicine

In recent years, there has been a growing recognition of the limits of traditional medicine with its extreme emphasis on pathology and acute disease as well as its reliance on drugs and surgery as the primary tools for treatment. While this materially oriented allopathic system is still capable of making enormous contributions, many critics such as Rick Carlson, Ivan Illych, and Robert Mendelson[21] call for the development of new, alternative systems of medicine. Energy medicine is one of these systems. This approach to health care includes the collective body of knowledge and practice wherein methods such as bio-feedback, meditation, acupuncture, visualization, psychic healing, and yoga are utilized to harmonize and balance the various physical, mental, and energetic processes of the organism in such a way as to diminish the impact of disease while simultaneously upgrading all aspects of health.[22] Within this context, it is believed that just as the mind has the capacity to create disease, so does it also have the power to consciously assist the body in its healing processes. Additionally, practitioners of energy medicine have come to recognize that the human organism is not just a collection of bones and muscles, but also a reflection of mind, emotions, and spirit, and therefore the whole person must be considered and included in the healing process.

While its potential is just being glimpsed for the first time by western scientists, there is a growing belief that continued development of this approach to medicine could lead to a time in the near future when all disease will be treated or prevented with mental or energy-related methods.

Organ Transplantation

Organ transplantation is another emerging area that could very well help to diminish the effects of age-related disease and add many healthy years to our lives.[23] Frequently when the body ages, one particular organ or system degenerates before the rest, as exemplified in a situation where a diseased liver lives within an otherwise vital body, or as in the growing number of cases of onset diabetes, in which the pancreas ages or degenerates long before the rest of the body. When specific bodily parts disease in this fashion, the entire system eventually degenerates, leading to premature death.

However, what if it were possible to replace individual diseased organs? It might become possible to live for 10, 20, perhaps even 100 more years with renewed health and vitality. Aside from the obvious moral questions involved in this possibility, the two major reasons that organ transplantation has not been successful to date are: the host body usually rejects the foreign organ, and there are very few healthy, compatible, spare donor organs available.

In recent years, however, there has been an increasing amount of research being conducted in the field of biological cloning. In whole body cloning, one cell from a donor body is isolated and then grown in vitro into a whole, healthy, and completely identical twin of the donor body. While this form of cloning seems more like science fiction than science fact, there has been some breakthrough recently into the modified area of single organ cloning. Through this process, donor cells from individual organs can be grown in vitro into countless numbers of identical organs. These organs can then be stored until the day when the donor's body begins to degenerate. If the area of disease can be aided with a healthy new organ (or organs), the donor need only go so far as a local "organ storage center" where he or she can have the aged organ removed and replaced with a brand new one. In this case, the body wouldn't reject the transplant because it would, in fact, be a perfect biological match. Similarly, with the capacity to grow dozens of spare parts, there would never again be a shortage of vital and easily transplantable donor organs.[24] Although hard to imagine at present, organ transplantation could very well become the practical life extending technology of the future.

Bionic and Prosthetic Devices

In recent years modern science has been committing a great deal of energy and money to the development of artificial parts and devices that are specifically designed to aid the body in functioning normally. Hearing aids and pacemakers were early examples of these kinds of prostheses yet the future may hold an unimaginable collection of bioengineered devices that would make the "Six Million Dollar Man" look like a wind-up toy in comparison.

Already on the drawing board are a host of soon-to-be complete bionic parts and substances including limbs, eyes, ears, joints and bones, tendons, ligaments and muscles, heart valves and blood, kidneys, livers, pancreases . . . there is even a growing body of research examining the possibility of creating a bionic brain. While most of us presently have negative feelings regarding the possibility of sharing our skin with a souped-up Chevrolet, history has shown that people will eventually begin to think more seriously about bionic assistance if it means an addition of quality and quantity to their life experience. . . . Or, of course, if it is the only solution to a life and death predicament. In fact, some futurists even envision a time when everyone will have some sort of bionic implantation possessing the capacity to continually monitor and control all normal biological processes as well as reprogram the body's natural capacities for extraordinary levels of performance and overall functioning. [25]

Enhanced Pharmacopeia

In recent years, researchers throughout the world have begun to search for natural and synthetic chemicals, elements, and substances that could effectively diminish the negative effects of aging while simultaneously heightening all aspects of physical, mental, and emotional functioning. Previously, most of the popular research on drugs has been narrowly focused on creating substances that suppress pain, such as barbiturates, and relieve anxiety, such as tranquilizers. In the future, the world of pharmacology may very well expand enormously to include anti-aging, mind-expanding, and body strengthening substances. In fact, there are already a number of such substances undergoing examination right now. If tests prove successful they could well be on the market and in our systems within this decade.

A sampling of these future drugs are: vasopressin, a pituitary related hormone that seems to have the capacity of enhancing memory and preventing senility;[26] ACTH/MSH (a combination of ACTH adrenocorticotropic hormone and MSH melanocyte-stimulating hormone) is a protein that has been shown to increase mental focus and attention span;[27] enkaphalins, which are naturally occurring brain proteins that can be isolated as well as reproduced synthetically. Apparently when a certain measure of enkaphalins are introduced into the bloodstream the result is an extreme elevation in mood . . . supposedly the supreme "high;"[28] vincamine, a compound derived from the periwinkle plant, seems to bolster the intellectual abilities of patients suffering from cerebrovascular disorders;[29] GH3, or Gerovital, is the highly touted Roumanian "youth drug," developed by Dr. Ana Aslan of Bucharest. Composed of procaine hydrochloride and haematoporphyrin, GH3 is reported to have the capacity to actually reverse some of the effects of age-related disease such as stiff joints, impaired cardiovascular functioning, and loss of mental vitality;[30] an overview of an enhanced future pharmacopeia would have to include all of the vitamin and mineral supplements such as Vitamin C, E, B-complex, pantothenic acid and pangamic acid that are now being more broadly utilized to strengthen the body's natural immunity systems and thereby make it less susceptible to disease and biological decay.[31] Many futurists feel that a more sophisticated, anti-aging oriented, future pharmacopeia could help to add healthy vital decades to all our lives by working in harmony with the internal nervous and glandular systems to diminish disease and maintain homeostasis.

Genetic Engineering

Another area that I think will be extremely productive during the coming decade is the field of genetic engineering. As explained earlier, there is a growing body of evidence that suggests that one of the primary determinants of physical aging exists as a piece of biological information deep within the nucleus of the cell. Inside this nucleus, within the DNA molecule, lives a boundless amount of information about every aspect of an individual's biological make-up—hair color, skin type, blood type, eye color, etc. Additionally, each DNA molecule contains a "biological clock" which dictates the maximum number of years each individual is capable of living. This longevity potential is diminished a bit with every exposure to stress, pollution, contaminants, and a host of lifestyle related factors such as lack of exercise, over-eating, or insufficient sleep.

Although the entire field of genetic engineering is still in its infancy, researchers are already beginning to speculate that one day we might be able to break the various biological codes that are programmed into each

DNA molecule. Once these codes have been broken and we know which part of the DNA double-helix is responsible for which activity, it could become possible, with the aid of micro-technology and electron super-microscopes, to tinker with the DNA code and reprogram it. The possibilities inherent in such a procedure are literally as boundless as the imaginations of all the people working in this newly emerging field. It's important to remember that the structure of the DNA molecule was first realized a short thirty-six years ago and the capacity to actually engineer this tiny molecule is just now being developed.

The implications of genetic engineering's effects on aging and disease prevention are profound. For if we have the knowledge and skills to alter the genetic code, a simple application of this technology would be to reprogram the biological clock so that instead of 50 lives, each of our cells might have 100, 200, even 1000 lifetimes, which would in turn extend our life spans to 200, 400, or 2000 years with a minimal amount of biological redoing (at least in comparison to the psychological, social, and planetary shake-ups this would precipitate). An additional application of genetic engineering is even closer to successful realization at present. Since most disease and premature death are due to the body's susceptibility to certain diseases as well as its inability to resist the wear, tear, and continual abuse of modern living, perhaps through gene recombining we could build tougher cells, ones for whom cancer or diabetes would be easy foes to conquer.

Now that the new technology of recombinant DNA has begun to truly blossom as a science, and is offering itself as a booming patent-producing industry as well, I think that it is reasonable to expect that in the coming years there will be enormous amounts of money and attention focused on this area, which is sure to lead to accelerated research and discovery. In fact, although the total implications of genetic engineering scare me with their immensity and uncertainty, I feel certain that it will probably emerge as the most extraordinary scientific field of the twentieth century. And if it works, then certainly one dramatic benefit would be the diminishing of disease and the radical extension of human life.[32]

Natural Life Extension

The last major potential contribution to extended life, and the one I support most, is what I call natural life extension. Although I strongly believe that methods such as bionics, genetic engineering, and organ transplantation will profoundly affect the future of aging, my personal orientation leaves me feeling somewhat cold and uncomfortable with these approaches. Perhaps it's the humanist in me. Or maybe I have a romantic picture of human evolution in which we utilize the best of our own human and natural means to stave off disease and prolong life.

Since the primary killers of today are no longer infectious diseases, but lifestyle-related disorders such as cardiovascular disease, arthritis, cancer, diabetes, and respiratory diseases, it no longer makes sense to blame genes, germs, or doctors for all our ailments. The actual cause of our illness seems to be ourselves, and our inability to deal effectively with ever-increasing stress. It has become obvious that fewer and fewer people are actually dying of old age and more and more people are beginning to suffer from the long-term chronic degenerative disease normally associated with unsatisfactory adaptation skills and negative health habits. Therefore the best way to diminish disease and extend life is to support the physical, psychological, social, and environmental elements and attributes that keep people healthy.

Although there is no absolute agreement as to what lifestyle is the most conducive to health and long life, there is a growing consensus that an optimally healthy lifestyle should include sufficient rest and relaxation, regular exercise, proper nutrition, a healthy and noncontaminated environment, an active sex life, positive and creative mental attitude, faith, meaningful social involvement, intimate contact with close friends and loved ones, and doing what brings joy and happiness.

A life of enhanced harmony and quality would lead naturally to life extension, not just another few years filled with the same emptiness and ennui, but the kind of life pictured in a positive image of the future of aging where people would have the opportunity to live to their fullest and most satisfying potential in the absence of disease and age-related anguish. From this perspective it is of equal importance that we look in every direction and attempt every means that will not only insure longevity but joy, communion, and happiness as well. For it is in the context of these basic life needs that health and a rich, long life could naturally emerge.

CONCLUSION: THE CHALLENGE OF THE FUTURE

As we approach the dawning of the third millenium, our country is about to face two dramatic trends that will deeply affect every aspect of our lives and may change the face of America forever. Both trends are related to human aging.

First, America is growing older; we are aging. Soon there will be more adults and elders alive in America than in any previous culture on earth. Second, as a result of impending breakthroughs in our understanding of the mind, the body, and the human aging process, we may soon be able not only to eliminate a great deal of age-related sickness and disease but also to slow down or even reverse the aging process. Consequently, we may soon be faced with a mass generation of healthy and vital elders with the capacity to live for ten, twenty, perhaps even hundreds of years longer than their current life expectancies.

Either of these developments would force a reshaping of our country's priorities; combined, they will challenge and shake every aspect of social, political, economic, commercial, and global dynamics. How we will change and alter ourselves in response to this coming revolution will be an issue of mounting concern during the coming years and may well prove to be the single most controversial issue in the twilight of this century.

And, like most other challenges that await us, in the near and distant future, the responsibility for creating the most ideal future from a countless assortment of alternatives lives with us . . . individually and collectively . . . for we are the future.

JOAN MARCUS

There are few individuals who have contributed more to furthering our understanding of human sexuality than Lonnie Barbach. Her landmark book For Yourself: The Fulfillment of Female Sexuality, *presented the first authoritative self-help approach to female sexual pleasure, and remains a basic handbook for women, therapists and clinicians around the world.*

Lonnie Barbach's investigations into female sexuality began early in her graduate studies at Wright Institute in Berkeley. Disenchanted with the sparse information available to women and clinicians in the field, she pioneered the preorgasmic group treatment approach, and later founded and became codirector of the Human Sexuality Program at the University of California Medical Center in San Francisco. After completing her graduate studies, her curiosity about sexual mores and values in different parts of the world launched her on a year of travel and study in Africa and Europe. On returning to the United States she resumed her clinical practice in San Francisco at Nexus Associates, and commenced writing Women Discover Orgasm, *a clinical guide for sex therapists working with preorgasmic women.*

Her most recent book, Shared Intimacies, *coauthored with Linda Levine, takes the field of human sexuality one step further by presenting ways of achieving and maintaining the highest degree of intimacy, enjoyment, and communication throughout the stages of sexual relationships. She is currently on the clinical faculty at the University of California Medical Center in San Francisco.*

In the following chapter on the future of sexuality, Lonnie Barbach combines a critical analysis of our sexual origins with her most imaginative speculation on the outcome of current trends in intimacy, the family, monogamy, and sex, now and in the next millennium.

LONNIE BARBACH # SEXUALITY

In the last century, the western world has undergone a sexual revolution of immense scope. Recently, these changes have focused on the area of sexual activities—earlier sexual experimentation among teenagers; experimentation with different sexual styles, including oral sex, anal sex, extramarital sex, and homosexuality. However, underlying these changes in sexual behavior is the real change accounting for the sexual revolution—a change in attitude about sex.

HISTORICAL PERSPECTIVE

Before the very late 1800s, books written about sexuality sought only to warn the reader of the sins and dangers of sex. The puritanical values that lie at the basis of our culture honor only those activities that are productive; that produce money or sustenance or that are performed for the good of others. Activities that merely produce pleasure are considered selfish, hedonistic, and therefore bad. This puritan heritage reinforced by prudery has endowed us with the belief that sexual activity should be engaged in solely for the purpose of procreation. Since it is necessary neither to enjoy sex nor experience an orgasm in order to procreate, the puritanical nature of our culture has created difficulty in justifying sexual activity purely for the sake of enjoyment.

Because of these attitudes, sexuality was not studied except as an act of procreation until Krafft-Ebbing's *Psychopathia Sexualis* (1886), which described variations of sexual behavior considered to be abnormal. Soon after, the English psychologist Havelock Ellis began to observe and collect information about individual sexual behaviors. His work, compiled in the seven-volume *Studies In the Psychology of Sex* (1897–1928) was an important influence in changing public attitudes toward sex (although the series was initially banned for obscenity). In the early 1900s, Freud became influential in changing sexual attitudes. He considered sexuality to be a vital driving force present in each individual from birth onward, but most of his theories were derived from his study of psychologically disturbed patients. Wilhelm Reich took Freud's work one step further—he believed that the utilization of sexual energy is the key to psychological health. His treatment of people based on this theory resulted in his censure and imprisonment. Considered to be a genius by some and a lunatic by others, Reich profoundly challenged the sexual attitudes of the times.

It was not until the 1940s when Kinsey's research detailing the sexual behavior of 12,000 American males and females of a variety of ages, backgrounds, and relationships that we had any idea as to the frequency and type of sexual activities being practiced. We learned that many people had what we would now consider sexual problems—men had erection problems and large numbers of women did not experience orgasm. Although Kinsey also undertook some physiological research, it wasn't until Masters and Johnson's work that we gained a basic understanding of sexual physiology. Among other things, their work corrected Freud's notion that women experienced two different kinds of orgasms—the "immature" clitoral orgasm and the "mature" vaginal orgasm. Masters and Johnson began designing effective treatment programs for those people who experienced sexual problems. The success of their work—and the field of sex therapy that it engendered—can be attributed to the combination of behavioral treatment and confrontation of puritanical or negative sexual attitudes learned in childhood which were often largely responsible for causing the sexual problems.

CULTURAL ATTITUDES

Every culture has its own mores or rules about sexual behavior. Sex is culture bound; it cannot be fully understood without looking at the values of a given culture. The role scripts we learn carry with them certain prescribed sexual attitudes and behavior. We learn to be boys and girls, men and women, mothers and fathers. In the American culture, both sexes have been given distinct roles that greatly affect their sexual interaction, expression, and ultimate satisfaction. For example, males should like sex, females should not—at least not overtly if they are to be considered decent by puritanical society's morals. If a woman is unmarried and sexual it is thought that she is either "being used" sexually or that she is using sex to catch a man. Since a woman has, in the past, needed a partner to feel whole and to survive economically, it is not surprising that women, lacking economic value, used sex as a powerful asset in attracting a husband and his accompanying financial security. There is a story that illustrates the point: A woman went over to a friend's house terribly upset and blurted out, "I'm so upset; I just caught my husband making love." "So?" replied her friend. "That's how I caught my husband."

In this society, women are socialized to be romantics, to believe that candlelight dinners and roses result in orgasms. Unfortunately, many of the women who grew up with these messages are having a difficult time unlearning them. And as a result of much of this training, plus the fact that the female's genitals are not as visible as the male's, many women also grew up ignorant of their genital anatomy. They simply never looked and so remained unknowing. Receiving no information about sex while receiving a generous portion of sexual orthodoxy may have kept some women from being promiscuous, but in many cases, it also prevented them from functioning sexually in a way that satisfactorily served them and their relationships later in life.

Men have suffered equally as a result of their role scripting. Men are expected to be the sexual experts. Without any information, without even the celebrated (although rarely occurring) father-son talk, all men are expected somehow to be totally knowledgeable about sexuality and about individual women. And given that every woman is unique sexually, this is no small order.

Considerable pressure has been placed on men because of their role as sexual authority. It is their responsibility not only to satisfy themselves sexually but to satisfy their partner as well. They must arouse themselves sufficiently to have an erection and maintain it until they have satisfied their partner, even if she is multi-orgasmic. He is totally in charge, much like an orchestra leader who is expected also to play all of the instruments as well. Quite a job.

Men are also expected always to be turned on, always ready for sex. As soon as an attractive female becomes available to them, they are expected to have an erection even if they are tired, stressed by work, preoccupied with other matters, or not particularly turned on to the woman. Even machines are acknowledged to require certain conditions in order to perform, whereas men, when it comes to sex, are expected to require none.

Male role scripting dictates that men always be in charge of their lives, never indecisive, never questioning their decisions, never illogical, always right, and always able to navigate their lives without letting their emotions interfere. A real man should always be able to control his emotions. Anything short of fulfilling these rigid requirements renders a man feeling inadequate.

Consequently, role scripting has had an adverse effect on male sexuality. Because men are not permitted to express emotions of sadness, uncertainty, and insecurity, many men seek caring and nurturing through the only acceptable form of personal contact and touching they know, through sex. Hence, many men who really need a hug instead find themselves attempting to perform sexually—often without an erection, for erections cannot always be willed, especially when other emotions interfere.

SEXUAL EQUALITY

Although the roles are beginning to change, there is still tremendous inequality between men and women. Men hold the strings of power. (For every dollar a man earns, a woman earns, on the average, fifty-nine cents.) Historically, women have been considered property with few rights of their own, and this has had an effect on women's sexual self-concept. Suffragists had to fight for more than seventy years simply to gain the right to vote. The Equal Rights Amendment (ERA) is still not ratified, though its directive is nothing more earthshaking than that women should be equal to men and as such deserve all the rights and privileges available to men.

But as more and more women begin to work outside the home, the balance of power is slowly equalizing and women are developing a greater sense of self-confidence. As a result, women are beginning to expect more out of their intimate relationships. No longer will a woman necessarily feel guilty if she does not want sex for a period of time, since she will not assume sex to be her marital duty. Sex will happen because both people want it. No longer will the woman be concerned about losing her partner if she makes certain demands.

As she begins to gain self-esteem, she will feel more deserving of the kind of relationship she really wants, more deserving of having her needs met, more deserving of sexual pleasure and satisfaction. Sex will soon be considered as important a part of female expression as it is of male expression. However, as women attain more freedom and power, men may find the transition difficult. Sexually, men are likely to experience transient periods of erectile or ejaculation problems as women become more assertive in expressing their sexual needs and desires. It will not be easy for men to change from their roles as sole sexual aggressors and seducers.

Initially, men will have difficulty adjusting to women taking the sexual initiative. As the rules now stand, men call the shots, and in so doing, can respond to their own level of sexual interest. This minimizes experiences of lack of erection since if a man feels he is tired or just not in the mood, he does not initiate sex. However, once women feel comfortable initiating sex, men will initially feel that they have to respond. After all, a "real man" is always in the mood for sex. However, real men aren't always in the mood, and as they react according to their role scripting and attempt to proceed sexually, their penises will inevitably get the message across—they won't get erect. And initially, this lack of response will cause men great distress. But men will have to recognize that they, like women, are not always interested in sex and will have to learn how to let their interested partner know that although they are not turned on at that particular moment, they still care.

In these ways, men can be expected to experience the same kinds of difficulties women currently experience in overcoming their role scripting. Initially, the process will be a bumpy one. Making changes in longstanding attitudes and behaviors is always difficult, but the payoff will be worth it for those men willing to take the risk. They will be freed of the impossible responsibility of determining the sexual needs of each individual woman they come in contact with. They will be able to relax more, sexually and in other areas, allowing their female partners to assume greater responsibility and perhaps permitting their own softer, emotional sides to show without embarrassment or inhibition.

These changing attitudes and expectations have affected the lives of young people. Adolescents and even young children are already being exposed to more explicit sexuality than their parents ever were. Television programs and movies on abortion, teenage prostitution, and homosexuality, with explicitly sexual scenes, are not uncommon. Teenagers are becoming sexually active at a younger age. Menses in females is occurring earlier and earlier, possibly a hormonal reflection of the growing sexual interest and indulgence among the young. Although girls still tend to have fewer sexual partners than boys of the same age, after the age of seventeen the percentage of girls having had intercourse now equals that of boys. In fact, teenagers today are experiencing pressure to become sexually active rather than placing value on their virginity. Girls in particular are experiencing conflict over changing sexual attitudes and values. Virginity is sometimes experienced as a kind of disease which one should rid oneself of as quickly as possible. This has always been true of boys who have experienced their virginity as a terrible stigma, and now this is becoming true for girls as well. As a result, many girls once at college have sex at the first available opportunity. Sometimes this "ritual deflowering" needs to take place in order for her to concentrate on her schoolwork, and many of these coeds don't repeat the sexual experience for quite a long time.

SEXUAL PROBLEMS

Early and more varied sexual experience, however, does not necessarily mean greater knowledge or satisfaction. Even though teenage girls are sexually active at an earlier age, as Aaron Haas has shown, 25 percent of these sexually active girls have never had orgasms with intercourse, and only 25 percent of them have orgasms 75 percent of the time or more. Meanwhile, teenage pregnancies are increasing at an alarming rate—one out of every ten teenage girls becomes pregnant—and teenagers account for 33 percent of all abortions.

Although perfected contraceptives may reduce the number of teenage pregnancies, the number is likely to remain high as long as conflict surrounding sexual activity exists, which results in inconsistent or lack of contraceptive use. Much of sexual relating is a developmental process and as such, relies on the emotional development of the people involved; some individuals are ready earlier than others.

Perfected contraceptive measures, however, will aid in reducing sexual problems among men and women who fear pregnancy. Some people enter a sexual experience with so much anxiety about pregnancy that they are unable to relax and enjoy themselves. For example, female adolescents had to learn to control their sexual feelings during necking and petting since the boy was expected to go as far as the girl allowed and it was up to her to stop him. After all, if things went too far, she was the one who got pregnant. As a result, many of these women found it difficult years later when they were married, or old enough to decide for themselves to be sexual, to let go of the control they had spent years developing. Some learned to control their sexual urges so well that they became unable even to recognize their physiological signs of sexual excitement.

For men, sexual problems frequently result from lack of information on controlling ejaculation and societal pressure for men to perform sexually and to satisfy themselves and their partners as well. Long ago, these sexual problems may have served a basic survival purpose. Rapid ejaculation in males and lack of orgasm in females was probably far more adaptive in prehistoric times than long, enraptured sexual episodes. When human life was vulnerable to beasts of prey, for reasons of safety it would have been far more advantageous for the male to ejaculate as quickly as possible while the woman remained alert and on the lookout for a lion or saber-toothed tiger. However, with sex taking place in the safety of the bedroom, with better contraceptives, more complete sex information, and changing sexual attitudes, sexual dysfunctions as we know them today (lack of orgasm, lack of erection, rapid ejaculation) could disappear.

With more leisure time and sex becoming more a form of pleasurable play than a survival mechanism, the sexual satisfaction of both people is becoming increasingly important. With a growing body of good literature available, people are learning the technical information. Also, as openness about sex increases, particularly on the part of the younger generations, negative attitudes are less likely to develop. Consequently, the types of sexual problems that will appear in the future are likely to be of a different nature than those that trouble us today. The most common problem I suspect we will encounter will be sexual dissatisfaction. Due to increased expectations raised by the media, people will not be satisfied with merely enjoyable sex, but will seek earthshaking sex. They will expect more orgasms, longer orgasms, skyrockets and cosmic experiences. When these events don't occur, people will more readily seek out new partners or even sex therapists who are becoming widely known for their effectiveness in treating people with sexual difficulties. Sex therapy itself, because of its effectiveness, may be responsible for creating sexual problems. Lack of orgasms, lack of sexual excitement or less than frequent sex, which may not have been of concern in the past, may now be acknowledged as a problem. People may feel that they are missing something if they don't benefit from the sex therapy experience.

At the other end of the spectrum, people will be seeking sex therapists to aid them with problems that are not really sexual in nature, but which have their basis in other relationship problems. Lack of interest in sex, sexual aversion to one particular partner, and certain cases of lack of orgasm, lack of erection or rapid ejaculation will continue to occur as symptoms of unexpressed anger and resentment when no other avenues for expressing these feelings are built into the relationship.

SEXUAL RELATIONSHIPS

In general, people are less willing now to continue on in the same old path simply because it was the route their parents took. And this broadened view of life with its elevated expectations is having its effect on relationships; people are also unwilling to maintain unsatisfying relationships for the sake of the institution of marriage or for the sake of their children. The result is a total change in the family structure. One sexual partner for life is not only becoming less of a reality, but also less of a desire.

The most obvious indicator of the changing family structure is the increase in divorce. In 1976, half of all marriages ended in divorce. Yet marriage does not appear to be dying off. In fact, in proportion to population growth, the marriage rate in 1978 was about equal to that of 1910. So people are still getting married; they are just more likely to do so two or three times. They expect more from their intimate relationships. When their current marriage is less than totally satisfying, they are more willing to end the relationship and to find another, more satisfying one with another, more satisfying partner.

The high divorce rate is, in a sense, a reaction to generations in which people remained in marriages long after the love had left them. Many of our parents and grandparents were willing to remain uncomfortable for the sake of the marriage or the children. Younger generations are less willing to be uncomfortable. Many of today's young adults experienced, as children, the discomfort of marriages that stayed together on their behalf. The result is often unwillingness to settle for anything short of total satisfaction. And the media has expanded our expectations of marital and sexual satisfaction. It has been instrumental in giving people a greater view of the world and making them more aware of the many options in life that are available. No longer are men likely to do the same kind of work as their father. No longer are people as likely to marry their high school sweethearts. People know that there are more opportunities available to them. They see this on television and in films. They read about them in newspapers, magazines and books. Women have careers; married people have affairs; normal people are homosexual.

More and more men and women are joining the ranks of the divorced and finding that not only are they capable of living alone and managing their lives without a spouse, but that many opportunities become available to them as divorcees. They need not be too lonely during the period between mates as there are interesting divorced or single potential partners available. And the ideal that there is just one perfect match among all the millions of people in the world is losing credibility. Now, with more career options available, women are less willing to adapt and persevere. Many realize that they can make it on their own and choose to exist on a lesser income in exchange for more fulfilling emotional opportunities. And men, in return, are gaining greater awareness of the rewards which can be reaped through spending more time in close family relationships rather than deriving their total fulfillment from work.

Also, as a result of the women's movement, women experience less of a stigma attached to being divorced or unmarried. In the past, a single woman beyond her mid-twenties was looked on askance. She was assumed to have some personality flaw that prevented her from finding a suitable man. If she were single and sexual, she was regarded as "loose" and "cheap." If she were not, she was labelled an old maid or a spinster, all terms which carry pejorative connotations, whereas single men were often envied for their carefree role as man about town. However, the high divorce rate and female equality have changed some of these attitudes and single women are no longer perceived in a negative light. In fact, career women are gaining the respect men have always enjoyed. Today, unmarried women can readily enjoy their sexuality without being stigmatized.

Due to the emerging equality of the sexes, the sexual double standard will disappear. Both men and women will participate equally in affairs outside of marriage. As women continue working more outside the home, they will have the same opportunities for extramarital affairs that men have always had. This trend has already begun. As reported by Morton Hunt and Linda Wolfe, the number of young women having extramarital affairs has doubled from the 1940s to the 1970s. Both men and women will be equally responsible for the sexual affairs they participate in.

This equal responsibility includes taking the initiative in expressing sexual interest. The following exchange that occurred at a recent social gathering exemplifies this trend. A young woman was attracted to a man she had just met that night. They spent some time talking and at the end of the evening she made it perfectly clear that she was interested in going home with him and spending the night. He felt flattered yet was not particularly interested in a sexual relationship, since he was seriously involved with a woman who happened to be away on business. To make a long story short, they went back to his apartment together and spent the night. Later when he related the story to me, he said with disbelief, "You know, I kind of felt used. All she was really interested in was my body, in having sex with me." The story illustrates the sexual role reversal. It is the man who should have scored and the woman who felt used. But in the future, without a double standard, women as well as men will feel free to be more open and direct in seeking sexual gratification as well as participating in unique and varied sexual experiences.

Hence, relationships of the future will be formed on different assumptions. Marital blackmail, where the woman is economically, socially, and sexually dependent on her husband will diminish as women become able to care for themselves economically. Single women will no longer be social outcasts, and sexually active single or divorced women will no longer be stigmatized. With the new sexual openness and permissiveness, sex will become a less powerful bargaining tool for men and for women. Instead, people will be able to come together to form meaningful relationships based on other, more important factors. The result may be more egalitarian relationships that are entered into only when they serve the needs of both people concerned.

Although many women may continue in the role of primary nurturer and child rearer, increasing numbers of men are beginning to assume this role, freeing their female mates to pursue career activities outside the home and releasing men from their goal orientation to explore their inner selves. Through the impact of the women's movement, roles have become less connected to sexual identification; instead, people are becoming freer to adopt the role that reflects their disposition, interests, and abilities rather than the role that reflects their sex. People will also be judged and acknowledged more on their own merits and less on expectations due to sex roles.

PROCREATION AND CONTRACEPTION

Medical advances in the areas of contraception and reproduction will also assist in reducing polarization of sex role scripts. As it stands now, if a woman does not take appropriate contraceptive action, she stands the chance of becoming pregnant. Once pregnant, if she chooses not to abort, she is responsible for the unborn child's health *in utero* and for the child's care after birth whether that means adoption, a foster home, or raising the child herself.

Originally, for the sake of preserving the species, social customs of monogamy and virginity became important parts of the culture. In order to best ensure survival of the infants born, both a father and a mother were necessary. Prohibiting sex before marriage was a way to stabilize society, by preventing family units without a male provider from developing and becoming a drain on the society. As the society became more industrialized and the nuclear family separated from the extended family, it became even more important to minimize illegitimate births. However, with the advent of effective contraception and more widely accepted abortion, women can involve themselves sexually as freely as men always have without fear of being responsible for an unwanted child. Consequently, some of the necessary restrictions to enjoying sexuality in the past no longer hold today and will be even less relevant in the future.

In fact, we are now coming dangerously close to overpopulating the planet, and it has become more and more important to restrict reproduction. Consequently, contraception of the future will be perfected, particularly male contraceptives. Given that men who are physically incapable of erections are already being implanted with an inflatable penile prosthesis, it should be possible within the near future to install a valve-like contraceptive that could be turned on or off, especially since vasectomies are already 80% reversible. The device could be installed at puberty to insure no unwanted pregnancies and then the mechanism could be reversed when children are desired.

The advent of contraception and the growing acceptance of abortion have not only reduced the number of births but have effectively separated sex from reproduction. With the fear of producing an unwanted child diminished, sex need not be limited to marriage and childbearing. It will be less necessary to restrict sexual relationships to ones that can support a child; hence sex will be indulged in more for pure pleasure, for physical release, recreation, joy, and the deepening of intimate relationships.

Then, as it becomes possible to reproduce artificially, sex may, for some, become totally severed from procreation. Even now, the first test-tube babies conceived *in vitro* then transplanted into the mother's uterus have been born. In the future, it may be possible for fetuses to be nourished by artificial means. Women who do not want to be subjected to the discomfort of pregnancy and childbirth could still have children by conceiving and nurturing them in installations designed to scientifically meet all the unborn child's physical needs.

In the future, with artificial means of conception and fetal nurturance, both men and women would be able to have children as single parents. Robot nannies and janitors might be used to relieve single parents of many of their custodial responsibilities, allowing them to spend time enjoying their children instead of just cooking for and cleaning up after them.

THE STRUCTURE OF THE FAMILY

What all this means is that the structure of families will change and the reasons for being in a relationship in the future will differ from those of the past. Living together before marriage is becoming more and more common and will continue to grow both in practice and acceptability. Sweden, which is far ahead of the United States in the development of equal roles for men and women, is experiencing a similar phenomenon, with even greater numbers of young people experimenting with living together before considering marriage. Marriage in Sweden is being postponed to the mid- or late twenties when it is entered into mostly for the purpose of having children. I believe this process will continue in the United States as well. As we become aware of our increasing options, we are less willing to settle down too soon or before the marketplace of available partners has been sufficiently explored. I think the time spent in the search for the ideal mate will continue to lengthen and marriage will finally be entered upon when the natural developmental stage of creating a family is reached.

Consequently, although more options will be available, I don't believe that the institution of marriage will necessarily become outdated. The natural propensity for pairing will continue. I suspect that the majority of these marriages and relationships of the future will espouse sexual monogamy. Although more people will experience extramarital affairs, given human nature, the natural territorial instinct and concomitant feelings of jealousy, monogamy will probably still be preferred. However, the changing of partners that will take place will produce a serial monogamy; one more or less monogamous relationship following another. And the pairings of the future will occur in a somewhat different fashion. People will not marry with the expectation that the marriage will last forever. Instead, they will continue to marry, but with the foreknowledge that they will be likely to do so two or three times during their lives. Even though at the time the marriage may feel permanent, in the back of their minds people may be more conscious of the fact that their current relationship may one day be replaced by another. In this sense, people will begin to see their relationships as serving a particular purpose during a particular developmental stage of their life.

For example, relationships in the early twenties may serve to supply the young man and woman with a home environment away from the parental home. This nurturing environment with a sexual partner will aid young adults in separating from their parents and at the same time help them to develop their sense of independence. Due to the great amount of growth and personal change that takes place during these years, this relationship may not last long. As with current early first marriages and living-together relationships, many, if not most, could falter or break up within seven years.

As in the stages outlined by researchers in adult developmental psychology, people in their late twenties and early thirties may move on to the stage in life where they will desire to create a family. Those with such needs may then enter a relationship or marriage for the purpose of raising children. This relationship may last through the children's young years, after which another pairing may follow, perhaps with another parent with children of his or her own. Or it may last until the children have reached their teen years or until after they have left home, at which time a relationship based solely on having children may not be able to adapt to a childless environment.

There is much valid concern about the negative effects on children of the parental unit dissolving. But I think that in the future, there are likely to be some benefits as well. In the first place, the part children play in the family has changed. In preagricultural times, children were property of the whole community. But once we changed to a society of nuclear families, children provided the manpower necessary for cultivation and became of economic value to their parents. In the current industrialized society, children have again become of little economic value. This is just one more factor that releases the family from having to remain together for survival reasons.

Since, in the future, divorce will be one of the societal norms, children of divorced parents will be more accepting of the situation as they find their friends in similar circumstances. As a result, children are likely to be less devastated as they grow to expect their parental relationships to change. Also, serial relationships will provide children with a number of parents. A new form of extended family will develop as aunts, uncles, cousins, and parents of a father's or mother's new spouse are incorporated into the family structure. For example, a typical child might have one or two stepmothers and stepfathers in addition to his or her natural parents. In addition, as many as twelve grandparents as well as numerous aunts, uncles, and cousins may take an interest in the child's development. The result will be a larger number of people available to nurture, support, and fulfill the child's needs. Relationships with favorite aunts, stepmothers, stepfathers, and uncles will be maintained well after the parental relationship has split up, providing the child with a variety of role models beyond his or her two natural parents. Children of these new extended families may develop better coping skills through their experience of a large support network. In the end, these children may gain insight into the qualities important in making relationships work as they perceive what succeeded and what failed in their parents' marriages.

After the children have grown, individuals might seek out a new relationship that reflects professional or personal change. The purpose of this relationship could be to grow old together as friends, to go back to school, to travel, or to develop a new career.

The general population is living longer; the average life span is currently seventy-three and constantly rising. Due to advances in medical science and increased awareness of the importance of proper diet and exercise, people now have the possibility of remaining healthier longer and hence maintaining active sex lives until severe illness or death prevails. Given the growing sexual permissiveness of the society, we will probably find that people will continue to expand sexually as they grow older. As a result, people in their fifties and sixties will be considered youthful and important contributors to society, having fifteen or more useful years left to devote to the society at large and to a loving intimate and sexual relationship. The idea that sex ends after forty-five is becoming widely recognized as a fallacy as people in their sixties and seventies report that sex not only continues to be good but can even get better as the years pass. As women are freed of their enculturated inhibitions and fears of pregnancy and men feel less performance anxiety, more relaxed and sexually satisfying relationships can result. And since in the year 2000, the majority of the population will be above the age of fifty, this age group will be a strong force in the creation of societal norms.

Aging also brings about greater openness and acceptance as people become all too conscious of the ephemeral quality of life. Friends begin to die and various illnesses and physical problems bring about the painful awareness that life is drawing to a close. The reality of the brevity of life often results in greater acceptance and breaks down prejudices that have been held for many years.

SEXUAL ATTITUDES AND ACTIVITIES

The breakdown of prejudices will free both males and females to express themselves sexually according to their own natural inclinations and preferences rather than according to some prescribed sexual role. Sex could become an important form of intimate communication not only between spouses but between close friends as well. Much younger partners, or partners of different races or religions, or even partners of the same sex may become more acceptable as society's sexual mores continue to relax.

Basically, there are limitless possibilities for enjoyment once the current taboos are lifted and sex becomes less shameful and takes a more open, acceptable place in our lives similar to that enjoyed by eating, playing golf, travel, or having intimate conversations. With more relaxed sexual attitudes, sex will become an activity for providing pleasure, fun, and closeness rather than solely for procreation. Sex can be an open, fun forum for the expression of closeness. It can be an area for experimentation, an area of physical and emotional liberation.

Hopefully men and women will not be coerced by new societal norms to become more sexually expressive than they want to be. In their attempt to be modern and free, many may initially act sexually in ways that are inconsistent with their own personalities. Some will try to have extramarital affairs or threesomes or have sexual encounters with the same sex when they are not constitutionally disposed to such experiences. However, reacting against their upbringing may be a necessary step before they can truly determine which activities and lifestyles are right for them.

With time, I expect the pendulum will swing back again away from socially prescribed sexual activity to sexual experiences that reflect the needs and emotional development of the individual. Instead of a sexual Olympics where each person tries to outdo all others by being more sexually "liberated," individual uniquenesses will be respected. Just as people are different in all areas of their lives, having been brought up in different families in different parts of the country, with unique physiological makeups and different ideas as to what constitutes fun, people differ in terms of what is right for them sexually. The nature of sexual stimulation, fantasies, activities, and sexual orientation will vary from person to person, and greater acceptance of these individual preferences will become manifest. I feel that with this true liberation will come more options—men will be more relaxed about sex, women more assertive. Idealistically, the definition of sexuality will broaden and the distinction between heterosexuality and homosexuality will blur. After an initial backlash, same-sex relationships will become less threatening to the general public. Stigmas attached to homosexuality or bisexuality will disappear as these forms of sexual expression become more the norm.

It will become more acceptable for people to go through periods of sexual experimentation that might include partners of both sexes, younger partners, and older ones. This is particularly likely given that people will be living longer and therefore will have more opportunity to change partners and experiment as one way of maintaining sexual excitement. People of all ages will be more open to experimentation. Having a number of sexual partners during one's lifetime will become the norm. Even more conservative people will become more experimental sexually. Oral sex, anal sex, and orgies, which have possibly always been practiced by a portion of the population, will be experienced by more people in the future, a trend already in evidence. The practice of oral sex among married males and females has increased from approximately 40 percent in the 1940s to approximately 60 percent in 1972. In 1980, 85 percent of women polled by *Cosmopolitan* reported engaging in oral sex and 15 percent of these women also regularly had anal sex. Twenty-three percent of these females had had at least one experience with multiple partners at the same time as compared with 17 percent of young males and 5 percent of young females in the 1972 survey by Morton Hunt. I would not be surprised if, in the future, some hot-tub parties or dinner parties even incorporate promiscuity hours.

Sexual experimentation might, in the future, include a greater use of drugs. The culture is in many ways becoming more passive and more drug-oriented. Chemical engineering is certain to be a booming technology of the future. Alcohol has long had a place in the sexual episode, but now marijuana is used almost as frequently; cocaine and amyl nitrate are growing in popularity as well. For some, drugs dull the senses and detract from the sexual experience. For others, however, the intensity produced by drugs enhances the body's natural sensations. Many people will begin taking drugs to create more ecstatic and exciting experiences such as those promised by *Forum, Penthouse, Playboy,* and other popular sex magazines. There has been and will surely continue to be, experimentation with sexual accoutrements such as vibrators. In the future, other mechanical aids will be available to intensify the sexual experience and will be utilized by more people. For example, the television is now in virtually every home and home video machines are growing in popularity. Home video could provide a whole new theater for sexual thrills. People will be able to relax in the privacy of their own bedroom and be passively stimulated by erotic films. With the small added expense of a video camera, they will be able to make their own home erotic movies.

Computers will impinge on our sex lives in the same way they seem to be affecting all other areas of our lives. The ultimate in passivity could consist of computerized chambers with push buttons for lighting, music, scents, textures, and temperature controls for creating the perfect sexual atmosphere. In addition, the machine would be able to translate brain impulses of fantasies and simultaneously project them on the walls of the chamber. Perfectly programmed to match our individual sexual delights, these machines could take the place of prostitutes. Since recent research by Harold Leif shows that the testosterone levels of couples who have good relationships rise and fall in synchrony, it could be possible for couples who enter the chamber together to have other biochemical and electrical aspects synchronized, leading not only to a higher state of intense pleasure but possibly a deepening of the relationship as well. Women are already being treated with mechanical devices such as vaginal myographs used in conjunction with biofeedback equipment for strengthening the pubococcygeal muscle to correct anorgasmia. In the future, other biofeedback machines and technological equipment similar to the orgasmatron in Woody Allen's movie *Sleeper* are likely to be used to help people intensify their sexual experience. Ancient practices of tantric sex and many of Wilhelm Reich's energetic techniques will, in all likelihood, gain greater popularity.

Taking sex into outer space totally boggles the brain as far as new possibilities for creative sexual novelty and excitement. First experiences always bring excitement to sex, and sex on the moon, Venus, or Mars would certainly fit that bill. Imagine all of the sexual positions that could be tried if you were weightless. Or the creative pleasure of figuring out how to do it with lead boots on.

There is also a good chance that sexual experiences in the future will be less genitally oriented. Sexual energy could enable sex, if desired, to be used as a profound expression of love in the spiritual sense. With the growth of the consciousness movement—the emphasis on spirituality, extrasensory perception, and telepathy—sex could become a more whole-body and even cosmic experience. True intimacy in a relationship may take the form of telepathic communication, and in the future, psychic monogamy may be more important than sexual fidelity in intimate relationships. In addition, sexual energy could possibly be transformed and harnessed to power creative work projects.

The future of our sexual relationships will also, of course, depend upon the well-being of the world. In the event of a nuclear holocaust or some natural disaster, people would turn inward, paying more attention to survival and using sex more for personal contact than pleasure. However, if we suppose that major catastrophic events are allayed for the time being, we can expect that our technological society will continue providing people with increasing amounts of leisure time, a part of which will inevitably be directed toward expanding sexual pleasure. After all, it is one of life's pleasures that is not only free in terms of cost but is available to virtually every human being.

Dr. Jonas Salk has left his mark on the lives of countless human beings. The discoverer of the polio vaccine, Salk has devoted himself to the improvement of human life through the elimination of disease and the promotion of social and individual health.

Born in 1914 in New York City, the oldest of a garment worker's three sons, Jonas Salk helped pay for his education by working after school and earning scholarships. After graduating from the New York University School of Medicine in 1939, Salk proceeded to the University of Michigan on a research fellowship, and quickly advanced to the position of assistant professor of epidemiology. While at Michigan, Salk developed a close working relationship with Dr. Thomas Francis, Jr., who was head of the department of epidemiology at Michigan's School of Public Health. This association proved to be a key element in Salk's life, for under Francis's guidance he developed his now-renowned ability as a medical researcher. It was during these years in association with Francis that Salk helped to develop the preliminary influenza vaccine that came to lay the groundwork for his monumental discoveries in the area of polio virology.

In 1953, Salk announced the development of a trial polio vaccine. Amidst much praise and joy, the Salk vaccine was pronounced safe and effective in 1955. For his brilliant and humanitarian contribution to health, Salk received worldwide acclaim as well as many honors, including a citation from President Eisenhower and a Congressional Gold Medal for "great achievement in the field of medicine."

Dr. Jonas Salk taught at the University of Pittsburgh from 1947 to 1964, when he moved to La Jolla, California to form the Salk Institute for Biological studies. Serving as the institute's director since its inception, Salk is still hard at work conducting laboratory research to improve his polio vaccine as well as to develop new vaccines for such diseases as cancer and influenza. In addition to his significant contributions as a medical researcher, Jonas Salk has authored several books on human behavior, including Man Unfolding and The Survival of the Wisest.

In this probing essay, Dr. Jonas Salk shares his feelings, beliefs, and insights regarding the way in which human evolution may presently be undergoing a dramatic shift—from an orientation based on the survival of the fittest to one which is primarily motivated by what he calls "the survival of the wisest." In postulating this evolutionary shift from brawn to brains, Salk creatively reformulates present evolutionary trends.

JONAS SALK # HUMAN
INTELLIGENCE

An unprecedented explosion of interest and movements concerned with
the survival of the species is now taking place. The idea of the extermina-
tion, by humanity, of various forms of life on the planet, and the danger to
human life, induces a fear that preoccupies increasing numbers of individuals, especially of the generations now maturing. Those who are ecologi-
cally oriented and those who are profoundly concerned about the quality of
life for the species as well as for the individual appear to stand in opposition
to others less aware of such problems, who are more concerned with
themselves in their own life spans. The fundamental difference between
these two attitudes is that the first expresses concern for *the individual and
the species;* the second reveals principally, and perhaps exclusively, an
interest in the *individual* and the *particular group* of which he is a part.
The more broadly concerned (*i.e., with the species and the individual*) fall
into two categories. One consists of those born after such threats came into
full evidence; the other, of those born earlier but who, having witnessed
the change, are now reacting to previously prophesied dangers which have
become realities. Those preoccupied only with their own problems are
either unaware or unperturbed in the face of a process in human evolution
to which others are sensitive and, if aware, feel frustrated, helpless,
or apathetic.

  A major threat to the species is attributed to the increasing size of the
human population, which, in turn, is ascribed to successes in science and
technology. This "explanation" has evoked an attack upon science and the
exploitation of its technology, to the development of which are attributed

43

many adverse effects upon the human species and upon other forms of life. "Polluters" who befoul the planet affect the "quality of life" and are regarded as a threat to the present and future equilibrium of the species and of the planet. Those who consider themselves *on the side of* nature, and therefore of the human species, see others in opposition to both nature and humanity. Hence we are to be concerned not only with humanity's relationship to nature but also with itself.

Viewed in this way we realize how much blindness to human nature actually exists. This may be understandable in the young, who have not lived very long, but it is equally true of those who have lived longer. How we grapple with our blindness is of the greatest importance for the present and the future; it is the central problem of our time.

If human life is to express as much harmony, constructiveness, and creativity as are possible for fulfilling the purpose *of* life, as "required" by nature, and the purposes *in* life, as "chosen" by humanity, an attitude will be needed, not of people "against" nature, but of humanity "inclusive with" nature. A more reasonable attitude would be for human beings to "serve nature" in order to serve themselves, rather than to "serve themselves" without regard for, or at the expense of, nature and others. By recognizing and respecting the natural "hierarchies of purpose" humankind would be better able to gauge its latitude to select and pursue its own "chosen purposes" without coming into conflict with the "purpose of nature," which appears to be the continuation of life as long as conditions on the planet permit.

As a process, evolution seems to be nature's way of finding means for extending the persistence of life on earth. This involves the elaboration of increasingly complex mechanisms for problem-solving and adaptation. The ability of the human mind to solve the problem of survival is part of this process. In this respect, humanity has evolved so successfully that it is now to be tested for its capacity to "invent" appropriate means to limit the harmful or lethal excesses of which it is capable. The conflict in the human realm is now between self-expression and self-restraint *within* the individual, as the effect of cultural evolutionary processes has reduced external restraint upon individual expression and increased opportunities for choice.

The fork-in-the-road at which humankind *now* stands offers either a path toward the development of ways and means for maximizing self-expression *and* self-restraint, by means of external restraints that are not suppressive or oppressive, or an alternative path of limitless license which would unleash destructive and pathological greed at the expense of constructive and creative individuals. In the latter case, a strong reaction can be expected to develop in response to the sense of order upon which their survival is based. The challenge is to establish an equilibrium between

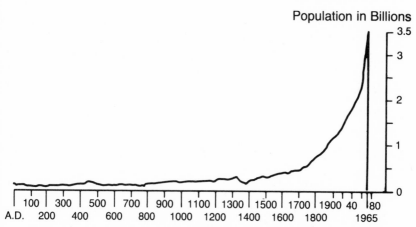

FIGURE 1. World population estimates, A.D. 0–1965. Adapted from
World Facts and Trends, by John McHale.

self-expression with self-restraint on the one hand and *self-protection with
self-restraint* on the other. If human beings are to take advantage of
opportunities to remedy difficulties that have arisen as a result of evolution, then they need to understand their relationship to the evolutionary
process which plays with and upon them.

As a logical overture, let us look at the growth of the human population
on the face of the earth and the present reasonable projection over the next
few decades to the year 2000. It raises vast and complex implications for the
character and quality of human life that concern relationships as well as
resources for the present and the future. It raises questions as to the means
that humankind or nature will invoke to deal with the excesses that have
developed and the insufficiencies that persist. Will humanity create its
own procedures to deal with them or will nature's simple ways come into
play, some of which may prove quite undesirable from humanity's point of
view? This, in fact, may already be occurring. Before turning our attention
to the questions and consequences of the rapidly mounting curve of population increase as drawn in Figure 1, or to the implications of its curtailment
or of its continuation, let us look at patterns of growth in other living
systems. For example, Figure 2 shows the growth curve of a fruit-fly
population in a closed system as observed by Raymond Pearl in 1925.

The S-shaped, or sigmoid, curve that describes the growth of fruit flies
is also seen in curves of growth of micro-organisms and of cells or molecules. Since the planet earth can be considered a closed system and *since
the sigmoid curve reflects the operation of control and regulatory mechanisms that appear to be associated with survival of the individual or of the
species* it would seem reasonable to expect that the pattern of future

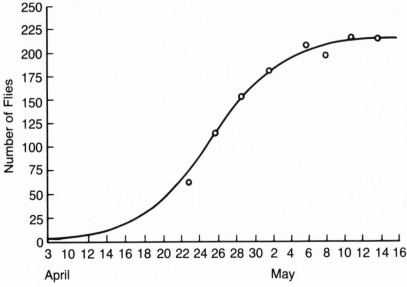

FIGURE 2. Growth of fruit-fly population. From *The Biology of Population Growth*, by Raymond Pearl. Copyright 1925 by A. A. Knopf, Inc. and renewed 1953 by Maude de Witt Pearl. Reprinted by permission of the publisher.

population growth of humanity will tend to stabilize at an optimal level described by an S-shaped curve. It is possible, of course, that an alternative pattern might resemble that of the lemmings (Figure 3), in which periodic catastrophe occurs with enormous loss of life. However, our attitude toward human life would have to alter significantly for such patterns to be endured; we are more likely to choose *other ways than catastrophe for*

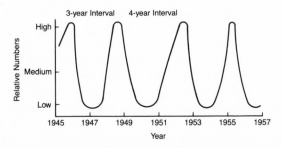

FIGURE 3. Generalized curve of the three-to-four-year cycle of the brown lemming population. From CRM Books, *Biology: An Appreciation of Life,* ©1972 by Communications Research Machines, Inc.

*maintaining optimal numbers on the face of the earth while remaining
within the limit of available resources.*

As humankind has still to complete a cycle of growth on this planet, its
biologically programmed pattern has not yet been fully revealed; it also
remains to be seen how this pattern will be influenced by factors for which
human beings are responsible, or by natural forces. Therefore we are
unable to know the pattern of humanity's trajectory in the short- or longer-
term future. The "catastrophists" and harbingers of doom *are in themselves
evidence that humanity possesses a signaling mechanism for sounding
warnings* of danger, sensed more acutely and more clearly by some who
alarmingly represent the problem of population increase as shown in
Figure 1.

If we assume, however, that humanity has the power of choice and can
influence the course of its growth curve on this planet, then it is of special
interest to look carefully at the sigmoid curve in terms meaningful for it.
Since our deeper purpose is to try to discern the nature of order in the
human realm in relation to the nature of order in the realm of life in
general, it is interesting to explore the possible meaning of the similarities
observed in the human population growth curve as manifested thus far, and
the first portion of the growth curve of the fruit-fly population and similar
curves in the subsystems of other living systems.

Since, through the process of natural selection, living organisms that
have survived have revealed their fitness for persistence thus far in the
evolutionary scheme, we would like to have some prevision of humanity's
program. Are we programmed for relatively short-term survival in which
our end may come of our own doing? Or are we programmed for a life in
which only those who have lost the power to discriminate, or who are
otherwise degenerate, will continue to inhabit the planet as long as reproductive activity continues to supply "victims" of life, struggling to preserve
itself in the "human" form? And what other alternatives exist?

It is likely that the human brain has developed as it has, in the course
of natural selection, partly in response to exogenous forces active against
survival. Does that same brain also possess the capacity to tame and
discipline those inner forces that act against long-term survival, in opposition to a life of high quality? The struggle for survival once manifest
principally *between humanity and nature now seems to be taking place
within the human species itself, between humanity and individuals* and
within the individual.

My purpose is to elucidate the factors and forces affecting the quality
of human life through ideas that emerge while "playing with" the growth
curve and reflecting upon the developmental and evolutionary processes of
humanity in the critical stage in which we seem to be at this point in time.

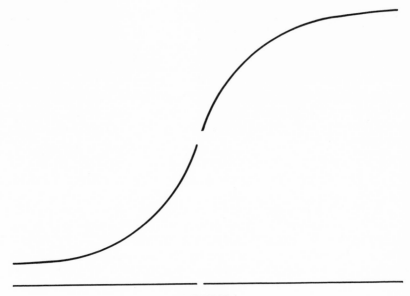

FIGURE 4.

As we study the curve in Figure 4 consideration of the lower portion only gives the impression of continuous, even explosive expansion, whereas consideration of the upper portion gives the impression of modulation and control of this expansion, so that finally a limit is established. At the junction of the lower and upper portions of the curve is a region of inflection at which there is a change *from progressive acceleration to progressive deceleration* and at which the influence of the controlling processes is clearly visible. The break apparent in this region suggests that a "signaling" mechanism of some kind must operate to bring about this change, producing an effect that, judging from the shape of the curve, indicates the existence of a uniform process, reflecting the operation of some kind of ordering principle in response to "signals" both from the environment and from within the organisms themselves. At different points in time along the curve, latent qualities and reactions are evoked appropriate to survival, the program for which is coded in the germ plasm, which also contains an accumulation of control and regulatory factors essential thereto.

At the plateau stage of numbers, the individuals in the fly population would be expected to "behave" differently as compared with those alive earlier in the growth curve, *i.e.*, before the zone of inflection when different "problems" prevailed. The extent to which circumstances differ, at different points in time along the curve, is graphically suggested in

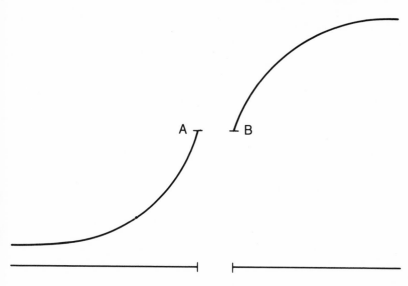

FIGURE 5.

Figure 5 by breaking the continuity at the point of inflection so as to create two curves, A and B.

These curves are intended to emphasize the difference in attitude and outlook in the two periods and help create a visual image of what can be sensed "intuitively." They also convey concretely what might be appreciated "cognitively" by means of an objective analysis of the increasingly complex problems generated by the growing numbers of individuals. In the discussion to follow, curves A and B will be used as symbols of the "shape" of the past and of the future, as we attempt to characterize each. When we speak of the fruit fly in anthropomorphic terms, it is to suggest, using this caricature, the nature of the forces operating in the human realm. For example, if we speak of the flies as possessing, individually or collectively, a "sense of responsibility" and "insight and foresight," it is to suggest the existence of the equivalent of conflicting forces by which they would, were they human, be impelled to "judge" and "choose." Such judgment would be exercised according to the contesting "value systems" that would be in operation during periods as different as those suggested by curves A and B.

The fact that the fruit flies are a product of a long evolutionary history, whose survivors react according to their genetic programming, leads us to think that humanity, which is of more recent origin and, moreover, at or near the point of inflection in its present curve of population growth on the planet, is about to find out whether it is programmed to behave in ways leading to a population growth curve similar to the fruit fly's, or to a curve of another shape. We have still to find out about the nature of the quality of life under circumstances that remain to be experienced. In being tested for survival, we still have a way to go not only quantitatively but qualitatively. The curves, however, provide some insight, their shapes suggesting the character of the problems that prevailed in the past, those now existing, and those likely to be encountered as humanity continues to move through evolutionary time.

The human species differs from other living organisms in possessing another "control and regulatory" system, for response to environmental and other changes, in addition to that genetically coded and automatically operative as in the fruit fly, which has been tested and selected in the course of its evolutionary history. Humanity is able to exercise learned behavior. A person also possesses individual will, which can be either in accord or in conflict with genetically coded patterns of response. In this sense we are more complex and more unpredictable than the fruit fly. We can learn to behave in ways that are anti-life as well as pro-life, anti-evolution as well as pro-evolution. We remain to be tested for this pattern of response to all that is implied in the need for changing values to make the transition from Epoch A to Epoch B. In view of the greed and ideologies of human beings as causes of their conflicts, attitudes as well as values will be put to test in the transition from Epoch A to Epoch B.

Genetic programming does not change as rapidly as the attitudes and values that also guide human behavior. Since genetically as well as culturally determined responses are "environmentally" linked, the circumstantial differences implied by the dissimilar "shapes" of the curves symbolizing Epoch A and Epoch B will be expected to evoke different sets of genetic as well as cultural potentialities. In Epoch B those attitudes and attributes which are of the greatest value will determine the "real" and not merely the "presumed" shape of the population growth curve and the quality of life. Value systems such as prevailed in Epoch A will, of necessity, have to be replaced by those appropriate for Epoch B, and new concepts will emerge about human nature and our relationship to all parts of the cosmos. Since the conditions into which future generations will be born are not yet determined, it will be of interest to see how individuals in different cultures, with different genetic backgrounds and capacities, will respond to the human and planetary changes now well under way. It is not yet possible to see how humanity will deal with attributes which dominated in Epoch A nor to forsee very clearly precisely what attributes will emerge in Epoch B.

Thus humanity is being subjected to a new and possibly more severe challenge than ever before, for which perspective and insight are needed.

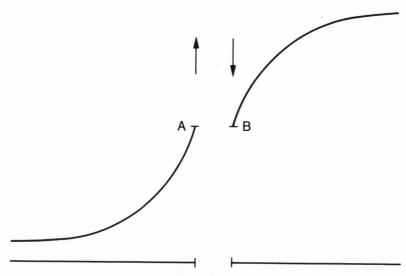

FIGURE 6.

We must become aware of the opportunities and the dangers that we will have to face when confronted by the conflicts resulting from a necessary inversion of such magnitude as implied by the diagram in Figure 6. The profundity of the change in values required for survival and for quality of life in the periods described by curves A and B makes it seem not only that what was of positive value in A may, in fact, become of negative value in B; but also, if "B values" had prevailed earlier they would have been of opposite value in the A epoch. From this point of view it is not difficult to understand the depth and meaning of the change that humanity is now experiencing in the various forms that have already become manifest under the specific historical circumstances in different cultures in all parts of the world.

This change is of such magnitude and significance that it may well be judged to be of major import in the course of human evolution. At this time humanity seems to be seeking tolerable levels quantitatively and is being called upon to develop qualitatively satisfying ways and means for living with self and with others that fit what might be thought of as the scheme of nature. Humanity's choices will be "judged" by nature, thus revealing the wisdom of its selections from among many alternatives.

We need to discern nature's "game," as well as humanity's. The choices that we make from the alternatives available to us will profoundly influence our own evolutionary destiny. The outcome will reveal the extent to which we will have succeeded in understanding the workings of nature, at a time in our own evolution when we are being tested for our capacity to accommodate ourselves to change, and for our ability to create the possibilities for existence under circumstances as different from those of the past as suggested by the shapes of curves A and B. Until this point in evolutionary time humanity has been selected for characteristics that were of value for survival during the A epoch. Now, quite abruptly, a new "selection pressure" has appeared, for which we are ill-prepared by experience but for which there may exist within us a reservoir of potential appropriate to the new circumstances such as are now developing.

In the course of evolution many more species have become extinct than have survived, each perhaps for particular causes very different from those which might cause the extinction of humanity. For in humanity's case, at this point in evolution, extinction might well arise for internal reasons. The way we deal with unresolved conflicts within ourselves individually and collectively might lead to our own destruction. The process of natural selection has developed survivors resistant to various infectious diseases and to some of the vicissitudes of the environment. It has also led to the selection for survival of those successful in escaping the ravages of war and those ingenious enough to escape human tyranny. Thus until now the qualities that have been selected for survival reflect the conditions and circumstances that have prevailed as much as the potentialities that exist in humanity. As nature continues its game of biological mutation and selection, and as humanity plays its own games of selection of ideas and of cultural innovations, nature will have the last word. Therefore it is up to us to look closely and deeply into nature's workings, not only at the molecular and cellular levels but also at the consequences of advancing knowledge and cultural practices as these bear on the question of survival and the quality of life. It is in this respect that wisdom will be required for which a balanced creative center for judgment is needed.

We must look to those among us who are in closest touch with the unfathomable source of creativity in the human species for an understanding of the workings of nature and for insight into nature's "game," as we enter upon an epoch in which new values are required for choices of immediate need as well as for those with longer-range implications. This is especially important when, as now, the number born in each new generation exceeds the number born in each of the earlier generations. For this reason, the character and quality of the individual that will survive and predominate in our period will have a very profound effect upon the character and quality of human life for a long time to come.

To what extent will we be able to affect the course of nature, in the short or in the long run? That remains to be seen. Nevertheless, we are fully conscious of this problem. How will we deal with this opportunity and this responsibility knowing as much as we do? What more do we need to know, being as aware as we are now of our limitations and our capabilities?

To help our understanding of our relationship to humanity and humanity's relationship to nature, in terms of their inherent complementary character, analogies have been drawn between the "games" of nature and of humanity. The point that has already been made is that the laws that govern nature's game require, under certain circumstances, "double-win" rather than "win-lose" resolutions which people must also develop.

Although each of us would like to be "winners," at least in terms of individual satisfaction and fulfillment, it is also clear that more luck, knowledge, and wisdom are required than are possessed by very many. Some are more fortunate than others, but none are born either fully knowledgeable or infinitely wise; hence humankind's search for perspective and guidance in dealing with the unknowns and uncertainties of life in all its complexity.

Since many of the problems for which we seek solutions are an inherent part of the process of human development itself, and since humanity is both a contributing cause as well as a sufferer, our position as both patient and physician is a difficult one. And yet we must be both. Fortunately, means do exist for self-correction, for self-cure, and for prevention even of those potentially harmful or lethal effects that are self-induced. The approach employed here in thinking about this dilemma has been to seek useful analogies in the self-correcting processes that are an essential and integral part of living systems. The assumption is that if the individual were aware of the existence of such processes and the way they operate, knowing that they are an integral part of the self as well, it might be possible to develop the desire to learn how to use them consciously and deliberately not only for survival but for fulfillment in one's lifetime. Such clues can be found in the way in which control and regulation operate in living nature, where success is evidenced in the persistence of life in spite of vicissitudes, difficulties, and seeming impossibilities. On the assumption that metabiologic evolutionary problems (that is, those surpassing the ordinary limits of living matter) are similar to problems encountered and solved in biological evolution, analogies are sought to serve as models helping us to deal more realistically, and therefore more appropriately, with some of our unresolved problems, and even, possibly, to accept the existence of insoluble enigmas.

Referring to humanity as a metabiological entity infers that it possesses self-correcting, self-controlling, and self-disciplining mechanisms, as well as biologically governed balance-mechanisms for each of two distinct yet related evolutionary purposes, *i.e.*, for improving the quality of life as well as for survival. It implies, also, that change in human behavior that will serve both biological and metabiological aims requires many steps and stages involving both error-making and error-correcting. In spite of our prior limitations, due to ignorance of the character or details of the processes involved in evolution, can we, now, with our increased knowledge of the nature of living systems, and of humanity, apply ourselves to conceive of ways and means of influencing the course of future events toward fulfilling humanity's evolutionary potential? In Epoch A it appears that greater success has been achieved in reducing premature death than in improving the quality of life in terms of individual satisfaction. Hence, to the gains made in Epoch A, facilitating survival by better hygienic conditions and other measures for the prevention of disease, new challenges will have to be accepted in Epoch B, testing humanity's ingenuity in developing the means to enhance the degree of fulfillment in the life of the individual and in the quality of life generally.

The difficulties and complexities involved in such a challenge are considerable; the mere existence of innate mechanisms for meeting them does not mean that the odds are in favor of success. Human history is replete with evidence that *de*volutionary processes also operate, with deterioration of the human condition, unless foresight, imagination, ingenuity, determination, and wisdom are brought to bear, to increase self-awareness and self-discipline in the choice of ends as well as means. To be able to prevent such deterioration, principles will be required by which to live, and by which to intervene judiciously in the process of biologic and metabiologic evolution with knowledge of the *de*volutionary as well as the evolutionary consequences of each action or nonaction when we face issues that affect our well-being individually and collectively.

The hypothesis has been proposed that if the human mind is exposed to the economy of nature, as revealed in the workings of living systems, it will be able to recognize the necessity of balancing values. Thus measure is established as the source of wisdom. By improving the quality of life, wisdom can influence the processes of metabiological evolution, just as the enhancement of physical fitness functioned in the struggle for survival in biological evolution. If we can come to recognize that the use of wisdom in the game of life leads to the reward of a greater measure of fulfillment and satisfaction, then we will value the development of such special skills; nowadays more individuals have the opportunity to do so for more years than was generally true heretofore. In this, everyone has much to gain.

If, in the course of this quest, a struggle arises between the wise and the unwise, the conquest or elimination of either one would result in loss to both, just as if Life and Death were to "conquer or eliminate" each other. The wise must avoid a "win-lose" conflict with the unwise, just as it was necessary in biological evolution for Life and Death to arrive at a "double-win" resolution in order for either one, and hence both, to persist. Even though Death eventually wins over Life so far as the individual is concerned, Life wins over Death in the perpetuation of the species. This is to say that Life "wins immortality" for the species and Death, mortality for the individual; the individual may be unwise, but not the species. For the quality of life to be improved, and for survival, humankind will have to respect those who are wise and expect the individual to behave wisely. If wisdom is, in fact, a new kind of fitness for survival, the operation of the equivalent of natural selection in the metabiological evolutionary processes will have been guided by the choice of human values.

In Epoch A humanity acted effectively on the side of Life, both of the individual and of the species, by reducing the incidence of disease and the frequency of dying prematurely. Correspondingly, in Epoch B humanity may be able to devise ways of improving the quality of life of the individual and of the species by reducing unwisdom or its adverse effects and by respecting and applying wisdom for increasing the possibility of personal fulfillment. Among individuals who now have less to struggle for personally in order to survive, as a result of the changes brought about in Epoch A, a new syndrome has developed, manifest in seeming purposelessness, for the treatment of which new experiences will be needed, possibly leading to new motivations.

Judgment is required in larger measure than ever before if humanity is to succeed in balancing the adverse effects, both upon the species and upon individuals, resulting from the increased knowledge and improved technology that reduce the need for struggle and also the opportunity to learn how to experience a sense of satisfaction. This is seen among the increasing numbers of individuals whose lives have been prolonged and made more secure by the metabiological evolutionary developments that have occurred in recent times, without effort on their part.

There is a further undesirable side effect of the benefits brought about in Epoch A. Among the individuals who feel purposeless, some become wantonly and pathologically destructive, threatening and interfering with the development and achievement of fulfillment of others. For resolving such problems as these, far more insight is needed than has as yet been activated.

By suggesting the idea of survival of the wisest I mean not only that the more discerning will survive but also that the survival of humanity, with a life of high quality, depends upon the prevalence of respect for wisdom and for those possessing a sense of the *being** of humanity and of the laws of nature. These are necessary for choosing from among alternatives, for

---

* "Being" is the center in which exist the possibilities that, when unfolded, reveal the essence of the person, both as a member of the species and as an individual.

fulfillment as well as for survival. Humankind's metabiological questions and problems still need answers.

The idea of wisdom as a pro-health, pro-life, pro-evolutionary influence still leaves open and unresolved the question as to how this might be developed and applied. Humanity's capacity to bring this about is also not known. The role of religious and political organizations has been to enlighten and to guide. Now new means are needed for inner self-regulation based upon naturalistic rather than on arbitrary moralistic formulations. In spite of the difficulties involved in devising and developing such formulations, this could provide an important purpose *in* life and serve the purpose *of* life individually and collectively.

The extent we have reached in our capacity to create, to destroy, and to move in space as well as over the surface of the earth has indeed been remarkable. To what extent do we have the ability to invent new ways to act wisely as a species even if our aptitude to so behave individually is relatively limited?

Exposing our minds to the laws of nature may help us discover and apply whatever insight and foresight we possess for dealing with the problems of relationships to ourselves and to others, and to the universe. This way of thinking about humanity and nature and relationship and wisdom is new to most, and to be of value will require modern patterns of perceiving one's self and others. New attitudes and behavioral patterns will follow.

It is simpler to conceive such notions than to apply them in everyday life. Nevertheless, it is far easier to reach objectives based upon sound concepts and hypotheses than upon those without basis. The challenge with which humanity is generally confronted at this point is to see itself as a biological and metabiological entity, possessing attributes capable of reversing some of the *de*volutionary trends. These attributes can also be directed and disciplined to facilitate and increase the probability of achieving a greater measure of fulfillment in life than has been possible until now.

Paradoxically, this challenge and hope exist in the face of enigmas more difficult to overcome than ever before, because greater opportunities for fulfillment are matched by correspondingly greater obstacles. For this reason, wisdom, understood as a new kind of strength, is a paramount necessity for humankind. Now, even more than ever before, it is required as a basis for fitness, to maintain life itself on the face of this planet, and as an alternative to paths toward alienation or despair.

Healing is perhaps humanity's oldest concern. Few scholars have investigated modern and primitive healing practices with as much depth and insight as Alberto Villoldo. His interest in ritual and magical healing began at an early age, when he would observe, awestruck, as local folk healers treated their patients in the outskirts of Havana, where he was born. His interest in optimal health would later take him to investigate healing practices around the world, from the Laplands to the tip of Tiera del Fuego in South America.

Pursuing his doctorate in psychology, he became interested in health education with young children, which led him to write The Multicultural Guide to Early Education, *highlighting and bringing together early education practices from numerous cultures around the world. The* Multicultural Guide *is now popularly used in school classrooms throughout the country.*

On completing his doctorate in psychology, and after publishing The Realms of Healing *(with Stanley Krippner) he went on to investigate the neuropsychology of the healing process itself. Under a grant from San Francisco State University he founded the Psi Self-Regulation Project. In his laboratory at San Francisco State University, where he is an Adjunct Professor, he has been researching the brain-body interface, and identifying and testing hypnotic techniques for accelerating healing, for strengthening the body's auto-immune system, and promoting states of optimal health and performance. His forthcoming book,* Future Mind, *describes these findings, and explores the possibilities of self-regulations and increased intelligence that await us in the near future. Dr. Villoldo has held faculty appointments at the University of California and the University of Mexico, and lectures throughout the world on hypnosis, health, and healing. He lives and practices in San Francisco, California.*

ALBERTO VILLOLDO # HEALING

On a spring day some sixty thousand years ago, a Neanderthal man was carefully buried in a bed of flowers inside a cave at Shanidar in the Zagros mountain highlands of Iraq. The evidence of a deliberate and ceremonious burial betrays a dawning sense of selfhood, for no other precursor of man until then had been known to bury their dead. It would seem that the man's family had gone off into the fields and gathered bunches of mallow, woody horsetail, St. Barnaby's thistle, and yarrow, and carefully laid them around the dead man's corpse in that cave at Shanidar. But even more fascinating is the discovery that many of the varieties of flowers found in the Shanidar grave have been used until recently in local herbal medicine.

The burial cave at Shanidar holds humanity's earliest accounts of herbal medicine. From the ceremonious use that these plants were put to we can assume the existence of early men and women recognized by their tribes as shamans, mediators with the natural and supernatural forces of health and disease that surrounded our forest-dwelling ancestors. In their world view, illness fell into two categories—the natural and the supernatural ones, the latter inflicted and cured by a pantheon of nature gods and demigods.

Primitive man considered the universe a living and intelligent being and personified it in numerous deities that the shaman could influence on one's behalf. Even in today's native American cultures, the shaman's stature is often determined by his ability to influence the forces of nature and the degree to which he is able to increase the tribe's well-being by keeping members healthy, protecting them in the hunt, and divining the location of the game. During certain states of trance the shaman is reputedly able to enter the realm of the gods and speak directly to them, then to return to the world of humans with a healing message or herbal remedy for his patients.

The healer's personal tie with the supernatural linked the community in its day-to-day existence with the divine and gave a sense of purpose and meaning to primitive life. The loss of a sense of connection with nature and the divine is perhaps one cause of civilized man's great sense of isolation, powerlessness, and lack of meaning in life. Psychiatrists like Viktor Frankl have pointed to this lack of meaning and sense of powerlessness as significant in the origins of many psychosomatic ills.

Although primitive medicine appears to us in the West as cumbersome and tainted with superstition, it did hit upon a formula of healing that worked. For if the herbal treatments were not effective (and the shaman was familiar with a great many natural medicines), the healing ritual often was. The ritual brought together the basic ingredients of healing: theatre, music, dance, family and community participation, natural pharmacopoeia, peer pressure, and rites of passage and transformation. The use of theatre in healing would later be recognized by the Greeks for its cathartic effects. Music and dance allowed the patient and shaman to jointly enter into an altered state of consciousness where personality structures that made one prone to disease could be changed. The dance also allowed the patient to externalize and act out the illness as well as the dark sides of their personalities such as anger, fear, and passion, which would normally not be demonstrated.

Above all, the shaman discovered that in an altered state of consciousness he was able to instruct his patient's unconscious mind to mobilize the body's self-healing mechanisms. For although the healer was not very knowledgeable about modern medicine, he was able to intuitively diagnose disease, and then through a combination of hypnosis, placebos, and healing mechanisms perhaps not fully known even to us, was able to effect a positive change in the patient's health.

The shaman often intuitively understood what was necessary for his patients to recover their health, though he could not describe it in contemporary medical language. In the same way, most of us are not aware of what happens when we think a thought, but this does not mean that brain specialists are better thinkers because they can describe the chemical reactions that take place inside the brain. The healer unconsciously recognized and understood the healthy state of an organ or the entire body and could transmit this information to the patient during the healing trance. The healing information was transmitted perhaps in a type of mime-dance ritual as well as literally through spoken hypnotic commands and chemically through different herbs and potions.

This type of healing involved a form of biological information transfer between the healer and the patient. It was an intuitive healing that would not be fully understood until the advent of modern hypnosis and contemporary physics. If you place a finely tuned violin on a table in front of you while playing a note of C on another equally tuned violin, the one on the table will begin to vibrate at exactly the same frequency of C. Similarly, the shaman's nervous system was being "played," while the healing information, stimulated a similar vibration in the patient. Physicist Evan Harris Walker discussed this concept of healing in his quantum mechanical theory of consciousness:

> There is the important question of how the consciousness knows how to rearrange the atoms, etc., to achieve "healing." The answer to this question is so simple that it is hard to understand. It is simply that the consciousness does not need to know the "path" from the sick condition to the healthy condition. All that is required is that (1) there exists an allowed or possible "path" from the sick condition to the healthy condition no matter how improbable—including the possibility that the atoms suddenly "tunnel" to the proper positions; (2) that the consciousness can recognize the healthy (and of course the sick) condition so that the proper state, if allowed by quantum mechanics, can be selected, and (3) that the healer's channel capacity be sufficiently high so that the selection of the desired state can be carried out—in other words, that the state can be found. Because the channel transcends time and space, it is intimately tied to the future state to be selected. Thus the healer feels the "healed condition" as though he were there in the future to see it—and to some extent he is. There is really no paradox here nor much real difficulty in understanding how this happens. The consciousness simply selects the appropriate state. The unwanted states are sluffed off as dead skin that does not feel good.[1]

Besides the transfer of biological information that occurred in the trance state, the patient was left with a number of obligations for maintaining his healed condition. These might consist of offerings to a deity or a particular service to the community. It was a reminder that the spirit had been made whole again and that the body, which was slower to change, would soon manifest the new state of health. And since the community had participated in the healing ritual, everyone was aware that the patient had been "renewed," and treated him or her in a new way.

While the shaman's power to a large degree rested on his ability to speak with the patient's unconscious, he also relied on the placebo effect, tricking the patient into believing he was receiving a potent medication. Yet the shamans who lacked this power of speaking with the unconscious and instructing it to heal the body soon fell into ill repute, for the body could only be tricked so many times before the placebo stopped having its impressive results. The chemical sensors in the body would soon recognize they were receiving an inert medication. The use of herbs, bio-information transfer healing, the placebo effect, and peer pressure during the healing ceremony combined to give the shaman an impressive cure rate, which would not be replicated by medicine until modern times.

Primitive medicine found itself in a continual state of flux, varying greatly from practitioner to practitioner and area to area. With their emphasis on the placebo effect, the practices that endured were not necessarily those that worked best, but those that worked last. There are, of course, notable exceptions, such as Chinese acupuncture, which dates back more than 5,000 years with the earliest written reference occurring in 500 B.C. Acupuncture is perhaps the only healing system that has endured unchanged over time.

MAGIC AND MEDICINE

It can be argued that primitive healers made the first major breakthrough in understanding the nature of disease. The medicine man understood in no uncertain terms that disease was nature's way of ensuring the survival and continuation of the species. This is not meant in a Darwinian sense, where only the strongest or the fittest survived, but rather that illness offers a rest from the body's usual steady state and allows the organism to adapt and evolve in a constantly changing environment.[2]

Perhaps more than at any other time in the history of our species, healing for primitive man was inexorably tied to the survival of the individual and the species. Only modern man makes a distinction between being killed by a lion or by a microbe, one being an unfortunate accident and the other the result of disease. For our early ancestors, the external and internal environments were two sides of the same harsh coin. Both disease and unfortunate accidents had to be survived if the individual and the species were to continue on the earth.

Magical medicine helped to ease the day-to-day ills and fears of our hunter-gatherer ancestors. Yet with the rise of agriculture and the emergence of cities and towns some 10,000 years ago, the effectiveness of the healer began to wane. The shaman held a hypothetical relationship with the world, where nothing was fixed and everything was subject to change and destiny could both be consulted and influenced. With the advent of agricultural communities, magical medicine gave way to religious medicine and a priest caste that instituted rigid and dogmatic laws about the nature of disease, its origins and treatment.

Religious medicine assumed that the props and aids that served the shaman to powerfully reinforce bio-information transfer and the placebo effect were actually valuable tools in their own right. During Egypt's decline, for example, a very systematized medicine developed that emphasized complex and often bizarre concoctions. Pig's bile was the prescribed remedy for eye trouble; the feces and urine of certain animals became highly prized medicaments. Egypt in its decline was also overrun with specialists who like our modern neurologists and others made exclusive claims to one or another part of the body.

Then, half a millennium before the birth of Christ, at the same time the earliest known manuscripts on Chinese medicine were being written, Hippocrates began upsetting the magical-religious tenets of Greek medicine of the time. Hippocrates' revolutionary contribution to medicine consisted first in the principle of careful observation and in detailed descriptions of symptoms. Before a magic potion or religious rite could be administered, the patient was to be carefully studied. Hippocrates also recognized the limitations of magical-religious medical knowledge in dealing with disease, and confined himself to prescribing rest, proper diet, and simple remedies whose effects were clearly known. The Hippocratic writings are full of aphorisms that encourage common sense and admonitions to follow the Golden Rule—that to eat, sleep, or drink either too little or too much is detrimental to health—in contrast to the earlier practices!

Hippocrates believed in the *medicatrix naturae*, or natural life force in man. He recognized the organism as a uniquely intelligent and self-regulating entity rather than a biological arena where bloody encounters between health and disease took place. Had these two theories been understood and generally accepted during Hippocrates' time, much suffering and a great many lives would have been spared from the effect of poorly conceived treatment and poisonous drugs with dreadful, sometimes lethal side effects.

Although Hippocratic medicine was both rational and effective, which magical-religious medicine was not, it met with an insurmountable obstacle—it required a rational society in order to work. In a highly superstitious society it is hard to find people who show much common sense when faced with illness. In fact, even to this day, people are not ordinarily rational about disease, or about pain or dying. Many practitioners at the time of Hippocrates took the opposite tack, reasoning that if illness was a weakening of the life force, why not take drugs and potions that would strengthen it, even if the effects of these substances were not fully known?

THE FIRST HOSPITALS

The religious fervor of the early Christians revived the age-old belief that illness is the result of a divine being's anger about one's actions. The primitive shaman could regard disease as an indication of disharmony with divine or natural forces, or the result of a hex against which he could muster his power or summon one of his spirit allies to appease the offended deity. But in a monotheistic religion where all the forces of nature and heaven stemmed from one god, the priest-healer was powerless to act—he could not direct his power against the one Supreme Being, and there were no minor deities he could cajole, bribe, or seduce to plead his case before the one god. The priest-healer's hands were tied behind his back, and religious medicine became more concerned with divination to find what caused God to become offended, or how one had sinned, than with prescribing treatment. And what treatment there was involved more the use of penance, prayer, and sacrifice than medication or diet.

The greatest legacy of Christianity to modern medicine, which would become a mixed blessing for the next thousand years, were hospitals. What better way for the faithful to follow the Christian admonition to help the sick, the poor, and the deprived than by being charitable to hospitals? More often than not, though, hospital conditions were appalling, with five or six sick patients often sharing one bed, and created more problems than they helped solve. For unless hospitals were well-endowed, which they seldom were, they became breeding grounds for disease and pestilence, and were a contributing factor to the plagues that scourged Europe. Both the healing arts and the civilization of the day would have been better off without the squalid, infection-ridden holes that were the hospitals of the time.

"IN PAIN THOU SHALL BEAR CHILDREN..."

The Middle Ages were also the darkest period in the history of women and childbirth. The towns' inadequate sewage and water supplies and the rampant infection resulting from lack of simple hygiene, such as washing the hands before delivery, made childbirth more hazardous than ever before. The ignorance of medicine of the time, combined with the prevalent religious barbarism of the era, made women pay dearly for bringing a child into the world. In the early 1200s, the Roman Church had put an end to abortions, which were practiced when the expectant mother suspected a difficult delivery or was nursing another child. Under the threat of eternal damnation, any woman attempting to abort was given a caesarian section, with no anesthesia or asepsia. In those days surgery was practiced by barbers or butchers, as it was below the dignity of the physician to bloody his hands, and the procedure consisted of a brutal slashing and wrenching of the fetus from the womb. Needless to say, few women survived the treatment.

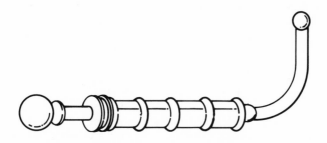

Baptismal syringe, designed in the seventeenth century, for baptising infants before birth in cases of difficult labor.

In the thirteenth century, religion assumed the supervision of midwives. The Dominican monk Albert Magnus wrote a manual on the art of midwifery, and the church passed edicts regulating the practice. Albert's manual was not intended for systematizing the care of the childbearing woman or alleviating her pain, but for ensuring that in the event of the mother's death there would be enough time to baptize the child before it died so that it would not be doomed to remain in purgatory for eternity. In 1280, the Council of Cologne further decreed that in the event of the mother's death during labor, the woman's mouth was to be kept open with a gag so the child would not suffocate while it was being surgically removed for baptism.

The Renaissance brought new light to medicine with figures like Ambrose Pare, who in the early 1500s was fortunate to train in the Hôtel Dieu in Paris. There were 1,200 beds in the then renowned hospital—480 for single occupancy and the remainder occupied by four to six patients each. The hospital was a breeding ground for the worst infectious disease, and patients often went without food or the most basic medical care, although the good nuns in the hospital would give sweets to the most pious looking or those that prayed the most fervently.

Pare broke away from the religious medicine of the time and reestablished in Paris the practices instituted by Hippocrates. To his credit, he was the first doctor concerned with improving the care of women during childbirth, insisting that deliveries and the care and comfort of the women were the responsibility of doctors and not barbers, for which he came under great criticism from his fellow physicians.

For medicine, though, the Renaissance was a second Dark Age, and the insight of men like Pare went neglected and unrecognized by their contemporaries. During this period numerous disgusting substances and therapies became common, including the powder of sympathy, a mixture of copper salts that was applied to the patient's blood-stained garment (to

his good fortune) rather than to the wound itself. Like the weapon ointment popular during the Middle Ages, this treatment is representative of
the medicine of the period, as described by H. W. Haggard, the Yale
historian of medicine:

> Weapon ointment was used for healing wounds, but, instead of being
> applied to them, the injured part was washed and bandaged and the
> weapon with which the wound was inflicted was carefully anointed
> with the ointment. This treatment was mostly used by empiric and
> ignorant barbers during the late Middle Ages, but it was advocated by
> Paracelsus and used by some of the respectable members of the
> medical profession. The ointment was usually composed of materials
> which appeal strongly to the imagination, such as human blood,
> eunuch's fat, and moss from a criminal's skull. The treatment was
> often successful; in fact it was a better form of wound treatment than
> that current among the medical profession at the time. A wound
> washed, bandaged, and let alone heals more quickly and with less
> infection than one to which is applied such healing ointments as
> were then used.[3]

Perhaps the most damage to modern medicine occurred during the
Renaissance, when most research and knowledge of the art was acquired on
the battlefield. As a result, medicine adopted the language of war to
describe the processes of disease and healing, a legacy which would burden
medicine for the next 500 years. People saw themselves the "victims" of
disease, and that their bodies were being "invaded," "attacked," "in-
flamed," "lacerated," or "assaulted" in every conceivable manner. It is easy
to understand how this language encouraged therapies and drugs that
"combatted" infection, "attacked" viruses, and "eliminated" symptoms, as
well as attitudes that encouraged people to think of their bodies as battle-
grounds for disease, where parts of themselves became the "enemy."

THE MODERN ERA

The nineteenth and twentieth centuries have been a golden era for technological and chemical medicine. One major breakthrough was the use of
vaccinations against the major contagious illnesses like polio and smallpox.[4] Discoveries in diagnostic medicine—from the stethoscope to X rays
to biochemical assays and the CAT scanner—made noninvasive diagnosis a
possibility for the first time in history. Up to that point, the physician was
blind as to what went on inside the body of a living patient and was forced to
work with calculated though frequently off-the-mark diagnostic guesses.

The state of the art of medicine in the early twentieth century, diagnostically advanced but still lacking in curative techniques, was perhaps best captured by Dostoevsky in *The Brothers Karamazov:*

> I've consulted all sorts of doctors; they can diagnose excellently, they will tell you all your symptoms, they have your illnesses at their fingertips, but they've no idea how to cure you. I happened to come across a very enthusiastic medical student. "You may die," he told me, "but at least you'll have a very good idea of what illness you are dying of."

To this date, epidemiology has yielded the greatest benefits to health, and the achievements of the World Health Organization in eradicating infectious disease and instituting sanitation and public health measures throughout the world have been notable, helping to make infant mortality and malnutrition a thing of the past.

LOOKING TO THE NEXT MILLENNIUM

The health revolution of the 1960s and 1970s has provided the first glimmer of the oncoming new age in medicine. In the early sixties numerous unorthodox healing practices sprang up under the banner of holistic health. They revived many of the techniques of primitive medicine, including faith healing, "energy healing," and long-distance cures. Many of the miraculous healings of the time were the result of a placebo effect, and mirrored the sentiments of a population anxious to vest their faith in medicaments that at least produced no harmful side effects.

The holistic health movement was an urban phenomenon that marked people's dissatisfaction with institutional and bureaucratic medicine. In April of 1978, medical care in the United States was costing one million dollars per hour. By December of the same year the amount had jumped to 2.67 million dollars per hour, and was increasing at a rate of 62% annually. Even greater controversy was stirred by the fact that life expectancy in the previous fifty years, while dramatically improved for infants through better nutrition and sanitation, had increased by only six months for the average person forty years of age. Furthermore, the quality of life deteriorated in that same fifty-year period due to the increase in cardiovascular disease, cancer, hypertension, and stress-related illnesses. Almost overnight, massive numbers of the population became interested in jogging, proper diet, cardiovascular self-care, and other health-oriented practices. America suddenly became aware of its own health and the responsibility for maintaining wellness. The population was no longer tolerant of the oppressive cost of medicine, although as yet no other option was available on a large-scale basis.

A number of realizations emerged from the holistic health movement, the most notable perhaps being that all healing is self-healing. Until then science had studied what doctors had done to achieve cures. Now medicine needed to study what people did to heal themselves. Another was the realization that there is a complementarity between psyche and soma. Both play an equally important role in the genesis of disease, its treatment, and the maintaining of health. Many people both in and out of the health professions realized that while there are thousands of possible ways of being ill, there are only one or two ways of being healthy, yet nobody knew what these were! The beginnings of a revolution of the magnitude of that brought about by Hippocrates was taking place. And as with the previous ones, its impact may not be felt by contemporary medicine, but in the years to come.

For the 1980s I see that new issues in healing will begin to be examined and much effort dedicated to studying the nature of pain, methods of tissue regeneration, the self-healing mechanisms of the body, and life extension techniques. A question that may typify the scientific inquiry of the next decade was raised by Nobel laureate Albert Szent-Gyorgyi, who pointed out that when you cut your skin, the cut activates a dormant mechanism that stimulates unprecedented cell growth in that area until the wound is closed again. What is it that keeps this mechanism dormant until it is activated by the cut? And when it is activated, what prevents it from producing rampant cell division such as you have with cancer?

The most notable medical breakthrough that we can look toward in the decade of the eighties will be as physics and biology meet, and quantum theory becomes integrated with the healing arts. Werner Heisenberg's uncertainty principle, which points out the interconnectedness between the person's subjective experience and the objective reality of science will become increasingly important in healing. At least in theory, medicine will be forced to abandon the mechanistic view that regards the body as a collection of parts like a machine.

Insightful healers who may or may not be medical doctors will begin to realize the role played by their patients' attitudes in creating and maintaining disease. For example, individuals who believe that heart disease "runs" in their families may be more prone to choose a life-style that predisposes them to the ailment. People's conceptions of themselves and of their maladies will be seen as a determining factor in both the onset and outcome of their illnesses. Illness, as well as health, will come to be regarded as the result of a life-style and one's attitude about oneself.

The Revolution in Biology

Repeated failures to find a chemical treatment for cancer and a host of psychogenic illnesses are resulting in popular disillusion with the drug-related therapies. Many pharmaceutical conerns will switch from a chemical orientation to a biological one, such as the pioneering development of man-made antibodies and the natural skin-growing process developed by Eugene Bell of MIT. In this new process, the person's own cells are induced to grow in any shape or form desired, promising new relief for burn victims and others having difficulty with the healing of wounds. Bell and his associates claim to be able to grow enough skin in their laboratory to cover the entire body in a month, to make a tube of any length or diameter to replace a blood vessel, and to grow new skin in the shape of a glove or an arm.

Space medicine also promises many surprises for future healing. The gravity-free environment of the space shuttle and of orbiting earth stations will open up a new chapter for a medical science whose 2,000-year history has been circumscribed by gravity. The first seeds of this new science were planted in the early fifties by A. S. Romen, a medical doctor and member of the Soviet Academy of Sciences. Romen set out to discover ways in which cosmonauts could learn to control physiological processes that would be useful during long space flights. His methods consisted of a synthesis of relaxation techniques, hypnosis, meditation, yoga, and zen through which the subjects were able to control heart rate, certain metabolic functions, and the displacement of internal organs, and to raise and lower temperature at will in designated areas of the body.

At the Biological Self-Regulating Project, which I direct at San Francisco State University, we have been testing the ability of our subjects to regulate their body's autoimmune system, as well as dopamine and beta-endorphin levels in the brain,[5] after they have undergone training in techniques similar to those used by Romen. Our preliminary findings indicate that there is an incredible potential for self-regulation and even self-healing in the human body-brain system. Furthermore, we believe that these same systems, when untrained, may be responsible for the genesis of many psychosomatic illnesses.

The next ten years will be crucial in illuminating the mind's role as healer as well as generator of disease. Self-regulation, both mind- and machine-induced, will become increasingly necessary for our future survival, for we have perpetrated changes in our environment that are too drastic for our DNA-based evolutionary mechanisms to respond to effectively. If left to biological evolution alone, it is doubtful our species would survive another 100 years in our increasingly toxic and polluted atmosphere. The DNA evolutionary code will have to be supplemented by new instructions from our brains and a new breed of computers that can interface with our biological systems, to allow our organisms to rapidly adapt to the new social and ecological environments that await us in the near future.

In the next ten years it is highly likely that all the biochemical parameters of the human organism will become known, leading to the eventual production of home Biological-Modulation units, which will enable individuals to regulate their mind sets and moods. These units may consist of a urinometer and telemetry system that projects on a television screen your hormone and brain chemical levels, and compares these to your normal levels, which are stored in its memory unit. You could then select a "normal" program that dimmed the room lighting and turned on soft lights of different colors and intensities. Simultaneously, preselected oscillating electromagnetic fields would surround you, and the room would be filled with a soft melody. These conditions would stimulate or depress the appropriate gland systems, reducing stress and altering the person's moods. We may also have the option of selecting from a number of states, from euphoric to contemplative to sensual enhancement to others you could "invent" yourself.

The two most important applications of home Bio-Modulation may be first, a new way of catalyzing ecstatic brain states, which could help reduce much drug and alcohol abuse. (So after a hard day of work or play you could punch the code for a mild "high" or a "two-very-dry-martinis" state and settle down to your favorite show.) The other may be a breakthrough in the healing of the now "incurable" diseases such as cancer. The treating of disease will very likely take on more of an information-based than a chemically- or surgically-based approach. This information would be encoded in magnetic and light waves, much like a radio transmission, and would "instruct" the affected cells or organ systems on the quickest path to recovery.

This new science may provide a connection between cybernetics and information theory. The scenario may unfold something like this: The problem posed by cancer is the chaotic reproduction of cells that have escaped all the body's usual controls. Both radiation and chemotherapy curtail the spread of cancer by jumbling the DNA strands in these cells, therefore inhibiting or slowing down their reproduction. They work by administering a large amount of poison to a small area of the body (radiation) or a small amount of poison to a large area (chemotherapy)—both treatments are, in cybernetic terms, conveying the signal STOP to the reproductive mechanism of these cells.

Poison is a very crude, not to mention dangerous way of transmitting the order to STOP. This conventional treatment method slows the growth of a cancer in one area but does not give the body the information it needs to reach a higher level of health and trigger the autoimmune and regeneration mechanisms of the body. Also, it does nothing to prevent metastasis and relapse. The new science may activate the body's self-healing mechanism by identifying the changes in energy fields in molecular groupings, then organ groupings, and then the entire body as it is treated with conventional chemical and radiation methods.

At first researchers may attempt to adapt Biological-Modulation units to supply the necessary healing information in the form of lights, sounds, and electromagnetic frequencies. It is likely that they will discover that these instruments work only at the neurologically higher frequencies, when in fact low biological frequencies are required to transmit information to the very primitive cancer cells. An innovative researcher may then conceive of the unconventional idea of surrounding the body in a low-frequency electromagnetic field, forming a closed feedback loop with the organism into which he would encode information that increases the cancer tissue's level of organization, possibly inhibiting chaotic cell division and metastasis.

It may become more evident in the years to come that there is no demonstrable relationship between the practice of medicine and the attainment of health. Indeed, we already are discovering the severe limitations of medicine. As Lewis Thomas, a noted physician and observer of science, pointed out:

> Sometime in the early nineteenth century, it was realized by a few of the leading figures in medicine that almost all of the complicated treatments then available for disease did not really work, and the suggestion was made by several courageous physicians, here and abroad, that most of them actually did more harm than good. Simultaneously, the surprising discovery was made that certain diseases were self-limited, got better by themselves, possessed, so to speak, a "natural history." It is hard for us now to imagine the magnitude of this discovery and its effect on the practice of medicine. The long habit of medicine, extending back into the distant past, had been to treat everything with something, and it was taken for granted that every disease demanded treatment and might in fact end fatally if not treated. In a sober essay written on this topic in 1876, Professor Edward H. Clarke of Harvard reviewed what he regarded as the major scientific accomplishment of medicine in the preceding fifty years, which consisted of studies proving that patients with typhoid and typhus fever could recover all by themselves, without medical intervention, and often did better for being untreated than when they received the bizarre herbs, heavy metals, and fomentations that were

popular at that time. Delirium tremens, a disorder long believed to be fatal in all cases unless subjected to constant and aggressive medical intervention, was observed to subside by itself more readily in patients left untreated, with a substantially improved rate of survival.[6]

Among other changes we can look forward to in the next decade is the gradual decentralization of hospitals. The existence of hospitals can be traced back to the fourth century A.D., and they enjoyed increased popularity in pestilence-wracked medieval Europe. While hospitals effectively remove the patient from all public contact, they often create more disease than they help resolve. And the incidence of iatrogenic (doctor-induced) and hospital-generated disease is continually on the rise. In the near future we can expect to see the traditional megalithic hospital, where all medical services are gathered under one roof, becoming highly specialized diagnostic and treatment centers. The more routine medical care will be relegated to community health centers, and the amount of self medical care practiced in the home will increase.

BEYOND 2000 A.D.

As early as the 1970s, cryogenics was becoming a popular practice for the well-to-do, and numerous concerns sprang up around the country sporting a slogan along the lines of "freeze now, live later." In general these fly-by-night operations are plagued with problems—their unfortunate clients will most probably thaw out quite lifeless. In a couple of instances, cryogenic companies that have gone bankrupt have abandoned their frozen clients in warm warehouses where they were later found half thawed and decomposing. As life-extension techniques become more readily available, cryogenics will most likely lose its appeal, save perhaps for those wanting to live their lives at some future time.

Following the 1980s, we can look forward to a Golden Age of Healing, with emphasis on life extension, optimal health, and cooperative evolution. First there will be major advances in prosthetic technology, and artificial limbs and organs that replicate the functions of the originals will become readily available. Aging, also, will come to be understood as happening more or less rapidly to the different organs in the body. As each organ begins to malfunction it is quite likely that it will be replaced with its mechanical counterpart.[7]

Despite the tremendous advances of prosthetics technology and implants, life expectancies will not increase dramatically until organ cloning methods are perfected. At first, organ cloning will be used to grow a "sheath" that surrounds a prosthetic organ, giving it a skin that the body finds compatible with its own and that will not be rejected by the neighboring tissues. With organ cloning methods perfected, life extension will finally become a reality for large segments of the earth's population. A common practice might be to draw cells from each organ during the person's youth. Then, through mononuclear reproduction, these cells could be used to create an organic replica of any malfunctioning part of the body.

Yet very interesting ethical questions will arise regarding organ cloning. For the easiest way to clone an organ is to clone the entire organism. Will we be making exact but brainless copies of ourselves that we can keep in clone banks from which to cannibalize any necessary parts?

The greatest issue in the early days of life extension will be "who." Will the wealthy, who can afford the costly prototype organs, be the first to benefit from them? Or will there perhaps be a national lottery to choose the lucky few who will reap the early benefits of life extension?

With life spans tremendously increased, perhaps even upwards of 200 years, childbearing will become an issue of great concern. Parenthood rights may have to be carefully parcelled so as not to overtax the dwindling resources of the planet, or greatly augment the exponentially increasing world population. Perhaps only families who choose to space migrate will be allowed more than one pregnancy. These groups of adventuresome space migrators may live in orbiting mini-earths where they can build pollution-free environments that suit their collective fantasies.

The most creative application of the medical technology of the future may be in cyborg engineering. A being that is half-human and half-machine will no longer be merely a science-fiction fantasy. Cyborgs may be in great demand as factory managers and for piloting interstellar freighters, as they would be able to instantaneously register and process thousands of bits of information through the ducts in the metallic half of their bodies directly from a computer and into the brains, bypassing the slower and often misleading senses. For the first time the human brain might directly benefit from the incredible processing and storage capabilities of modern computers, at the same time supplying the machine with a human mind. Interstellar pilots could then issue commands in microseconds while navigating their ships through hazardous meteorite regions.

Public health may again become a concern in the early part of the next century as travel to other planets in the solar system becomes possible. Health authorities may fear that extraplanetary viruses could be introduced by foreign life forms that will be purposely or accidentally brought back by our astronauts, resulting in a rash of new and unheard-of epidemics for which we had no known treatment. Yet alien organisms will most likely be so foreign to our own that we will have a natural immunity to them. It's possible the only infectious diseases remaining on the earth in the next century will be in laboratory vials and museums. What illnesses remain on the planet may be of an autogenic or self-inflicted nature, and only will "befall" artists and others wanting to experiment with them for creative or self-exploratory purposes. It may even be in vogue at some future time to use self-inflicted hepatitis to enter into the depths of depression, but the fad will be a passing one, as the population maintains increasingly high levels of health.

It should be noted that the human body had begun to gradually but unmistakably change toward the mid 1900s, when major ecological changes began to take place in a short period of time—decades, in fact—from oil spills to acid rains to radiation leaks. In our evolutionary past Homo sapiens had numerous generations to adapt to the new environments that resulted from the earth's geophysical changes. The human organism was not geared by nature to adapt in the course of decades, but rather over generations. In effect, no perceptible change in the human organism has taken place in the last 100,000 years. Simultaneously, modern medicine has enabled even the physically weakest members of the species to survive. And every time there is a heart or kidney transplant that prolongs a patient's life and that person's tendency to a weak heart or kidney is inherited by his or her offspring, the species itself is debilitated. Genes that would have previously been weeded out by nature are now inherited by future generations. The renowned biologist, Sir Julian Huxley, noted a generation ago that "the quality of the world's population is not very high, is beginning to deteriorate, and should and could be improved. It is deteriorating thanks to genetic defectives, who would otherwise have died, being kept alive."

How do we go about improving the quality of humanity's stock? A future historian may well describe the following fictional scenario: "When a mechanical kidney was transplanted, it was equipped with new baffles and filters to eliminate impurities in the blood, resulting from new chemicals in our habitat and diet. As the rate at which changes in planetary ecology increased, other adaptations of the human organism became necessary. By 2150 our internal organs held only a small resemblance to those of the early 1900s, although our physical features remained the same. Consequently, by the age of fifteen, most children had their digestive and eliminatory tracts, which were nothing more than a vestige from our hunting and foraging days, replaced with compact mini-processors that rapidly assimilated the potent tablet or liquid nutrients it received. There were no body wastes, which had been virtually eliminated from the planet, for a population of 40 billion people would drown in its own wastes."

The technologically inspired mutations that may take place in the next century, with each advance in prosthetics and in recombinant DNA should be instrumental in allowing our species to survive our ever-changing environment. For example, thicker, more porous skin will enable us to tolerate higher temperatures resulting from a "greenhouse effect" that may raise ambient temperatures to as high as 44 degrees Centigrade when the great forests are cut down toward the end of the twentieth century. Some scientists may decide that from the neck down the human body is most suited to survive in the wild, with a digestive apparatus designed for foraging in the bush and limbs constructed to hold weapons and build shelter, all of which machines already do better than man. At first unconsciously and then more and more actively, we may decide that we do not have the time to wait for nature's slower rhythm of change. With the genetic engineering technology currently available we are in a position to not only play alchemists, but to actually play God. Science has already given us the power of genetic predestination, to use or abuse in the future.

We are inclined to see ourselves today at the brink of an enormous precipice that may mark the end of the human era on earth. Yet there is another, more optimistic perspective that I see for our future. The term *Homo sapiens*—sapiens knowing, knowing man—has become in vogue to describe our species today. Yet we don't really understand ourselves or nature at all. We don't understand why people fall ill, or even how they get well. We don't even understand, or have a description for being healthy and well. We are just knowing enough to become conscious of our ignorance. And while total ignorance is bliss indeed, it is painful and depressing to be halfway on the path of knowledge.

We need to look to our own neurological apparatus—our brains—as the foremost tool for acquiring knowledge. And we need to do this both as individuals and communally. There is no question that we have become co-creators of our future. If this task is left to government institutions and big business and genetic engineering, we will have no say over our destiny.

To me the most important direction to look is within ourselves. It is our own minds that bring about our illness and that also heal us and maintain our health. As we learn to mobilize our self-healing capabilities, we will not only be able to influence the state of our health but also break new territory into heretofore unknown areas of human potentialities, and to re-create ourselves in whatever image we choose, through techniques like meditation and bio-self-regulation.

Few Americans have done more than Michael Murphy to promote the exploration of human potential. Keeping a consistently low profile and a humble demeanor, Murphy has for nearly three decades been at the very heart of the Western search for expanded consciousness and enhanced mental and physical capabilities.

Michael Murphy's interest in human evolution was sparked in the early 1950s while he was a graduate student in philosophy at Stanford University. Finding himself disenchanted with the limitations of Western philosophy and traditional university life, he journeyed to India, where he began his serious study of Eastern psychology, philosophy, and transformational disciplines such as meditation and yoga. It was during this period that he had the opportunity to become a student of meditation at the Sri Aurobindo Ashram in Pondicherry. After returning to the United States and continuing his long daily meditation practice, he was inspired to form the Esalen Institute in Big Sur, California. Initially founded as a center to explore "those trends in education, religion, philosophy, and the physical and behavioral sciences which emphasize the potentialities and values of human existence," Esalen has developed during the past two decades to become the most renowned and successful growth center in the world, presenting seminars on all aspects of human transformation to thousands of students and seekers from throughout the world. Murphy was president of Esalen until 1973 and presently remains chairman of its Board of Trustees.

In recent years, Michael Murphy's specific interest has centered on the human body and its latent capacities for enhanced functioning and performance. His curiosity led to the creation of the Transformation Project, established in 1976 as a computer-based research program to explore, compile, and analyze information about extraordinary physical functioning mediated by the human mind. This fascinating involvement has drawn him into all endeavors related to the human body, from sports to psychic phenomena. From this research, Murphy and his staff hope to present a new image of the human body and its evolutionary potentials.

These years of study and examination have also produced a number of highly acclaimed books, including Golf in the Kingdom, The Psychic Side of Sports, *and* Jacob Atabet: A Speculative Fiction.

In the following chapter on the future of the body Michael Murphy presents his most imaginative speculations about the nature of human life—now, as well as in the near and distant future.

MICHAEL MURPHY **THE BODY**

The future of man, if it is to be progress and not merely a standstill or a degeneration, must be guided by a deliberate purpose. And this human purpose can only be formulated in terms of the new attributes achieved by life in becoming human. . . . Progress is a major fact of past evolution; but it is limited to a few select stocks. It may continue in the future, but it is not inevitable; man, by now become the trustee of evolution, must work and plan if he is to achieve further progress for himself and for life.

                                                          Julian Huxley

The human being is unique among animals in having reduced the impact of natural selection on the survival of individuals. Medical care, sanitation, and social welfare have ensured the survival and reproduction of individuals whose physical makeup would have caused their extinction in earlier times. Biologists agree that the processes of natural selection will play a minimal role in the further development of the human body.[1]

In the absence of natural selection, can there be a future development for the human body? Scientists and science fiction writers have envisioned several basic scenarios in this regard. These possible futures tend to fall into three categories: *the cyborg,* in which the human brain would eventually be housed in a conglomeration of elaborate prosthetic devices . . . . a bit like the "Six Million Dollar Man;" *genetic engineering* and *selective eugenic breeding* which involve the scientific manipulation of the genetic code to create a superior race of humans; and *conscious bodily transformation* mediated and assisted by a variety of psychological and physical disciplines. It is this third possibility that will be the primary focus of this essay.

77

THE CYBORG SCENARIO

The possibilities for human self-transformation through prosthetic devices are immense. The aftermath of the Vietnam war has seen enormous advances in the technology of artificial limbs. Artificial cardiac pacemakers, arteries, corneas, heart valves, and implanted hearing aids are common. Batlike sonar devices are now used to aid the blind. Implanted electronic brain stimulation is a recognized treatment for certain types of depressive psychoses. Artificial hearts, lungs, and kidneys are fairly well developed, although not presently implanted.

The term "cyborg," coined in 1960 by Manfred Clynes and Nathan Kline, is an abbreviation for cybernetic organism. The original notion was that artificial implants might be placed in future astronauts to aid them in maintaining normal body functions during the long, hard months in space. The term is now more broadly used. Future cyborgs may be equipped with devices having no natural counterparts. It might be possible, for example, to build sense organs that receive and transmit radio waves or devices that would release hormones, enzymes, and other chemicals into the blood stream. The following prospect is suggested by Robert Prehoda in *Designing the Future:*

> In the future, a stroke-prone person may sleep with a device resembling a football helmet which would constantly monitor brain waves on an attachment evolving from the electroencephalograph (EEG). At the first signal of a stroke, powerful anticoagulants and antimetabolites would instantly be injected into the brain arteries, dissolving the blood clot causing the damage. The antimetabolites would limit brain tissue destruction. The device would also automatically summon the patient's doctor. Micro-miniaturization might permit a cyborg implant in which this entire system is made into a synthetic skull over the brain with direct EEG electrode-brain contact. The normal scalp would cover this skull-bone cyborg replacement, and it would be operational twenty-four hours a day.[2]

The variety of artificial implants will probably continue to grow beyond the limits of contemporary speculation, increasing our personal options for health and well-being. There is an industry now developing such prosthetic devices, with its own burgeoning research effort. There is a literature about the promise of cyborgs. And we have a set of bionic heroes commanding large television audiences. Arthur Clarke and other science fiction writers have created characters that make cyborgs more plausible and attractive. All this imagination, research and industry may indeed produce men and women with at least some of the supernormal capacities we see on the television screen: people who can run faster, jump higher, see further. But will the prosthetic device, humane and necessary as it has proven to be, enhance the quality of our consciousness? The cyborg scenario, it seems to me, when carried to extremes would lead to a cold, machine-ridden future.

GENETIC ENGINEERING

The possibilities for human transformation through genetic manipulation are even more far-reaching than the cyborg scenario. One eugenic measure, sometimes called "eutelegenesis," was first suggested in the Soviet Union by A. S. Serebrovsky, and independently in America.[3] It proposes that the sperm of men judged to be superior be used for artificial insemination, thereby increasing the frequency of desirable genes in the human gene pool. Sperm banks now exist, and egg banks might be established as well. The recent controversy over several Nobel Prize winners offering their sperm for a fee to interested mothers attests to the fact that selective artificial insemination has moved out of the realm of science fiction into that of science fact.

Over thirty years ago the French scientist Jean Rostand removed rabbit ova, stimulated them into beginning embryonic development, then placed them in host female rabbits—foster mothers that subsequently gave birth to normal rabbits with only one parent. This process of developing an egg without fertilization, called "parthenogenesis," allows the offspring to receive a double charge of heredity from the mother. In a similar process, the maternal chromosomes are removed from the rabbit ova and replaced with the father's chromosomes alone, from a sperm cell. Such "androgenesis" could permit a man to be the sole parent of millions of children.[4] In "superovulation," another recent reproductive achievement, special hormones cause as many as 100 cattle ova to ripen at one time. Such mass ovulation is followed by artificial insemination and removal of the embryos by surgery so that they can be reimplanted into the uteri of other cows. Thus one pedigreed cow can be the parent of thousands of calves.

The possibilities of genetic engineering go even further. As we gain more knowledge of the genetic code, direct tampering with the genes could subtract from or add to the instructions received by a cell. Many biologists believe that intelligence, memory, and the body's capacity for self-repair could be improved. Genetic engineering might increase the human life span and put more bodily function under the kind of conscious control that can only be obtained at present through extensive biofeedback or yogic practice. Perhaps physical beauty could be enhanced. It has even been suggested that we could design genetic modifications to facilitate states of consciousness comparable to the Zen "satori" or Yogic "samadhi." Or it might be possible to grow people with three arms and five legs.

It is clear, however, that the wonders of eugenics and genetic engineering will create many social and ethical problems, the solution of which will require much collective wisdom. Such wisdom is not likely to come from the biologists alone, because it involves moral issues beyond their expertise. As with prosthetic devices, there already is an industry to develop these various kinds of genetic manipulation, an industry with its own research effort. As benefits from such research become more evident, there might be increasing support for genetic engineering in general. When that happens the ethical problems involved will arise with growing urgency. Who will have the right to manipulate genetic changes? What kinds of changes will be permitted? The scientific control of our genetic inheritance presents us with a prospect that is both promising and dangerous.

BODILY TRANSFORMATION THROUGH
PSYCHO-PHYSICAL DISCIPLINE

Evidence from yoga, contemplative practice, hypnosis, sport, psychotherapy, spiritual healing, shamanism, and modern psychical research suggests that humans can effect life-giving transformations of the body through a combination of spiritual, psychological and physical disciplines. A significant frontier is revealed by this kind of evidence, one that is richer and more promising, I feel, than the cyborg and genetic engineering scenarios. Indeed, many programs to explore these possibilities are already emerging in Europe, Russia, and the United States.

A group of colleagues and I are presently exploring such experience, gathering research material and anecdotes from every field of human experience that seems fertile in this regard. To date we have collected several thousand examples of supernormal bodily change—some of it spontaneous, some of it consciously self-directed—from the lore of yoga and contemplative practice the world over, from work with hypnosis, autogenic training and Soviet psychical self-regulation, from sport and athletic training, from research with hallucinogenic drugs, from spiritual or "mind assisted" healing, from the reports of artists, and from several other fields. As far as we know, this is the first systematic attempt to collect evidence from a variety of fields for the human capacity to achieve extraordinary bodily function. From this data base we are developing an analysis of the talents, belief systems, personality structures, and environmental conditions of the people involved, as well as certain psychological processes that accompany the emergence of new physical capacities.

In the pages that follow I will present an overview of some of the material we are studying, then describe some features of supernormal function that seem likely to appear in the transformed body of the future.

EXAMPLES OF SUPERNORMAL BODILY CAPACITY

Running

At every distance up to several hundred miles, human running speed has increased steadily over the past fifty years. New records are set at most Olympic Games. Roger Bannister, the first man to run the mile in less than four minutes, has predicted that the first three and a half minute mile will be run within thirty or forty years. A *Scientific American* article presented data on the performance of male runners who set world records at distances from 100 yards to thirty kilometers over the past fifty years.[5] The rate of improvement has averaged about .75 meter per minute per year. Most coaches and fitness experts believe that improvement in performance is almost certain to continue.

Running influences a number of physiological parameters. Aerobic capacity—the ability to utilize large quantities of oxygen per second per kilogram of body weight—increases with developing fitness and running ability.[6, 7] Structural and functional changes occur in the heart, allowing more blood to circulate during peak effort. Many questions regarding the effects of athletic training are still being researched, but there is a strong belief among health experts that the practice improves health, increases resistance to disease and prolongs life.[8, 9, 10, 11, 12]

Placebo Research

A placebo is a sugar pill or inert substance that is given to someone who believes it is a medicine or drug. By accepting the authority of the doctor or experimenter, persons taking such a pill often rally their own powers to produce the changes they have been led to expect from the drug. The fascinating aspect of this phenomenon is that it suggests that the individual has the innate capacity to alter his or her bodily state in very subtle ways in order to eliminate disease, enhance mental functioning, or simply to fall asleep. Since the only actual function the inert placebo serves is to convince the subject's mind that the desired event can and will take place, all of the actual biological and chemical changes inherent in this event are induced by the subject. Although this incredible mechanism is yet to be completely understood, placebos can help lower the amount of fat and protein in the blood, change the white cell count, reduce the trembling associated with Parkinson's disease, relieve depression, increase sleepiness, reduce postoperative wound pain, relieve the symptoms of arthritis, eliminate the symptoms of withdrawal from morphine, and produce various specific effects of both stimulant and depressive drugs. Through placebos we apparently become motivated to mobilize our own self-regenerative powers.

Hypnosis and Suggestion

Hypnosis and suggestion have now been proved effective for a variety of problems including pain control, shyness and serious medical illness. Researchers have successfully used hypnotic induction to alleviate congenital ichthyosis, a devastating disease characterized by skin that is black, horny, and covered with scales; by using hypnosis and suggestion, at least four researchers have helped victims of this disease achieve from seventy-five to ninety percent remission.[13, 14, 15, 16]

Using hypnosis, James Esdaile, a Scottish surgeon, performed several hundred operations without anesthesia in India during the midnineteenth century. These operations included the amputation of arms, fingers, and toes; the removal of tumors; the extraction of teeth; the removal of cataracts. His patients not only felt less pain, but their wounds healed faster than those of patients who were not hypnotized. Esdaile's operations were observed and described by many reliable witnesses, including sceptical British doctors and government officials.[17, 18] Even with today's remarkable advances in anesthesiology, hypnosis is sometimes used as the sole anesthetic for major operations.

Results like these have been achieved in many experiments during the past 150 years. These studies clearly demonstrate that through hypnosis many people can win significant freedom from pain, disease, and allergy, change the structure of their bodies, and increase certain skills and capacities.[19]

Spiritual or Mind-Assisted Healing

Dr. Carl Simonton and his wife, Stephanie Matthews, maintain a cancer treatment clinic in Fort Worth, Texas. Based on the premise that an individual's mental and emotional processes are significant contributors to the formation of cancer, their treatment program consists of regular exercise, psychological counseling, radiation therapy, and mental self-healing. Participants in it visualize a scenario in which their natural immune systems are seen fighting the cancer as a healthy body does. Patients might be asked, for example, to visualize an army of white blood cells swarming over the cancer to carry off malignant cells which have been weakened or killed by radiation therapy. These white cells are then visualized as breaking down the malignant cells and flushing them out of the body. Finally, just before the end of the meditation, the patient sees himself well again. The Simontons' positive results to date indicate that mental activity of this kind helps rid the body of disease. One of their patients was a sixty-one year old man with extensive throat cancer; by using mental imagery and radiation therapy, he was healed after a year and a half of treatment. In the course of his remission he drew pictures to represent the state of his disease, and Dr. Simonton was amazed to observe his accurate representation of the cancer's size and shape. He seemed to see internally what Dr. Simonton could see with the aid of an instrument. After his cancer was gone, this man used the same mental techniques to eliminate arthritis and sexual impotence. Seven years later, in 1978, he was still free of disease or disability.

In a study of 152 patients, Simonton found the greatest success with those who were most optimistic and committed to full participation in the entire therapeutic process. These patients also showed fewer distressing side-effects to the radiation therapy.[20, 21]

Autogenics and Biofeedback

In recent years, there has been a growing body of evidence to suggest that subtle biological changes can be brought about through self-directed control. Since a host of disease symptoms relate to such basic physiological factors as blood flow, pulse rate, blood pressure, skin temperature, muscle tension, and brain rate, an effective way to alter these symptoms is simply to induce the appropriate change in the related bodily function. For example, when people are extremely tense and stressed, there is a corresponding constriction of the musculature, a decrease in temperature in the extremities, and an elevation in temperature in the forehead. Through methods such as autogenics (which involves repeated self-suggestion regarding desired physical states) and biofeedback (in which physiological conditions are immediately reported back to the subject for the purpose of self-manipulation) patients can learn to bring about the desired bodily states and thereby diminish the disease or physical condition.[22]

Dr. John Basmajian has reported on the voluntary control of single nerve fibers through auditory and visual feedback from electrodes placed in thumb muscles. Subjects learned such delicate control that they could produce neural rhythms such as "doublets, triplets, gallop rhythms, and drum rolls" after sixty to ninety minutes of training.[23] In another study, Bernard Engel showed that some people can learn to control individual sections of the heartbeat.[24] Yet another study has demonstrated a person's ability to influence blood sugar levels at will. These various investigations suggest that any aspect of a person's chemistry or physiology that can be brought to awareness, either directly or through instruments, can become accessible to conscious control.

Autogenics and biofeedback are currently being used throughout the world as alternative medical therapy for a variety of common diseases such as peptic ulcers, migraine headaches, asthma, arthritis, lower back pain, sexual disorders and Raynaud's disease.[25, 26]

Russian "Psychical Self-Regulation" (PSR)

PSR is defined by its Russian authors as "a directed, purposeful regulation of the various actions, reactions, and processes of an organism realized by means of its own psychic (mental) activity." The system was pioneered by A. S. Romen, a medical doctor, to discover ways cosmonauts could control their physiological processes during space flight. The research, which began in the mid-fifties, involves a synthesis of yoga, zen, Chinese medicine, progressive relaxation, hypnosis, autogenic training and the martial arts. In it, mastery of muscle relaxation and breathing rhythms; achievement of temperature changes in the arms, chest, abdomen, and head; and control of heart rate are developed in preparation for more selective control of various psychological and physiological functions. More advanced forms of self-control have included induction of isolated contraction of abdominal muscles, displacement of the internal organs in the abdominal cavity, alteration of sensitivity to pain, control of blood sugar metabolism, decrease of reaction time and increase of memory abilities.

Russian researchers report that we all have the capacity for psychical self-regulation to various degrees. They maintain, although their work is still in its early stages, that mental self-influence of this kind occurs through normal physiological pathways such as the central nervous system, and at the micromolecular level down to the most fundamental structures within the living organism (molecules, atoms, etc).[27, 28, 29, 30]

Psychokinesis

The ability to affect physical objects and the bodies of others without the mediation of any known physical medium has been studied by parapsychologists since the 1880s. In 1970, Dr. Helmut Schmidt introduced a reproducible and consistent approach to the scientific study of psychokinesis. Schmidt designed and built a random-event generator triggered by the radioactive decay of strontium-90 nuclei. The electron emission from such decay is one of nature's most random processes. Since then at least forty-five psychokinesis studies using this device or similar equipment have been reported in the parapsychology literature. In most of these studies, subjects were able to influence the generator mentally, being aided by sensory feedback whenever a decrease in the randomness occurred. Interestingly, experienced meditators seem to learn the task more easily than non-meditators. [31, 32]

These studies strongly indicate that there is a human capacity for intentional psychokinesis. In showing that order can be imposed upon randomness by meditation or mere intention, they give us a clue about the mind's role in self-transformation. [33, 34, 35, 36, 37]

THE BODY OF THE FUTURE

The collective body of information and knowledge that has begun to form around the research described above suggests that we could undertake a systematic program to develop our untapped potentials. What such an exploration might produce is uncertain, but we can make some guesses based on the evidence we now possess. What follows are some of my own speculations about the body that could emerge from intensive, long term, sophisticated disciplines growing out of approaches that are now in existence. Such disciplines of course would have to draw upon the growing insight into psychological processes that modern clinical work provides and would have to be guided from beginning to end by a wise set of ethics. The moral implications of a program like this will require far more consideration if these dreams are seriously pursued.

In some cases, the speculations that follow are based upon direct extrapolations from the body's capacities as they exist today. In other cases I will present visions which have no present counterpart. In these instances, it will be more my own hunches and wishes than logical extrapolations at work.

In the body of the future, there would be less filtering of perception in order to maintain organismic balance and less reduction of sensory input. The world would be seen and felt with new richness and depth, revealing unknown vistas and transparencies. The luminous perception of textures, colors, contours and vibrancies that so many artists and contemplatives claim would be a natural function of the senses.

This perception of the external world would be accompanied by a similar awareness of the world within. Specific sensations from organs, muscles, cells and tissues, and from even finer structures would be more readily accessible than they are at present for most of us. We see such kinesthetic sensitivity in distance runners who read the subtle shifts of glucose and hormones during a race, or in yogis who can redirect their blood flow when their bodies seem unbalanced. All or most of the transformed body's systems would be directly perceivable, but their teeming information would be finely orchestrated. Kinesthesis would not be the confusion that prevails in certain psychoses and drug states, but would cohere instead to form a harmony.

With this greater awareness, a body would control itself in marvelous ways. Awareness inevitably increases self-mastery, but self-control would be sensitive, well-organized, intelligent and selective. Feedback among the various bodily parts and systems would always operate harmoniously to balance and orchestrate the whole. This body would know itself as an intricate network of systems able to maintain its identity and organismic integrity while simultaneously adventuring and exploring new powers. It would be a master of both homeostasis and radical change, with increasing capacity for reconstitution and receptivity to further evolution. This combination of staying power and mutability is prefigured, I believe, in the ability of certain athletes to move from sport to sport, event to event, changing their physical capacities and physiques as they go (witness the development of the modern decathlon champion); in the dramatic alterations of musculature that champion bodybuilders achieve from year to year (Frank Zane came into successive Mr. Olympia contests with significantly different proportions); or in the radical physical changes of yogis like Sri Ramakrishna or Swami Rama who demonstrate the capacity to gain or lose weight, alter body temperature and shift muscular tone instantaneously. Such mutations of structure and capacity depend upon the renewal of elements throughout the body's many systems. Such renewal is constant in our bodies already, but it would become even swifter and more efficient. In strenuous exercise the release of somatotropin or growth hormone speeds up protein synthesis so that tissues can be repaired more readily; this and similar mechanisms are paradigms for others that might develop. Through all of evolution, new bodily structures and processes have continually appeared to facilitate adaptions to the environment (gills developed into lungs, fins into legs, etc). This process would continue, giving the body increasing powers of survival and rejuvenation. The development of such mechanisms would be aided by the formative powers of imagination and awareness, just as changes in the bodies of athletes are aided by the various mental disciplines I have described above.

Such self-mastery could promote superior health by enabling the body to recognize and ward off injury and disease. It could also bring increasing longevity. As subtle physiological changes came to be monitored and altered, deteriorating structures could be repaired more easily. The body would begin to free itself from its various "aging clocks" and programs for termination.

Super-health and increasing longevity can be seen as enhancements of the body's homeostasis, but its capacity for change would also develop. Because its systems would be more flexible and efficient it would have a wider repertoire of states and behaviors. It would be more resourceful, more teachable, more agile. The physical feats of a Nadia Comaneci or Mikhail Baryshnikov would come more naturally to such a body. And such agility might correspond to the subtle psychical events triggered by religious ecstasies. It might be possible then to move in and out of radically different energetic states in the manner of yogic legends. Some people might adapt their bodies to travel in space, developing physical structures suited to outer space environments. Others might learn to create the subtle, disease-free, radiant body described in Neo-Platonic, Islamic, Buddhist, Taoist, and Hindu scriptures.

These powers would enable the body to resonate and harmonize with its surroundings more freely. In the contemplative traditions, the power to blend with the environment was a sign of enlightenment. The yogi, it was said, could make himself invisible as he became one with the world around him. When such blending occurs, life is less impeded. Both emotionally and physically, we do not grate against resistances caused by our own limitations and rigidities. In the body of the future this ability to blend and adapt could happen at all levels, down to the subtle entrainments of cells and molecules. A marvelous resonance exists among our elements already, but generally in the midst of great imbalances among internal systems and between our bodies and environments. We are at best a harmony of discords. The body of the future would become a harmony of harmonies

In studies we have made of athletes, I have often heard stories about players who changed their size and shape for brief instants in the midst of games. I have found similar accounts among artists, dancers, and people who practice meditation. There are stories of this kind in the contemplative traditions—tales of Jinn who appear to the Sufi sage bringing powers to change his shape, of yogis who shrink to the size of an atom, of Tibetan masters who take on the aspects of angels or demons. The power of metamorphosis exists in the myths and fairy tales of every nation. I believe this image has endured because it prefigures the mutability our bodies might someday possess. The mutability we see in our cells and molecules might eventually be extended to the whole system—for brief moments at first, and then for longer periods. The human face would reveal a wider range of feelings and ideas, a richer sea of emotions. We would have a larger repertoire of gestures.

Most highly creative people report times in their lives when they could work continuously with little or no recreation. Some, like Thomas Edison and Mahatma Gandhi, have needed only two or three hours of sleep a night for most of their creative lives. In the yoga sutras it is said that enlightenment liberates the body from the strains that require recuperation, thus giving the yogi boundless energy. In our own research we have heard about athletes who were suddenly filled with forces that seemed superhuman. If we can extrapolate from these examples, the body could become more energetic, requiring less and less sleep. Experiments in the Soviet Union with psychical self-regulation and similar disciplines seem to confirm this possibility.

With this marvelous kinesthesis and sensory release, bodily pleasure would increase enormously. One's feelings would fluctuate as now, but in a richer way. Instead of oscillations between depression, boredom, and pleasure there would be changes at a higher level, from serenity and calm to ecstasy. The Indian scriptures invariably end with the celebration of *Ananda*, the Delight that rules the world. This outcome of so many sacred teachings would become manifest in the transformed body. I believe that any body of this kind will require a moral and spiritual transformation that would broaden all our nobler emotions, our sympathy for others, our courage, our sense of unity with the world at large. Our joys would be linked with the well-being of our fellows. Their sufferings would be ours. The developing strength and pleasure of a transformed body would be a resource for everyone, I feel. Its joyous state would be contagious.

And with this delight would come beauty. We all glimpse this already in the bodies of dancers, in the movements of great athletes, in the faces of lovers, saints and seers. We are fatally attracted to it. A developing beauty of the human form would quicken our efforts to explore these possibilities.

Throughout his inventive and colorful career, Dr. Karl Pribram has distinguished himself as a scientist, physician, and brain researcher. There are few, if any, people alive who have contributed more to our understanding of the brain.

An ambitious student, Pribram gained both his B.S. and M.D. degrees in less than five years at the University of Chicago. After a residency in neurosurgery, he joined renowned brain scientist Dr. Karl Lashley at the Yerkes Laboratory of Primate Biology near Jacksonville, Florida. He served in the position of neurosurgeon on Lashley's research team while simultaneously helping to write up more than thirty years of Lashley's monumental research on the nature of memory. These early experiences sharpened Pribram's interest in the nature of the mind while developing his skills as a surgeon. In fact, it was the wedding of Pribram's varied talents that eventually gave birth to the hybrid field now known as neuropsychology.

After a short term as director of the Yerkes Laboratory following Lashley's retirement, Pribram went on to Yale, where during his ten-year stay he taught courses in neurophysiology and physiological psychology while continuing his research into the workings of the human brain. After leaving Yale, he joined the faculty at Stanford University, where for the past twenty years he has served as professor of neuroscience in the Departments of Psychology, Psychiatry, and Behavioral Sciences.

Throughout his life, Dr. Pribram has repeatedly been in the forefront of brain/mind studies. In the early 1950s his discoveries of the nature of the brain's limbic system forced a complete restructuring of existing knowledge about mental functioning. Again in 1960 his findings refuted popular behaviorist views of brain function. Pribram's innovative research in collaboration with George A. Miller and Eugene Gallanter proved that brain cells do not work as a simple reflex arc, but instead are part of a sophisticated feedback loop. Declaring themselves "subjective behaviorists," the three scientists gave impetus to the cognitive movement, now one of the dominant fields in psychology.

In recent years, Pribram's studies and research have taken an entirely new and somewhat startling turn. Proposing that the brain does not function in a linear fashion, as has always been believed, but instead functions more like a hologram, Pribram has caused his greatest scientific stir to date. In the following essay Dr. Pribram uses his own history as a brain pioneer to demonstrate the dramatic ways in which our understanding of human behavior has broadened and deepened in recent years.

THE BRAIN

Recent scientific endeavor has been characterized by a peculiar happening: While laboratory scientists have been learning more and more about less and less, the impact of their findings has repeatedly scuttled reductionistic theories in favor of more encompassing holistic views. This trend has accelerated to such an extent that I see a major paradigm shift taking place in all of science.

In *Structure of Scientific Revolutions* (1962), Thomas Kuhn pointed out that much of everyday scientific effort is directed toward substantiating major world views, theories that have become established in various fields of inquiry. However, from time to time the weight of evidence demands revision of these views. At this point, fresh views have a chance to overturn the old, provided they can satisfactorily explain those very irritating points that produced difficulties for the older theories.

Three such revolutions in thought have occurred during my research career, and I was privileged to be in the center of the storms that always surround such upheavals. In each instance, the revolution—the overturning of then currently established thought—took us back to earlier, perhaps more basic formulations. However, where the earlier views had been vague and general, the new theories took on great precision and became instrumental for gathering the data that comprises most of any scientific effort.

The first revolution came about when the conception of a horizontally organized central nervous system in which higher levels simply control lower levels was replaced by a concentric view in which the core and outer portions of the nervous system perform different functions. The second revolution replaced the reflex arc with a self-regulating elementary behavioral unit. Thus a linear, causal, and stimulus-response behavioral science gave way to an understanding of the nervous system and behavior based on feedback and feedforward organizations. Finally, a model of a distributed memory store was achieved, giving rise to a precise, mathematical, holistic formulation that had heretofore been completely lacking in science.

REVOLUTION I:
THE COREBRAIN AND THE
CHEMICAL CONTROL OF CONSCIOUSNESS

The first of these revolutions came as a result of innovations in the study of brain function after World War II.

The overall configuration of the brain is much like that of a mushroom—a stem with an umbrellalike outer layer or cortex. Early investigators analyzed brain function by dividing the cortex from the brainstem and by "cutting" the stem at various intervals. Principles of organization were noted: the top levels regulate complex experience and behavior, while the lower levels regulate more automatic and reflex processing. Further, the higher levels act upon lower levels essentially by inhibiting the more or less continuous neural discharge. Just as the heart beats spontaneously (in fact, it does so because of the discharging of its neural system), so do many nerve cells "beat" continuously throughout the life of the organism. When the controls from above are severed, the spontaneous discharge becomes excessive and reflexes run loose, producing spasticity and disorganization.

Since World War II, this rather simple view of the organization of the brain, brainstem, and spinal cord has been augmented by more sophisticated approaches. The brainstem and spinal cord are now seen not as the stem of a mushroom, but rather as a stalk of celery. Similarly, the umbrellalike top of the brain is now studied not as a homogeneous organ but more as if it were layered like an onion. Thus, the functions of the outer shells can be contrasted with those of the inner core in both the brainstem and the brain.

When the core portions of the brain are injured or stimulated in some special way, changes in the individual's emotional state occur. A most dramatic illustration of such changes occurred in a patient who had suffered a bullet injury during World War II. The bullet had lodged within the ventricles of the brain and would float about in the fluid-filled cavities. Depending on which way the patient held his head for a period of time, he would experience sadness or elation and all of the concomitant behavior that attends profound changes in emotional state.

The advent of psychotropic drugs has generated an outpouring of studies that relate changes in emotion to the chemistry of the core parts of the brain and brainstem. These studies have shown that not only emotional and motivational states, but also one's feelings of effort and comfort and the integration of experience into memory are a function of the chemistry of these systems. States of consciousness thus devolve in a large measure on the neurochemical processes of the core brain. A considerable number of these processes are being investigated. I will here focus on three of special interest that are beginning to comprise a coherent body of knowledge.

One such system converges forward onto the amygdala, an almond-shaped accumulation of nerve cells deeply buried in the lobe of the brain. (*Amygdala* is a Greek word meaning "almond." Having removed hundreds of amygdala from monkeys, I was startled to hear street vendors in Athens hawking their wares: "Amygdala! Amygdala!") Removal of the amygdala in monkeys produces marked changes in the animal's reaction to abrupt environmental change. Such reactions are called orienting reactions and as a rule are brief, such as the startle reaction when we are interrupted by a novel sound or flash. When the sound (or flash) is repeated, the reaction progressively diminishes as we become accustomed to it. The manifestations of orienting such as turning toward the sound reaction are accompanied by visceral responses, many of them mediated by the autonomic nervous system. Removal of the amygdala disturbs the entire pattern of orienting and habituation.

This disturbance of the orienting reaction is a part of a larger pattern of changes in emotional reactions—reactions that can most easily be remembered as the 4 F's: Feeding, fighting, fleeing and sex. The changes are in each instance very specific—once begun, the behavior of the animals subjected to amygdalectomy does not stop as readily as in the ordinary course of events. One group of experiments has shown that the chemistry of the amygdala modulates the mechanisms that usually signal satiety.

To summarize—the amygdala deals with the interruption of ongoing behavior—interruptions due to interest in sex or food, to sudden events that might prove dangerous, and the like. Whenever ongoing behavior is stopped or is to be stopped, the amygdala and its system become involved, and we ordinarily label such involvement as an emotional or affective reaction.

But what about ongoing behavior per se? What keeps it going in whatever direction it is headed? A different core brain system is involved, this one centered on the basal ganglia of the forebrain. The basal ganglia have for a long time been known to regulate postural and thus muscular attitudinal sets (i.e., motivation). More recently, work in my laboratory and in others has shown these structures to be involved in attention (experiential attitudinal sets)—as well as in motivation. Furthermore, the basal ganglia systems are the locus of the origin of Parkinsonism, a disease which yields to a recently discovered treatment by dopamine, a chemical found almost uniquely in these neural systems.

The amygdala and basal ganglia systems do not function in isolation. A third, and perhaps the most interesting, system coordinates the motivational "go" of ongoing behavior with the emotional "stop" of interruption. This third system intimately involves the hippocampus—an elongated structure just behind the amygdala in the human brain that looks much like a seahorse (Hippocampus in Greek) when dissected free from the brain. Our research has indicated that this coordinating system regulates attention in the sense that an organism is constantly balancing ongoing activity against distraction. The coordination apparently takes *effort* whenever a situation occurs which is beyond the experience of the organism: He must "pay" attention.

The chemistry of this system is a focus of current interest. The hippocampus selectively absorbs a substance produced by the outer portion of the adrenal gland—a chemical that is secreted whenever the organism is under prolonged stress. This secretion is regulated by another from the pituitary "master" gland—and once again the hippocampal system shows special sensitivities to this chemical and its near relatives. What is most interesting, however, is that these pituitary secretions can protect the organism against pain and suffering much as does the drug morphine. An extremely active area of research at the moment concerns isolating a family of morphine-like substances secreted not only by the pituitary gland (the enkephalins) but by many nerve cells in the core brain systems.

These startling discoveries suggest that we are all "addicts" in a sense—but that our "addiction" is internally regulated for most of us. Our ordinary state of consciousness is not so ordinary, it seems, so perhaps we should not view alternate states as so extraordinary.

Thus, the earlier theories of hierarchical control of "lower centers" by "higher brain functions" have been radically modified. Hierarchical control has not been done away with—as we shall see in the next section. Rather, it has been shown to be more limited than earlier theories had held and the substrates—the "lower centers"—have been shown to have a much richer complexity than had been suspected. It is the chemical and physiological organization of these core structures of the brain that in fact exercise primary control, and the "higher functions" only modify and modulate these lower levels.

When these studies began, only the hypothalamic region was viewed as a central control mechanism for emotional and motivational behaviors, and this in the earlier tradition as the "head ganglion of the autonomic nervous system." Walter Cannon's classical studies at Harvard University during the 1920s and 1930s had established the principle of homeostasis as describing hypothalamic function. The work of Horace Magoun and Donald Lindsley at the University of California at Los Angeles brought the core of the lower brain stem—the reticular formation—into prominence during the 1950s. And the studies accomplished at Yale by Paul MacLean and myself during the same period showed that these core brain functions extended forward to the (limbic) forebrain, as well.

The suggestion that this portion of the forebrain—and the core brain as a whole—might regulate conscious states, though acceptable to neuroscientists, was certainly not even venturable in experimental psychology until the recent past (1970s). A strict behaviorism which excluded all mind-talk held sway until 1960. How this change has come about is the topic of the next section.

REVOLUTION II: THE ORGANIZATION OF BEHAVIOR

The revolution of 1950 which I have briefly reviewed above produced a change in the way we conceptualize gross brain function. We replaced the concept of centers with that of systems. And we replaced the upstairs *vs* downstairs organizational scheme with the concentrically layered approach to these systems. These changes in thinking and new accumulations of data ushered in another revolution which in my experience culminated with the publication of *Plans and the Structure of Behavior* (authored by George Miller, Eugene Galanter, and Karl Pribram) in 1960. This revolution changed our conception not so much of the organization of the brain as it changed our views about the organization of behavioral processes.

Since Descartes the reflex has been the unit of analysis of behavior. Early in the century Sir Charles Sherrington proposed, on the basis of his own experiments and the earlier ones of Bell and Magendie, that the reflex, at least at the spinal level, is an arc composed of an input neuron, an interneuron and an output neuron. Behaviorists were delighted with this simple model and attempted to build a science on this foundation: a stimulus-response psychology that could define its constructs by operations on the input (stimulus) and output (response). What could not be accounted for directly would be inferred as an intervening variable (a presumed function of interneurons). Precise particulate minitheories were developed upon these premises and even larger conceptual frames such as those of Hull and Spence were attempted.

Two major experimental results emerged during the 1950s that were difficult to contain in stimulus-response terms. The first of these was the finding by Miller and Stevenson at Yale that rats with hypothalamic lesions would overeat and become obese in an ad libidum feeding situation but would starve if they had to work even slightly for their food. Any theory based on a stimulus-provoked "drive" simply had no plausible explanation for such results. By contrast, a concept of "effort" related to some brain representation of the work involved in eating and metabolizing could readily account for the data. But "effort," a term linked to the subjective realm, was taboo to behaviorists and so the finding remained unexplained—though not unheeded by experimentalists.

The second major finding was that a large portion of the output fibers from the spinal cord to muscles ended not on contractile tissue but on muscle *receptors*. These receptors are connected in parallel with muscle tissue and serve to gauge tension. The finding that the receptors could be influenced by a signal from the central nervous system (including the brain) as well as by changes in muscular tension made it necessary to totally revise our ideas about the organization of the reflex.

Sherrington had, in fact, invented the reflex arc as a simplification in

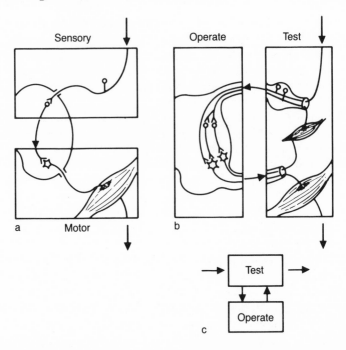

FIGURE 1. Development of the TOTE from the reflex arc concept. Note that the γ-connectivity of the muscle spindle demands that a "test" be performed.

an attempt to understand the interaction among reflexes. He never meant the "arc" to become neurophysiological or behavioristic dogma on which a whole scientific enterprise should be built:

> A simple reflex is probably a purely abstract conception, because all parts of the nervous system are connected together and no part of it is probably ever capable of reaction without affecting and being affected by various other parts, and it is a system certainly never absolutely at rest. But the simple reflex is a convenient, if not a probable, fiction.

Believers in the reflex arc fiction had to face the evidence that these receptors could be influenced by a signal from the brain as well as by the environment. Obviously the simplest, most direct modification of Sherrington's fiction is to add the output fibers from the central nervous system to the receptor. The consequences of this apparently minor revision are far from trivial. Imagine for a moment that, isolated from other stimulation, you are monitoring receptor activity. When a change occurs, how will you know whether that change is the result of an event outside the organism or an activity within the central nervous system? Some computation, some test must be applied to discern "reality"—i.e., a stimulus originating outside the organism (Figure 1).

Much behavioral evidence supports the concept that some sort of active test is performed on input. Many of the pertinent observations result from experiments in which the visual image is distorted or inverted by prism glasses worn by the subject for a prolonged time. Given an opportunity to move about and manipulate his environment, that person can right his perceptual world in a matter of hours or days (depending on the extent of the distortion). Should such manipulation or movement be proscribed, however, there is considerable delay in the correction of the distortion if it can be accomplished at all. The manipulative experience appears integral to some phase of the construction of the corrective mechanism.

A generalized diagram of the reflex, the unit of neurobehavioral analysis, can therefore be attempted (see TOTE Fig. 2). To be effective, input must be compared to and tested against central neural activity; the results of this comparison initiate some operation which then influences either other parts of the nervous system, or the external world, as in the manipulation of the environment in the prism experiment above. The consequences of this operation are then fed back to the comparator and the loop continues until the test has been satisfied—until some previous setting, indicative of a state-to-be-achieved, has been attained (exit).

This modification of the reflex arc results in a diagram familiar to engineers. Tracking devices of various sorts are built to just such specifications. The apparatus, known as a servomechanism, matches the effects of

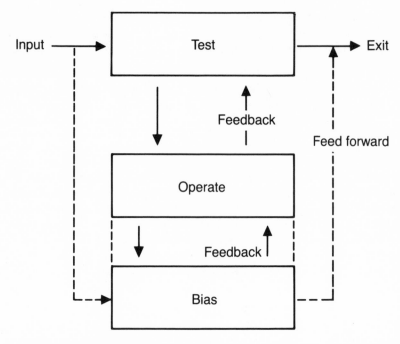

FIGURE 2. The TOTE servomechanism modified to include feed-forward. Note the parallel processing feature of the revised TOTE.

an input against the effects of the outcome of an activity aimed to deal with that input. The thermostat is probably the most familiar servomechanism.

The reflex arc was a conception used by Sherrington to explain data he had before him. The success of his explanations made the reflex arc an extremely useful fiction. The TOTE diagram is also a fiction when applied to neurobehavioral analysis. It is a somewhat higher-order fiction than the reflex arc—the reflex arc is the limiting case of a servo in which feedback can be accomplished only via the organism's environment and in which the operation performed is insensitive even to this feedback, i.e., the effect, once initiated, runs itself off to a predetermined state. The usefulness of a higher order fiction must lie in its ability to handle a broader range of facts. The TOTE concept was brought to bear for just this reason: the reflex arc cannot encompass the data that demonstrate the central control of receptor mechanisms.

The essence of the change from the reflex arc to the TOTE is the Test mode. The test implies an active comparison between input and some central state—a state that can be updated by the consequences of behavior. The state therefore becomes in some sense a *representation* of the environment with which the organism interacts. In opposition to behaviorists, Gestalt and other psychologists (such as psychophysicists) less averse to taking into account reports of subjective experience had always emphasized the importance of representational mechanisms (maps, schemata, neural processes isomorphic to stimuli, etc). In *Plans and the Structure of Behavior* we also drew upon representations and worked out the implications for psychology of the then recent neurobehavioral and neurophysiological findings. The reviews of the book were almost all dismal ("...unfortunate that such hardheaded scientists have gone soft—is it their age or the California climate where the book was written?"). But for many years every president of the American Psychological Association and recipient of the Association's prize for scientific contributions mentioned the book as seminal to their own thinking—and almost two decades of experiments by cognitive psychologists attest to the vigor of the conceptions put forward.

This favorable response was in part due to the fact that our proposal used the digital computer as a model for the processes we were describing. Thus experimentalists could for the first time perform *in vitro* tests in the behavioral sciences—types of experiments abstracted from life situations that have proved so invaluable in the work of biochemists. So much of academic psychology is now cognitive that one can safely say a revolution in thinking has occurred. But as noted earlier, revolutions simply overturn the present in favor of an earlier, less articulated past. The initial behaviorist revolution was responsible for making psychology an operational science that brought quantitative experiment to bear on psychological problems. The cognitive revolution simply readmitted reports of subjective experience to this quantitative scientific enterprise (we first called ourselves subjective behaviorists, before the cognitive label became the more common).

REVOLUTION III:
THE HOLOGRAM AND THE
ORGANIZATION OF EXPERIENCE

The computer is not, however, the only artifact that has proved useful in allowing *in vitro* experimentation to occur in the brain and behavioral sciences. Computers provide the key to the way in which TOTEs (feedback units, homeostats) can be assembled into higher order control operations, the operate part of the TOTE. Computers do not furnish the tools for understanding the organization of the test portions of the TOTE, the representational mechanism and its interaction with input.

New data and novel artifacts contributed towards producing the current 1970's revolution in thinking. This revolution may be the most far-reaching, since it encompasses not only the brain and behavioral sciences but the physical sciences as well.

The new data concern the mechanisms of perception of the physical world. Over a century ago, Georg Ohm—who is responsible for the ohm as a measure of electrical resistance—suggested that the ear and the auditory brain analyze the periodicities of sound waves. Herman Helmholtz provided evidence for this view of the auditory system as a wave form analyzer. More recently, evidence obtained by Fergus Campbell and John Robson and their associates at Cambridge University (and by others at Harvard, Berkeley, and our own Stanford laboratories) indicates that pattern vision may also be based on wave form analysis. In vision the wave forms are made up of light and dark regions over *space* (rather than over time as in the auditory system). The complex of frequencies of alternating light and dark (called the "spatial frequencies") is analyzed (decomposed into its fundamental frequencies) much as a complex sound is registered in distinct melodies and harmonies by the auditory system.

The importance of a wave form analytic mechanism in brain function appears not to be limited to hearing and seeing. Bekesy showed, with a brilliant series of demonstrations (akin to the demonstration of a stereo effect when the phase of the frequencies of two loudspeakers is properly adjusted), that the touch (and perhaps even the taste) systems also operate in this fashion. Thus our perception of the physical world is dependent on a brain mechanism that processes wave forms—vibrations of occurrences (over time and space and perhaps other dimensions).

The novel artifact in this third revolution is the hologram, a photographic process that stores the wave forms generated when light falls on an object rather than simply storing the intensity reflected by that object as in ordinary photography. Storing the wave fronts encodes the relationships between their frequencies (their phase) in addition to intensity information. Thus when properly illuminated, the hologram reconstructs a three-dimensional image of the original object. Interestingly, this image is constructed at a plane remote from the photographic film (as in stereophonic reproduction of music). Looking at the film without proper illumination shows only a relatively haphazard (random-appearing) distribution of developed silver grains.

The hologram derives its name from another interesting property: every reasonably sized part of the hologram encodes the entire image. Essentially the hologram is a blurred record—the light reflected by any and every point of a scene is spread over the entire film surface. The blur is not as haphazard as it appears to be, however, but is akin to the wave fronts produced in a pond by a pebble. If one could momentarily freeze a pond into which several pebbles had simultaneously been thrown, one could "reconstruct" the site of impact of the pebbles from the waves that had been generated. In a similar fashion image reconstruction from a hologram deblurs the information by decoding the encoded wave forms. Mathematically the encoding and decoding are inverse transforms of each other, that is, the same operation of wave form analysis produces both the blur (by spreading the information) and the image (by reconstruction).

Thus, in addition to helping us understand perception, the evidence that the brain mechanisms of perception involve wave form analysis helps explain something that has been a puzzle to students of brain function for a long time: the distributed nature of the memory trace. Even with massive brain lesions, specific memories are never lost in isolation. For example, if a person has a stroke and half of his brain is inoperative, he does not recognize only half of his children. Memories are not localized to specific regions.

If sensory coding is done by means of wave form analysis, the problem is solved. The input is automatically distributed across a small part of the brain cortex as a series of interfering wave front patterns. This is to say that when an input is analyzed by a two-dimensional frequency transform, this information is automatically (or axiomatically by virtue of the process) distributed in the form of a hologram.

There are certain important consequences of this new model of cortical brain function. First of all, as we have noted, it explains a great deal about brain function that until now has been inexplicable. Second, in holography we are storing information in a form that does not have a space-time dimension. What is stored is everywhere and records only frequency of occurrence—not place or time—although space and time can be reconstructed from the stored information.

I was once asked how it is that an image can be reconstructed from memory when its holographic-like representation is, so to speak, spread over large extents of brain cortex. Where and who is the little man doing the reconstructing? It finally occurred to me that not only was I not going to be able to answer that question, but that it might be the wrong question to ask. A more appropriate question seemed to be: What makes us believe that we see things the way they are? The lens of the eye focuses the world of light on the retina, producing an image and then, through the processing that we have been discussing, the brain dismembers this image. So let us ask: *What* is the nature of the world of light that the lens is focusing? What would we experience if we used other ways of viewing the world than through lenses? Quite possibly the world outside might appear to us as a hologram. In fact, many physicists (e.g. Heisenberg, Bohr, Wigner, Bohm, to mention a few of the most outstanding) who have been struggling to understand the fundamental nature of matter have proposed just such a possibility.

In suggesting this, I am not forgetting classical mechanics and the "objective" view of the ordinary sensory universe. However, this "objective" view can only partly account for observations at the ultramacro and ultramicro levels. As David Bohm has pointed out, since Galileo science has essentially taken its view of both the macro-universe and the micro-universe through lenses. When, however, science uses other procedures (such as looking at the world through interferometers), we obtain different results. Perhaps we have focused far too long on one type of organization while ignoring other possible types.

All this has direct implications for an understanding of the physical as well as the psychological universe. We in the Western world are just beginning to be aware that there might be several orders that characterize the universe. If holographic representations *within* the brain do not exist in terms of the familiar space-time coordinates, then perhaps there are orders of the universe *outside* that also do not exist in ordinary space-time. Leibniz called such an order monadic. His conception derived from the mathematics he had invented—or discovered—the integral calculus which in Gabor's hands led to the invention of the hologram—a set of spread functions that would aid the recording of interference patterns (spatial frequencies). The hologram and its predecessor the monad were initially mathematical inventions and occurred long before current technology made possible the artifacts we now use.

What makes holographic theory so revolutionary is the fresh view that the wave form domain brings to all of science. Wave "numbers" can refer to densities of occurrences with respect to any number of dimensions other than or in addition to time-space. This could mean that physical orders exist in which synchronicity rather than causality operates as a basic principle. Encoding in the wave form domain gives the appearance of random distributions, but with the appropriate transforms this apparent randomness can be decoded into ordinary perceptible forms. This could mean that beyond every appearance of randomness lies hidden an order that awaits discovery.

The hologram is holistic in that every part represents the whole and the whole is represented in all its parts. This holistic organization distinguishes it from others in which the whole is considered to be more than or different from the sum of its parts. Holism derived from holograms describes an enfolded order which can be readily unfolded into the ordinary sensory order produced by lenses and lens-like receptors. The enfolding and unfolding transformations are the product of a highly precise mathematical operation, even more precise and predictable than the statistical probability operations that now form the hard core of ordinary scientific calculations. Does this not augur for a paradigm shift in all of science? Suddenly holism becomes respectable.

My experience, as I have recounted it here, may be idiosyncratic. But I do not believe it is. Rather, I find it significant that every time a series of precise data has accumulated, it has overturned theories that seemed up to that time extremely precise in formulation, and replaced them with more holistic theories that up to then had been less well articulated. I have thus begun to suspend disbelief in more holistic views even when they cannot be completely understood on the basis of available data. One never knows when the tacit knowledge that produced these views will become explicit because of better technology or inventive thought. Further, I have come to suspect that scientific procedure in the near future will shed light not only on the physical and biological universe, as it has in the past, but on the psychological and even *spiritual*, as well. After all, mathematics is a psychological process that underlies all of science, and mathematical insights have proved not altogether different from spiritual ones—as for example Leibniz' monads. The extensive changes in human material weal that science thus far has brought may thus be only a prelude to even more profound influences in a realm that heretofore was considered outside the purview of science.

PAUL SCHNECK

Dr. Stanley Krippner is recognized through-out the world for his distinguished work in many new, untapped areas of scientific study. Currently the Faculty Chairman of the Humanistic Psychology Institute in San Francisco, Dr. Krippner was director from 1964 to 1973 of the Dream Laboratory at Maimonides Medical Center in New York. It was during this decade of intensive research on the nature of sleep and dreaming that Krippner first began to probe the inner depths of the mind. Specifically, he began to chart the extraordinary world of psychic perception, with particular attention to ways in which the human mind seems to have the capacity to link with other minds geograph-ically distant and to influence activities and thoughts with no apparent physical involvement.

In addition to his involvement as a researcher, educator, and lecturer, Stanley Krippner has published numerous books and articles, including Dream Telepathy, The Realms of Healing, Song of the Siren, The Kirlian Aura, *and* Human Possibilities.

Arthur Hastings is a transpersonal psychol-ogist of worldwide reputation. As dean and professor of psychology at the California Institute of Transpersonal Psychology, he develops curricula and teaches courses about the many aspects of Eastern and Western psychology and philosophy that emphasize human potentialities and the evo-lution of human consciousness.

Dr. Hastings's publications include Ar-gumentation and Advocacy, Group Com-munication Through Computers, Changing Images of man, *and* Health for the Whole Person.

In this lively essay on the future of parapsychology, Arthur Hastings and Stanley Krippner give us a fascinating glimpse into the world of psi phenomena. Believing that psi phenomena hold the potential for both posi-tive and negative use, they illustrate several ways in which the future evolution of the human species could be constructively or destructively affected through the further development and proliferation of psychic abilities by members of the world community.

STANLEY KRIPPNER
and ARTHUR HASTINGS

PARAPSYCHOLOGY

In 1893, Hans Berger, a student of astronomy at the University of Berlin, had a dramatic experience while out riding. His horse slipped on the narrow ledge of a steep ravine, causing him to fall into the path of a horse-drawn artillery unit. The battery came to a stop just in time, and he escaped injury. That evening, Berger received a telegram from his father asking about his well-being—the only time in his life that he had received such a query. Berger's sister had told her parents that she knew for a fact that her brother had been involved in an accident. Berger later wrote, "This is a case of spontaneous telepathy in which at a time of mortal danger, and as I contemplated certain death, I transmitted my thoughts, while my sister, who was particularly close to me, acted as the receiver."

Berger's experience represents just one of countless examples of parapsychological phenomena reported throughout the ages. These occurrences were known in primitive times when people reported experiencing dreams that appeared to transmit thoughts of another person, altered states of consciousness in which they "saw" or became aware of distant events, rituals in which future events were predicted, and shamanic procedures that reportedly produced direct action on a distant object. These events may have been instances of what parapsychologists now call telepathy, clairvoyance, precognition, and psychokinesis.

Collectively, these phenomena are referred to as psi: interactions between organisms and their environment (including other organisms) that are not mediated by known sensorimotor functions. Telepathy is an organism's acquisition of awareness concerning another organism's thoughts or mental state without using the known sensory channels. Clairvoyance is an organism's acquisition of knowledge concerning external objects and events by other than the known sensory channels. Precognition is the noninferential knowledge of future events. Psychokinesis is influence exerted on objects or events in the environment without the use of the known physical means. The first three of these phenomena are referred to as extrasensory perception (ESP) because they provide information that does not appear to depend on the known functions of the senses. Psychokinesis (PK), however, does not appear to depend on the known functions of the muscles or motor system, or other physical mechanisms.

The observation of psi moved from the anecdotal level to that of clinical and experimental study in the late nineteenth century with the advent of psychoanalysis and the founding of the various psychical research societies. C. G. Jung hypothesized the existence of a "collective unconscious," the deep basement of the psyche in which the individual is connected with all humanity. Jung felt this "collective unconscious" served as the foundation for each individual's psi experience. The Society for Psychical Research, founded in London in 1882, became the first major organization to attempt the scientific assessment of psi, publishing the *Journal of the Society for Psychical Research*. The society attracted the attention of many distinguished scholars, including the philosopher Henry Sidgwick and the physicist Sir William Barrett. Similar organizations emerged in other countries, including the American Society for Psychical Research, founded through the efforts of psychologist William James and his colleagues.

The early investigators focused most of their efforts on the task of authenticating individual instances of purported psi. Spontaneous cases were difficult to assess adequately because of the possiblity of such contaminating factors as coincidence, unconscious inference, sensory leakage, exaggeration after the fact, faulty memory, and occasional outright fabrication. As a result, laboratory experiments were designed to prevent such contamination from taking place. In the early 1600s, Sir Francis Bacon, in his book *The New Atlantis*, had made several suggestions for conducting psychical research. He advised that shuffling cards or throwing dice could be used to test the "binding of thoughts." The experimenter, according to Bacon, could then record whether the subject had "hit for the most part." Bacon's advice proved to be prophetic. The application of probability theory to the assessment of deviations from chance outcomes was introduced by the French Nobel laureate Charles Richet in ESP experiments involving card guessing. The most extensive use of card-guessing procedures was initiated by William McDougall, J. B. Rhine, and L. E. Rhine in the late 1920s and early 1930s at Duke University. The Duke experimenters found that subjects could successfully identify cards in shuffled decks under laboratory controls that eliminated every explanatory factor but ESP. The subjects could do this under telepathic conditions, with another person looking at the cards one at a time, or as a clairvoyance test, with the deck sealed and the order of the cards not known by anyone. The distances between the subjects and the cards were as great as several hundred yards, which seemed to indicate that ESP is not affected by distances. (Later experimenters extended successful ESP tests to several thousand miles.)

J. B. Rhine published his first major work, *Extrasensory Perception*, in 1934. A flurry of critical articles appeared, challenging the evaluative methods and experimental conditions used in the card-guessing studies. Most of the criticisms of Rhine's mathematics were dispelled when the president of the Institute of Mathematical Statistics, B. H. Camp, approved the evaluative techniques. In 1937, Rhine initiated the *Journal of Parapsychology*, a scientific periodical that reported on psi experimentation and employed a statistician to check the mathematics of each article before it was published.

Additional criticisms included the allegations that scoring errors accounted for the significant data, that only successful experiments were published, and that no other researchers were reporting evidence for psi. However, between 1934 and 1939, thirty-one ESP studies were reported from other laboratories; of this number, twenty-one produced significant data supporting the existence of ESP.

In a 1955 issue of *Science*, the official publication of the American Association for the Advancement of Science (AAAS), G. R. Price claimed that those ESP and PK data not dependent on clerical and statistical errors "are dependent on deliberate fraud or mildly abnormal mental conditions." Price retracted his accusations in 1972, but the initial article was widely distributed and is still used to debunk parapsychology.

In 1966, C. E. M. Hansel, in his book *ESP—A Scientific Evaluation*, suggested that subjects as well as investigators could have cheated during parapsychological experiments. Parapsychologists agreed that fraud should be guarded against but pointed out that Hansel's accounts of the critical experiments were often less than accurate.

Meanwhile, psychologists and researchers in other laboratories had begun to study ESP and PK. The type of experiment and information sought varied greatly. At Maimonides Medical Center in New York, Montague Ullman and Stanley Krippner studied telepathic dreams in the 1960s, creating laboratory experiments in which a sleeping subject received images from pictures and photographs and incorporated them in dreams. Later, Charles Honorton reported that subjects could obtain ESP impressions of pictures while relaxing in a state of light sensory deprivation. At the City College of New York, Gertrude Schmeidler attempted to identify personality traits that related to high ESP scores. Other researchers have carried out significant experiments on parapsychology at the University of Virginia, UCLA., the Psychical Research Foundation in North Carolina, Stanford Research Institute in California, the Mind Science Foundation in Texas, and the University of Edinburgh.

In 1965, J. B. and L. E. Rhine left Duke University and organized the Foundation for Research on the Nature of Man (FRNM). In 1969, the Parapsychological Association, composed of professional psychical researchers, was admitted to affiliate membership in AAAS, an indication of the growing acceptance of psi research by other scientific disciplines. This favorable attitude was strong enough to allow parapsychology to ride out its greatest scandal—the discovery, in 1974, that a medical researcher at FRNM had been caught tampering with data from an experiment with animals. J. B. Rhine promptly revealed this discovery in the *Journal of Parapsychology*, and other parapsychologists observed that stringent controls were needed as well as further attempts at cross-validation.

After a century of laboratory and field studies of psi, some major findings have emerged:

1. ESP and PK do exist and can be produced under laboratory conditions, though not at all times.

2. Believers in ESP generally have higher scores than nonbelievers on standard tests of psi.

3. Motivation and emotional interest are important for ESP ability; high motivation usually produces higher scores.

4. Personality traits affect ESP—extroverted persons tend to be better at ESP than introverts.

5. Persons do better at ESP in relaxed states, when their minds are quiet and their attention turned inward.

However, there still exist controversies about parapsychology, and issues that need to be addressed. For many scientists, the issue of cross-validation is more important than any other issue in parapsychology. Since Richet first applied statistics to psychical research in the 1880s, no experimental procedure has emerged that would invariably produce the same results no matter who followed it. Furthermore, no mechanism underlying psi operation has been discovered. Finally, no practical use of psi has been developed by laboratory research. If any one of these three possibilities should develop—a repeatable experiment, a mechanism of operation, a practical use—parapsychology could leave the fringes of science and sweep into the mainstream of scientific inquiry.

These three possibilities are visions in need of actualization. During a century of scientific inquiry, parapsychology has been handicapped by a lack of adequate financing, resulting in the inability of the field to engage in long-term planning of experimental approaches. In addition, the field cannot offer job security for most of its research workers. The direction that parapsychology will follow over the next several decades depends largely upon the funding issue.

In the pages that follow, two different dramatizations are offered. One or both of these may be confirmed by the events of the future. Possibly an altogether different picture will emerge. The first scenario is presented in the form of a report submitted to an international organization, the second as a transcript of U.S. congressional hearings on innovation in science. Both are fiction, though yesterday's fiction very often becomes tomorrow's fact.

SCENARIO ONE

Secret Report to the League of Uncommitted Nations, Prepared by the Director, Office of Strategic Technology

Almost twenty years ago, the League of Uncommitted Nations was formed by those countries that hoped to preserve their autonomy in the face of the strength exhibited by the superpowers. That we have reached the year 2000 with so few defections from the league's ranks is a tribute to our organization's success. It is also a tribute to the Office of Strategic Technology, which I have been privileged to direct for the past decade. This office was founded in the first few years of the league's existence; its mission was to devise new technological systems for the purpose of protecting our independence.

From the beginning, it was obvious that the league could not match the arsenals of the superpowers in conventional weaponry. We league leaders also knew that we could not depend upon them to sell us arms that could be used, in an emergency, against their attempts at hegemony. Most of all, we were aware of our limited budgets. However, our first director had the remarkable insight that in the folk traditions of undeveloped countries rested untapped reserves of strategic value. The early warning systems, the protection fields surrounding our key leaders, the trance-inducing rituals, and the deadly poisons we have developed in the last several years bear witness to her insight. Although officially retired, she continues to search the deserts, jungles, tundras, and rain forests for devices and practices that will assist our cause. In fact, she has identified many of the witch doctors, shamans, and wizards who have since become our most dependable psychic operators.

It is also a testament to the insight of our league's founders that six percent of our military budgets are earmarked for research and development. Although this is a small amount by the standards of developed nations, it exceeds the total amount of money spent in the last century by all the scientists conducting parapsychological research in the universities and institutes of the superpowers! The purpose of this report is to summarize our progress.

The psi-based operational processes and procedures now available for use can be classified into three categories: ESP weaponry, PK weaponry, and spirit weaponry. Extrasensory perception is the acquisition of knowledge without recourse to the conventional senses; clairvoyance, telepathy, and precognition are examples of ESP. Our "Consensus Clairvoyance" project has been rewarding. We station four or more clairvoyants in different parts of the world and ask them to concentrate upon a site selected by our intelligence agents as a high probability location for a missile base, a mass troop deployment, or an air attack locale. If our clairvoyants reach consensus, we consider the site's function identified and send the results to all member nations of the league. If the clairvoyants do not reach consensus, we send another team of four to the locations. If they do not agree, we simply tell member nations about our efforts and give them a majority impression. Having used this procedure for many years, we have had the opportunity to see our clairvoyants' statements confirmed or refuted whenever a secret base is revealed. In this way, we have been able to identify our most accurate clairvoyants and bring considerable sophistication to a procedure that is far less costly than the spy satellites used by the superpowers.

Our "Team Telepathy" project operates in a similar fashion. Each of our specially trained telepathic teams is assigned a superpower leader. There are usually four telepaths on each team operating from different parts of the world. They concentrate upon the world leaders and record their impressions, especially in the weeks before a leader is due to make an important decision that might affect league members. Those items on which there is consensus are related to member nations. Once again, feedback is provided by the positions those leaders finally take on an issue; our telepathic team's consensus is then confirmed or disproved. Over the years, some teams have proven to be virtually infallible in their judgment. Unfortunately, telepathy is subject to personality changes, emotional cycles, and the aging process. We are, therefore, constantly attempting to identify new telepaths.

The "Precognition Poll" is another of our ESP projects. Trained prognosticators enter altered states of consciousness by taking drugs, receiving electrical stimulation, or simply through meditation and dreams. Hypnosis has prepared them to direct their fantasies toward future world events. We have nearly one hundred prognosticators involved in this project; they send us hunches every week that are recorded in computer banks. A control group of political analysts also sends in hunches based on their experience and judgment. As one might expect, there is a great deal of overlap, and the events agreed upon by both groups have proven to be the most likely to occur. Through this project, we were prepared for such developments as the oil depletion crisis, the moon base, and the outbreak of plague, which took several of the superpowers by surprise.

Psychokinesis is the movement of objects or the influence of matter without recourse to the conventional abilities of one's motor system. "Project Trojan Horse" is the most successful of our PK enterprises. A talent search was launched for the most effective voodoo priests, hex casters, sorcerers, witches, and warlocks in the league. If they were able to demonstrate PK one or more times under controlled conditions—either in their villages or our laboratories—we offered them a position with our office.

Our craftspeople worked with these practitioners to design a mask, statuette, or other art object that was an appropriate gift to a head of state, a foreign affairs officer, or a prominent diplomat. Our analysts then identified the world leaders whose policies were most detrimental to world peace. These individuals were given a gift from one of our countries, usually in a dignified ceremony. Each gift was imbued with an average of five hundred hex hours supplied by a number of practitioners. The success of "Operation Trojan Horse" has been striking; recipients of these gifts often became confused and muddled to such an extent that they were demoted or removed from office.

One example of spirit weaponry—our third category—involved the foreign minister of a superpower who proposed to establish televiewing monitoring centers in all Third World countries, ostensibly to promote massive cultural exchange programs. But our intelligence agents warned us that the monitors to be used contained all the equipment needed to create a massive global spy network. The person in question worked privately, neither attending social functions nor leaving his country. Therefore, we could not give him one of our Trojan Horses. Instead, we directed our most talented mediums to direct malevolent spirits in his direction. They did this by posting his photograph in their seance quarters; each time they exorcised an evil spirit from a patient, they would direct the spirit toward its next host, the man in the picture. Many of them used doll-like representations of the diplomat into which they would stick pins, creating openings that the spirits could enter more easily. The TV monitor notion faded into obscurity once this foreign minister suffered a breakdown.

There have been some positive byproducts of our research. We now have a registry of unorthodox healers available to our citizens and—at slightly extra costs—to foreign tourists. In addition, we are test marketing stone pendants that have been held for a minimum of one hundred hours by six different healers. In their spare time, our clairvoyants have been responsible for locating lost children, solving crimes, and identifying geological sites containing natural resources, archeological treasures, or precious stones and metals. We look forward to the day when the world's superpowers allow the smaller nations to live in peace and the function of this office can turn from politics to the betterment of life for everyone on the planet.

SCENARIO TWO

Testimony Given to the Joint Congressional Committee on Innovation in Science by the Science Advisor to the President of the United States

COMMITTEE CHAIR: Dr. Slocum, we have requested your testimony before our committee for an important reason. In 1979, the world situation was such that our State Department had no less than six contingency plans ready for use depending on which trouble spot would plunge us into global war. Following the presidential elections of 1980 and the power shift in the Soviet Union, SALT III was negotiated in terms that for the first time enabled a thorough inspection to be made of military sites. This, combined with the new cordiality between the United States and the People's Republic of China, enabled the great powers to put pressure on the opposing parties in the Middle East to reach an agreement. In 1984, our military budget was reduced by fifty percent; an even greater reduction was made the following year. Some of the funds recovered by cuts were channeled into psi research.

There appears to be general agreement that the efforts of the past fifteen years have dispelled all doubts concerning the reality of psi phenomena. Our committee is interested in a summary of these findings as well as their implications.

DR. SLOCUM: Thank you, Madame Chair. In 1980, I had no idea that I would be reporting on parapsychology, a topic that only twenty years ago I relegated to the world of the starry-eyed and the fuzzy-minded. Today I set before you our progress in the second decade of the Psi Impact Enhancement project, or PIE, as it is known.

You probably know that ESP and PK—what we call psi—began to be acknowledged in the early 1980s. We began to see that these are natural abilities that can be learned or enhanced. This acceptance of psi was furthered by the emergence of concepts and paradigm-stretching ideas such as black holes, holographic models, quarks, quantum equations, bootstrap theory, catastrophe theory, and mathematical formulations of consciousness, including new concepts in horizon theory. These opened up windows on the universe, enabling us to see psi as a phenomenon of consciousness that is modified as it transacts with material or mental states and is directed by need or intention at many levels.

In 1986, we held the pivotal state-of-the-art conference, an important portion of which was the discussion of theory. Most of the long-range research was designed to check out one or more of these theoretical approaches to the operation of psi. The theories that impressed us the most did not hypothesize any new "energies," simply some type of relationship between the subject and the parapsychological effect. Furthermore, these theories clearly indicated that it was not in the nature of the psi process to lend itself to a repeatable experiment. Indeed, a truly repeatable experiment is an unlikely event in any of the social and behavioral sciences. A more productive approach has been the identification of repeatable experimenters. Throughout the history of parapsychology, there have been a few scientists whose success rates with subjects in ESP or PK tests has been remarkably high. In one or two instances it was discovered that they simply altered the data to make the results appear significant. But in the other cases there is no doubt of their legitimacy.

In the 1970s, some parapsychologists were asked to take two tests to determine what personality traits correlated with success in eliciting psi from subjects—one, an established personality inventory, the other, a test of ESP. No relationships between personality traits and the conducting of successful ESP experiments were identified. However, the experimenters who obtained high ESP scores were the same ones who produced consistently significant ESP test data in their laboratories.

This finding led to a cooperative effort in which the theoretical approaches to psi were tested by the repeatable experimenters. Each of the designated experimenters was assigned studies for which his or her past record indicated that the experimenter would obtain useful data. For example, one experimenter who had an admitted bias against the possibility of precognition—the only area in which he had never attained significant results—was simply assigned other tasks. The new data opened up to us a perspective quite different from the Western world view of 1980.

Locality of an event in space and time has proven to be an arbitrary way of describing events in our universe. Western science has made the mistake of assuming that we are studying reality as we observe and measure it. However, it would be more correct to say that we create reality as we observe and measure it. The observer is a part of what is observed. Our reality cannot help but be influenced by our observations. In psi research, for example, we have found that a subject's eventual knowledge of the results is often the crucial variable that will determine the way the experiment turns out. In addition, the researcher's expectations often affect the experiment, especially if the researcher is gifted in ESP or PK.

Parapsychological studies have also advanced our understanding of consciousness. We find that consciousness is present in all forms of matter, all types of energy, and in the transformation between the two. We now know that psi is neither matter nor energy; rather, it is a manifestation of consciousness. One need not speculate how a force at one point can exert an effect on another point if the effect is potentially at the second point, waiting to be actualized. C. G. Jung came close to these models with his concept of synchroneity because meaningful coincidences do not depend upon cause and effect. Now we have finally begun to explain how synchroneity takes place. The coincidences are meaningful because what seems like two events is really one event.

Basically, all events are interrelated and all forms of life are intertwined. In the years ahead, as the culture at large realizes this fact, there may be a shift away from racism, sexism, and nationalism. Sexual stereotypes do not make sense because we all have the potentials of either sex. The concepts of a "master race" or a "chosen people" are sheer nonsense; we all share common genetic and information pools at some level of our being.

The links that connect each of us are now being put to use in the healing arts. With the advent of national health insurance, physicians and psychotherapists have had to find new ways to deliver health services. Herbalists, midwives, pastors, shamans, spiritualists, medicine men, and curanderas have been brought into the mainstream of the helping professions. When a patient's belief system matches that of the healer, and the healer approaches the healing task with love and compassion—with medicines and techniques that make a modicum of sense—the patient's recovery is almost assured.

As a result of these new applications, we turned our attention to ways of training or developing psi skills—not producing pure, antiseptic psi, but applying it to everyday situations. For example, psychics were already being used by some police departments to find missing persons, and dowsers were providing individuals and some communities with water locations. You probably recall the incident in Southern California during the recent drought in which one of our dowser trainees was deluged by the sudden eruption of water from the artesian well that he located.

Recognizing these skills to be related to basic human and social needs, we saw that psi might work best if it were humanly motivated rather than separated and isolated. Thus, our current program is to inform, encourage, and in some cases, financially assist this approach to psi, which is being carried out through public and private projects. I have with me today several persons who are participating in this endeavor, representing many facets of psi applications. First, I would like to introduce Dr. Sandra Fellheimer, a clinical psychologist and psychic counselor.

DR. FELLHEIMER: Let me say that I am only one person who has begun to use psi in my counseling and clinical work with individuals. There are two or three thousand others who have had some training, and many other counselors use the same procedure, but simply view it as "intuition." For many years we have known that the therapist who assists persons with problems, goals, and decisions must be sensitive to the client. What we have discovered is that the use of psi in such a counseling situation often facilitates understanding of problems and possible avenues to their solution.

SENATOR SNEED: Excuse me, Dr. Fellheimer. I am not familiar with this procedure. Could you give me an example? Suppose I asked you for advice on how to break this habit of mine of chewing on my pencils.

DR. FELLHEIMER: Senator, it is possible to do that, but I can't guarantee anything! If I allow myself to empathize with your problem, meditate on it for a moment, I get an impression of a small boy in a classroom chewing his pencil and spitting the pieces on the floor to annoy his teacher—perhaps a Ms. Tower or Towser. Does that mean anything to you?

SENATOR SNEED: Good Lord! I had forgotten all about Old Lady Tower. I say "Old Lady" because she was at least three times my age, and I was seven. (LAUGHTER) Is that where that started? Do I do it to annoy people?

DR. FELLHEIMER: Yes, you chew pencils when you are frustrated or can't speak your mind plainly. That insight may be of use to you, Senator, or it may not, but we are finding that a good counselor can use psi in many ways—to uncover emotional motivations, discover underlying conflicts or goals, and gain understanding.

SENATOR ATKINSON: That is very impressive, but isn't it also dangerous? Can you read someone's mind? Don't you dare look into my thoughts, young lady!

DR. FELLHEIMER: I appreciate that concern. For most, this ability cannot be turned on and off at will. It requires attention, mental quiet, and a relationship of trust. It is not mind reading, like reading a newspaper. It is an implicit communication based on feelings and impressions, sometimes specific, sometimes general, and dependent on a relationship. We are just beginning to learn how to build that kind of relationship. What we are learning may also apply to friends and acquaintances, not just to a counselor/client relationship.

DR. SLOCUM: Our next witness is John Malwyn. Mr. Malwyn is a resident psychic diagnostician at Mt. Mercy Hospital in Florida, where he specializes in identifying diseases and health problems with psi.

SENATOR KENNEDY: *Mr.* Malwyn, not *doctor?*

MR. MALWYN: No sir. I am not an M.D., although I have some training in biology. There are about two dozen psychic diagnosticians in the United States now working in clinics, hospitals, and holistic health centers. Some are physicians and nurses; others, like myself, work alongside the health–care professional. What we do is psychically identify diseases or conditions that are difficult to identify without extensive tests.

SENATOR KENNEDY: What is the process used? Do you read their palms, read their minds, or what?

MR. MALWYN: Each one of us has a different technique. My way is to see mental pictures of what is going on in the patient's body. This is technically called clairvoyance. I can often see concentrations of bacteria or toxins like a dark mass or tiny dots in the bloodstream or in some part of the body. Some of my colleagues can sense functions of organs by seeing them in color—sick livers are a different color than healthy ones, for example. One of our trained diagnosticians in a Chicago hospital says he clairvoyantly sees written labels with the name of the disease hanging around the patient's neck.

SENATOR KENNEDY: That is hard to believe.

MR. MALWYN: That's what we keep telling him!

REP. McNEARMORE: Let me ask you a practical question. Admitting that you can do this, and I have studied your very impressive statistics, why bother? Don't we already have very sophisticated tests and diagnostic procedures?

MR. MALWYN: Indeed, Congressman, and these procedures are almost always used to confirm our diagnosis. However, clairvoyant diagnosis often provides an immediate indication of which tests to make; it gives direction to a preliminary understanding of the person's condition. You would be surprised at the number of diseases that are difficult to identify, and psi may enable us to recognize the site and nature of the problem long before we have an inkling of its name. Also, we know that every patient interacts with his or her disease in an individual way. An introverted person with pneumonia may have a different disease condition than an extroverted person. Psi can help us to see differences in individual cases.

DR. SLOCUM: Since our time today is limited, let me summarize some of the other projects that have had some degree of success. A group of five or six individuals are working with the NASA space program in one of the few projects that includes both ESP and PK—the Group Psi Project. They call the project "Psi in the Sky," I understand. This group assists the planetary probe flights by using psi to view possible landing sites. After the probe has landed they use it as a "homing beacon" and have been able to retrieve information about the landing site for guidance in manipulating the probe mobile units.

SENATOR LaFOLLETTE: Where does the psychokinesis come in? You aren't going to tell me our rockets are really run by psi power. Not after the budget increase we just voted that program!

DR. SLOCUM: We have not yet reached the stage of rocket propulsion. What we are doing is exploring the use of group PK in energizing some of the relays and microcircuitry. It appears that some of the molecular circuits are especially amenable to accepting psi interactions. Our psychics can operate those circuits in outer space by remote PK.

In other areas of life, teachers are learning to use telepathic transmission in the classroom to help students learn on several levels of awareness. Psychic and paramedical healing techniques are coming to be accepted modes of treatment by physicians and lay healers in many hospitals, hospices, and health centers.

REP. WHORT: I fear, Dr. Slocum, that this genie, if I may use the metaphor, may be too far out of its bottle, that it may wield a two-edged sword. Psi may heal, educate, create, and inspire, but can't it also kill, threaten, and destroy? Can it be used for aggression, for attack? Are our enemies even now beaming confused thought waves toward Washington, muddling our brains and sapping our will to uphold the Free World?

DR. SLOCUM: Thank you, Mr. Congressman, for that very penetrating question. I hope that your fears are not realized. However, I do believe that psi abilities, like all human potentials, can be used for good or ill. They are a part of us, of you and me. They serve our needs, our hopes, our fears, our good intentions, and our mistaken ones. We believe that if we can grow equally in the understanding of ourselves and psi abilities, then we can use them wisely. As we keep them in a human context, with public communication and personal responsibil-

ity, Congress, our citizens, and men and women of good will over the
world will support the uses of psi for the general welfare of humanity.
SENATOR SCHELLING: Dr. Slocum, can psi tell me if I will be reelected next
November?
DR. SLOCUM: Ah, Senator. There are some things that we are simply not
meant to know.
CHAIR: The committee thanks Dr. Slocum and his colleagues. The hearing
is adjourned.

WHITHER PSI?

We have described two scenarios of how psi might develop by the year
2000. There is no way to know which will emerge, or whether our use of psi
might take an entirely different direction.

In centuries past, persons who had psychic abilities—and those who
pretended to be psychic—often were ostracized, with little appreciation of
their social contribution. Although sometimes revered, prophets and seers
were often driven from villages and countries in fear of what they might
see. Witches were portrayed as possessing demonic supernatural powers,
and were persecuted with ferocity. In more recent times, psychics were
seen as mediums, able to talk with the spirits of the departed, a shady
occupation at best.

Now we have a new view of psychic abilities. We believe that psi is a
natural part of human experience. It is a skill, a normal ability that opens
onto new dimensions of ourselves and the universe. We are entering a
world in which psychic abilities are supported socially and psychologically.
Persons reporting psychic perceptions are increasing—with experiences
through dreams, hunches, and intuition in times of emergency and threat
to survival—and are interested in learning and developing psi.

It may be that psychic talent is an art, like baseball playing or virtuos-
ity on the piano, and that a few of us are exceptionally gifted. However, the
research evidence indicates that almost everyone has some degree of
psychic talent, just as almost everyone can play baseball, pick out a tune on
a piano, or hum into a kazoo. It is likely that more and more persons will
have the opportunity to develop psychic abilities in the years ahead.

If we develop our psychic talents, we may find ourselves using telepathy as well as the telephone to be close to spouses, lovers, and friends.
Indeed, we may develop intimacy in ways that we can now barely imagine.
If I can know who you are and you can know who I am, then lying and
deception are unnecessary, and we can nourish and appreciate each other
at a deeper level than we have previously experienced. There is no guaran-

tee of this. Undoubtedly we will have to cope with fear and embarrassment, with self-conscious shyness. But we will all share the same condition, and with understanding comes sympathy and caring.

We may be able to psychically tell what events are emerging from the
future, using precognition to prepare for natural disasters, to prevent
accidents, to explore alternate choices, and to plan our future. Clairvoyance may give us valuable information unavailable to our senses—signs of
early toxicity in our bodies, rapid diagnosis of disease, and information to
further our interests, such as how much snow is on our favorite ski slope,
where to hide to spot the rare bird we are seeking, or how to find the
location of the parking place we need.

Those who develop psychokinesis may learn to promote healing and
enhance wellness. Kidney stones may be dissolved through PK as well as
the sophisticated technologies of medicine. Technology itself may be more
efficient as we learn to use PK to better interact with computers, type-
writers, cars, and sewing machines.

The world in which we live may be different, or it may be similar to our
present world. But if we use psi, *we* will be different. Psychic abilities will
not make us enlightened; we must still do that for ourselves. Yet they do
offer a new avenue of awareness and action. They offer an opportunity to
explore our universe, to nourish ourselves and each other.

BONNIE FREER

"A *leaderless but powerful network is work-ing to bring about radical change in the United States. Its members have broken with certain key elements of Western thought, and they may even have broken continuity with history."* These words, quoted from Marilyn Ferguson's highly con-troversial bestselling book The Aquarian Conspiracy *capture the spirit of Ms. Fergu-son's belief that our culture is presently un-dergoing a radical transformation of con-sciousness. Originating from countless sources simultaneously, Ferguson proposes that this transformation deals with nothing less than a profound shift in the way we perceive the world, manage our lives, choose our mates, and perhaps even fulfill our destinies.*

In this illuminating essay on "The Future of Relationships," Ms. Ferguson draws upon her comprehensive research into this snowballing phenomenon. By examining closely the many aspects of social/sexual bond-ing, she colorfully explores a variety of ways in which the human expres-sion of and need for love and intimacy may dramatically change in form, process, and rhythm in the coming decades.

Marilyn Ferguson is herself a model for tapping the human potential. A tireless campaigner for expanded consciousness and a holistic orienta-tion to the social and physical sciences, she is perhaps best known for her role as creator and publisher of the Brain/Mind Bulletin, *the most widely read newsletter in the areas of humanistic medicine, learning creativity, brain research and the physics of consciousness in the world, with readers in forty-five countries. Her prior bestselling book,* The Brain Revolution, *published in 1973, was selected by fourteen book clubs and translated into several languages. Recently, she expanded her involvement in researching and promoting the latest advances in the area of human transformation by creating a new newsletter,* The Leading Edge, *which focuses specifically on worldwide frontiers of social transformation. In addition, she is pres-ently at work on a new book to be titled* Awakening: The Aquarian Conspir-acy Papers, *a collection of seminal writings on various aspects of evolution-ary development.*

Relationships

Certain forms of the sexual adventure will be lost, but this does not mean that love, happiness, poetry, dream will be banished. . . . Our lack of imagination always depopulates the future.

Simone de Beauvoir
The Second Sex

Romantic love becomes the pathway not only to sexual and emotional happiness but also to the higher reaches of human growth.

Nathaniel Branden
The Psychology of Romantic Love

The form and purpose of human relationships is undergoing profound changes—evolutionary, historic, and cultural—as we approach the next millennium. From the narrowly defined personal relationships of the mid-twentieth century, married couples and nuclear families, we are moving into an age of variety, synthesis, and relationships whose ultimate goal is to foster growth.

At the moment, what we see most clearly is the variety. For example, there are "extended family" structures much like the kinship systems of old, but these new ties are based on shared values rather than blood relationship or tribal loyalties. People are living together, living alone, getting married, refusing to get married, having children, remaining childless by choice, adopting children as single parents, forming ad hoc families and "reconstituted households."

A diversity of living arrangements is here to stay. It is unlikely that the pendulum will swing back to the postwar norm of the nuclear family: breadwinner-father, housewife-mother, children. Too many irreversible trends—economic, social, technological, political, psychological—are generating change.

Our relationships and their stresses are microcosms of struggles and revolution going on in the larger society, issues of values, power, and rights.

Power is changing hands, through grassroots activism, the women's movement and movements for the rights of minorities, children, political dissidents, sexual dissidents, the handicapped, the elderly. Economic dislocations and mobility have created many temporary households: individuals joining forces for survival. Others form "intentional families" for emotional as well as practical support. Increasing numbers of divorced fathers are being granted child custody, sole or joint, creating a relatively new phenomenon, the single-father household. The number of couples choosing to live together without marriage increased eight-hundredfold between 1970 and 1978.

There is no longer even a clear consensus as to what comprises a family. The White House Commission on the Family, meeting in 1979 and 1980, was sharply divided on this issue. Traditionalists wanted to limit the definition to the nuclear family, but other commissioners preferred broader definitions, like that offered in 1979 by the American Home Economics Association: "Two or more persons who share resources, share responsibility for decisions, share values and goals, and have commitment to one another over time. The family is that climate that one 'comes home to,' and it is this network of sharing and commitments that most accurately describes the family unit, regardless of blood, legal ties, adoption, or marriage."

Birth control and legalized abortion have not only freed women sexually but greatly reduced their once overwhelming economic dependence. And, at the same time, many men are choosing to change their work in mid-career, often at a lower rate of pay.

The authority of institutions—church, state, medical and educational establishments—is dwindling rapidly. The growing sense of self-responsibility manifested in the holistic health movement and community activism is also reflected in the changing institution of the family.

A broad cultural revolution is altering the old territory of relationships. These stresses were noted in a 1980 survey of thirty thousand married readers by a traditional women's magazine, Ladies' Home Journal. The editors remarked that those women who were attempting to sustain traditional roles were suffering more anxiety and illness than those (a minority) adapting to change.

The women who answered our survey... are caught up in what may be the greatest period of transformation that has ever challenged American women, their partners, and their families. And there is a price to be paid for this coming of age.

Change brings stress, and the more traditional a woman, we found, the more she suffers. But a new woman is emerging, a happier woman. We call her a changing woman. . . .

These changing women are leading lives they were not brought up to expect or even want for themselves. They are laying their own ground rules.

The rising tide of change is pervasive, overturning old forms and raising up new, tentative ones. Relationships are changing because people are changing. Unprecedented millions have been drawn, seduced, recruited, or catapulted into journeys of the spirit. Collectively, they are moving into unexplored landscapes of transformation.

As we begin to relate differently to ourselves, all other relationships are also shaken. As we begin to trust ourselves and think of ourselves as strong, creative, and capable of learning, we are slower to conform. We chafe at the old compromises.

The journey has many departure points. For some, it is social concern: a movement that asks new questions about the environment, human rights, schools, or politics. For many, it is crisis: poor health, financial hardship, a broken relationship, a bereavement. Or it may be challenge: sudden success, new responsibilities, new demands. Anything that unsettles the old assumptions and compromises can initiate the process of personal change.

The greatest impact probably comes from the intentional systems, the modalities available at every hand: pop psychology and self-help books, psychotherapy, meditation, dream journals, bodywork, yoga, biofeedback training, running, weekend seminars, esoteric teachings. The inquiring mind, the drive for self-expression—once considered the hallmark of artists, mystics, and other nonconformists—is now an everyday phenomenon. The heroic pathway into the self is no longer the stuff of legend but the potential of Everyman and Everywoman.

Learning to trust oneself often leads to a set of values quite unlike those imprinted and endorsed by society. The conflict between these new values and traditional values sets off tremors, even earthquakes, in existing relationships. New priorities create their own agenda.

As the first wave of the population shifts its greater loyalty to this new agenda, those bound to the old are threatened. We are in for at least a decade of turbulence, not only between marriage partners and within families but also in our friendships, our work relationships, and within the larger society.

THE VALUES WAR

Heaven is living in your hopes and Hell is living in your fears. It's up to each individual which one he chooses.

Tom Robbins
Even Cowgirls Get the Blues

The emerging values shift has already become the subject of corporate, psychological, and anthropological scrutiny. Polltakers like Harris, Gallup, and Yankelovich have attempted to sketch its outlines. SRI International has projected its possible shape and numerical makeup in a major study for its business clients; the rise of an "inner-directed" consumer will mark the 'Eighties and 'Nineties. These polls and projections cite compelling evidence that a significant number of us are turning toward spiritual values and self-actualization. Rapidly growing segments of the population express concern about stewardship of the planet, global interdependence, the poor credibility of institutions.

The conflict that at first appeared to center around changing life-styles and behavior is, in fact, rooted in opposing realities—mutually contradictory sets of values, based on a belief system.

These systems, which we will call *Protection Values* and *Growth Values*, are like old and new scientific theories. The Protection Values have been our consensus. They are rewards appropriate to a dualistic, us-against-them way of seeing the world. They emerge from fear—of ourselves, of others, of a hostile, death-dealing universe. The Growth Values, on the other hand, are grounded in trust—of oneself, of others, of life, of the human capacity to survive and even transform adversity.

PROTECTION VALUES

Safety. Avoiding risk. Protection via external restraints and constraints (rules, burglar alarms, borders) to define the places safe from danger, "us" from "them." Survival a goal.

Comfort. Avoiding pain, contradiction, threats to belief systems.

GROWTH VALUES

Spontaneity. Freedom, willingness to risk, move into the unknown. Survival taken for granted.

Meaning. Willingness to confront life as it is, including uncomfortable contradiction and paradox. Tolerance of ambiguity.

(Continued on next page)

PROTECTION VALUES

Image. Meeting or exceeding cultural expectations. Conforming to norms, fitting oneself to the "job description." Status and role valued.

Self-control. Ability to restrain emotional responses or control the situation. Repression of anger, fear, sexuality, sentiment. Or *self-indulgence*, which is also an anesthetic against fear for some people.

Ego defenses. Protection of one's self-image by making others wrong or by rationalizing one's beliefs and behavior. Feeling right or righteous.

Permanence. Long-range commitments, preservation of traditions, repeating and recalling past triumphs, longevity. Effort to freeze and memorialize the past.

Information. Having answers, facts, training, experience, data. Being sure.

Adjustment. Belief in human limitations, which excuses one from great effort. Human beings seen as limited in what they can accomplish. War, starvation, and poverty viewed as inevitable, effort as futile.

Power over others. Being boss, judge, authority, Top Dog; or being helpless, manipulative, flattering, coercive.

GROWTH VALUES

Authenticity. Meeting or exceeding one's own expectations. Flexibility. Willingness to diverge from cultural norms out of curiosity or integrity. Acceptance of nonconformity in others.

Self-knowledge. Awareness of one's feelings and their role in behavior; transformation of fear and anger through self-understanding and trust; inner confidence that comes from having let go of illusions and survived fears.

Vulnerability. The "transparent self" acknowledges its weaknesses and draws from its strengths. It does not identify with the ego's need to be perfect.

Potential. Recognition of the flux and dynamics of life, the impossibility of holding the present moment. Belief that change represents possibility, a future whose capacity to surprise is relished, not feared.

Insight. Asking the right questions, eager to learn. Acceptance of uncertainty.

Aspiration. Belief in human potential. Human beings have built great cathedrals, flown to the moon. Any of us might accomplish something beyond the ordinary.

Power with others. Cooperation, communication, mutual support, alignment.

(Continued on next page)

PROTECTION VALUES	GROWTH VALUES
Feeling superior to others. Protection from feelings of inadequacy by being special: more attractive than others, or more intelligent, more successful, harderworking.	*Feeling connected to others.* Identifying with all human traits. Acceptance of oneself and others.
Freedom from responsibility. Whatever happens is the fault of other persons, social forces, fate. Sense of impotence.	*Freedom in responsibility.* Acknowledgement that one has chosen in the past, chooses now, and can choose in the future. Sense of personal power.
Relationship as completion. The self perceived as needing another, one's missing self.	*Relationship as enrichment.* The self experienced as whole, relationship as an opportunity for growth.

Movement toward the Growth Values is experienced more as a dawning realization than a sudden conversion. Initially we may simply notice that it feels good to drop pretenses, that cooperation is more fun than competition, that our half-conscious choices help create the drama of our lives day by day. At a certain point the new insights coalesce into a system more coherent and logical than the old. Although we fluctuate between these two value systems, we have our basic allegiance in one column or the other. There is a point of no return, a commitment to the Growth Values, comparable to the acrobat letting go of one trapeze bar to reach for another.

It is easy to see why relationships become strained when one partner defects from the Protection Values, the agenda on which the relationship itself was built. There is no middle ground. How do you compromise between living a role and living authentically? Between feeling superior or inferior to others and feeling connected to them? Between feeling yourself a victim and feeling powerful?

The shift is from No to Yes. As someone remarked, most of the time we are running away from what we're afraid of rather than running toward what we want. The Protection Values of our past have been attempts to ward off anticipated pain or loss. The Growth Values are a reaching out.

No one can persuade another person to make that shift. Only experience and courage and the inner urge to live life to the fullest show us that we can move through the mine field of our fears to freedom, to a richer existence.

Until recently our culture has had no initiation for this journey—no rite of passage. Typically, those who undertook the process have had to face not only their own fears and misgivings along the way but also the disapproval of their peers, friends, and families. Only now, with the emergence of hundreds of popular systems of personal transformation, is there any moral support for the journey.

Why do most of us embrace the Protection Values in the first place? After all, as young children we were spontaneous and free in many ways, vulnerable and candid, eager to explore and experiment. But it is important to remember that human beings are also pain-avoiders. Even small children are timid at times in the face of the unknown; they are fond of the familiar, anxious for approval.

Both fear and risk are inherent in the human equation; the biology of our brains and bodies allows us to shut down—or to transcend conflict, learn, change.

The Protection Values are reinforced by the environment. The family, the school, advertisers, and authorities give us the subtle Protection messages of our culture: Wear your galoshes, don't guess, don't speak to strangers, buy brand names, walk, don't run. We crystallize around these values, which promise us the good life. If we achieve status in the community, financial robustness, a desirable partner, control over our emotions, a good education, material comforts, and adequate insurance, we will be happy... won't we?

Little wonder that the greatest number of defectors from the Protection Values are members of the upper middle class who have tried them and found them bankrupt. Many of the most fortunate in society have discovered that these supposed hedges against danger fail to answer our deepest needs.

The ultimate goal of the Protection Values—security—is not to be found through them. Seeking protection where the culture has mapped it, we are like the character in the famous Sufi story who sought diligently for the key where the light was good rather than in the darkness where he had lost it. We seek meaning, completion, peace, and safety in externals, but we can only find them in ourselves.

An old Hasidic scripture says that man is afraid of things that cannot harm him and craves things that cannot help him. "But actually it is something within him that he is afraid of, and it is something within him that he craves."

Safety, we learn, is not to be found in blue-chip investments or promises to love forever but in oneself, one's own *spontaneity*—the ability to enjoy innovating in the face of the unexpected. In the Protection Values, we think of survival as a goal. In the Growth Values, we take for granted that we will survive—and aspire to more. When there are choices to be made, we ask not merely, "What is the worst that could happen?" but also, "What is the *best* that could happen?"

Another paradox: *comfort*, the avoidance of pain and conflict, is only temporary and partial. Determined to avoid suffering, we suffer nonetheless. At an unconscious level, we are made uneasy by the hidden contradictions in our lives and relationships. These conflicts translate into psychosomatic illness, depression, anxiety, irritability, insomnia. The commitment to finding *meaning*, although it requires confronting painful conflicts, can lead to ultimate resolution and understanding. We seek *permanence*, hoping to stave off the unknown, to protect ourselves from loss—but the only permanent attribute of life is change. *Potential*, the gift of change, offers us a stream of new possibilities and challenges.

Image is meant to impress others, to make us seem perfect enough to be loved and admired, an appearance rather than a sturdy reality. *Authenticity*—congruence within and without—does not depend on others. It cannot be destroyed or undermined. Love requires that we know one another intimately and therefore authentically; image defeats its own purpose.

Self-control, one of the Protection Values, is inherently contradictory. Who is controlling whom? If there is something that is controlling, what is it—and what is being controlled? How do "I" keep "me" in line? *Self-knowledge*, on the other hand, leads us to an understanding of our various selves and inner drives, not from managing or smothering these parts but allowing them all into awareness.

Ego defenses, erected to protect the personality, prove to be a bristling fortress around that which needs no defense: the self, stronger than the fearful ego. When one is *vulnerable*, on the other hand, others tend to respond to that humanness and trust; they often abandon their usual attacking or advantage-seeking behavior. The best defense is often no defense at all.

We hope that *power over others* will protect us from uncertainty about what they will do, but people remain unpredictable. Even if we control their behavior, we cannot control what they think. If we have *power with others*, if we are aligned with them, we will have a strong sense of what they are thinking, what they will do.

Feeling superior to others, meant to make us feel valued and important, often just makes us feel isolated. *Feeling connected* means sharing humanness with others; it allows us to feel good about ourselves in a mutually supportive relationship—more satisfying and workable than one-upmanship.

Adjustment, as a dominant philosophy, defines and limits the "possible," arming us against disappointment in ourselves or others. Yet a belief in human limitations is contradicted all too often by the aspiration of individuals too naive or hopeful to have given up. Human potential keeps asserting itself in our midst, reminding us poignantly of our own unrealized possibilities.

Information, having all the answers, is false protection in a world where the questions keep changing. There is less security in static facts than in knowing how to ask intelligent questions. *Insight* and a willingness to learn are of more use than accrued knowledge.

Freedom from responsibility rewards us by pardon. If we are victims, we cannot be held to account for failing to fulfill our promise. We can avoid self-blame and we can avoid change. But if we find our *freedom in responsibility* we realize that we have cocreated situations and attitudes in the past. Acknowledging past choices, we can choose now and in the future. We need not blame ourselves for the past, only concede that, consciously or unconsciously, we helped make it happen.

Relationship as completion only works so long as the other person feels a complementary need for completion; if he or she achieves a greater wholeness, the old dependency disappears. The relationship is then on a different, perhaps shaky, basis. If we experience our *relationships as enrichment* we are together by choice. As the poet Rainer Maria Rilke described it, "a wonderful living side by side can grow up, if human beings succeed in loving the distance between them which makes it possible for each to see the other whole and against a wide sky!" Unfortunately, no one taught many of us to love the distance.

As one set of values is gaining adherents and the other losing membership, the cultural seesaw becomes pronounced. Because most existing relationships were initiated under the old system, the defectors find themselves branded as troublemakers, the agents of unwanted innovation, or even revolt.

THE TRANSITION: DANGER AND OPPORTUNITY

The values war—symbolic, guerilla, open combat—will take its toll of old agreements. For example, one parent decides to risk giving a child or teenager more freedom and responsibility while the other prefers the security of rules. One partner may ask for a reassessment of the relationship, its form and purpose. Perhaps a couple has given high priority to material ambition, and suddenly one member begins to define the "quality of life" as the quality of *inner* life, losing a measure of interest in money, career aspirations, socializing, creature comforts.

During this transition, we can see clearly how crucial the safety/security issue is in most adult relationships. If we have not learned to trust ourselves as children, we seek a kind of pseudo-parental protection in our marriages. Too often we have used each other as parent substitutes, talismans against danger. The controlling mother-wife buffers the fear that "I can't be trusted, you'll make me be good." The protective father-husband speaks to the childhood faith that "Daddy will make me safe."

As we break out of the old fears that we are not enough, that we don't know enough, we are liberated from our present bondage and from a lifelong pattern of imposed limitations, the warnings of parents, teachers, our mate, all of those who remind us that we *can't*. We no longer bargain away our rights for the wish to be safe.

Seeking meaning, confronting the contradictions in our lives, may lead to disruptions. Ordinarily we tend either to avoid direct conflict or fight about behavior. When a couple discovers divergent values beneath the divergent behaviors, their differences are more frightening and harder to deal with. They may seem unresolvable.

Like pictures talking to pictures, couples have supported each other's facades. If one person wishes to quit pretending, to become more real, the delicate consensus is jarred. For one thing, the partner may prefer the old mask to the new reality. The person who appeared powerful and controlled, now expressing self-doubts or hidden hopes, may lose respect. The person who was self-effacing and is now strong has changed the dynamics of the relationship.

Furthermore, people have defined themselves by their relationships, proud to be the wives, husbands, children, parents, or associates of people who are glamorous, powerful, special. If, for example, the surgeon decides that he would rather be a potter, where does that leave "the doctor's wife"?

One who no longer needs to defend the ego, who refuses to enter the old win-lose game, has changed the rules of a game that may have been vital to the relationship. Many couples, once characterized by a companionable commiseration about the world or a shared critical attitude, may feel lost for something to talk about if one partner is no longer miserable or critical. Others have developed their own miniculture, their family dogma. When one partner abandons what "we" always believed, the new openness may seem to be instability, a lack of discrimination, betrayal.

Our transitional crises also reflect the gains and hesitations in our efforts to get beyond limiting sexual roles. Already women are expecting and getting a fairer share of life's challenges, the "action" of public life. Men are discovering their intuition and their gentler traits, they are claiming their right to feelings. Women are learning to treasure their noncompetitive, deep friendships with women. Men, no longer able to rely exclusively on women for warmth and nurturance, are finding that they can support each other. These discoveries are freeing the sexes to love each other as equals.

Once freed from the old issues of security and dependency, women seem naturally endowed to shift to the Growth Values: to be communicative, expressive, empathetic, real, vulnerable, spontaneous. During the transition there is an understandable oscillation in both sexes, women wavering between independence and dependence, between giving and withholding, men being alternately democratic and domineering, torn between controlling and letting go. Neither sex is yet fully trusting. Women fear they will be cut off from love if they lose their dependency; men are ambivalent about their role as protectors, wanting to keep it and to relinquish it, uncertain of the new expectations of women.

TRANSFORMATIVE RELATIONSHIPS

If love can't recreate lovers, what good is it?

Tom Robbins
Even Cowgirls Get the Blues

The Growth Values, responsible for stress when they are embraced by only one partner in a relationship, are the cause for celebration when shared. When two people have formed a relationship on this basis, they engage in an experiment and an adventure. They are pioneering a new social form.

In the age of transformative relationships we will ask more than ever before: more intimacy, more honesty, more depth. At the same time, we will ask less: less external evidence of our bonding, less identification with roles, less focus on the relationship as an end in itself.

Aware that we cannot bind others to us by claims of blood or ceremony, we are coming to appreciate the richness of human possibilities, the ways in which complex human beings need to express themselves in relationships to many different persons, not limited to one closed relationship, me-for-you and you-for-me. In the future sexual exclusivity will be less an issue than the whole notion of possession. People will not expect to 'belong to' or possess another. For many, marriage will continue to be a mode of commitment, but it will be more egalitarian, more realistic: new marriage vows, already in use, supplant "till death do us part" with promises to support each other "in the changes to come" and "to speak the truth in love."

Ironically, as there is more flexibility and acceptance, relationships may be more enduring. Although we will expect more in the way of enrichment and potential, we will acknowledge that a relationship cannot replace one's calling in the world, just as a vocation cannot substitute for deep human connection.

Even now, parents who have gone through personal transformations are rearing their children differently, giving them acceptance and the courage to assert their own needs over a lifetime. These parents also emphasize to their children that we create our lives by our choices.

Perhaps schools in the Third Millennium will teach young people the lessons our own generations are learning painfully. In the future it may be "common wisdom" that we must confront pain, that freedom is worth the risk of facing down fear, that we can find our authentic way and must not sabotage the efforts of others to find theirs. Just as our schools now teach courses on "Marriage and the Family" emphasizing budget and sexual information, they may someday teach young people the "Seven Deadly Warning Signs in a Relationship." Everyone may know the ways in which we erode and undermine our relationships.

Perhaps in times of stress we will even turn to "values counselors." We will cheer each other on in the search for meaning. Our relationships will be contexts, not goals.

Relationships grounded in trust demand a fearless and unsentimental love. This ruthless love was described in *The Way of Transformation* by Karlfried von Durkheim: "The man who, being really on the Way, falls upon hard times in the world will not, as a consequence, turn to that friend who offers him refuge and encourages his old self to survive. Rather he will seek out someone who will faithfully and inexorably help him to risk himself.... We should have the courage to face life and encounter all that is most perilous in the world."

As we move into another historic age, as explorers and adventurers, we can ask no more and no less of one another: loving support for the exciting journey ahead.

NOZIZWE S

There is little disagreement that Carl Rogers has done more to promote a humanistic approach to personal and social behavior than any other twentieth-century psychologist. Few, if any, of the thousands of people involved in human-centered research or practice during the past forty years have not been deeply influenced by his pioneering work. Born in 1902, Carl Rogers received his doctorate from Columbia University where he immediately began a career that has led him to become one of America's most honored and respected social scientists. Throughout his life, he has always stressed the importance of human expression, dignity, and respect and has been an unrelenting social crusader for the "self-deterministic" orientation. His well-known debates on humanism versus behaviorism with Dr. B. F. Skinner have become classics in the field.

Prior to his present position as Resident Fellow at the Center for Studies of the Person in La Jolla, California, Dr. Rogers worked at the Institute for Child Guidance in New York, and held professorships at Ohio State University, the University of Chicago, and the University of Wisconsin. In addition to his broad activities as a writer, lecturer, educator, therapist, and consultant to government and industry, he presently holds teaching posts at Harvard University, UCLA, Columbia University, and Brandeis University.

Dr. Rogers was initiated into Phi Beta Kappa six decades ago in 1922 and has since received numerous honors worldwide, including the Distinguished Scientific Contribution Award, the Distinguished Professional Psychologist Award, and the Award of Professional Achievement from the American Board of Professional Psychology; he was named Humanist of the Year in 1964 by the American Humanist Association.

Dr. Rogers is widely published in journals and books, many of which have appeared in translation, reflecting his international influence and involvement. His most widely read publications include: Client Centered Therapy, On Becoming a Person, Freedom to Learn, Carl Rogers on Personal Power, *and* A Way of Being.

After all his years of involvement in people-centered activities, Dr. Rogers feels that the greatest potential for human good and for loving human development rests within the community. What follows are his personal thoughts and reflections on the most essential ingredients of human relationships as well as a fascinating glimpse into their personal future.

CARL R. ROGERS # **C**OMMUNITIES*

THE FORMING OF COMMUNITY

For the past fifteen years, I, together with colleagues from all parts of the world, have attempted to understand and facilitate the delicate process of building communities. We have worked with small groups, larger groups of 50 to 200, and occasionally with very large groups of 600 to 800—in the United States, Mexico, Brazil, Venezuela, Japan, England, and Spain—in an effort to learn the subtle mechanisms of bringing people together so that power is truly shared, individuals are empowered, and groups are perceived as trustworthy and competent to handle problems. Despite our mistakes and frequent bewilderment at the process, it is clear that we have become more effective in facilitating the formation of temporary communities in which most of the members feel both a keen sense of their own power and a sense of close and respectful union with all of the other members of the community. In these groups we have focused our efforts on providing a climate in which the individual can make his or her own choices, participate equally with others in planning or carrying out activities, become more aware of his or her own strength, and become increasingly autonomous and creative as the architect of his or her own life. Because of this absolute focus on empowering the individual, we have come to think of our work as a person-centered approach to creating community.†

---

* In the writing and thoughts which make up this chapter, I am indebted to many people, but especially to Maria Bowen, Joann Justyn, Jared Kass, Maureen Miller, Natalie Rogers, and John K. Wood.

† This approach, the foundation of what I shall be describing, is not the only basis possible. In China, for example, it is the collective purpose that is important, and the individual is helped to become less autonomous, more of one cell in an organism. In this country, some groups are formed around charismatic leaders or certain religious or other dogmas. I am, for the moment, ignoring those other possible bases for forming communities and am speaking only of our own experiences, growing out of a person-centered philosophy.

135

This approach stands at odds with the dominant trends in our culture. Our schools, governments, and businesses are permeated with the view that neither the individual nor the group is trustworthy. The paradigm of power—power *over*, power to control—is the very cornerstone of our society. Most Western religions regard individuals as basically sinful and therefore in need of discipline and guidance. Psychoanalysis takes a similar view, that at the core of each individual lie primitive, unconscious, destructive impulses that would wreak havoc if they were unleashed on society. The individual must, therefore, be taught, guided, and controlled by the superior authority of our social institutions.

Yet our experience, and that of an increasing number of humanistic psychologists, has shown that another paradigm is far more effective and constructive for the individual and society. We have found that given a suitable psychological climate, humans are trustworthy, creative, self-motivated, powerful, constructive, and capable of releasing undreamed-of potentialities.

A Way of Being in the Staff*

My experiences with person-centered communities have been sharpest and most vivid in working with colleagues in six summer workshops beginning in 1974. These have been held in six different locations, three in California and one each in Oregon, the Adirondacks, and Nottingham, England. The number of participants has ranged from 65 to 135.† The staff has been relatively constant. The membership has ranged in number from five to seven, and there have been a few changes, but the feeling is one of continuity. During the year we work separately, but we come together before each workshop. The way we function and meet each other's needs has changed over time.

Initially we saw our function in somewhat traditional ways. In preparatory meetings we spent much time in making alternative plans and designs for the program involving small groups and other special activities. We wished to "give" as much freedom of choice as possible (as though it were ours to give). We saw ourselves primarily as specialists having different interests and skills to offer; as teachers and facilitators. We endeavored to be prepared and to offer a wide variety of resources for learning. Within the

---

* In this section especially, and to some extent in other portions of the chapter, I have drawn on material produced by the staff of the person-centered approach workshops, which includes Maria Bowen, Joann Justyn, Jared Kass, Maureen Miller, Natalie Rogers and John K. Wood as well as myself.

† For a detailed description of one of these groups, see Rogers (1977).

staff itself we spent time working through interpersonal frictions and differences, which we did not wish to expose to the participants.

Gradually we have come to see our function as a staff in a very different way. Briefly, we believe that our major task is to *be ourselves.* To this end we spend several days together before the workshop convenes so that insofar as we are capable:

We can be fully open to each other, and later to the whole group.

We can explore new and unknown areas of our own lives.

We are truly accepting of our differences.

We are open to the new ideas and insights we will receive from our fresh inward journeys, all stimulated by our staff and group experiences.

Thus it can be said that we now prepare *ourselves,* with much less emphasis on plans or materials. We value our staff process and want that to be available to the group. We have found that by being as fully ourselves as we are able—creative, diverse, contradictory, present, open, and sharing—we somehow become tuning forks, finding resonances with those qualities in all the members of the workshop community.

While we do not persuade, interpret, or manipulate, we are certainly not laissez-faire in our attitude. Instead we find that we can actively share ourselves, our feelings, potentialities, and skills. We are each free to be as much of ourselves as it is possible for us to be.

Part of that way of being has become ingrained. It is our desire to *hear.* During periods of chaos or criticism of staff or expression of deep feelings, we listen intently, accepting, occasionally voicing our understanding of what we have heard. We listen especially to the contrary voices, the soft voices, those that are expressing unpopular or unacceptable views. We make a point of responding to a person if he or she spoke personally and no one responded. We thus tend to validate each person.

We do not stop here. We as a staff are continually exploring new facets of our own experience as individuals. It has meant facing openly the increasingly intuitive and psychic aspects of our lives. As we push on into these unknown inner areas, it seems to enable each new workshop community—individually and collectively—to probe more deeply into their own worlds of shadow and mystery. This has brought us findings we did not anticipate.

One striking example is that the community has an almost telepathic knowledge of where the staff *is,* in its own process. One year, in meetings of the staff, we discussed in depth the sexual overtones and behaviors that appear to be a part of workshops, and we openly shared these same sexual aspects in ourselves. Later, in the workshop community, this topic, without any suggestion from us, was for the first time openly talked about and considered. One staff member puts it this way: "The mystery that remains for me is the uncanny way the community seemed to live out the ideas we generated in our staff meetings, right down to the psychic happenings."

One final statement about the way we function. We are a thoroughly open staff with no leader and no hierarchical organization. Leadership and responsibility are shared. We have become a very close team, living our relationship in the most person-centered manner we know.

My Own Experiences

I have found my experience with the workshop staff to be most nourishing. It has made it possible for me to take risks I would never have dared to take alone. I know that even if I behave in stupid ways in a large workshop community or try something new that fails, there is still a group that believes in me and accepts me. This makes it possible for me to dare to try the new and the impossible.

It is most helpful to me to feel that I have no special responsibility for the success of the workshop community, that that responsibility is completely shared. No longer does my gut tighten up when I sense something going "wrong" in a group. I can relax and simply *be* whatever I am at the moment. My trust in the collective wisdom of the staff has now become a deep trust in the collective wisdom of the entire community.

It is a tremendously releasing experience to have a human environment where I can completely let go. In the three or four days prior to the workshop, by meeting with the staff, each of us pours out our problems, our predicaments, our feelings. We share as deeply as we are able. This exchange is restorative, it is therapeutic, it gives an incredible security. During the workshop this kind of sharing continues in our staff meetings and makes it possible for us also to share deeply with the larger community. But there is also more feedback during our community experience. We astonish each other with our creativity and ingeniousness. We anger each other by the way we have handled relationships and situations. We are critical of one another, we are at times proud of one another. We learn from each other, and we work out feelings together. We are a marvelous support group for each other. We have become a catalytic force.

THE PROCESS OF THE GROUP

So complex is the process within these workshop groups that I despair of doing more than hinting at its multifaceted aspects. Yet there are some characteristic elements that I think are significant and deserving of mention.

Unity out of Separateness

For one thing, the sense of community does not arise out of collective movement or a conforming to some group direction. Quite the contrary, each individual tends to use the opportunity to become all that he or she *can* become. Separateness and diversity, the uniqueness of being "me," are experienced. This very marked separateness of consciousness seems in an odd way to bring the group to a oneness of consciousness.

We have found that each person not only perceives the workshop community as a place to meet personal needs, but actively forms the situation to meet those needs. One individual finds new ways of meeting a difficult transition in marriage or career. Another gains insights that enable inner growth. Another learns new ways of building community. Still another gains improved skills in interpersonal relationships. Others find new means of spiritual, artistic, and aesthetic renewal and refreshment. Many move toward more informed and effective action for social change. Others experience combinations of these insights. The freedom to be individual, to work toward one's own goals in a harmony of diversity, is one of the most prized aspects of the workshop.

One participant, writing some months following the workshop, stated very well the way in which community develops out of separateness:

"Each moment of the nine days seemed to add more threads to a kind of complicated tapestry that was unfolding before our eyes and being woven by participants . . . some using strong threads, others bold colors, others delicate touches. For me it became so awesome, so complicated a masterpiece of artwork, that until I could stand back from a distance and view the entire tapestry against an uncluttered background, it could not be fully understood or appreciated. Even then, in its fullness, it would still appear to change each day and never be completely finished. The still unfinished part is all the insights that are hitting me at the most unexpected times."

The diversity of the threads in this tapestry can be explained by the incredible variety that exists among the participants. A youth of eighteen and a woman of seventy-five, in the same group. Ardent Marxists and conservative business and professional people in the Spanish workshop. Devoutly religious persons of many faiths and those who scoff at religion. Athletic people and paralyzed persons whose lives are spent in wheelchairs. All of these persons have been active participants, each contributing his or her distinctive self in the process.

The Chaotic, Painful Aspects

I would not want it to appear that the group develops smoothly. The initial sessions are often chaotic. Usually there is disbelief that *the workshop plan is to arise from all of us together*. There is suspicion of the staff. (In the international workshop community in Spain, there was a general dislike of the United States and its economic imperialism—a feeling that extended to American staff and participants.) There is confusion because of the lack of structure and a criticism of the staff for not having made plans—a reluctance of the participants to own their own power. There are sometimes violent disagreements. There is a tendency to make "speeches" without listening to what has been said. There is rivalry and power-seeking as members attempt to take control over the group or "give leadership." There are arguments over how to divide into small groups, a step that nearly everyone desires but for which a dozen methods are proposed and rejected.

But in the presence of the facilitative attitude created by staff and by many participants, individuals gradually begin to *hear* each other, and then slowly to understand and respect. The atmosphere becomes a *working* atmosphere, both in the large and small groups, as people begin to delve into themselves and their relationships.

As this working process goes more deeply, it can bring great personal pain and distress. Nearly always the pain has to do with insights into self or with the fright caused by a change in the self-concept, or distress over changing relationships.

So there are experiences of frustration, distrust, anger, envy, and despair in the group. In the individual there are the personal experiences of suffering through change, of being unable to cope with ambiguity, of fear and loneliness and self-depreciation. But both group and individual experience these sufferings as a part of a process in which they are involved and which they somehow trust, even if they could, at the moment, give no rational reason for doing so.

The Basis of Value Choices

In these groups, a shift in the basis of value choices occurs. Values based on authority, which derive from sources external to the person, tend to be diminished; values that are experienced tend to be enhanced. What the person has been *told* is good and valuable, whether by parents, church, state, or party, tends to be questioned. Those behaviors or ways of being that are *experienced* as satisfying and meaningful tend to be reinforced. The criteria for making value judgments come more and more to lie in the person, not in a book, teacher, or set of dogmas. The Locus of evaluation is in the person, not outside.

Thus the individual comes to live increasingly by a set of standards which have an internal personal basis. Because he or she is aware that these standards are based on ever-changing experience, they are held more tentatively, less rigidly. They are not carved in stone, but written by a human heart.

The Process of Decision Making

One of the astonishing aspects of such large group experiences is the incredibly complex ramifications of any decision. In ordinary life, a course of action is ordered by authority, and unless it outrages us we tend to obey the order, follow the rule. Although there may be mutterings, it appears that, in general, everyone accepts the regulation. All the complex reactions are hidden.

But in a community such as these workshops where persons feel a sense of their own worth and a freedom to express themselves, the complexities become evident. Someone in the workshop community proposes a way of dividing into small groups. "Let's draw numbered lots. Then all the ones' will constitute a group, all the 'twos' another, and so on." It is hard to imagine the variety of responses. Reasons are given for this idea. Points are raised against it. Slight variations are offered. Exceptions are suggested. One discovers that there are not one or two, but dozens of personal reactions to this seemingly simple plan. Often the group seems on the verge of consensus when one more member speaks up. "But I don't like this because it doesn't fit *me*."

Such a process can be seen as a cumbersome, complicated, irritating, frustrating way of arriving at a decision, and often is. After all, does the wish of *everyone* have to be considered? And the silent answer of the group is that, yes, every person is of worth, every person's views and feelings have a right to be considered. A solution is reached by a process that ensures that each individual feels that his or her contribution was respected, weighed, and made a part of the final plan. The sagacity of the group is extraordinary.

This process seems slow, and participants complain about "the time we are wasting." But the larger wisdom of the group recognizes it as valuable, since it is knitting together a community in which every soft voice, every subtle feeling has its respected place.

The Transcendent Aspect

This leads me into another characteristic of the community-forming process as I have observed it—the transcendent or spiritual aspect. These are words that in earlier years I would never have used. But the broad wisdom of the group, the almost telepathic communication, the sense of a "something greater" seem to invoke such terms.

As in other instances, a participant puts in a more eloquent fashion what I have felt. She wrote, some time later:

"I found it to be a profound spiritual experience. I felt the oneness of spirit in the community. We breathed together, felt together, even spoke for one another. I felt the power of the 'life force' that infuses each of us—whatever that is. I felt its presence without the usual barricades of 'me-ness' or 'you-ness'—it was like a meditative experience when I feel my self as a center of consciousness, very much a part of the broader, universal consciousness. And yet with that extraordinary sense of oneness, the separateness of each person present has never been more clearly preserved."

A PARADOX—ITS POSSIBLE RESOLUTION

I have endeavored to sketch some of what we have learned in our work regarding the formation of community and to identify some aspects of this complex process. I would like now to call attention to the bearing that our experience may have on one of the strange aspects of our Western culture. We are a part of an incredible paradox. On the one hand we want self-sufficiency, independence, privacy. Each person, even each family member, wants and "needs" a car so that one person never has to adjust to the schedule or the wants of another. The family acquires a dishwasher so that family members need not cooperate in washing the dishes. A separate room for each member of the family is always the goal, if not an absolute "must." When we commute by train or bus, we bury our respective noses in our newspapers or books so that we can avoid communicating with the person next to us. It is very clear that the utmost in privacy is none too private. Our slogan could well be that of Greta Garbo: "I vant to be *alone.*" As Phil Slater (1970) has shown so clearly, we *pursue* privacy and self-sufficiency in almost every possible way.

Yet in our workshop communities there is an opposite tendency. Strangers room together without complaint. Sometimes a dozen people share an uncomfortable dormitory and simply joke about it. Communal and coeducational bathrooms are usually regarded as welcome places for more communication. In particularly intensive workshops, it is not at all unusual for a person to be in constant interpersonal and communicative contact with others for eighteen or twenty hours in a day—and to be excited and positive about the experience. As the workshop concludes, there is a great sense of sadness at leaving. Plans are made for the continuing closeness of support groups originating in the community. We do everything possible to continue the depth of intimacy that in daily life we so assiduously avoid. We wish to continue the very personal sharing, the honest feedback, the open confrontation, which we work so hard in our everyday situations to escape.

How is it possible to account for this paradox? One aspect of it can be easily understood. Many of us abhor superficial communication—chit-chat, long conversations on trivial topics, cocktail party burbling, lengthy arguments over everything from politics to baseball. So to avoid such "a waste of time" we remove ourselves from situations in which such superficiality is the expected level of communication.

But there is more to it than this. We seem as a culture to have made a fetish out of complete self-sufficiency, of not needing help, of being completely private except in a very few selected relationships. This goal would be completely impossible during most of our history, but modern technology makes it achievable. With my private room, private car, private office, private (and preferably unlisted) telephone, with food and clothing purchased in large, impersonal stores, with my own stove, refrigerator, dishwasher, washer-dryer, I can be practically immune from intimate contact with any other person. What with massage parlors and call girls for men and "escort services" for women, even sexual needs can be satisfied without any personal intimacy. The utmost in privacy of personal life can be—and often is—achieved. We have reached our goal.

But we pay a price. From our alienated young people come our criminals, capable of senseless violence. From our private middle life we "progress" to a very lonely "senior citizen" status. Both the young and the old are considered to be almost completely useless in our modern society, and are made keenly aware of that attitude. They have no place. They feel private, isolated—and hopeless.

It seems as though in our workshops, with participants from age eighteen to seventy-five, we are acknowledging by our behavior, that the pendulum has swung too far in the direction of separateness. We discover that we prize deep intimacy, that it helps us to grow, and empowers us to act in our society. We are sad with each other, and we rejoice with each other. We are quite willing to put up with discomfort in order to *be* with each other. We enjoy nourishing each other. We find our private selves lost in the larger endeavor of forming a community, and yet discover that this gives us a deeper and more solid sense of self.

Some Unresolved Problems

Though I believe our experience contains significant implications for the future, there are still problems we have not satisfactorily resolved. I will list them briefly.

1. Our experience is limited almost entirely to the formation of temporary communities. We need more experience with permanent communities.

2. We have been only partially successful with groups in which the members are bound by their constituency to voice a "party line" and do not feel free to enter the process as persons. That this situation is not impossible to deal with is best shown by the astonishing effect of the Camp David experience on President Sadat and Prime Minister Begin, who were able to drop their assigned roles temporarily and converse and embrace as persons.

3. We do not yet feel sure of our ability to deal with violent revolutionaries and terrorists, though we moved in that direction in a group containing militant Catholics and Protestants from Belfast (see McGaw, et al., 1973).

4. We have not resolved the "reentry problem," the person who seems to lose the gains he or she has made in the workshop upon returning home. We are making progress in this area by discussing the issues in advance and forming support networks that continue after the workshop.

IMPLICATIONS FOR THE FUTURE

Opportunities for Resolving International Frictions

The nine European Common Market nations are to elect a European Parliament of some 400 members. It is reported that its function will be more symbolic than legislative. This opens still more opportunities, since they will not be rigidly bound to "party lines" but can be open and responsive persons. I have little doubt that a competent international facilitative staff could initiate in this European congress the same sort of process I have been describing, one that was strikingly illustrated in the intercultural workshop community in Spain, creating a harmonious unity out of citizens of twenty-two countries. Imagine the members of such an international parliament reaching the point where they could truly hear and understand and respect each other, where a cooperative sense of community developed, where humanness had a higher priority than power. The results could have the most profound significance. I do not mean that all problems would be resolved. Not at all. But even the most difficult tensions and demands become more soluble in a human climate of understanding and mutual respect.

This is only one example of the way in which our know-how in forming community might be used to resolve and dissolve intercultural and international tensions. A plan is ready for working with Arab-Israeli relationships. Whether it will be tried is problematical. What is important is that such a plan is within the realm of possibility. If such hostile, antagonistic individuals are willing to gather in the same room together, we know the attitudes and skills that can move them in the direction of a communicative mutual respect, and eventually toward becoming a community.

The Significance of Education

Many experiments in a more person-centered mode of education are under way. I would like to paint, in broad strokes, a picture of what education in the future might achieve utilizing the know-how we have today.

It could build a climate of trust in which curiosity, the natural desire to learn, could be nourished and enhanced.

It could free students, faculty, and administrators alike to participate in decision making about all aspects of learning.

It could develop a sense of community in which the destructive competition of today would be replaced by cooperation, respect for others, and mutual helpfulness.

It could encourage students to prize themselves, to develop self-confidence and self-esteem.

It could enable both students and faculty increasingly to discover the source of values in themselves, coming to an awareness that the good life is within, not dependent on outside sources.

It could imbue students with an excitement in intellectual and emotional discovery, which would lead them to become lifelong learners, in a community of such learners.

These are not "pie-in-the-sky" statements. We have the know-how for achieving every one of these goals. Whether, as a culture, we choose to bring them about is the uncertain element.

Pilot Models

I do not deceive myself that our communities or similar efforts growing out of a humanistic, person-centered philosophy have any chance of directly affecting the mainstream of world events or the lives of the multitudes who inhabit our planet.

I do know, however, that we are developing pilot models that can be utilized on a larger scale when and if society so wishes. Our Belfast group had, even in the long run, only an infinitesimal impact on the troubled Irish situation. But, as a Belfast observer remarked, "If there could only have been a group like this in every block in Belfast, *that* would have made a difference!"

My point is that we wait upon the social will. If the time comes when we tire of the endless homicidal feuds, despair of force and war as a means of bringing peace, become discontent with the half-lives we are living, then we may seriously look for alternatives. When this time comes, we will not find a void. We will discover that there are means for facilitating the resolution of feuds, find that there are ways of building community without sacrificing the potential and creativity of the person. We will realize that there *are* ways, already tried out on a small scale, of enhancing learning, of moving toward new values, of raising consciousness to unexpected levels. We will find that there are ways of being that do not involve power over a group. We will discover that harmonious community can be built on a basis of mutual respect and enhanced personal growth. That I see as our basic contribution as humanistic psychologists with a person-centered philosophy—that we have created working models on a small scale that our culture can use when it is ready.

Part II

THE CULTURE
AND BEYOND

THE DISCOVERY OF AGRICULTURE SOME 10,000 YEARS AGO, ostensibly marked the dawn of civilization, the emergence of the first communities, and the promise of plenty for all. At the excavation of one of the most ancient cities known to man outside of Jerusalem, only the ruins of a colossal watchtower remain as a testament, demonstrating that the rise of communities coincided with the accumulation of goods and the need to protect these from neighbors.

At the time the walls of Jericho were first being built, the population of the planet was a scant 10 million people, mostly hunter-gatherers, who coexisted sharing the abundant game and wild vegetation. Today, 10,000 years later, there are over 4,000 million people on the planet, and despite all the advances in agriculture, two-thirds of these people are starving. The promise of agriculture, of feeding the earth has never yet been realized. Instead, man the hunter, became man the warrior and began to increase his land holdings at his neighbor's expense, eventually developing the great feudal estates of the middle ages.

Some 200 years ago a group of daring men gathered in Philadelphia to forge a new vision of man. The ensuing document of the 1st Congress of the United States under Thomas Jefferson put an end to the feudal system in our country, and set the blueprint for similar revolutions around the world. Today a daring group of men and women are forging yet another vision of the possible human. Like the vision shared by the signers of the Declaration of Independence, it is a political vision yet one in which the individual rather than the government is the prime agent of change, growth, and self-realization.

Jean Houston leads the charge with her chapter on education. We need to develop the complete child, Jean explains and brings in supportive facts and anecdotes from Teihard de Chardin and other figures from her wonder-filled life. Willis Harman describes a future where only the fortunate may be able to work, while the rest of us are kept merely as "pets," with nothing to do but spend our leisure time meaningfully. Will play and pleasure be the mainstay of our future automated society? Don Mankin explores the issues raised by the evolving hedonistic lifestyle.

In his essay on the future of art, Livio Vinardi states that we are in the throes of a scientific renaissance. The cyclical nature of history is bringing us to a marriage between art and science, and a cross-fertilization of style, technologies, and aesthetic modes. Frederick Pohl raises the somber question of whether we're doomed to forever reenact humanity's first political act, where one of our ancestors clubbed a presumed enemy to his death over an historically-insignificant argument. Will a new political form emerge to carry us through the next millennium of human history? The author prescribes several inventive methods for enhancing each individual's political power and choice.

We are approaching the era of the super-healthy, claims Rick Carlson. The end of disease-oriented medicine is at hand and in its stead institutions that promote health and optimal development are rising. Harvey Cox explores the possibility of a new religion emerging from the hearts and minds of humans, a religion that will build upon our most noble and self-transcending qualities.

In their chapter, Planetary Cycles, Barbara Marx Hubbard and Barry McWaters describe the planet as a conscious, living organism. Our destiny lies in participatory evolution, they claim. Timothy Leary presents the Academy Awards for the most exceptional scientific discoveries of the 21st century, to the men and women whose legendary discoveries have brought us one step closer to the future.

The changes forecasted for our species for the next millennium are so dramatic that they may require a quantum leap forward. But quantum change as a vehicle into the future is hardly implausible. It takes only one individual discovery to set off a chain of events that can radically alter life as we know it. We have seen this throughout recorded history. The following story recounted by Lyall Watson demonstrates that this principle is true not only for our species but for other forms of life as well.

"Off the coast of Japan are a number of tiny islands where resident populations of macaques have been under continuous observation for more than twenty years. The scientists provide supplementary food, but the monkeys also feed themselves by digging up sweet potatoes and eating them dirt and all. This uncomfortable practice continued unchanged for many years until one day a young male monkey broke with tradition and carried his potato down to the sea where he washed it before eating it. He taught the trick to his mother, who showed it to her current mate and so the culture spread through the colony until most of them, let us say 99 monkeys, were doing it. Then one Tuesday morning at eleven, the hundredth individual acquired the habit, and within an hour, it appeared on two other islands in two physically unconnected populations of monkeys who until that moment had shown no inclination to wash their food."

 *Jean Houston has devoted her life to closing the gap between human potential and human performance. A tireless researcher, writer, and educator, she brings a unique combination of wit, energy, charm, and intelligence to the human sciences. Her unending curiosity regarding the many faces of human evolution has taken many forms and turns. In the 1960s it led to her now classic work on the nature of altered states of consciousness, as detailed in* The Varieties of the Psychedelic Experience, *written in collaboration with her husband and colleague Robert Masters. Over the years, her interest in the expansion of consciousness broadened and deepened to embrace literally hundreds of methods, strategies, and rituals for accelerating the learning process, gathered from sources as disparate as primitive cultures and modern biofeedback laboratories. In recent years, her interest in human education has taken a more holistic bent as she has turned her attention to the study of the relationship between the mind and body and optimal states of learning. This deepened involvement in full organismic education culminated in the publication of* Mind Games, Listening to the Body, *(both coauthored by Robert Masters), and* Lifeforce.*

Dr. Houston's contributions to the area of human potential are distinguished by a deep committment to sharing her ideas, discoveries, and methods with people of all ages from all walks of life. Unlike many researchers who remain isolated in their laboratories and teaching auditoriums, Jean Houston has for nearly two decades "taken her show on the road"; she has traveled throughout the world instructing people in ways to increase intelligence, creativity, self-care, and body/mind harmony.*

Presently Dr. Houston is director of the Foundation for Mind Research and educational director of the Dromenon Institute, a training center that researches and designs programs and curricula in the areas of mental and physical development. She also serves as developer and chief consultant of the Curriculum in Human Capacities at the New School for Social Research in New York City.

In her chapter on the future of education Jean Houston identifies what she feels to be the most important ingredients in the educational process and explores ways in which the learning process could be improved, expanded, and accelerated in the coming decades.

EDUCATION

I would like to begin my remarks with two contrasting statements about the nature and possibilities of education. The first is a negative meditation which I recently composed. I call it, "Consider the Stradivarius . . ."

We are given as our birthright a Stradivarius and we come to play it like a plastic fiddle.

Consider the Stradivarius. Consider the child—the star brighter than any star man's mind can create a conception of, this God-stuff rendered freely as spillover of an abundance of which we are largely unaware. This nuclear divinity which radiates an unnameable glory when it comes is in fact a creation of such inestimable worth that, were a cosmic scales to be employed, the infant child placed on one tray and all the precious jewels on the other, there would be no possibility of outweighing the child. Talents to last a million years are the mother lode of its molecules. Its body is celled of mysteries which are incomprehensible yet existent and responsive to all that is, and therefore is the container and active channeler of all that is. There is no need here to speak of Evolution to come. All the future tunings and turnings are already here, latent givens in the once and future child.

Its arms and legs enter into conversation with the bright of mornings, in perfect diaphony it knows the shapes of nature for its own. Sunbeams shaping grasses, trees parting skies, waters rushing over rock, these are the mirrors and progenitors of all its movings, the visible likeness of its earth-partnered life.

Come then society's teaching time. The child is ushered into the presence of the Guidepost to the relevant life. And this post, assigned the teaching talk, begins the process of informing the child of its smallness in relation to the far larger, its ignorance measured against great intelligences, its ineptitudes contrasted to vast skills, its lacks opposed to fullnesses, its basic inconsequentiality within the context of "things that matter."

Knowledge of its own divine origins begins to be quite systematically removed from its consciousness. First, the fullness of nature is removed. The trees are taken out of its arms, the rushing waters out of its blood. Body and brain are hunched and coerced. Doors slam in its bones, gates are built in its muscles, its brain becomes a fortress against all vastness, guarding against the remembrance of who it is and where it came from. This done, the child is deemed acceptable.

But it is not yet over. The internal world must be put to rout. At one point, a serious point, the child will be taught that what is imagined is unreal, and an arterial siphon will draw from near his heart that much strength of impulse which was necessary to keep up his commitment to the inner realms. What is imagined, what has a reality of ponderables which simply doesn't lend itself to physically calibrated scales, this is said to be not real, and the child is halved so to speak. If the heart siphon is not wholly effective, another siphon is put into the veins of the inner elbow and all that society thinks impractical is drawn from the elbow's crook. Put various other siphons into alcoved places, the armpit, the groin, the bend of the knee, the arched chamber of the eye-socket. Tell the little child that the world out there is only this, or only that, or perhaps phrase it *merely*, make less than worthy the notice of it. Only a tree, and all the trees are cut down; merely a small lake, and the deeps have lost their mystery; only this and merely that and the magnificences of nature are made into shoddy stage sets, and the siphon has drawn nerves of vision from under the roofed brain, taken the full life of seeing from the eyes.

Belittle another human being, categorize him with a label having to do with his color, his race, his lack or surfeit of academic training, his societal affiliations, pin him, like a butterfly specimen, for the child to inspect minus all his full lifeness, his essential human-divineness, his proper dimensionality, and you've siphoned out generative power that reaches deep into the groin that could have meant the reseeding of the world.

One of the greatest moments in the history of education occurred in the early life of Helen Keller, who was both deaf and blind. It is a powerful and poignant example of transformation from darkness and almost animal-like muteness to luminous humanity through the dawning recognition of the purpose of symbols. It is the tale of a plastic fiddle that became a Stradivarius.

"For nearly six years," she wrote, "I had no concepts whatever. I was like a clod of earth." Helen's teacher, Anne Sullivan, tried in vain for weeks to help her pupil associate hand motions with objects so that some form of communication could break through the imprisoned flesh to the mind within.

I had not the faintest idea what I was doing. I do not know what I thought, I have only a tactual memory of my fingers going through those motions, and changing from one position to another. One day she handed me a cup and spelled the word. Then she poured some liquid into the cup and formed the letters w-a-t-e-r. She says I looked puzzled, and persisted in confusing the two words, spelling cup for water and water for cup. Finally I became angry because Miss Sullivan kept repeating the words over and over again. In despair she led me out to the ivy-covered pump-house and made me hold the cup under the spout while she pumped. With her other hand she spelled w-a-t-e-r emphatically. I stood still, my whole body's attention fixed on the motions of her fingers as the cool stream flowed over my hand. All at once there was a strange stir within me—a misty consciousness, a sense of something remembered. It was as if I had come back to life after being dead! I understood that what my teacher was doing with her fingers meant that cold something that was rushing over my hand, and that it was possible for me to communicate with other people by these signs. It was a wonderful day never to be forgotten! Thoughts that ran forward and backward came to me quickly—thoughts that seemed to start in my brain and spread all over me. Now I see it was my mental awakening. I think it was an experience somewhat in the nature of a revelation. I showed immediately in many ways that a great change had taken place in me. I wanted to learn the name of every object I touched, and before night I had mastered 30 words. Nothingness was blotted out! I felt joyous, strong, equal to my limitations! Delicious sensations rippled through me, and sweet, strange things that were locked up in my heart began to sing. That first revelation was worth all those years I had spent in dark, soundless imprisonment. That word "water" dropped into my mind like the sun in a frozen winter world. Before that supreme event there was nothing in me except the instinct to eat and drink and sleep.*

That symbolic act opened the door to a life of such depth, learning, and compassion that Helen Keller came to be one of the great inspirations of the twentieth century—the friend and teacher of people all over the world. When I was 8 years old I was taken with my fourth grade class to

*From *My Religion* (New York: Swedenborg Foundation, Inc., and Twayne Publishers, 1974), pp. 120–122.

meet Helen Keller. She was a very old woman by then but her face was lit with a radiant smile and she spoke to us in the strange and awesome voice of one who has never heard speech. After a while I found myself so moved that I stepped forward and presented my face to her hand so that she could read my lips. I knew that I had to speak to her and without knowing what I was going to say, finally blurted out, "Why are you so happy?" She laughed and answered, "My child, it is because I live every day as if it were my last, and life in all its moments is so full of glory."

Both tales that I have just told are our own stories, and their possibilities are our own possibilities. They are relevant not only for what they tell about our potential for being crippled and our capacity for waking up, but also because both are allegories of our time. We are in the time of the darkness before the awakening. We are living in the last quarter of the 20th century with the end of the millennium coming up as a major construct in our lives. And the end of the millennium warrants far more serious concern and challenge than do the fears and fancies which accrue around the *fin de siècle*.

The age in which we live is shivering amidst the tremors of ontological breakdown. The moral mandates, the structural givens, the standard brand governments, religions, economics, the very consensual reality is breaking down, the underlying fabric of life and process by which we organized our reality and thought we knew who and why and where we are. The world by which we understood ourselves, which began in its essential mandates two thousand years ago with certain premises about man, God, reality, and the moral and metaphysical order, and which in terms of our existential lives began about 300 years ago with the scientific revolution, is a world that no longer works, and no longer provides us with the means and reference points for understanding ourselves. We are not unlike the cartoon cat who runs off the cliff and keeps on running, treading air over the abyss before he discovers his predicament and says, "Oops!"

There is a lag between the end of an age and the discovery of that end. We are the children of the lag, the people of the time of parenthesis. We are Americans, and that means a great deal, for we are probably the oldest modern nation on earth. By that I mean that we were the first to move through the consequences of the industrial revolution, the urban revolution, the cross-ethnic revolution, the democratic revolution, the materialistic revolution, the atomic revolution, the outer space revolution, and now, the inner space revolution. We are an old people in terms of the expectations of the modern world. We are fast becoming post-moderns.

Despite the awakening pulsations of the third millennium A.D., we are gravely threatened by problems peculiar to the time of lag, problems having to do with the lack of a story and the lack of depth and vision in an age of frenetic activity.

We look about us and see a growing wasteland with its hazards of mass destruction through nuclear and biological weapons; its threats to privacy and freedoms; its growing overpopulation and exacerbated unemployment; its increasing pollution and depletion of the earth's resources; its information overload and vulnerability to collapse and breakdown; its dehumanization of ordinary work; its proliferation of institutional megastructures which have left us with a vast chasm between public and private life so that the political order has become detached from the values and realities of individual life, and the individual gives neither moral sanction nor legitimacy to the political order.

We are all aware of a governmental disunity so pervasive, and pummeled by so many special interest groups that no coalition of interests is apparently strong enough to set priorities for the overall public good, to effect reforms that have wide public support, to root out inefficiency and corruption, and to inspire confidence in political leadership or in leadership of any kind.

The voracious rise of special interest groups is especially distressful because of the way it has separated so many levels of government and so many levels of education. Legislators can afford to become paranoid about the separation because that is their job. Educators cannot become so paranoid for their tasks involve the growth and resolution of human beings.

And yet we desperately need a global sensibility. We are not regional people any more. We are about to become planetary people. This is a time of emerging and converging global sensibility, but we have neither the psychology nor the education to know what to do with it. The irony is that the majority of Americans still live under balkanized local governments, regional rivalries, and warring layers of government which prevent the establishment of needed national policies, much less international ones.

Now that we are in an age of frightening interdependence, the old territorial imperatives must give way to the necessities of a mutually shared planet. The knowledge that we have entered into a planetary community, with its binding together of peoples, compels an organic vision of what must be done to achieve an ecology of cultures, races, and sensibilities.

As a professional in human behavioral research, I have discovered that if you want to explore the full range of human potentials, you cannot look at just one kind of person or culture. Most of the human potentials of our planet have been manifested by different races, cultures, and societies around the world. It is only in crosscultural inquiry that one discovers the genius of a human being. No longer can a single society try to overwhelm all others with a presumed "rightness" of its religious, economic, or political ideology. We need the full complement of known and unknown human capacities in order to respond to the enormous problems and complexities of our time. And it is only in the tapestry of cultures that we begin to gain any notion of the range and variety of these capacities.

Right now, most thinking about complex problems is linear, analytical, and hierarchical. The whole world is at hand, everything in the planetary existence is resonant with everything else, and yet we keep plodding along as if everything were separate, doing one thing at a time, and inevitably failing. Part of the mess we are in comes from using 19th century ways of thinking and learning in a third-millennium world. In such a world things must be learned in multimodal ways. This is heterarchical thinking, a thinking and learning style in which one becomes aware of many patterns at the same time, as well as of *the* pattern that connects them together. Hierarchical thinking which persists in linear analytic discrete modes of knowing is a crippling atavism which distorts and inhibits the learning process. Many educators suspect this but are prevented by school bureaucracies from doing anything about it.

The extraordinary range and dimension of human knowledge and experience, both personal and cross-cultural, are not being used to solve today's problems. Instead, we apply a patchwork quilt of bandaids to solve critical problems. A great number of our complex short-term solutions to social and economic problems have resulted in long-term failure because of their psychologically simplistic bases. Here are some examples:

Success: Reducing infant and adult mortality rates.
Result of Excessive Success: Regional overpopulation and problems of the aged. We do not know what to do with so many old people. They have great genius to give us, but we have not yet understood the genius of the elderly.

Success: Highly developed science and technology.
Result of Excessive Success: Hazards of mass destruction from nuclear and biological weapons, threats to privacy and freedom, surveillance technology, bioengineering.

Success: Machine replacement of manual and routine labor.
Result of Excessive Success: Exacerbated unemployment.

Success: Advances in communication and transportation.
Result of Excessive Success: Increasing air, noise, and land pollution, information overload, vulnerability of a complex society, and breakdown. Disruption of human and biological rhythms.

Success: Efficient production systems.

Result of Excessive Success: Dehumanization of ordinary work. Efficient rather than effective education.

Success: Affluence and material growth.

Result of Excessive Success: Increased per capita consumption of energy and goods leading to pollution and the depletion of the earth's resources.

Success: Satisfaction of basic needs.

Result of Excessive Success: Worldwide revolution of rising expectations and rebellion against nonmeaningful work.

Success: Expanded power of human choice.

Result of Excessive Success: Increasing gap between the have and have-not nations, frustration of the revolution of rising expectations, exploitation, and growing pockets of famine and poverty.*

What we see in this chart is the story of the *Sorcerer's Apprentice* enacted on the field of history. The apprentice, understanding almost nothing of the subtle dynamics of the powers he is dealing with, and of himself in relation to these powers, is overwhelmed by his evocation of the automated brooms. When he says the magic word, the broom starts to multiply itself, and before long a battalion of brooms is pushing rivers of water through the castle. He is nearly done in by the sheer excess of his success as the brooms and pails of water flood the castle in their mindless mania for cleaning and efficiency.

What was lacking in the success of the apprentice and of western technology is a sense of the vital ecology that links inner and outer worlds. The dominant social paradigm of a reality perceived in largely economic and technological terms is deficient, and it is bound only by the objective external dimension of things. It contains, therefore, no internal limiting factor. The external environment is strictly limited in its resources, so each solution yields ten new problems, and our successes become world-eroding failures. Our response is always to stay in a state of crisis reaction.

Education is characterized by the same kind of patterning. So much of educational planning and decision making has been primarily that of crisis decisions. Suddenly a school is overcrowded. Suddenly district enrollment dramatically falls. Suddenly test scores are too low. Suddenly the newly elected board wants a new superintendent. Suddenly something must be done for the mentally gifted. Suddenly a group of parents is angry about the new bus routes. Everything runs on a crisis mentality, and the poor ad-

*Based on J. Campbell, et al, *Changing Images of Man* (Menlo Park, California: SRI International 1974), p. 7.

ministrators scurry to put out existing fires before the next one erupts, and the needed revision of education goes by the boards.

Expanding federal curriculum efforts modeled on this emergency approach have institutionalized a crisis mentality. New emergencies have led to a rapid proliferation of subject-oriented projects and the emergence of a patchwork curriculum at the precollegiate level. These programs now include drug abuse education, ethnic studies education, metric education, environmental education, moral education, consumer education, driver education, sex education, global education, economic education, leadership education, health education, energy education, and nutrition education. The present federal effort in the area of curriculum leaves out the essential dimension of any balanced curriculum, the fusion or integration of the topical material into an interdisciplinary instructional program. The present band-aid approach diverts attention and scares resources away from what is really needed in educational reform: basic education with contemporary social concerns presented in a dynamically integrated way so that students learn to read, write, and compute, and become aware of the planetary process. We have to move from isolated, topical treatment of curriculum issues to comprehensive curriculum renewal for total education.

There have been wonderful attempts to revise education. In the 1960s, extensive revision was attempted, but in such a piecemeal manner that all those successful, innovative programs died. Remember how, during the 1960s, innovation in education was the byword? Hundreds of conferences were conducted. The Kettering Foundation sponsored a network of innovative activities. Millions of dollars were expended. Educators traveled throughout the United States to visit model programs, and the literature was filled with success stories and change processes. For a while it was one successful fad after the other. Do you know what happened? Everything worked, and practically nothing failed.

Everything worked because the great innovations of the 1960s were patterned after the successful experimentation of the 1930s. They tried to change from efficiency to effectiveness. They tried to improve with solid scientific data the affective, psychomotor, and cognitive development of children. Wonderful efforts of team teaching, flexible scheduling, and individualized learning helped many students. Many better programs were developed. Now this is important: those programs had been developed in the university by innovative educators who then went with their assistants to put them into the schools. As long as that educator was there, it was wonderful; and it worked. But after the innovative leader or program director went back to Harvard or Stanford, the majority of the programs reverted to more conventional approaches or settled into middle-of-the-road compromises that tried to satisfy everybody and satisfied no one. What we have seen in education is exactly the same pattern of breakdown that we have seen in every arena of society. Education and the process of educating is a total integral, contextual situation which includes students, teachers, parents, administration, and environment. The context, the pattern that connects, was not served by hotshot educators who came in from a university. Innovation has to be worked in relation to the whole educational system. Unless something grows as part of the organism as a whole, there will be nothing but fragments.

Why is it that Johnny cannot read, spell, or balance his checkbook? How could he, when his education was so fragmented?

The liberal programs failed because they were not involved in the pattern that connects. No one has ever really looked at what it means to educate an entire society contextually. Why? Because the richness of human psychological and educational processes has been ignored and derided during the recent reign of quantity. The popular absorption with the prodigies of technology not only inhibited the development of a mentality attuned to more subtle inward understandings of reality and social process, but it also encouraged a dangerous interface and modeling of human personality with mechanistic forms. These forms are fine for machines. They do not work for human beings. When human beings become secondary to the so-called efficiency of a given system they almost invariably fail in large numbers.

Look what we did. We took a European system that was intended to educate an elite and which was itself based upon an archaic understanding of the nature of intelligence. We then took this same system and tried to educate everybody and create a mass elite. In so doing, we created a mass failure rate such as the world has never known. Never before, at least as measured by tests, has there been so much failure on the part of so many people. Before long, the failing people, or people who perceive themselves as failures, will begin to create a failing culture, a failing nation, and a failing civilization. The response to failure in the schools has been to add programs, not to rethink education and get everybody to succeed—which from my perspective, and from what we are now beginning to discover about the mind and brain, is very possible. The human brain is incredibly endowed. We use about ten percent of our physical capacity and far less of our mental capacity. With a holistic integral education it is quite possible that many students can learn to use a much greater range of their innate capacity. This assumes that there are many different kinds of intelligence and different ways of educating that intelligence.

Educational transformation is the time for waking up. It is enormously significant that the current crisis in consciousness, the loss of a sense of reality felt by so many, the destruction of, and disillusionment with, education, and the rising tides of alienation occur concomitantly with the ecological destruction of the planet by technological means. We are forced into the awareness that we are not encapsulated bags of skin dragging around dreary little egos. Rather, a human being is an organism-environment.

If we are to survive, we have no choice but to reverse the ecological, technological, and linear-analytic plunder. That will mean discovering forms of consciousness and fulfillment and forms of human energy and learning apart from those of consumption, control, aggrandizement, pass-the-test, and manipulation. Clearly, the human race is about to take some major growth steps—as Helen Keller did. We have evolved physically and culturally to a remarkably fine psychosocial instrument. Now the time has come for that instrument to work, explore, and create with levels and capacities of existence that hitherto have remained more mythical than real.

At a time when we are experiencing a loss of hope in the social domain, the vision of what human beings can be has never been more remarkable. We are living at the onset of the golden age of brain, mind, and body research that is beginning to show us the full dimension of human capacities and how we can use these capacities more productively. We may well be standing, with regard to the understanding of our brain, where Einstein stood in the year 1904 when he discovered the special theory of relativity that helped accomplish the great revolution in physics.

For the first time in human history people may become what they are—fully human. Not that this planet has not seen thousands of richly actualized human beings before. Obviously it has, but only with the random individual and never, as far as we know, with great numbers of humankind. We may be in the time of the opening up of the ecology of inner space to humanity at large—because the problem of human survival may no longer be that of discovering new economic or political solutions, but rather one of a growth of the qualities of mind and body of a human race. That should be education's concern.

Most of us have been raised to have the experiential intake and the faculties of a much more limited and bounded culture. We have not educated our brains, bodies, and our conscious receptors to take in the enormous amounts of information and multiple levels of knowing that we need for modern decision-making. In some ways we are still being educated, in the family, by the environment, and in the schools, for the demands of about 1825, not for the twenty-first century. We have a nineteenth-century psychology whose paranoid insularities and aggressions are trigger happy with the twentieth-century technology. It is all going to burst very fast. The ecological and technological crises may force us to do the work on ourselves that we avoided for too many centuries. We use but a fraction of our capacities and live as crippled, distorted versions of who we are.

This came home to me in a remarkable experience I once had. I live not far from a leading center on the East Coast for mentally retarded people. Every year the center puts on a show, generally a musical comedy such as *Oklahoma, Carousel,* or *Fiddler on the Roof.* All the parts are played by the mentally retarded patients. I went the year they put on *Fiddler on the Roof.* You could tell that the people in the chorus were retarded, but you could not tell about the principals. The man who played Tevye was so magnificent, so full of high drama, rhythm, and theatrical brilliance that I turned to my friend, and said, "What a fake, what a fake! He is an out-of-work off-Broadway actor who is using these mentally retarded people as a showcase for himself. Isn't that terrible!" My friend said, "No, Jean. It says in the program that he is one of the patients." I replied with great disdain, "Listen, I am the professional. I know. He is a fake. Or else he's a doctor who should have been an actor."

After the show, we went backstage to meet the man who played Tevye. I went up to him and said, "Hi, you were very good. What was the last show you did off-Broadway?" He stared at me mutely and continued to do so as I plied him with more questions. Finally, I was so shocked at my own tactlessness that I shocked myself into doing the right thing. I grabbed his hands, and I began to dance and sing to the music of *Fiddler:* "My name is Jean Houston, and I certainly loved your show . . ." His eyes leaped into knowing, and he grinned at me as he sang, "My name is Aaron Schwartz, and I am glad you found me out . . ." Then he began to tell me about his life and demand in his singing that I tell him about mine. He did it in rhyme. I was too dumb and couldn't keep up the rhyme. As he sang he told me that when he was singing and dancing he knew who he really was, for when he sang and danced he found himself. He went on and on and on. He told me that when he was as others were, it was as if a curtain fell in front of his mind. When he was singing and dancing, however, the world moved into meaning.

The story of Aaron Schwartz is also our own story. There are many different modes of knowing. He happened to have minimal brain damage, but in music he used other areas of the brain in which different kinds of connections occurred. This is true of so many of us. There is an innate genius in all of us, but we have to find the pattern that connects.

What would happen to human beings and to society generally if we could recover as well as discover the use of our own potential? Much in the new scientific research and the vision of the possible human is predictive of this recovery and its consequences. It points to capacities which we all have and which have been demonstrated in the laboratory with thousands of research subjects. These capacities are then learned, integrated into daily life, and even applied constructively to the improvement of many social programs such as enhancing educational programs, teaching "non-learners," rehabilitating ex-prisoners, and even greatly restoring and extending the physical and mental capacities of the elderly.

I have been involved with the creation and implementation of such programs for the last fourteen years at the Foundation for Mind Research, and through this work I have found that human capacity is a vast and inexhaustible resource. We have discovered, for example, that most people, given opportunity and education, can realize more of their potentials, in varying degrees. Their bodies can be psychophysically rehabilitated for optimal physical functioning. As physical capacity is extended, mental awareness increases. When the abilities to move and to sense are enhanced, cognitive and feeling functions improve also, for the extensive changes in the brain's motor cortex which must precede changes in the muscular system affect adjacent brain areas as well.

In our applications of these methods to education and the rehabilitation of the elderly, we have found that these movement exercises frequently result in enhanced capacities in learning, remembering, and problem solving. We find throughout our work that if you wish to extend the capacities of the mind, you must at the same time extend the capacities of the body which is the instrument of that mind.

In other areas of our work, people learn to think in images as well as in words, to practice in subjective time the rehearsal of skills, and to experience the acceleration of thought processes. They can learn to think kinesthetically with their whole bodies, they can experience cross-sensing, the self-regulation of pleasure and pain, and acquire voluntary control over some of the autonomic functions by means of biofeedback and autogenic training. As an exciting extension to this kind of research we find that subjects can be taught to speak to their own brains directly, so entering into conscious orchestration of mood, attitude, learning, and creativity.

In our laboratory, individuals are enabled to experience the extensive range of consciousness. Most of us exist with regard to the dimensions of consciousness, as if we were inhabiting only the attic of ourselves, with the first, second, third, and fourth floors, and the basement, going uninhabited and remaining unconscious. When we begin to take up residence in these other realms of ourselves, when we extend the domain of consciousness, the pragmatic effects are numerous. People can learn how to work with dream content, how to better concentrate and how to remember more effectively. There is a tapping of the creative process and an experiencing of those levels of the self where one's personal existential life finds analogies with universal constructs and broader formulations.

To evoke and work with these capacities restores the ecological balance between inner and outer worlds. It produces a wider use of the self, and a larger measure of self-knowing. It moves us beyond the conditionings and cul de sacs of our present environment and problems and brings each of us into very different relationships in our world.

The extensions of learning are grounded in the extended use of our sensory perceptions. By the time we reach maturity, our sensorium is, most often, a shrunken, crippled version of what it could be. As people grow older in our culture, they undergo a progressive diminishing of sensory acuity and sensory knowing. They become progressively less able to see, to touch, and otherwise to utilize their senses. This loss would seem to be attributable in part to our verbalizing, conceptualizing, mental processes and not just to impairment by age. In many hunting and tribal societies, for example, it is the adult and not the child who evinces the most acute and orchestral balance of his senses. In our own culture we have the evidence of professionals who have to keep up a certain sensory acuity for the sake of their art—the musician's ear, the artist's eye, the perfumer's nose. The blunting of perception has led me to formulate Houston's law: *concept louses up percept.*

Conceptualization, of course, is essential to the continuance of culture—it sustains the very fabric of civilization. But civilization as the Patriarch, Sigmund Freud has warned us, has its profound discontents. In societies where sensory experience is depreciated as a cultural norm (so that one can put most of one's energies into mastering the environment), the body itself suffers attendant harpies—the neuroses, obesities, aggressions, and even the widespread deathwish which seems to characterize much of psyche and history in the twentieth century. Is it worth seeing as through a glass darkly, or touching as if one were wearing gloves, or hearing as if through wads of conceptual cotton wool? Such simple matters may be the stuff out of which historical catastrophes are made.

Now there is a great deal that can be done to regain sensory acuity in one's adult years. Part of it is just paying attention. I think the establishment of preventive educational programs calls for more public decisions. Education for children, especially for small children, should in part be education in sense perception—education in enhancing and intensifying the senses and the child's awareness of a physical state of being so he or she can keep a good body. This is not just to give people good health and sensory acuity. It is to make them much more alert.

With the enhancement of sensory and perceptual knowledge, with the recovery of imaginal and symbolic structures, the child learns the virtuoso capacities of brain and body and its mind grows in kind. Ironically, conceptualization in its finest forms is grounded in a refinement of perceptualization. In our research we find that there is a real equation between the ability to entertain and sustain complex thinking processes and the richness of sensory and kinesthetic awareness.

In the dozens of cases that we have explored of high actualizing intelligence, of people who use their intelligence for creative accomplishment, the great majority of them were stimulated as children with rich sensory and arts-related experiences.

Perhaps the most intelligent and sensitive person I have ever known also had the greatest subtlety of sensory refinement. Her name was Margaret Mead and she was far richer and more interesting than her public image, remarkable as that was. She thought more, felt more, gave more, and got more out of life than virtually anyone I had ever met. In knowing Margaret Mead, I was experiencing a new style of human being, a new way of being human.

With her cooperation, I eventually began a formal study of Margaret Mead, especially of her thinking and perceptual processes. This study, which lasted five years until her death in 1978, is especially germane to our consideration of the education and preparation of the possible human. Her early years particularly tell us much about the important effects of sensory and aesthetic styles of learning on cognitive development.

She was born in Philadelphia in 1901 into a family of educators. Her father, Edward Mead, was a brilliant, rather eccentric economist and professor. Her mother, Emily Fogg Mead, was a sociologist much involved in causes and community projects. Her grandmother, Martha Ramsay Mead—one of the principal influences in her life—was a strong-minded, innovative schoolteacher. After kindergarten, Margaret was periodically educated at home because her family had thought so much about education that they disapproved of formal schooling. Her mother gave her poetry to memorize; her grandmother dispensed hardy maxims for her to take to heart while her hair was being brushed. She learned basketry, carpentry, weaving, wood carving, and other manual skills requiring fine eye-to-muscle coordination (in which she surpassed nearly everyone else we have tested).

Following a suggestion of William James, her mother exposed her to numerous sensory stimuli when she was still an infant—colors, textures, pictures of great works of art, and masterpieces of music, including an ancient Greek hymn to Apollo retained in the Byzantine church. She was encouraged to use all her senses in any kind of activity, even the most abstract ones. Dualisms were discouraged; she was trained to accept the unity of mind and body, thinking and feeling. If you ask Western people where "I" exists, many point to their foreheads. If you asked Margaret Mead that question, she responded matter-of-factly, "Why, all over me, of course."

Of course.

Given this base of rich sensibility, Margaret acquired an unusual ability to store memories and learn abstract material rapidly. When a sensorium is as consciously developed as it was in young Margaret, then the child and the adult she becomes has more conscious use of proprioceptors, more "hooks and eyes" as it were, to catch and keep the incoming information and then relate it to other information stored in the sensorium. Nor was she limited to five senses. Throughout her life she kept up her childhood capacity for synesthesia (cross-sensing) which most children lose because it is discouraged. A synesthete can hear color and see sound, taste time and touch aromas. Here is a classic exchange with a natural synesthete:

ME: Margaret, what does this room taste like?
MARGARET: Something in which spices were put last week.
ME: What do you hear in Bob's face?
MARGARET: I guess . . . a symphony.
ME: What is the touch of my voice?
MARGARET: Your voice is a brush. It's a brush that's made of very non-bristling material so it isn't like a brush made of pig's bristles, but it isn't as soft as the kind of silk brush that you use to do a baby's hair. It's somewhere in between.
ME: Not nylon, I hope!
MARGARET: No, not nylon! It's something live.

Her kinesthetic sense was also developed early and sustained throughout her life so that as an anthropologist, she had the physical empathy to understand, through body sensing, the special skills of primitive cultures. She could feel a complex fishing procedure in her bones and sinews, sense an intricate dance as a kinesthetic rhythm in her muscle fibers. Photographs of her on the field reveal her assuming some of the sensibility of the cultures she is observing. She appears soft among the Arapesh, tense in Manus, unfocused and "away" in Bali.

Grandmother Mead insisted that she learn how to do entire procedures from beginning to end, so she learned not only how to weave, but also how to build a loom. Throughout her life whenever she began or joined a project, she invariably followed it through to its natural conclusion (which made for an extraordinary number of projects in progress at any given time).

In contrast, other people often dilute their actions and decisions, becoming observer bound, abstracted from social responsibility, and with no sense of the need to follow through the organic sequencing of a process. One begins to lose the sense of how to guide the beginnings, middles, and ends of things. At The Foundation for Mind Research we have tried to remedy this by helping many schools develop a rich arts-related curriculum in which children learn to think from a much larger sensory and neurological base. According to current theory the left hemisphere of the brain is the seat of analysis and sequential learning, including verbal and mathematical skills, while the right is the site of visual and spatial abilities. The entire spectrum of intelligence—thinking, learning, adaptation, problem-solving, re-constructing, creativity—is at its best the result of the cooperation of both hemispheres working together and informing each other. The neurological dominance of one hemisphere over the other could only diminish the nature and capacity of this intelligence. Thus the need for educational programs that develop both sides of the brain, that evoke both reason and imagination, thinking and feeling, concept and percept, abstraction and immediate concrete experience, words and images, body and mind.

In the arts-related curriculum which we have developed, children very early become capable of using many different kinds of materials and methods with success. The child is taught how to work with clay, with glazing, with block printing, papier mâché, tissue collage, weaving, batiks, as well as more complex uses of chalks and paints. In learning these things, the child also has to learn in a tangible and expressive way many of the mathematical principles needed to carry out the work: principles of design, line, form, color, texture and structure. Measurement and fractions are learned naturally and with ease as the child constructs art work. In order to weave, the child has to learn something about making grids and this occurs with far less pain and confusion than if he or she learned about grids in an abstract context. Since learning is occurring with both right and left hemispheric functions, the child is much more fully engaged. Children educated in this way, when measured by standard tests, are routinely scoring one to four grade levels above normal. * Also, since arts-related education involves the child in entire cycles of any process, these children, like the young Margaret Mead, become far more resourceful and responsible in

* For further information see the Arts and Minds issue of Dromenon. (Dromenon, G.P.O. Box 2244, N.Y., NY 10001. $3.00).

initiating, carrying out, and completing other kinds of projects with which they involve themselves.

Grandmother Mead had other techniques she applied to Margaret's early education. Grandmother Mead didn't care for drill, believing that it inhibited originality and spontaneity in children. If something was to be learned, it had to be learned right away, a skill Margaret retained all her life. In Margaret's experience, this involved employing more senses and ways of knowing in the learning situation—combining both left and right hemispheres of the brain for acquiring information. When she learned a poem, for example, she would join simple rote memorization (left hemisphere) to an inner process in which she actually saw the images described in the poem, felt the situation or event as vividly as if she had been there, experienced the textures and tone of the poem, and took its emotions for her own (right hemisphere).

In our own research with "problem learners," we have developed techniques quite similar to Margaret's multi-perceptual learning. The child is taught to think in images as well as in words, to learn spelling or even arithmetic in rhythmic patterns, to think with the whole body—in short, to learn school basics from a much larger spectrum of sensory and cognitive possibilities. Thus, if a child shows inadequacy in one form of learning—say, verbal skills—we try another form of learning—such as sensory-motor skills, in which the child may show a greater facility to learn to read and write faster and with greater depth and appreciation. Some years ago, while developing new teaching methods for what was bureaucratically referred to as "minority group slow learners," I asked an eight-year-old boy, "Tommy, how much is this: five plus three plus two?" Tommy made a face indicating boredom. I then upended the chair I was sitting on and began to drum on it, asking, "Tommy, how much is this: bump bump bump bump bump—bump bump bump—bump bump?" Tommy grinned and said, "That's ten, man." "Why didn't you tell me before?" I asked. " 'Cause you didn't ask me before," he replied.

He was right. Most of our questions and answers in the schoolroom are addressed to one very small section of the brain, and arise out of one very small section of the planet, northern Europe. Much in northern-European-derived education and understanding of intelligence discriminates against one whole half of the brain, and tends to reward only left-hemispheric-dominant students who respond well to verbal, linear styles of education. And yet we humans are as different as snowflakes, one from the other. Our brains are as different from each other as are our fingerprints, with enormous variations in styles and talents of perception and learning. Some people are naturally kinesthetic thinkers, others think in images, others in sounds. Classical education tends to inhibit these and frequently causes nonverbal thinkers to feel inferior and begin a process of failure that will last all their lives. From many years of observation I have found that I have rarely met a stupid child, but I have met many stupid and debilitating, and yes, even brain-damaging systems of education. As we subsequently discovered, a child can learn math as a rhythmic dance and learn it well (the places of rhythm in the brain being adjacent to the places of order). A child can learn almost anything and pass the standard tests if he or she is dancing, tasting, touching, hearing, seeing, and feeling information. In using much more of his mind-brain-body system than conventional teaching generally permits, the child can take real delight in the learning process. So much of the failure in school comes directly out of boredom born of the failure to stimulate all those areas in the child's brain which could provide so many more ways of responding to the world.

The message of the bilateral brain is that we are Both/And; we are artistic and intellectual, emotional and practical, and much, much more. In the case of Margaret Mead we see ways of educating the Both/And so that one learns to play the Stradivarius that is the possible human. In today's complex reality we need to have access to all our parts. We can no longer afford to short-change our brains and impoverish our spirits. Those limitations have now become desecrations of our humanity, the fullness of which is needed in ways it never was before.

Willis Harman is probably the only contemporary scientist and theoretician who has contributed as much to the field of futuristics as to the rapidly developing fields of humanistic psychology and human potentials research. A diligent researcher, prolific writer, sought-after lecturer, and a true humanitarian, Willis Harman is thought of by many as one of the most brilliant visionaries of our time.

During the past thirty years, he has been an active researcher and spokesperson in the areas of futures research and social policy. After receiving his doctorate in electrical engineering from Stanford University, he joined the Stanford faculty where he has since served as professor of engineering-economics systems. During the 1950s he was a Fulbright lecturer on communication theory at the Royal Technical University of Copenhagen. Throughout the 1960s his personal interest in human evolution led him to become an active participant in the newly forming Association for Humanistic Psychology where he served as a member of the Executive Board of Directors. In 1978 Dr. Harman became president of the Institute for Noetic Sciences. In 1980, he was awarded one of the highest possible honors in California when he was named to the prestigious State Board of Regents of the University of California. Willis Harman's highly acclaimed book An Incomplete Guide to the Future *was published in 1979.*

In this chapter on the future of work Dr. Harman draws upon his vast experience as a social policy analyst to illuminate a historical view of the nature and purpose of work in human life. Many of our past and present attitudes toward work may be inappropriate for the future, he suggests, offering instead a complete context from which work, leisure, and human development may creatively emerge in the coming decades.

WORK

There may be no aspect of the future about which we are more confused than the role of work in the life of the individual and in society. The reason is, simply, that the roles are undergoing fundamental changes that we have not yet recognized. Our present conceptions were formed in an era when the primary societal function of work was the production of necessary or desired goods and services. Yet today, economic production is faced with an assortment of resource and environmental constraints, limiting the expansion of job opportunities. This presents us with a dilemma. If labor productivity does not continually increase, U.S. industry becomes noncompetitive in the international market; yet if productivity does increase, it is either at the cost of fewer jobs or of having to produce and stimulate more demand for stuff and nonessential "services." Either option may lead us down dead-end corridors. In effect, the ethic of "work in order to eat" seems to be changing to "the fortunate may work; the remainder will be kept as pets—supported, with little more demanded except that they be housebroken."

The problem of "superfluous people"—those marginal human beings not fortunate enough to be employed—grows more serious as society becomes more highly industrialized (or "postindustrialized"). As far back as 1930, the British economist John Maynard Keynes warned in his *Essays in Persuasion:*

> If the economic problem [the struggle for subsistence] is solved, mankind will be deprived of its traditional purpose. . . . Thus for the first time since his creation man will be faced with his real, his permanent problem—how to use his freedom from pressing economic cares. . . . There is no country and no people, I think, who can look forward to the problem for the ordinary person, with no special talents to occupy himself, especially if he no longer has roots to the soil or in custom or in the beloved conventions of a traditional society.[1]

171

To see what future resolution is possible, we need to examine how we got here. The problem is as much one of attitudes, goals, and basic premises as of technology, economic growth, and manpower training. The problem of work is ultimately inseparable from the problem of meaning in individual life and in the evolution of society.

HISTORY

The fundamental social doctrine of colonial America strongly emphasized the dignity of labor. It stressed the virtue of diligent application to one's task and promised that earnest industry would be unfailing in its rewards. The virtues of diligence, sobriety, and thrift, characteristic of the rising middle class in England, were transported to America and became a dominant influence in the colonies. While accomplishment tended to be measured in material progress—the transformation of nature and development of useful arts and knowledge—personal aggrandizement tended to be considered incidental, and there were injunctions against waste, extravagance, and ostentation. Labor was scarce, returns from the individual's work were high, and opportunities to move to higher status were abundant. It was assumed that the idle poor brought poverty upon themselves; poverty was made so disgraceful that a man would labor to the extent of his capacity to avoid such a stigma. If not everybody prospered, the great majority of honest, hard-working men made their own way and improved their lot. Additional rewards of the virtue of work were found in the good opinion of others and the sense of having fulfilled one's "calling."

By the nineteenth century, a greater emphasis on self-improvement had developed. The self-made man, less moved by piety and virtue, still owed his advancement to the cultivation of God-given talents and habits of industry, sobriety, moderation, self-discipline, and avoidance of debt. Aiming to surpass the previous generation and provide for the next, he deferred gratification and lived for the future, patiently saving and accumulating. Wealth became an end in itself, and compulsive industry, discipline, and self-denial were the means to that end. The public schools, available to all, inculcated industrial discipline, self-reliance, orderly habits, punctuality, workmanship, versatility, and obedience. They offered vocational training and served for industrial recruitment, selection, and certification.

The early twentieth century evidenced more stress on the will to win. The advent of mass production had brought an ever-growing hierarchy of supervisors and managers, and increasingly large staffs for engineering, management, distribution, and sales. Ambitious young men had to compete with their peers for the attention and approval of their superiors in order to advance in the corporate structure. Advancement was assumed to depend on willpower, self-confidence, energy, and initiative. The new ethos was one of salesmanship, boosterism, pursuit of wealth, and success as an end in itself. There apparently was no reason to question the role of work in the life of the individual or in society. It was self-evident that the individual worked to support himself and his family. As for society, the assumption shared by economists from Adam Smith to Karl Marx that the role of work is industrial production became widely accepted.

The Great Depression of the 1930s signaled the end of labor scarcity and the beginning of a persistent fear of job shortages and chronic unemployment. But this fear has been sublimated through reassuring proclamations made by economists with frequent reference to the doctrines of Keynes, who believed the "age of leisure and abundance" would not be upon us for many generations. As summarized by Kelso and Adler, the basic elements of this post-Depression Keynesian reasoning are:

1. Mass consumption is necessary if all members of a society are to have a high standard of living. What is more significant, mass consumption is necessary to support mass production in an industrial economy.

2. Mass consumption cannot exist or continue unless there is a mass distribution of purchasing power.

3. The proper method of creating a mass distribution of purchasing power is mass employment, i.e., full employment, or the employment of every person who would like to be employed.

4. Prosperity and well-being depend upon the successful distribution of purchasing power. This can be achieved through progressively raising, by union pressure and legislation, wages, social security payments, unemployment compensation, agricultural and other prices, and through the free use of income taxing power and other powers of government to promote full employment.[2]

The inevitable result of acting according to these principles would be, it was promised, a high standard of living for all, freedom from toil, and personal liberty.

Accompanying this shift in economic reasoning came a profound shift in the value and certainty of the future, which has transformed work attitudes and the definition of success. The new ethic tended to be "live now, consume now, pay later." As Christopher Lasch put it in *The Culture of Narcissism*, "the happy hooker stands in place of Horatio Alger as the prototype of personal success."[3]

The social costs of unemployment are recognized as being high. To be unemployed is to suffer a severe blow to one's self-esteem. The connection in industrialized society between employment and psychological health is reflected in statistics on mental disorder, alcoholism, heart attacks, drug use, and crime, and in the experience of numerous counselors and social workers. If it were possible to create ample, satisfactory work opportunities for all, many of the social problems of the nation would disappear. The federal budget would be more easily balanced. Teenagers could enter the work force and elderly persons could find part-time employment. The poor, blacks, and other minorities would meet less discrimination, and they could move to areas providing more wholesome environments and better job opportunities. There would be less waste of human energy and resources and more opportunity for individual self-fulfillment. Welfare problems would be reduced, and the necessity for governmental interference in private lives would be diminished. Urban decay could be slowed or halted, bringing relief in a host of related problem areas—crime, drugs, safety, housing, schools, and city financial crises.

But if the natural and social limitations on production and consumption of stuff and "services" are such that full employment in the mainstream economy *cannot* be provided in the future, what then?

CHRONIC UNEMPLOYMENT IN THE FUTURE

The likelihood of long-term chronic unemployment and underemployment (working at less than one's full productive capacity) rests on two propositions: (1) in the long run, economic growth may not continue to generate enough jobs to accommodate the expanding work force; and (2) the quality of available jobs may not be compatible with the rising educational levels of the work force.

The problematic character of economic growth arises primarily from the tension between growth and the cluster of problems relating to resources and the environment. These problems could be eased if economic growth were modified to lessen resource utilization, but since the economy displays a built-in correlation between employment and resource utilization, a slacking of growth tends to increase unemployment. Despite a commitment to growth and full employment, environmental constraints and resource limitations will tend to keep the economy from generating enough satisfactory jobs to meet the demand.

Economic and demographic trends will partially obscure this problem through the mid-1980s. The labor force has been increasing at a rate of something like two million persons per year. This high growth rate is partly due to the entrance into the labor market of individuals born during the postwar baby boom and to the rapid rise in the percentage of employed women. It is projected that both of these growth rates will drop dramatically in the next few years, so that by the mid-1980s the rate of increase will be halved. There are indications that the rate of labor productivity increase will drop and stay significantly below the long-term three-percent rate of the past, so that the rate of job creation as the economy grows will be higher. New energy-related projects (finding new supplies and taking conservation measures), together with further expansion of the services sector, will create new jobs. Furthermore, increasing numbers of people will probably voluntarily reduce their participation in the work force to attain a more leisurely lifestyle.

Thus, the short-term prospects may well result in a temporary easing of the national unemployment problem, although there will still be severe regional problems, particularly in New England and in areas experiencing high rates of international migration. The long-term prospects are another story.

In his *Cybernation: The Silent Conquest*, social psychologist Donald Michael forecasted in 1962 that a shortage of jobs caused by the rapidly expanding cybernation of production processes would be the key problem in the future.[4] For some years following this warning, conventional wisdom regarded Michael as an alarmist and argued that new technology and mechanization would continue to generate more jobs than they displaced. Any fears that automation and technological change would cause unemployment seemed temporarily laid to rest by the report of the National Commission on Technology, Automation, and Economic Progress in 1966. However, during the 1973–1975 recession and the accompanying increase in unemployment, the belief that technological progress causes unemployment suddenly revived.

The effects of automation and technological change vary from industry to industry, though technological advances have generally permitted growing demands for goods and services to be fulfilled by smaller and smaller proportions of the work force. Technology may eliminate some jobs and the demand for some skills, as when linotype machines began to be replaced by phototypesetters. Technological progress may also impoverish jobs by reducing the amount of variety and craftsmanship in the work itself. One example is the decline of some carpentry skills with the advent of mass-produced, prefabricated buildings. At the same time, technological progress may enrich jobs by extending basic human sensory, perceptual, cognitive, and motor abilities, as may be the case with human-computer systems for editing book manuscripts.

There are no statistical analyses able to identify satisfactorily the impact of automation on unemployment. In *Human Factors*, Kenyon De Greene paints a future "characterized by the spread of mechanization, rationalization, and cybernation to most institutions of society, and by the development of machines and systems capable of at least some of the higher-level perceptual, cognitive, and adaptive capabilities of human beings. These developments are likely to render millions of workers superfluous and present societal problems defying easy solution."[5]

Despite these indications of trouble ahead, economists and social scientists do not yet agree that chronic unemployment and underemployment will be a fundamental problem of the future. This lack of agreement probably reflects, in part, different perceptions of the extent to which the problem already exists. For example, it seems apparent that the U.S. economy since the 1930s has been able to maintain a politically acceptable level of employment only by preparing for war and by becoming an arms supplier to the world (a role that Americans harshly criticized Germany for playing over a half-century ago).

One hidden aspect of unemployment shows up in the pressures on older employees to leave the work force by retiring early (a form of age discrimination now being challenged). The true extent of the unemployment problem is also reflected in inflated age and education criteria for job entry, delays imposed on job elimination, automation of routine operations, subtle forms of featherbedding, and panic reactions when there is talk of canceling a defense contract or space project. The spectre of unemployment is a key factor in the energy policy issue: it is feared that a major reduction in the demand for energy would cause an unmanageable unemployment problem.

Various estimates have been made of the *real* unemployment in the U.S., taking into account the despairing who no longer seek work, workers who are quite clearly in featherbedding or make-work situations, and dropouts in holding institutions such as reform schools or mental institutions. These estimates range from twenty-five to thirty percent of the potential work force, with well over forty percent among some urban minority groups. Statistics are not available on either the underemployed who work at jobs that do not use their skills and abilities or on the involuntarily retired. Studies indicate that between thirty and forty percent of retired persons did not retire by choice and would have preferred to continue working.

THE PUZZLE OF UNDEREMPLOYMENT

Underemployment is rapidly becoming a major source of alienation and workplace problems. As the educational level of the work force rises, discontent and alienation spread among highly educated workers forced to take jobs previously performed by workers with less schooling. In 1980, one in four American workers had a college degree. Half of these college-educated workers were under thirty-five, while half of all the workers with only an elementary school education were over the age of fifty. More workers were in white-collar jobs, though these can be as stultifying, repetitive, and unchallenging as any blue-collar work.

The proportion of the adult labor force with one or more years of college rose from nineteen percent in 1960 to twenty-seven percent in 1970. However, the proportion of total employment represented by managerial, administrative, technical, and professional positions rose more slowly, going from twenty percent in 1960 to twenty-two percent in 1970. Yet the rise in expectations continues—nearly fifty percent of young adults indicated that they expect these kinds of work, with upper-middle-class income and status and opportunities for creativity and self-expression as well.

A greater percent of the future work force will be well educated and demand jobs that offer challenge, growth, and self-fulfillment. Those jobs will not be there. Persons of high educational achievement tend to expect that work should utilize their talents and develop their potential. But a significant fraction of the jobs in industrialized society are neither instrinsically challenging nor obviously related to inspiring social challenges.

Education is no longer a sure route to increased status, power, and income. But that is not all there is to the underemployment problem. One is reminded of the two medieval stonecutters who were working on the same project. Asked what they were doing, one answered, "I'm squaring up this damn stone." The other replied, "I am building a cathedral." The first was underemployed; the second was not.

Must we conclude that underemployment is a state of mind? Clearly what counts is not so much *what* work a person does, but *what he perceives he is doing it for*. The frontiersman, the old-time craftsman, the farmer blessed with a fine piece of land all would have scoffed at the idea that they were underemployed. But once mechanized agriculture appeared on the scene, one could no longer spend the day behind a horse and plow in the same spirit as before. "Meaningful work" is not necessarily work that is exciting and challenging every moment, but may rather be work that is part of a larger endeavor that has meaning. If the society has a "central project" in which people believe—e.g., conquering the Western frontier or the technological frontier, or building a new society or world democratic order—then even routine tasks take on meaning.

THE FUNCTIONS OF WORK

We have established that the work dilemma is intimately related to society's advanced stage of industrialization, approaching what sociologist Daniel Bell has termed a "post-industrial society."[6] Or, to put it another way, the dilemma that Keynes anticipated is upon us, a fact that we have been trying desperately to conceal from ourselves because any resolution necessitates a fundamental change in our thinking, and that is never easy or comfortable.

The required new thinking can be simply stated: In a technologically advanced society where production of sufficient goods and services can be handled with ease, *employment exists primarily for self-development and is only secondarily concerned with the production of goods and services.* This concept of work represents a profound shift in our perceptions with implications that reverberate throughout the entire fabric of our society.

Some of these implications can be better seen if we examine the various functions of work in modern society. The institutions of education and work together have historically performed four quite distinct functions:

1. Promoting the education and development of the individual citizen
2. Providing the individual with a role to play in the meaningful activities of society with the opportunity to achieve a sense of contribution, belonging, being appreciated, and to develop a healthy self-image and sense of self-affirmation
3. Accomplishing certain service needs of the society (e.g., production of goods, protection of life and property)
4. Distributing the total income of society in a way that is generally perceived as equitable

In the past, these four functions—*education, social roles, production,* and *income distribution*—have been delegated largely to schools (education), parents and peer groups (social roles), and jobs (production and income distribution). As we have seen, this arrangement has been increasingly less effective. The production economy has difficulty providing an adequate number of suitably challenging work roles for the ever-increasing educational levels. Through increasing labor productivity, it is no longer true that all of the potential labor force is needed to produce the goods and conventional services to fill previously felt needs. The "solution" in the past was to teach us to "need" more. A consumption ethic replaced the frugality ethic on which the nation's economy was founded. But limitless consumption, even of services, eventually runs into difficulties with resource limits and consumer resistance.

Reduction in the importance of labor in production is inherent in industrial development. Each worker can produce more wealth because of the employment of capital-intensive technology. As industrialization proceeds, the increases in wealth produced are more and more the result of technological and managerial expertise, and less and less the contribution of routine, narrowly trained, or unskilled labor. Nevertheless, the real wages of unskilled or semiskilled laborers have risen as fast as, or faster than, the wages of managers and technically creative workers. Thus, wage levels have become quite divorced from the real value added by the worker. As this happens, and the percentage of persons involved with production decreases, jobs in the production economy become less and less satisfactory as an equitable basis for income distribution.

In response to the manifest inequities of income distribution according to productivity, the government's role in redistributing income has grown vastly over the past century. Governmental redistribution is accomplished by direct transfer payments, such as social security and public assistance programs, by the graduated income tax and other differential monetary and fiscal policies, and by controls on wages, prices, and interest rates. These policies have weakened still further the link between productivity and income. For all practical purposes, the notion that an individual's income is determined by the productivity of his labor (plus return from property) has become obsolete. As a substitute, society is confusedly attempting to rationalize income distribution with vaguely defined principles of welfare and equity. Work is still the least controversial form of income distribution, but it is becoming increasingly less suitable for that purpose.

A similar situation exists with regard to the social function of work. Work is one of the most socially acceptable, potentially constructive ways for people to spend the major portion of their waking hours. But in the advanced industrial economy, satisfying work opportunities become an increasingly scarce commodity.

Finally, the old concept of education as job preparation is totally unsatisfactory from the standpoint of both the individual and society. For a host of reasons, lifelong learning is the only kind of education that makes sense. Thus, the workplace can also be considered a learning place. But the economy has difficulty accommodating to this concept. According to its rules, work is something you get paid to do, and education is something you pay for.

Having examined these four functions, we are now in a position to restate the work dilemma in terms that better suggest what options are available. The problem is to redefine the four functions of work and education so that the unsatisfactory aspects just described are eliminated.

It is important to remind ourselves that we are dealing with the problem of success. In terms of its own goals of efficiency, labor productivity, material growth, and consumption, industrialization must be judged an unqualified success. In economic terms, the problem of production seems solved once and for all.

If human beings basically sought to escape from work, industrialization might be considered a success from a social standpoint as well, since it has made possible the elimination of so much work that humans once had to do. But both from observation of worker behavior and from the findings of psychological research, there is ample evidence that persons seek meaningful activity and relationships. Humans thrive not on mindless pleasure, but on challenge. Thus, although full employment is no longer needed from a production standpoint, full participation is essential from a social standpoint. But we have already seen that the process of production will eventually fail to provide enough work roles either for satisfactory fulfillment of the income-distribution function or the social-roles function. There seem to be basically two different approaches to this situation. Let us call them the *transfer payments* approach and the *"appropriate technology"* approach.

The Transfer Payments Approach

The term *transfer payments* refers, in the jargon of economists, to income payments and transfers of purchasing power by governments to people deemed needy or worthy, without their having to provide a specific service in return. Examples include welfare payments, veterans' pensions, and Medicare. Since the depression, the economic strategy of the United States has been the promotion of growth and consumption and the manipulation of the economy to achieve the fullest employment possible and hence to minimize such transfer payments as unemployment compensation and welfare. Minimizing transfer payments was considered desirable not only for economic reasons but also because of the deleterious social consequences presumed to accompany welfare programs.

If the economists' usual definition of a transfer payment is broadened to include transfers from institutions and individuals as well as from governments, we note that there are at least four distinct kinds of transfer payments:

1. Those based on membership, entitling a person to support simply by virtue of belonging to a particular group such as the family, community, organization, or society (e.g., transfers to wives, children, students, or commune members)

2. Those that are a social investment based on promise (e.g., some research grants and competitive scholarships)

3. Those based on need, but conditional (e.g., the Canada Works program wherein unemployed individuals must propose and carry out socially constructive tasks to qualify for payments)

4. Those based on need, but otherwise unconditional (e.g., welfare and unemployment payments, assistance to the aged)

Using broadened definition, if all four types of payments are included, more than sixty percent of the population (mostly housewives, children, and students) are already supported wholly or in part by transfer payments. All but five percent are receiving one of the first three types of payments; nevertheless, the negative aspects of the fourth type tend to give undesirable connotations to income transfers in general.

Some aspects of the work-roles problem could be alleviated by greatly expanding the number of transfer payments available to the second and third categories. Because these two types comprise such a small percentage of all transfer payments, the numbers involved could be multiplied many times without appreciably increasing the overall percentage. If a significant number of people had the opportunity to extend their education, shift careers, or make some voluntary response to societal needs, their moving out of more structured work roles would free up places for those who want and need those more structured jobs.

The term *enhancement income maintenance* seems appropriate for this form of aid to distinguish it from the *subsistence income maintenance* that will always be required for those who are not able to work because of disability or other reasons. The purpose of enhancement income maintenance would be to provide support, on either a temporary or permanent basis, for those who have demonstrated an ability to hold structured jobs but who want to carry out some project of manifest social merit. Such activities could include study and research (now generally provided for only a small elite group through scholarships and fellowships), providing educational opportunities for the elderly, preserving and beautifying the environment, carrying out a social experiment, assisting the handicapped, creating in art, music, or writing, and providing companionship for the young or aged. Funds for individuals or group projects would need to be available on a competitive basis to keep incentive levels up. Preferably the funding would come from diverse sources in public, business, and non-profit sectors.

Enhancement income maintenance might also be used to provide rewarding work opportunities, increase job mobility, and subsidize public works projects to accomplish socially desirable objectives that are not likely to be achieved by the private or voluntary sector. Subsistence income maintenance for those who require it and some form of universal unemployment insurance could also be a part of this type of transfer payments policy.

The "Appropriate Technology" Approach

A very different approach is represented by the social movement designated by the term "appropriate technology." Basically, the term refs to technology that is environmentally benign, resource conserving, frugal in the use of energy, and understandable and usable at the individual or community level. It tends to complement a strong ecological ethic; identification with nature, fellow human beings, and future generations; a lifestyle characterized by voluntary frugality ("doing more with less"); appreciation of the simple life and simple virtues; and the work that fosters these attitudes.

Inherent in this approach is the reversal of a number of aspects of the long-term industrialization trend. This is particularly true of the emphasis on small, decentralized technology and the removal of many production and service activities from the mainstream economy. Were society to move in this direction, production would become more decentralized, with a significant proportion of it returned to the household and community. As Burns points out, the relative importance of the household economy vis-a-vis the market economy, which had been decreasing since the early 1800s, seems now to be increasing.[7] The household economy is far from negligible; were its exchanges counted in such economic indicators as the GNP, the household economy would be about one-third the size of the market economy. The products from a household economy represent more tangible national wealth than all market economy structures and inventories. Working in the household economy can provide rich benefits in terms of human environment. (A half-century ago, pundit Ralph Borsodi hailed the development of the small electric motor with the observation that it would permit returning much industrial production to the household, "where it belongs.") Furthermore, the increasingly burdensome taxation of market economy transactions creates an incentive to spend time and capital outside the market economy.

The social-roles function of work is enhanced when work is done in the environment of the home and the community rather than the factory. The best solution to having sufficient and satisfactory work roles is found not in some form of job enrichment in the main market economy, but in the multitudinous activities involved in a learning and consciously evolving society. Such a society needn't run out of constructive social roles—that situation only occurs when all such roles must come from the activity of economic production. The voluntary sector can play a central role in providing social roles (and even in the production of goods).

Income distribution is far less of a central issue in a society where much of the exchange takes place outside the formal market economy, such as through barter and trade. Nevertheless, some amount of government transfer payments would no doubt be necessary.

Two scholars who have written about the sort of person-centered future society that might accompany the "appropriate technology" approach—Lewis Mumford describing "biotechnic culture" and Robert

Hutchins describing "the learning society"—both stress the Greek concept of *Paidea*. As Hutchins envisions this society, learning, fulfillment, and becoming human are the primary goals, and all its institutions are directed to this end. "[The Athenians] made their society one designed to bring all its members to the fullest development of their highest powers. . . . Education was not a segregated activity, conducted for certain hours, in certain places, at a certain time of life. It was the aim of society. . . . The Athenian was educated by the culture, by Paidea."[8] Paidea was the educating matrix of the society, involving all its institutions. It is perhaps worth noting that the highest, central theme of Paidea was the individual's "search for the Divine Center." Of course, the Greeks had slaves rather than technology, so the case is not completely comparable. Nevertheless, the principle of lifelong learning taking place in all society's institutions is fully applicable.

THE LONG-TERM MODERNIZATION TREND

We have observed that the "appropriate technology" approach really involves reversal of some of the components of the industrialization trend. To fully understand its significance, we need to look more closely at the origins of industrial society in that long, multifold trend of modernization and economic development that Robert Heilbroner calls the "Great Ascent."[9] This trend started eight to ten centuries ago in Western Europe and has since affected all parts of the globe. It contains such dynamic stages as the development of capitalism, the growth of empirical science, the Industrial Revolution, and the wedding of science and technology in the late nineteenth century. But it all started inconspicuously with a fundamental shift in the basic premises underlying European society during the Middle Ages.

In preindustrial society, most people were involved in work to meet their own needs and those of a limited community. There was some long-distance trade, but not much. The money economy was not central; most exchanges occurred outside the money economy. Behavior fell largely into traditional roles, and society's guiding values were rooted in religious tradition.

The "Great Ascent" began with a gradual shift of values from those based in tradition to a more utilitarian set centering around a new concept of material progress: the idea that man could by his own efforts control and improve his physical environment. The most important components of this long-term modernization trend included:

Increasing secularization, i.e., rational organization of society's activities and institutions around impersonal, utilitarian values in place of the traditional cultural and religious values.

Increasing industrialization of human activity and inclusion of an increasing fraction of this activity in the mainstream economy.

Increasing dominance of economic rationality in social issues and decision making.

Increasing "technification" of knowledge, that is, emphasizing the kinds of knowledge that lead to manipulative technology to the exclusion of other types.

Some societies, ours included, have been on this path for many centuries. Others are just starting on it. The tensions between these two groups will dominate the globe in the decades to come. In the so-called advanced societies, people are questioning how much farther along this path it is advisable to go, recognizing that the social and environmental costs began to outweigh the benefits some time ago. The secularization of values seems to have brought society to the point of being able to do more and more, and being less and less sure what is worth doing. It is no longer obviously desirable to industrialize more and more of human activity in the main economy. Especially questionable are activities and exchanges that involve living organisms, human or otherwise, e.g., health care and agriculture. We are coming to question the ever-increasing dominance of economic rationality, e.g., recognizing only those exchanges that "count" in economic calculations like the GNP and applying standard discount rates to the rights and welfare of future generations. Most fundamentally, perhaps, the shape of society's knowledge base is up for reassessment. The biasing of human knowledge towards technological ends has brought obvious and highly praised technological benefits; the costs have only recently been widely acknowledged.

Perception of the role of work is part of the larger awareness of what is real and what is important. If the cultural perception, the social paradigm, changes, so will the perceived role of work. Here we encounter a curious fact. We hear a good deal these days about the difference between "left-brain" (rational/verbal) and "right-brain" (intuitive/imaginal) activities and the tendency of modern culture to overemphasize the former. But a far more fundamental distinction passes relatively unnoticed: the distinction between what we learn of reality through the physical senses and what is learned through inner, intuitive, aesthetic, noetic sensing. Knowledge about the former is elaborately articulated in conventional science. The prestige and influence of materialistic, measuring, positivistic science has succeeded in persuading us that it is not possible or useful to construct a systematic knowledge of the world of inner experience.

This situation is now changing. Cultural shifts and frontier explorations in the nascent "noetic" sciences both embody a return of the ostracized "other half" of human experience. Human development is being seen once again as involving inner, spiritual growth as well as the acquisition of skills and knowledge. The view of society in which the economy dominates is being vigorously challenged. Work is seen once again as important opportunity for inner development. Described in alternative language, to be sure, people are once again concerned with what used to be termed finding their unique "calling" or "vocation."

MOTIVATION

A principal feature of the industrial paradigm has been the concept that man is motivated largely by economic concerns. Whether an individual is concerned with a real need for food and shelter or a perceived need for a vacation in the country, his economic behavior and the responses of the economic system are assumed to be fairly dependable and predictable. Indeed, a science of economics has been erected positing that people's economic behavior, like the movement of molecules in a gas, is both predictable and easily depicted in models. We tend to forget that this dominant, institutionalized concern with economic motivation could turn out to be quite transient and parochial. Other societies and social groupings have placed more emphasis on other motivations, such as the social forces of tradition, identification with the common welfare, tribal loyalty, patriotism, moral righteousness, or the search for enlightenment.

Abraham Maslow, among others, has noted that there are basically two kinds of motivation observable in human behavior: deficiency motivation and self-actualization motivation. Put still more simply, there are motivations essentially based on fear and those based on love, on awareness of and desire to actualize one's potentialities, on a desire for union. The institutions of industrial society assume the prevalence of a fear motivation and incorporate fear-based incentives, both economic and noneconomic, into the system. The transindustrial society toward which we seem to be headed may rest more on assumptions of love-based motivation.

The consume-and-waste ethic of recent industrial society may be replaced with an ecological ethic and a self-realization ethic. The ecological ethic involves identification with the whole of nature, from the smallest life form to the planet itself and the evolutionary forces that exist. It calls for man to act in partnership with nature in protecting the complex life-support systems of the planet, to husband resources appropriately, to modify ecological relationships wisely, to reestablish satisfactory recycling mechanisms in harmony with natural ones, and to move toward a new economic-ecological system that makes a clear distinction between wholesome and cancerous forms of growth.

The self-realization ethic affirms that the proper end of all individual experience is the furthering of individual awareness and the evolutionary development of the human species. Hence, the appropriate function of all social institutions is to create environments that will foster this development.

We have already indicated that learning will occupy a key position in the transindustrial society. Learning in the broadest sense—education, research, exploration, self-discovery, and participating in the community of concerned citizens to choose a better future—contributes to human fulfillment and betterment. These activities are humane, nonpolluting, and nonstultifying; they can absorb unlimited numbers of persons not required for other sorts of work. Unbounded opportunities become apparent once the mind is freed by separating the functions of creative work and income distribution.

CONCLUSION

There should be no minimization of the depth of social change we are postulating here. In the short term we have a fraction of the population "dropping out," choosing alternative work styles, forming small work-centered communities, designing alternative technologies, creating their own worlds of meaning in the behemoth of industrial society. We are postulating a transformed society in which Keynes's bleak vision has miraculously become an age of creative work and sufficiency for all, one in which the problem of superfluous people has been permanently solved. This possibility is clearly open to us.

We started by observing that the problem of work is ultimately inseparable from the problem of meaning. We end with the observation that the same transformation that is returning to society a sense of meaning and worthwhile destination will transmute the problems of unemployment and underemployment to the opportunities of a learning and planning society.

 What sort of person would become an authority on leisure? Whereas most of the contributors to this book are noted for their unceasing committment to study and work, Dr. Don Mankin is unique in his unrelenting search for the "perfect leisure life." Yet the leisure life as identified by Don Mankin is not an empty one filled with shuffleboard and soap operas, but is instead a vigorous, energetic, and highly imaginative lifestyle replete with learning, travel, interpersonal stimulation, personal assessment and development, and, of course, some work as well.

In this chapter on the future of leisure Don Mankin examines the historical as well as present beliefs on the nature and importance of leisure. After identifying the positive as well as negative aspects of leisure, he proceeds to illustrate the many ways in which life in the twenty-first century may make more effective use of leisure time and activities to heighten intelligence, enhance social behavior, and improve all aspects of personal/cultural functioning.

The themes and challenges inherent in integrating creative leisure into contemporary lifestyles are well exemplified in the life of Don Mankin. After receiving his undergraduate degree in electrical engineering from Drexel University, he completed his master's and doctoral degrees in experimental psychology at Johns Hopkins University. While studying the many faces of work and leisure, he has served as a research associate and professor at Lehigh University, in the graduate program in Studies of the Future at the University of Houston, and at the Center for Future Research at the University of Southern California.

He presently divides his time between serving as a researcher in residence at the Rand Corporation, where he is writing a book on the future of work and leisure; and as a faculty member at Antioch College West, where he is designing a graduate program in organizational psychology. In addition to his academic and formal research pursuits, however, Don Mankin spends a major portion of his life in a broad assortment of leisure activities.

In addition to his ongoing work as a lecturer and consultant, he has published several books, including Classics in Industrial and Organizational Psychology, Toward a Post-Industrial Psychology: Emerging Perspectives on Work, Education and Leisure, as well as numerous papers and articles in professional journals.

LEISURE

There is little doubt about the growing interest in leisure in our everyday lives—the evidence is all around us. Television commercials and ads in magazines and newspapers urge us to buy recreational vehicles, vacation homes, and video games. New restaurants, discos, travel clubs, athletic facilities, and "growth" centers open up almost overnight. And if these phenomena aren't enough proof of the increasing importance of leisure, the unconvinced need only walk through a shopping center any evening or weekend, try to get a campsite in a national park during the summer or a ticket to a professional football game in the fall.

As we approach the dawning of the 21st century, we are heading toward an era when people may be spending more time involved in leisure activities than working; when leisure may replace career as a central concern and focus of people's lives; and where individuals may define themselves and their roles in terms of their leisure pursuits rather than their work (e.g. "I am a student, a skier, or a gardener"—rather than "I am an accountant").

If this is so, what might a leisure-centered society look like? Is this a desirable state? Would the leisure activities that characterize this society be mere extrapolations of what they are today—modified by technological change, social and environmental constraints, and consumer taste but varying little from today's activities in purpose and essential character? Or might we be heading for an entirely new vision of the "leisure life," one that has never been considered before?

To best gain insight into these issues it would be most helpful to take a look at the nature and meaning of "leisure" particularly with respect to the personal and cultural needs it is believed to satisfy.

Portions of this article originally appeared in expanded form in D. A. Mankin, *Toward a Post-Industrial Psychology: Emerging Perspectives on Technology, Work, Education and Leisure* (New York: John Wiley, 1978). Reprinted by permission of the publisher.

THE MEANING, FUNCTIONS, AND ACTIVITIES
OF LEISURE: PAST, PRESENT AND FUTURE

Central to all definitions of leisure is the idea that it is free, relatively uncommitted time allowing the exercise of choice. In addition, leisure is supposed to fulfill certain functions in the life of the individual. What are these functions? According to sociologist Max Kaplan,[1] leisure functions fall into two primary categories: those associated with the classical interpretations of leisure and those consistent with the Protestant work ethic.

The classical interpretation is the oldest, having its roots in the traditions and philosophies of the earliest days of ancient Greece. In essence, this interpretation views leisure as an end unto itself. Included within this framework are activities such as scholarship, contemplation, self-expression, self-realization, and self-development. In ancient times, leisure was viewed as the most desirable state of being for a citizen with high social status whereas work was identified as an inferior activity to be performed, as much as possible, by slaves.

From the perspective of the Protestant work ethic, the importance, role, and purpose of leisure are quite different. As an essential element of the Industrial Revolution, the Protestant work ethic stressed the primary importance of work and saw the function of leisure as "therapy, rest, relaxation, social control, re-creation for subsequent productive effort— and generally, therefore, as instrumental in character."[2] That is, leisure served the function of resting the individual so that he or she could work harder and more efficiently. This interpretation, according to Kaplan, was broadened towards the end of the last century by economist Thorstein Veblen to include leisure as a symbol of wealth. Since then, as leisure changed from the exclusive domain of the wealthy elite to the mass phenomenon it is today, the symbolic function has similarly changed to encompass its use as an instrument of rest as well as status by the general population.

This distinction between the classical and instrumental interpretations is a useful point of departure for exploring the kinds of leisure functions and activities that might be available in a future, leisure-oriented society. At present the instrumental interpretation, and the consumer-oriented activities that are associated with it, are the dominant mode in advanced industrial societies.[3] If this situation remains unchanged, in the coming years we could expect to see more exotic, sophisticated, and expensive versions of existing amusement parks, night clubs, recreational vehicles, travel clubs, television programs, electronic games, and so on. No doubt technological innovations could add unique dimensions to these activities as well as provide new opportunities for inventive entrepreneurs to devise activities, goods, and services of an unprecedented kind.

But, if the recent past is any indication, new entertainments, diversions, and gadgets may become passé at even faster rates than they do at present. If so, how certain can we be that technological innovation and the imagination and expertise of the leisure industries will be able to keep at least one step ahead of the constantly changing needs of an increasingly well-educated, sophisticated, and somewhat jaded populace?

Another problem is that many of our leisure activities require the depletion of natural resources. Raw materials make up the goods on which these leisure activities often depend and energy is used to convert these raw materials into finished products. Energy is also used to power many of these goods—recreational vehicles, for example—and to transport us to vacation spots and areas where these leisure resources can be used. As the costs of raw materials and energy continue to rise, leisure activities that are dependent on these resources could become prohibitively expensive and increasingly unavailable.

If consumer-based leisure became less available and desirable, one of the most important consequences might be an increase in leisure time! This somewhat surprising result follows from the well-known economic relationship between income and time, i.e., increases in industrial productivity (typically caused by technological innovations in work processes) create potential choices between higher incomes or decreased work time or, as is usually the case, some tradeoff between the two. [4] Therefore, with leisure products and services less available and desirable, periodic increases in income would not be as important, and therefore a larger percentage of future productivity gains could be taken in the form of shorter work hours (e.g. the 5 day, 40 hour week might be replaced by a 3 or 4 day, 25–30 hour week). So, an alternative to the "instrumental" form of leisure would be characterized by increases in leisure time but not necessarily by comparable increases in leisure goods and services. [5]

Fortunately, the classical interpretation of leisure, described earlier, fits just such an alternative—a contemporary version of the contemplative, self-regarding, and developmental mind set extolled by the ancient Greeks. This "neo-classical" interpretation of leisure might focus on self-generated activities that are relatively independent of private goods and services and require little more than an individual's own imagination and spontaneity and the abundant stimulation offered by the presence of other people and the natural and constructed environment. For example, thinking, reflecting, self-exploration, and problem solving can be forms of self-generated leisure that require little more than time, quiet, and one's own imagination. Similarly, interaction with other people can be an entertaining leisure activity since it can increase the diversity of the activities in which we engage; it can fill our off-work time with interesting sources of stimulation and knowledge and offer valuable social feedback to be used to increase self-knowledge and self-esteem. Hiking and camping in the natural environment are also relatively inexpensive leisure activities that are personal and self-generated. In addition, constructed environments such as cities can serve a valuable leisure function as anyone who has spent time sightseeing in places like Paris, London, New York, or San Francisco, to name just a few of the best examples, can easily attest. Clearly, leisure activities of this sort can be effectively limitless, relatively inexpensive, and potentially highly satisfying as well.[6]

Comparing the Alternatives

Basically, the role of the participant in "instrumental" activities is passive since he or she is usually dependent upon external agents such as TV sets, vehicles, devices, or rules. The activities are structured for individuals rather than by them and the primary function is not self-development but rather entertainment or a simple respite from work. On the other hand, the "neo-classical" alternative suggests activities that are more spontaneous, self-initiated, and self-directed. In this case the individual is responsible for creating whatever structure is necessary, without dependence upon external means, and can be more flexible in the use of leisure time. In effect, the person is the creator of his or her own leisure.

In a sense, the difference between these two alternatives is similar to the distinction social critic and historian Theodore Roszak makes between "play" and "games." He describes "games" as:

> human activity that absorbs people in the orderly pursuit of arbitrary—usually competitive—goals according to arbitrary rules. . . . "Game" is the word we reserve for . . . *organized* play. But it is not always to the regularity and orderliness of game that play gives itself. Playing is clearly a much more generalized and lawless form of activity. Babies and animals "play" in a perfectly chaotic fashion. In fact, playful babies have very little patience with rules and regulations. They *play* quite naturally, but they must be taught their *games*.[7]

The important distinction is that "games" are more highly structured and the source of this structure is external to and imposed upon the individual, while the relatively little structure present in play is generated by the "players" themselves. We can see from this that the concept of games corresponds to the consumption of leisure-related, technology-dependent goods and services whereas play corresponds to non-consumptive, self-generated leisure activities. In other words, the distinction between these two types of leisure activities lies not only in the cost, but, more fundamentally, in the degree and source of the structure, which is the usual, but not necessarily inevitable result of the commercialization of technological change.

Theory and research on the psychology of play suggests several fascinating advantages associated with "play-like" leisure. One of the foremost authorities on the psychology of play, Brian Sutton-Smith, describes these advantages. "Other things being equal, there is some optimal level of play participation, which contributes to the subject greater autonomy, greater enjoyment of life, a greater potential repertory of responses, and a greater potential flexibility in the use of these resources."[8]

Elaborating on this, we could say that to the extent that leisure is play-like it has the potential for being intrinsically more satisfying and will better fulfill its classical functions of self-expression and personal development. According to this view, "playful" leisure can lead to increased knowledge about the world and our abilities to deal with it as well as aid in the further development of our adaptability, spontaneity, independence, and imagination. In addition, play-like leisure activities usually place less of a burden on the resources of society—energy and materials, commercial ingenuity, technology—to provide new and continually increasing outlets for the leisure needs of its citizens. The spontaneous ability to generate novel and absorbing activities, perspectives, and experiences suggests a leisure resource of almost limitless variation. In effect, the whole world, internal and external, can serve as a potential leisure resource to the person with the flexibility and imagination to take advantage of it.

Of course, the line of demarcation between the two alternatives is not always a sharp one. For example, some TV programs and movies invite an active mental involvement on the part of the viewers to interpret, analyze, and find meaning relevant to their own experience. Travel is another example. Travelers can always insulate themselves by interacting exclusively with fellow tourists and viewing the travelscape through the windows of a tour bus, an experience not unlike watching a travelogue. On the other hand, one can also travel in a far less structured fashion, experiencing diverse natural and cultural environments on their own terms. The important difference is in the attitude and the state of mind with which we go about our leisure; that is, in our ability to play with and within the structures we generate and the external environment rather than being restricted by them.

A similar point can be made with respect to the relationship between leisure activities typically associated with the consumption of goods and services and those that could help to fill large blocks of free time. To consume goods and services in pursuit of leisure does not necessarily preclude participation in more active, less structured activities and in some cases might even make it easier. For example, to take advantage of the leisure resources available within the city, one must make relatively small expenditures for admissions to museums, zoos, and cultural events, fares for public transportation, and for the diverse ethnic foods for which most of the major cities of the world are known. Similarly, the exploration of wilderness areas is made considerably more comfortable and enjoyable by the purchase of good equipment. Once again it is a matter of degree; that is, the activities associated with the classical or playful class of leisure resources generally require relatively less spending than the more common forms of commercially dependent leisure activities. In addition, it is often the case that more highly structured activities also tend to be more expensive. Compare, for example, the cost of a conversation with a friend with the cost of a TV set! The important point, in any case, is that an optimal intentional and humanistic leisure-centered future would offer a balance and diversity of integrated and complementary leisure alternatives which would serve a wide range of needs and conditions.

But would the "leisure society" be a satisfying place in which to live? Even if it is possible, is it desirable?

Futurists frequently translate ideas, observations, and speculations about the future into a variety of narrative forms—scenarios, future histories, science fiction stories—to convey a feeling for what a particular alternative future might be like and to identify problems, opportunities, and contingencies that might be otherwise overlooked. The following story is offered with this purpose in mind. In this scenario, I present a future in which nearly all work has been eliminated and replaced by an abundance of leisure resources that reflect aspects of both types of leisure discussed in the preceding pages. As you read this story, please bear in mind that this particular glimpse represents some of the ideal aspects of a "leisure lifestyle" as well as some of the more frightening and hollow characteristics of this vision. My purpose is not to create another "utopia" vision but rather to illustrate and make more obvious many of the issues that will increasingly challenge us in the years to come.

ENNUI, 2080 A.D.

The gnawing feeling of uneasiness that had been Aaron Richter's constant companion since his job at the Institute for Forecasting, Planning, and Decision Analysis was phased out several weeks ago began to grow once more as he boarded the high speed pneumo-tube exiting from Municipal Leisure Park #27. Another day spent in the carnival-like atmosphere of the largest and most popular of the 106 Municipal Leisure Parks in Northwest Megalopolis had left him as empty as the blur of other days spent in other MuniLeis Parks since he left the Institute. He settled back into the yielding cushions of the acceleration couch and absentmindedly punched out his regional destination on the panel at the front of the cab. The gentle whine of the cab picking up speed lulled Aaron into the reverie which had become an increasingly common state in recent weeks. One by one he reviewed the day's activities in an attempt to find an answer to a question he still wasn't able to formulate adequately.

The memory of his outstanding performance on the racquetball court reminded him of the satisfaction and optimism with which he had started the day. Although his skill at gravity-free six-wall racquetball was legendary at the Institute, he hadn't expected to gain the proficiency he demonstrated today on the eight-wall courts for at least another few weeks. It was almost too easy.

"It might be interesting to play 'against' someone next time," he thought. He had at times participated in competitive athletics, but, like many others of his generation, derived little satisfaction from this archaic form of activity.

Although the short time he had spent in one of the many Multi-Sensory Fantasy Pavilions in the park was interesting, as it almost always was, he had left there with the same vague feeling of emptiness that had accompanied many of his other recent activities. The DiscoSex Pavilion had left him completely cold. Although he had passed all of the screening tests for the Psychedelic Dens, he felt no strong urge to begin the "Quest" just yet. Even when the time did come, he did not think he would go that route anyway. It definitely did not appeal to him as a means of diversion either.

The vast array of games, sports, entertainments, and devices for fantasy, diversion, and activity spun through his mind. His reflections on these activities were punctuated by the hiss of the opening door as the cab glided almost soundlessly into the delivery dock. The task of getting from the cab to the regional traffic conveyor through the surging mobs of people forced Aaron to put his thoughts aside for the moment.

Aaron was able to work his way into the center express conveyor with a minimum of effort. He wedged himself into a seat between a rather stout woman with the ear plugs and glazed eyes of a "media addict" and an elderly, distinguished gentleman whose slim attaché case and smug expression immediately marked him as a "functional." Through the background hum of whirring machinery and the murmur of voices, Aaron was just able to hear the tinny voices from his neighbor's ear plugs. "A soap opera, no doubt," he thought, a barely perceptible smirk conveying his tolerant amusement at those members of the older generation who still subsisted on the diet of dull but innocuous serialized stories they needed to help fill up their idle days. He couldn't control the slight shudder that shook his body as he tried to imagine himself spending day after day following the adventures of fictitious people in fictitious regional subdivisions pursuing lives as empty as those of their listeners.

It was with equal curiosity that Aaron glanced at the man to his left. He found the air of self-perceived importance in which this man, like most functionals, cloaked himself to be rather ludicrous, especially at a time when the need for "functional" work in the old, traditional sense was rapidly disappearing. Aaron remembered, from his studies of the industrial and early post-industrial society of the last century, that at one time a great deal of "status" (an archaic expression very popular in those days) was attributed to the historical predecessors of the functionals. Now that most of the few jobs still in existence were allotted more on the basis of psychological needs and personality characteristics than on ability, questions of status and importance were quickly fading. Few of his contemporaries defined function in terms of formal contributions to society, in any case, since most people defined their role and function in society in a very personal sense—many somewhat facetiously referring to this role as the "Quest." Aaron did not pretend to understand fully what this meant but he realized that the restlessness and uneasiness which he had been only recently experiencing often acted as a spur to the launching of this lifelong activity—or so he had learned in his course in Psychology 397 at EducInst, the Psychology of the Existential Crisis.

The man's smug, self-assured expression began to irritate Aaron. "Doesn't he realize that the automational planners and engineers will soon eliminate his job just as they have so recently done to mine?" The recollection heightened Aaron's feelings of loss, uncertainty, and anxiety that had begun when he was first notified that his job was to be terminated. While he realized when he took the position of "Futures Analyst/Generalist, Level II" that it would eventually be automated, he expected the complexity of the job to confound the automational engineers for far longer than it apparently had. He was clearly not prepared for the termination announcement when it came. He was even less prepared for the forced idleness that followed.

Aaron, almost mischievously, wondered how much of this man's job was really functional and how much was designed by the vocational engineers to appear as if it were. In the course of his work at the Institute he had learned that this was frequently done when an individual's psychological profile revealed a pathological inability to adjust to the unstructured conditions and nonproductive role necessitated by unlimited leisure. The bureaucratic system and its associated hardware were so complex that it would be relatively easy to design an activity that at least looked functional to the person performing it. If this were actually the case and if it ever became public, the reaction among those who were being deceived could cause serious problems. Of course, their numbers were considerably less than those displaced by the Automational Revolution at the beginning of the century. As a consequence, there was little chance for a recurrence of the massive riots of the idle which had swept the technologically advanced nations of the world at that time. In any case, with the planned evolution of consciousness currently under way, this was less likely to be a problem in the future. "Or so the Meta System Planners hoped," he noted to himself with more than a touch of irony.

A movement at his side snapped him out of his reverie. The woman sitting next to him was rising from the seat and preparing to exit from the express conveyor, reminding him that he also would be exiting shortly. Rising from his seat, he glanced back once more at his other neighbor and noticed that the expression on his face had changed from smugness to one that looked slightly pained. "Probably indigestion," Aaron reflected, recalling from his studies at EducInst the name of a common physical malady which often plagued functionals in the days before the Automational Revolution.

Without further thought, he devoted his complete attention to preparing his exit from the conveyor. He easily worked his way out from the high speed express conveyor to those of successively lower speeds until he reached the slow, outermost exit conveyor just as it passed the Residential Park and Local Leisure Area marking the edge of his residential sector. In a few seconds he had exited, descended to the next level, and entered the local residential exiting conveyor system which ran perpendicular to the regional conveyors. Within a matter of a few more seconds he stood at the entrance to the delivery tubes for ResidBldg #637, Sector 23, N.W. He entered the tube cab and simultaneously spoke his Residential Rental Unit (RRU) number into the voice key and slipped his right hand into the security viewer. In what appeared to be no time at all his palm and fingerprints were cross-checked with those under file for his RRU number and, with the check completed, he was soundlessly whisked off home.

None of the other members of Aaron's living group was there. Although the membership of the group frequently changed, what with various members leaving for one reason or another, and new members, friends, and transients on Quest moving in for a time, there was a core that had remained fairly stable for the past several months. Of that core, Boyce was still in attendance at EducInst though he was showing signs of restlessness and was beginning to look for alternative ways to spend his time. Janna's job had been terminated several months before Aaron's but so far she seemed perfectly content with the distractions of the MuniLeis Parks. Aaron smiled to himself as he recalled the first few days following her arrival in Northwest Megalopolis. She had been brought up in one of the few remaining areas of the North American Federation in which the customs and mores of the previous century still flourished. After an initial period of reluctance and a rather quaint embarrassment and shyness, she had begun to avail herself of the more sensually oriented activities available in the leisure parks and elsewhere. It did not take long before her curiosity turned into what could only be described as dedication. Her enthusiasm for these activities showed no signs of diminishing, and the sheer size of her network of intimate partners and occasional lovers would exhaust all but the most hardy and committed.

Although Robin and Vika could be more accurately described as transients, they had been in residence with the group almost long enough to be considered long-term members. Unlike the others, they had a formal marriage contract and were already well into their first five year renewal term. Since the earliest years of their contract they had traveled together between megacities, towns, wilderness sanctuaries, ashrams, growth centers, schools, and living groups throughout the world. These two, more so than anybody else Aaron had ever known, were on the Quest. Although there were no formal criteria or identifying characteristics for those involved in the continual process of attaining personal self-fulfillment and full realization of potential which was the ultimate state of leisure—or so it was taught—it was clear to everyone who met them that it was the most appropriate description for what they were doing. In spite of the widespread acceptance and official encouragement for the Quest, Aaron could not help but feel that these activities were frequently self-indulgent and narcissistic and generally a poor substitute for the feelings of pride, accomplishment, and worth that he had derived from his recently terminated job. Nonetheless, Aaron respected Robin and Vika and was confident that if they stayed around much longer, he would have a better understanding of the nature and purpose of the Quest and its relevance to his own circumstances. As things stood, however, they were planning to leave shortly for a prolonged stay at a Zen monastery on an island off the northern coast of Scotland.

At least one other member of the family had also been greatly influenced by his contact with Robin and Vika. Brooke, a shy and withdrawn young man who always seemed to be somewhat set off from the other family members, had recently decided to enroll in one of the Federal Wilderness Survival Institutes in preparation for embarking on his Quest. The emphasis of these Institutes on techniques of solitary survival, independence, and self-reliance seemed ideally suited to Brooke's solitary nature. It was never quite clear why he had chosen to live with a group in the first place. Maybe it was some kind of personal experiment to determine how much he needed or desired interpersonal contact. Whatever his initial reasons for joining the living group in RRU #73282, it was obvious that he had gained a great deal from his contact with several members of the group, particularly Robin and Vika, and the solitary nature of his chosen approach to the Quest was in no way contradictory with these important interpersonal influences.

Of the four remaining members of the constantly changing extended family presently residing in RRU #73282, Nikaya was the only one with a child. Nikaya, a world-class megamarathon runner, was off with his daughter Sky visiting the recently established Heritage Museum of New York. The restoration of this 20th century urban district had long been awaited and gave every indication of rivaling the popularity of its counterpart across the continent, the Circus of Los Angeles. Nikaya's present lover, Alissa, had remained behind to begin her new job as a Psychic Image Artist in a local Multi-Sensory Fantasy Pavilion. Aaron and Alissa had once held a dual marriage contract that was not renewed after its initial 6 month period. A strong bond of affection still remained between them, and when the occasion still arose they made love with the same fervor that marked the early days of their contract.

Aaron was so absorbed in his thoughts that he failed to notice the entrance of the tenth and last member of the semi-permanent population of RRU #73282. Jon Newman was the only member of the group engaged in a planned, synthetic leisure activity.

Jon looked at Aaron with concern and asked, "How was your day?"

"Okay, I guess," Aaron replied somewhat halfheartedly.

"Getting bored, huh?"

"I guess so, how could you tell?"

"It's pretty obvious. For one thing, you're beginning to look uneasy, sort of nervous—there's an air of restlessness about you."

"No wonder. I just don't know what to do with myself anymore. I liked my job—it challenged me almost every day. I discovered abilities that I never realized I had; I used skills that are a source of pride to me; I was constantly learning new things, and I was rarely bored. Besides, I could see that my job was important—I guess that made me feel important as well. Of course, I've had a lot of fun since leaving the job but that's beginning to wear thin. It's just not the same—something's missing."

"I know what you mean."

Of all the members of the family, Jon was in many ways the most like Aaron. His job had been terminated several months before Aaron's. Since then he had sampled many of the diversions provided by the leisure parks in this megacity and others and even spent some time in several of the vast international wilderness sanctuaries including the recently established regulated-access park in Antarctica. After several months of this he decided to return to Northwest Megalopolis and try a synthetic activity designed specifically for him by AVOCOUNS, the official government agency for avocational counseling. For the past two months he had been engaged in this activity and appeared to be happy, at least to Aaron. Because of the similarity between Aaron's present condition and what Jon had gone through several months ago, Jon seemed especially attuned to Aaron's apparent discontent.

"Have you thought of contacting AVOCOUNS?"

"To tell you the truth, I have been thinking of getting some counseling. I've never had to utilize AVOCOUNS, though. How does it actually work?"

"There's really not all that much to it. You spend a couple of hours taking tests, and then they assess your situation. Afterwards they contact you to explain your activity and give you all the necessary details. They make all of the arrangements and you just follow the instructions. If there is any aspect of the activity you don't like, they will put you in touch with a counselor and the two of you can work out the necessary changes. Once you start, you can alter the activity in consultation with the counselor, and you can terminate whenever you like. The AVOCOUNS center can give you all the information you want. Even if you don't want to pursue it any further, it's pretty interesting learning about it anyway."

"I guess I don't have anything to lose."

"Good. I'll be in my suite meditating for the next hour. If you have any more questions, I'll be glad to talk with you any time after that." With a look of encouragement Jon turned around, walked down the hall to his living suite, and slid the door shut behind him.

Aaron stood another moment or two and then walked down the hall to his own suite. As soon as he entered he headed directly to the compunications[9] console sitting unobtrusively in the corner of the living room. With some hesitation he took a seat in front of the console. Resisting the temptation to try out the new video-computer game in the Historical Issues Series, he carefully intoned the designation "AVOCOUNS" into the voice encoder. Almost instantly the words, "HELLO. CAN WE HELP YOU?" appeared in the middle of the screen above the keyboard.

Aaron responded, "Yes, I would like some information concerning AVOCOUNS."

DO YOU HAVE A SPECIFIC QUESTION OR WOULD YOU LIKE GENERAL INFORMATION?

"General." Aaron set the scan rate on the viewer to accommodate his usual reading speed.

In the middle of the screen appeared: AN INTRODUCTION TO THE GOALS, PURPOSE, AND HISTORY OF AVOCOUNS. Shortly after Aaron had finished reading the title, lines of text began moving from the bottom of the screen to the top. He leaned forward so he would not miss anything.

AVOCOUNS—AN ABBREVIATION FOR AVOCATIONAL COUNSELING—IS A SERVICE PROVIDED TO ASSIST AND GUIDE THE DESIGN OF INDIVIDUALIZED AVOCATIONAL ACTIVITY. THIS SERVICE WAS ESTABLISHED BY THE UNITED FEDERATION AS PART OF THE PROGRAM OF SOCIAL EVOLUTION INITIATED AFTER THE "TWO YEARS OF RAGE" IN RESPONSE TO

WHAT IS POPULARLY REFERRED TO AS THE AUTOMATIONAL REVOLUTION. THE LONG-RANGE GOAL OF THE PROGRAM FOR PLANNED SOCIAL EVOLUTION IS TO COMPLETE THE TRANS-FORMATION OF OUR HISTORICALLY WORK-CENTERED SOCIETY INTO A LEISURE-CENTERED ONE. AVOCOUNS—IN CONJUNCTION WITH THE CENTRALIZED EDUCATIONAL INSTI-TUTION (EDUCINST), THE WORLDWIDE SYSTEM OF LEISURE PARKS, AND THE SMALLER INFORMAL NETWORKS OF WIL-DERNESS SCHOOLS, ASHRAMS, LIVING GROUPS, AND GROWTH CENTERS—IS CONCEIVED OF AS A TEMPORARY SER-VICE TO HELP FACILITATE THIS TRANSITION. WHEN THE TRANSFORMATION IS COMPLETE THE NEED FOR AVOCOUNS WILL HAVE DISAPPEARED.

THE SHORT-RANGE GOAL OF AVOCOUNS IS TO AID THIS TRANSFORMATION AT THE LEVEL OF THE INDIVIDUAL BY DEVELOPING ACTIVITIES DESIGNED TO PROMOTE PERSONAL GROWTH UNTIL THE INDIVIDUAL FEELS CAPABLE OF CON-TINUING THIS PROCESS ON HIS/HER OWN. AN ADDITIONAL GOAL OF AVOCOUNS IS TO FULFILL THE FEW REMAINING WORK NEEDS OF THE SOCIETY BY ASSIGNING THEM ON A VOLUNTARY BASIS TO INDIVIDUALS CONSISTENT WITH THEIR PERSONAL CHARACTERISTICS AND ABILITIES.

THE METHOD OF AVOCATIONAL ACTIVITY DESIGN CON-SISTS OF A COMPLETE ASSESSMENT OF A CLIENT'S CHARAC-TERISTICS INCLUDING PERSONALITY, NEEDS, INTERESTS, ABILITIES, IMAGINAL PROCESSES, AND SO ON. VARIOUS AC-TIVITY COMPONENTS FOUND TO BE RELATED TO THESE CHARACTERISTICS ARE THEN SYNTHESIZED INTO AN INTE-GRATED ACTIVITY. THE CLIENT IS FREE TO MAKE SUGGES-TIONS BEFORE THE ACTIVITY IS SYNTHESIZED AND CAN AL-TER IT TO BETTER SUIT HIS/HER NEEDS—SUBJECT TO CERTAIN PRACTICAL CONSTRAINTS—AT ANY TIME AFTER THE ACTIVITY HAS BEEN INITIATED. A COUNSELOR IS AVAILABLE AT ALL TIMES TO ASSIST THE CLIENT IN WHATEVER ADJUST-MENTS HE/SHE MAY WANT TO CONSIDER. THE CLIENT CAN ALSO TERMINATE THE ACTIVITY AT ANY TIME. IT IS IMPORTANT TO EMPHASIZE THE VOLUNTARY NATURE OF THIS PROCESS. THE CLIENT AT ALL TIMES HAS THE RIGHT TO REFUSE, TERMI-NATE, OR REASONABLY ALTER THE DESIGNED ACTIVITY. THE FUNCTION OF AVOCOUNS IS TO PROVIDE GUIDANCE AND SER-VICE TO THE CLIENT AND *NOT* TO PRESCRIBE A MANDATORY ACTIVITY. IT IS UP TO THE CLIENT TO DECIDE WHETHER TO AVAIL HIM/HERSELF OF THESE SERVICES.

DO YOU HAVE ANY QUESTIONS?
"No."
SHALL WE START WITH THE ASSESSMENT PROCEDURE?
"OK, what the hell . . ."
THE LAST COMMUNICATION WAS INDECIPHERABLE.
Aaron smiled briefly. "Sorry, yes, go ahead."
BEGIN: FOR THE FOLLOWING QUESTIONS PICK THE AL-
TERNATIVE. . . .

Several hours later, Aaron slid wearily into the comforting, weightless confines of his gravity bed. Although he was still too keyed up to fall asleep, he did not want to take a relaxant but preferred to reflect on the events of the past few hours while calming down enough for sleep to overtake him.

"It's funny," he thought, "how anxious I was about contacting AVOCOUNS—I guess I'm still a little nervous at the prospect of actually starting my activity tomorrow—I don't know that many other people who have used AVOCOUNS but most of them seemed to have taken it much more in stride than I have—I guess I'm just basically more insecure than most people—probably a leftover from the days when I had teenage pimples." Aaron almost laughed aloud recalling his early fascination with the samples of mid-1900s popular reading which he had come across in the archives at EducInst. "What were they called—comedy books? Something like that, anyway." Nonetheless, Aaron was considerably less anxious now than he had been for the past several days. In fact, for the first time since his job had been terminated, he felt as if he had a new and exciting direction to his life.

His activity, as it had been described to him briefly by AVOCOUNS and later in more detail by the counselor, consisted of a program to help him in developing more of a capacity for internal experience. The tests indicated that he possessed undeveloped skills for the generation and utilization of "stimulus-independent thought" such as fantasy and self-reflection. He was described as introspective and somewhat aloof. In addition, his personality tests had indicated that his interpersonal skills were substantially above average and that he was capable of effective interpersonal interaction with a broad range of people. The tests had also indicated that his independence needs were high, as was his ability for adaptation and flexibility. As well as Aaron could remember, these were the most important variables considered in the design of the activity.

The counselor had explained to him that while he possessed the ability for a rich and satisfying internal life, he could use these thought processes far more effectively than he had been doing. Specifically, with some practice and training he could learn to use fantasy as additional mediums for play and satisfaction, and as a means for evaluating the leisure potential of many other activities as well.

They had also discussed and altered some of the details of the activity but the general outlines had remained unchanged, it combined a variety of individual and group techniques for the expansion and enrichment of internal experience. The individual aspect of the activity would involve research and personal experimentation with techniques used by different cultures throughout history, such as meditation and visualization, in addition to several that had been recently developed. The purpose of the group was to share and relate experiences and to use the various group members as facilitators for the experiences. All in all, Aaron was quite satisfied with the activity as it had been described to him and was looking forward with anticipation to his orientation conference the following day.

Aaron began to feel drowsy and relaxed his body to welcome the inexorable approach of sleep. As he began to drift off, he recalled the sense of déjà vu he'd had as he viewed the smiling and sympathetic face of the counselor just before the communication ended, informing him again that the activity was voluntary and he could terminate it any time he wished. Finally he realized the source of that feeling with a slight pang of uneasiness. He recalled the one day he had spent viewing videotapes of old television commercials dating back to the days when that form of advertising was still used by large, competitive, privately-owned businesses. Memories of the smiling face and ingratiating voice of the counselor merged with those of the announcer in the commercial as he extolled the virtues of a, "what was it now? 'A miracle washday' something or other . . . whatever that was. . . .

CONCLUSION

In effect, one could view the society described in this story as a relatively benevolent solution to the problems of work that might arise from a continued pursuit of the goals of efficiency and productivity. To be more specific, there are two basic assumptions that underlie this view:

1. Technological innovation will continue to make it possible to replace more and more human work functions with machines and automated processes (this would include the possibility that "artificial intelligence" could eventually be substituted for such complex human cognitive skills as judgment, decision-making, relational thinking, and creativity); and

2. These machines and processes are potentially more efficient than the humans they would replace.

Of course, the "Meta System Planners" referred to in the story realize that in the interests of social stability, alternative ways of filling time, finding meaning, and exercising skills and competence must be found for those displaced from their jobs by automation—which ultimately includes everyone. For many people, the entertainments and diversions of the leisure parks would suffice. Others might find an adequate substitute by pursuing their own personally defined goals—developing valued skills (athletic, artistic, etc.), seeking enlightenment and transcendence, learning—through a variety of means of their own choosing or invention; in other words, the "Quest." Recognizing that some people are totally incapable of deriving contentment from a life that in traditional terms is essentially nonproductive, the Planners allot to those individuals the few jobs that still remain, or when that is not possible, deceive them by fabricating "make-work" jobs that only *appear* socially productive. For those individuals who fall somewhere in between—those who are not entirely dependent on a structured, well-defined and productive work role but who nonetheless find the "nonproductive" alternatives to be generally unsatisfactory—there is always AVOCOUNS. And finally, all of this will ultimately be unnecessary, the Planners hope, because the planned evolution of consciousness will eventually produce a society in which self-development and its related leisure activities becomes the natural state of humankind.

The problem with this scenario, as illustrated by Aaron's "ennui" and uneasiness, is the assumption that the increased availability of a wide range of leisure activities can be adequate compensation for a life without meaningful work. In effect, this belief is a third assumption underlying the view that the kind of leisure society depicted in the story is a desirable and feasible alternative future. And it is this third assumption that the author finds particularly troubling, even when applied to a society where personal growth and development is at least as important as the consumption of leisure goods and services. The limits of the former may not be as obvious as they are for the latter, but exist nonetheless. These limits are, perhaps, best illustrated by their contemporary example in the quasi-therapeutic, human-potential, narcissistic, "growth-oriented" life styles of the affluent, sophisticated and trendy upper middle class that are so effectively satirized in Cyra McFaddin's *The Serial* and criticized by Christopher Lasch in *The Culture of Narcissism*. For these people—who in many respects may be the vanguard of the leisure-dominated society—the idea of "working-on-oneself" seems to have replaced working in a socially productive work role as a central and meaningful focus of their lives. Given the conditions and constraints of modern work, is it any wonder that they turn to therapy, human potential programs, and pseudoreligious spiritual movements for meaning and growth?

Another contemporary example, more populist and less sophisticated than the preceding, may also be a precursor of the leisure society and, as such, is no less troubling in its implications for the future. What I am referring to is the kind of *Guinness Book of Records* mania and death-defying daredevil challenges that seem to have inflicted people at all levels of society with time on their hands and without meaningful activities to pursue. While the number of times one can spin on a skateboard, jump rope, or leap over rows of automobiles on a motorcycle without personally catastrophic consequences may be a satisfying test of skill for some, is this a feasible or desirable future for many? And if it were, what would this suggest about the judgment, vision and commitment of tomorrow's citizens? I recognize that this kind of activity may not coincide with the idea of "leisure for personal growth and development" as understood by the classical philosophers or their contemporary counterparts, but it probably does to those engaged in these activities. And after all, who is best qualified to judge the personal significance and meaning of an individual's pursuits?

In conclusion, then, it is clear to this observer that a wide range of leisure alternatives cannot, or at least should not, be adequate compensation for a life without meaningful work, a conclusion that is buttressed further by the limited scientific evidence presently available concerning this issue.[11] If this is indeed the case, then the viability of a leisure society must be seriously questioned. As a result, any strategy for the future that emphasizes a dominant role for efficiency, productivity, and unlimited leisure as societal goals should be viewed with some skepticism.

Of course, it is possible that in time we could evolve into a society where these goals and assumptions are more valid than they are at present, but the risks of pursuing the appropriate strategy with this in mind are great and may be unnecessary, in any case, since a reasonable alternative does exist. Instead of consciously moving toward a society where work no longer exists, what if we focused our efforts on increasing opportunities for individuals to derive a sense of competence and meaning from their work and to determine to a substantial degree how, when, and where they worked? These work characteristics would be compatible with the kind of leisure advocated earlier in this article, and a holistic approach to the design of both work and leisure would be more successful than strategies that emphasized one while neglecting the other.

JAY KAY KLEIN

Frederik Pohl has spent the last half century living in the future. As one of the leading writers and editors of science fiction in the world, his novels have won all the major awards in this field: Man Plus (1976) won the Nebula Award; Gateway (1977) the Nebula, Hugo, Campbell Memorial Awards, and the Prix Apollo; Jem (1979) won the American Book Award. Throughout his life, Pohl has been a tireless student of all aspects of human experience as well as an extraordinarily prolific writer, having written or edited scores of books related to science fiction, fantasy, and science fact. Kingsley Amis, the well-known literary critic, called him "the most consistently able writer science fiction, in its modern form, has yet produced."

Currently, Pohl is president of the international body of science fiction professionals, World SF. Although he is best known for his imaginative and prophetic science fiction works, he has also proven his writing talent and wisdom in other fields; he is the author of the fascinating handbook Practical Politics (1972) and of various contributions to the Encyclopedia Britannica on early Roman civilization.

On the special subject of future studies, he has written and lectured throughout the world, has served as an advisor and management consultant to major corporations and industry associations, and as visiting instructor at several colleges and universities.

Pohl's lifelong interest in human experience, culture, and political process has made him perhaps the most practical of today's science fiction visionaries. His warm and humorous style, his insistence on improving the human experience, and his undying curiosity about the future of humankind inform his unique perspective on the future of politics. In this essay, he explains our current predicament, offers us a peek into the future, and suggests a variety of practical future-minded systems and methods for making our political system more relevant, functional, and purposeful as we approach life in the twenty-first century.

POLITICS

There is a skull in a museum in Johannesburg which constitutes what may be our earliest record of a political act. The skull was smashed at the jawline by a blow from a weapon, perhaps the thigh-bone of an antelope. We do not know what motivated the hairy little small-brained creature who bashed his fellow. It may have been only anger, or hunger, or jealousy. But it may also have related to the wielder's desire to take over the management of their tribe's affairs, and thus have been political. For "politics" is the process of transferring or maintaining power in society.

Since that australopithecine act there have been a couple million years of social evolution, and the political strategies for keeping or acquiring social power have benefited from a continuous flow of social inventions. In fact, it may even be argued that "society" itself is one of these social inventions. Since society in the abstract is a set of rules governing behavior, it seems plausible that politics existed before society and that the rule of "might" preceded the rule of "rules." Seen from this perspective, politics and the struggle for power may be older than the society in which they come to function.

Over the eons, the social inventions have included an immense variety of political institutions and strategies. Aristotle, the first systematic thinker on political questions whose writings have survived to our time, distinguished three kinds of governments: *kingly rule, aristocracy,* and *constitutional government* (each of which had a subset or "perversion," which he identified as *tyranny, oligarchy,* and *democracy*). Aristotle was a remarkably clear thinker, and, twenty-three centuries later, it is still possible to classify all known governments into one or another of his categories.

Aristotle's taxonomic categories blur and overlap as ingenious politicians find ways to achieve their own purposes in spite of accepted political theory. To the rule of brute force was added the concept of higher authority. Sometimes the authority was divine or superstitious, so that priest-kings and God-anointed sovereigns could call on supernatural forces to strengthen their hold on terrestrial affairs. What kept the supernatural authority in power was physical force in some form, from crucifixions through the Inquisition, to the Ayatollah's firing squads. Often the authority is grounded in patriotism or racial superiority—again, backed up by the jails, the gallows, and the concentration camps. The thigh-bone of the antelope remains in contemporary disguise. A form of social structure free of compulsion and punishment has often been dreamed of, and may some day be tried, but not one has ever existed long enough to leave its mark on history.

About three hundred years ago in England, philosophers John Locke and Thomas Hobbes began to suggest a better source for political power than divine right or even custom. It came to be called "the social contract." It formed the basis for what we would now call consensual government, and its appeal was so powerful that now there are few societies on earth which do not at least pretend to government by consensus.

The principle of consensual government is set forth clearest in the American Declaration of Independence:

> We hold these truths to be self-evident, that all men are created equal, that they are endowed by their Creator with certain unalienable rights, that among these are life, liberty and the pursuit of happiness. That to secure these rights, governments are instituted among men, deriving their just powers from the consent of the governed.

The appeal to supernatural authority remains, but the operative phrases represent a majestic statement of a revolutionary ideal. It is no derogation of the Declaration of Independence to say that its ideals have not fully been attained even now, much less in 1776. Progress toward any ideal is a process of giving tangible reality to a wishful fantasy. "Men," in its application, did in fact mean only men. Women were not included in any formal sense in the giving of consent. And the word "men" was interpreted quickly enough to mean only *some* men—certainly not, for instance, slaves.

Still, what it says is clear enough: "the consent of the governed" legitimizes all "just" powers of government. From that concept flows all the structure of ballot and legislature, courts and tax-collectors that mark American (and, at least in theory, most other) political systems today. In fact, Aristotle's despised "perversion," democracy, has won the day . . . at least in theory.

Even in theory, consensual democracy presents many problems. Not the least of them is that human beings do not always agree on what is "just," and in many cases they do not choose to accept the consensus.

To provide for these exceptions, within the democratic structure there usually remains some absolute authority to which even the consensus must bow. For the United States it is the Constitution, some kinds of treaties, and the common law. A whole congeries of customs and precedents gives even dissenters a bundle of rights which they can use to meet their special needs, as they perceive them. Because dissenters do not always perceive these measures to be adequate, a whole series of unlegislated and un-planned procedures has come about. One of them, "single-issue politics," has become an increasingly significant part of contemporary American politics. In this situation, legislators frequently give up comprehensive political careers in order to focus all of their attention and expertise on single issues and causes such as prohibiting abortion, or legalizing the possession of firearms.

Even more worrisome (if fortunately far less frequent) are the strate-gies of terrorism, letter-bombs, kidnappings, and hijackings. Terrorism is a relatively minor part of the political process in the United States, at least compared to countries in Europe and the Near East. But to the person who finds himself in a hijacked plane or caught in the blast of a time bomb it is certainly a significant one. And so we have come from the political breaking of an opponent's jaw to the political smashing of an opponent's kneecap, and it has taken only a few million years.

What are the root causes of political violence? In my experience I have found that impatience and mistrust are frequently at the heart of political strife and struggle. Even Aristotle, who was notably uncomfortable with the whole idea of democracy, had no deeper distrust of democratic govern-ment than many people now living in one. And, there is no question that a certain level of cynicism is well justified. For between the high sentiments of most political documents and the low practices of many political leaders there is such a wide gap that it is the nearly universal fashion to view politics as a dirty business, and the people who practice it as a career as not much better than con-men.

Perhaps the worst effect of this cynicism is that it makes itself true. The low esteem in which politics is held deters many people from taking any serious part in it, thus making it all the more difficult for those who do to achieve worthwhile ends.

It seems probable that no nation in the history of the earth has provided so fully for the rights of its citizens to participate in government, to view its inner workings, and to be protected against its excesses. Yet at the same time it seems probable that no government has been more scorned, derided, and distrusted by its citizens—regardless of which party is in power or what individuals hold office. Each of the last four presidents (at least) has been viewed by large segments or even majorities of the citizens as villain, fool, or both. In most recent two-party elections it appears that the actions of the voters are motivated not by the desire to vote for the candidate they prefer, but to vote against the one they most detest. It is not exclusively an American phenomenon. The dominant political mood of the late 20th century is distrust. "They're all crooks," says popular wisdom.

Popular wisdom can cite good evidence for its opinion. Public service remains one of the best ways for a poor boy to get rich. Of the American presidents elected in the past half century, two—Roosevelt and Kennedy—were born to wealth, and two others—Carter and Reagan—acquired money before entering a political career. All of the others—Truman, Eisenhower, Johnson, Nixon, and Ford—started poor, ended rich, and owe it all to politics.

Perhaps it is meet that the republic should reward its chief heroes. But it also rewards hundreds of thousands, even millions, of others, from the township or city election district on up.

A great deal of the profit in politics is plainly illegal, in the form of bribery, extortion, expense-padding, and general graft. Not all. Much is marginal, or even quite safely within the law. Political authority requires decision-making, and there are few decisions to be made that do not produce benefits for some and difficulties for others. All are convertible into cash. Conflict of interest laws do not prevent conflicts of interest. If a town mayor, for instance, also owns a car dealership, the law may make it difficult for him to sell the cars to his town's police force, while if a county supervisor also owns a lumberyard he may not be able to buy building supplies from himself. But if the county buys its cars from the mayor, and the township buys its building supplies from the supervisor, the law remains technically unbroken, and both parties prosper. If a municipality floats a bond issue (and what municipality does not?) an attorney must be appointed to handle the sale. His fee is customarily a percentage of the total amount of the issue, and six-figure payments for a month's work are not uncommon. The attorney who gets this plum is invariably someone with good political connections. If a state builds a highway, someone must select a route and acquire the land. Tens of thousands of individual parcels may be involved, at a cost of hundreds of millions of dollars—and every one of them subject to bargaining, litigation, or bribes. Or simply, again, to "good political connections."

It is not necessary for a politician to seek favors. They are thrust on him as a matter of course—it is how "good political connections" are built. Shortly after my handbook, *Practical Politics*, was published in 1972, some reformers in a small eastern city got hold of a copy, followed its directions, and elected a mayor and majority of the city council in a stunning upset. A little later the new mayor had occasion to seek a mortgage loan from a bank, at a time when mortgage money was tight. "Of *course* you can have the mortgage," said the bank president, ushering the new mayor to a seat. "It is this bank's practice *always* to get along with the mayor." The practice operates at all levels, from top to bottom—I can testify from personal experience as to the bottom, since for a good many years I held the absolute lowest elected office in the United States. I was a county committeeman; the largest number of votes it ever took to put me in office was about thirty and the smallest was two, my own and my wife's. As I was a notorious reformer I was seldom offered any truly illicit perqs, but there were a variety of others, from free tickets to a ballgame to a $1500-a-year no-show job on the local Mosquito Control Commission.* The dollar fallout from the political process is most spectacular at the federal level, where single decisions about locating an army base or a dam can involve many hundreds of millions of dollars. But in the aggregate the amounts siphoned off in local and state decisions probably far exceed even the federal.

Corruption in politics is expected, and therefore tolerated. When a congressman is found guilty of padding the payroll or taking kickbacks he may wind up in jail. If he does not, his constituents as often as not will re-elect him, presumably on the grounds that everybody does it and it was only their boy's bad luck to get caught. To enter a career where it is common wisdom that corruption is the norm takes a certain kind of person—either a crusader, or an ambitious candidate for a little corruption of his own. Only extremes of conscience fit a person for a career in politics. The average person in between, whose conscience discourages him from personal wrongdoing but does not drive him to right the wrongs, prefers to stay away.

There is no doubt that corruption and dishonesty interfere with and diminish the impact of the democratic political process. But even if it were not so, there is still the question of what function this government is supposed to serve. I imagine that we would all prefer to be governed justly by a political structure that truly represents our needs and dreams. Yet, the will of the people is not easily determined. Even when it is evident, it does not always seem a trustworthy guide to action. For example, several years ago a study was performed on popular attitudes toward desegregation, as they changed over time. In one set of communities, opinion strongly opposed racial segregation at first, then a few years later marginally favored it. In another, opinion was strongly opposed in both surveys. The difference between the two was that in the first, the Supreme Court decision had been enforced and desegregation had actually occurred. In the other it had not. The study showed that when events in which people live are altered,

---

* My record is not wholly clean; I accepted one offer. For two weeks I held a patronage job as a urine collector at the local trotting track. It paid more per hour than editing two magazines, which I also did at the same time.

their perspective on those events changes somewhat. In this case the will of the people did not *cause* government action, it was a *consequence* of it.

Nor does the will of the people (if by that is meant the preference of the majority) reliably protect minority rights. Some majorities, e.g., the ancient Romans, clearly did not think that some minorities, e.g., early Christians, had any rights to protect. Others, such as the Aryan Germans of 1933 to 1945, did grant certain rights to the minority population of Jews and Gypsies. Minority property rights, for example, were the subject of so much legal concern, that the expropriation of Jewish property was done with meticulous attention to the forms of law and much taking of inventories and signing of receipts. But there was no parallel concern with such a basic right as being allowed to remain alive. In the United States, as recently as the 1950s, there was little visible majority concern for the rights of Communists.

Even more troublesome, the will of the majority sometimes espouses contradictory, or even impossible goals. Public opinion polls at the end of the 1970s showed a whole set of widely held goals among the American people, including large majorities favoring (1) full employment, (2) tax cuts, (3) an ever-increasing GNP per capita, (4) no inflation, and (5) a strong international dollar, all at the same time, namely right now. Americans also want (6) plenty of gasoline to put in their cars, (7) low prices, and (8) no rationing or other controls; and those too they want right now, before next weekend's drive to visit the grandparents.

So even a democratic government cannot, and surely does not, simply follow the will of the people. To some extent, it must shape that will, as well as abide by it. It must also interpret it when it is obscure, and mediate it when it is contradictory. To make all these things possible, the American Constitution provides for a complicated set of governmental institutions and divisions of power, entrusting the fundamental lawmaking power to the Congress.

The theoretical reasons for that delegation include the proposition that the common citizenry are simply too concerned with their own affairs to become expert on all the myriad concerns of modern government. That seems reasonable enough, although it may be asked whether congressmen do much better. Historically, there were other, more practical reasons. At the time of the framing of the Constitution, travel and communications were difficult and slow. At that time it seemed necessary to entrust major decision making to a small body of men who could assemble in a single place, and stay there until all necessary decisions were reached. Technology, in the form of jet aircraft and the telephone, have made the distances shorter, but at the same time the population has grown immensely. The original Constitution was designed to meet the needs of thirteen scantily populated ex-colonies huddled along one coast. The fifty states of today's U.S.A. stretch across a quarter of the earth's time zones, and from the tropical to the Arctic; they contain close to a quarter of a billion human beings. So we have stayed with delegated authority for more than two centuries.

Perhaps the distances and magnitudes have contributed to the alienation of Americans from the political process. They see their federal legislator only when he returns to check out the grass roots. He hears what his constituents want and then, back in Washington, his vote, submerged in a sea of 99 or 400-odd others, helps to make the law. It is impossible for him to please all his constituents; but in a few months, or at most a few years, those constituents will either return him to office or throw him out of it, in the next election. So he gives lip service to most causes, and action on a few, and the cynicism grows.

Is there any hope for democracy? Is there any real evidence that the will of the people and the consent of the governed are trustworthy guides? Fortunately for all of us, there is. There is the historical record, first of all. Under its rule the United States has survived for more than two centuries, and—though it may still be a long way to Utopia—its people are freer and more prosperous now than they were when the republic was founded.

There has been an occasional wiggle in the curve, but the net trend of two hundred years of American history has been toward an increase in freedom, an expansion of decision making and a general amelioration of individual injustices. The Civil War gave the vote to former slaves, World War I to women, the Vietnam War to eighteen-year-olds. A higher proportion of American citizens now possess the franchise than ever before in history, several times as high as was envisaged by the authors of the Declaration of Independence. The activist Supreme Court of recent memory nailed down the rights of blacks and other minorities to equal opportunity for jobs and education, and the rights of all accused persons to be protected against wrongful police and court procedures. Particularly since Watergate, such measures as the Freedom of Information Act, new limitations on campaign fund raising and spending, financial disclosure laws for federal legislators and executives and a host of other innovations have given the force of law to the citizens' right to know what their government is doing and to prevent abuses.

Another bit of evidence lies in the jury system. Simple citizens, chosen almost at random, are entrusted with complex tasks of evaluation and decision, even with the power of life and death. Trial by jury is not perfect, and mistakes are sometimes made. But by and large American courts are as fair and just as the world has ever seen.

What does the future hold?

It is easy to guess that in America and elsewhere there always looms the possibility of an escalation of repression. Another Great Depression, a war, an increase in urban violence, a wave of crippling strikes, an epidemic of large-scale terrorism—any might lead to counter measures that could extend to full-scale dictatorship.

There is no guarantee that such a scenario will not be acted out, but we can take assurance in the fact that America has survived foreign wars, depressions, two near impeachments and a protracted and devastating Civil War without interrupting the orderly and lawful succession of elected governors. The direction of future evolution seems to me almost certain to be toward more democracy and freedom, rather than less.

Nevertheless, change is in the air. I feel certain that some will occur in the relatively near future—evolutionary changes rather than revolutionary, perhaps, of the order of magnitude, let us say, of some of those that have already occurred, from the direct election of senators to the enfranchisement of women, ex-slaves and under-21s.

The Electoral College, for example, seems to many to be a vestigial organ that should be cut out. In theory it could thwart the will of the voters entirely, since the electors need not vote for the candidates who receive the largest popular votes in their states (although they almost always have). In practice, it has in fact put into the office of the presidency persons who received less than a majority of the popular vote, and even less than a single opposing candidate. A constitutional amendment providing for the direct election of presidents and vice-presidents would ensure that the person who received the most votes would attain the office.

There are schemes, now being explored, for permanent voting registration and for decreasing residency requirements, so that any citizen who wishes to vote will be able to with a minimum of red tape and a maximum of convenience.

Finally, there are any number of measures and proposals for providing codes of ethical behavior for elected and appointed officials at all levels; for requiring full financial disclosure, of the sort now imposed on many top federal officials, at all lower levels of government; and in general for exposing possible wrongdoing to public scrutiny, or even punishment.

All of these have their strong proponents. Some (like the proposal for direct popular election of presidents) seem to have little opposition, except for inertia. I feel that all of them could become law over the near future period, with no doubt considerable benefit to the democratic process.

But these do not exhaust the possibilities of change. Farther in the future, and farther out, are considerably more far-reaching proposals.

For example: Are the units of government too large?

The models of effective participatory democracy are usually held to be the Greek *agora* and the New England Town Meetings. It seems clear that many of the problems of modern government would be at least ameliorated if government were practiced on a smaller scale. B. F. Schumacher argued persuasively that "small is beautiful," and such current political theorists as Karl Hess have suggested dividing the United States into a hundred thousand self-governing "neighborhoods."

One major difficulty with any proposal for reducing the size of governments (or nations) is that it is hard to see how to accomplish it. The traffic seems to go all the other way. Nations which have divided usually do so only under outside pressure—e.g., India-Pakistan, Germany, and Ireland —and even the State of Texas, which has the treaty right to divide itself into five separate states, with five times as many senators to represent it in Washington, has shown no inclination to do so.

There is also the question of whether small is viable. As long as there is a perceived risk of conflict with external adversaries, it seems clear that small countries would be easier to gobble up piecemeal than one super-power like the present U.S.A. (But the counterargument is that conflicts might be less likely: if the U.S.A. were not such a super power it might be less likely to engage in destabilizing adventures like the Vietnam War. Nevertheless, few Americans would seriously consider splitting up the United States unless, as a minimum, the Soviet Union conspicuously and irrevocably did the same, an event which does not seem probable.)

An alternative proposal came from the Center for the Study of Democratic Institutions. In September 1970, after years of deliberation, consultation and revision, Rexford Guy Tugwell, the Center's resident political thinker, produced a model "Constitution for the United Republics of America." Under it, federal powers would be sharply reduced and the present fifty states would disappear, replaced by a loose alliance of "republics," each with a population in the more manageable range of tens of millions rather than the quarter-billion of the present U.S.A. Today, a decade later, there seems no detectable desire on the part of any political leader or group to put the new constitution into practice.

It seems unlikely that any great change in the present physical size or basic constitution of the United States will occur in the next few decades, at least—barring defeat in all-out war, or some other cataclysmic change. But if we cannot reduce the size of the political arena, there may be ways of overcoming some of its worst handicaps.

One such proposal has nothing to do with elections or the usual mechanisms for exercising popular control over government; it has to do with taxation, and with the spending of tax money.

Governments govern as much by spending money as by passing laws. One of the sharpest irritations for many citizens is to see their hard-earned tax money spent on projects they consider iniquitous, or merely silly.

California's Jarvis amendment and the many similar popular initiatives that it spawned are one reaction to undesired government spending, but a crude and imprecise one. More to the point, during the Vietnam War a number of taxpayers calculated the proportion of their income-tax payments which went to support the conflict, and tried to withhold it. If more precise, this was less successful since the IRS took a dim view of their actions, and simply raided their bank accounts.

It is not only war expenditures that divide citizens. Many voters wholeheartedly support, for instance, the space program, while others consider it a shameful diversion of funds from public health, welfare—or their own pockets.

By permitting the deduction of certain kinds of charitable and philanthropic contributions, tax law does recognize a limited right of individuals to decide how tax money should be spent. For every dollar an average taxpayer gives his church, for example, perhaps thirty or forty cents comes out of the public pocket—since he is excused paying a tax on that dollar. He can help support schools, libraries, hospitals, and a few other kinds of public institutions in that way, at his private discretion—in fact many public services, including such essential ones as volunteer fire departments in rural and suburban areas, derive the bulk of their funding from such donations.

But one can conceive of more substantial ways of giving individuals some control over how their tax money is spent.

THE FIVE PERCENT LEVER

Let us suppose that the federal budget were divided into two parts:

1. Mandatory spending: debt service, military costs, contractual obligations like Social Security and pensions, and basic services of all kinds.

2. Optional spending: federal funding for urban redevelopment and highway building; subsidies for agriculture and public transportation; school aid; the space program; support to scientific research; and any other "frills" or special projects.

When Congress passed a budget, the mandatory Category 1 items would be allocated from the general treasury. Allocations of optional Category 2 funds would be enabling rather than committed; expenditures could be made only as funds were available. And the extent to which funds were available could be decided by the taxpayers themselves, on an individual basis.

Each taxpayer would be allowed to earmark any or all of his income tax payments, in $100 units, by paying a five percent surcharge. If his total tax payment in a year is $2000, he can elect to contribute to the optional causes he endorses for any part of it. He might designate $500 for the space program, $400 for basic scientific research, $500 for subsidizing the arts, and $600 for social welfare programs: so that by paying $100, all of his income tax money would go to such causes except for the $100 surcharge itself. He also has the privilege of not paying any surcharge at all, which would mean that his entire $2000 tax payment would go into the general treasury, to be used in conventional ways as Congress decides.

Similar schemes could be applied for state, county, and municipal taxes as well, although the tax base might then be on real estate rather than income, or even (though with more complicated accounting) on sales, gas, liquor, or cigarette taxes.

Experience might show that a five percent surcharge is too little (or too much?) to allow the ordinary taxpayer a proper voice in how his taxes are spent. It is at least possible that so much of the tax receipts would be dedicated to "frills" like science, education, and the arts that not enough would be left to pay for navies and nuclear missiles. It could also be argued that such a result would only mean that the wrong items have been termed "frills."

THE CAFETERIA CREDIT CARD

A related plan is based on the concept, now at issue in some labor negotiations, of what is called the "Cafeteria Fringe Benefit." As proposed in labor contracts, each worker is given a fixed annual amount for fringe benefits, with the privilege of selecting, cafeteria style, which particular fringes he wants: longer vacations, dental insurance, free meals in the company cafeteria, higher pensions, etc. The idea is to respond to individual workers' individual needs. The same proposition could be applied to the payment of taxes.

Particularly on the local level, the variety of "fringe" benefits paid for out of tax funds is immense, from free parks and playgrounds to swimming lessons, ethnic fairs and parades, and open-air concerts. Free libraries, free adult education, free museums and zoos are all, of course, not free at all, except at the point of purchase when the operating expenses are met by tax money. Under the Cafeteria Credit Card plan, each citizen would be given a magnetically imprinted card, resembling the American Express or Diners Club card, good for some arbitrary amount of annual expenditure on "fringe" benefits. His taxes would be applied in part to cover the maximum amount of validity of the card. The "fringe" institutions would be allocated only enough tax money to serve as a start-up fund; to survive, they would need to show use, as each user inserted his card into an appropriate machine each time he entered a zoo or borrowed a library book or attended a free concert, and had an appropriate amount deducted from his allot-ment.

The flexibility of such a plan would permit such fine-tuning as a sucharge for library services at night, or a higher fee for admission to a museum specializing in subjects of very limited popular appeal. Nor need it be limited to the extreme fringe. Mass transit—subways, buses, com-muter trains, etc.—could be financed in the same way, probably thus increasing their use as commuters confronted a choice between paying for a subway ride with the use of tax money already spent or driving a car at an immediate out-of-pocket cost.

Both the Five Per Cent Lever and the Cafeteria Credit Card would return some measure of decision over government spending to the gov-erned, so that "the consent of the governed" could be meaningful in more ways than the authors of the Declaration of Independence ever considered.

Abuses are possible under both schemes, but their importance does not seem significant. A person possessing a Cafeteria Credit Card might wish, for instance, to sell it to someone else, presumably at less than face value; it is hard to see how that would do any harm. The options possible to a taxpayer under the Five Per Cent Lever would surely be diverse, might be confusing, and probably would be susceptible to tampering, as the persons who wrote the enabling legislation attempted to divert funds in deceptive ways; but the same problems exist in even greater form in the present ways of allocating public funds.

More traditional prospects of change lie in the conventional areas of the vote and the choice of policies and of officials to carry them out.

There have been endless proposals for limiting the franchise to the people who really deserve it, and will make proper use of it, from Aristotle to Robert A. Heinlein. Aristotle's criterion was substance, meaning mostly wealth; Heinlein's is service to the nation, meaning usually military. Many others have proposed a licensing test for voters, limiting the vote to persons who can demonstrate that they are capable of using it wisely. But as all such schemes have in practice been used to exclude those whose need for good government seems most acute, that is, the poor and the racial minorities, it is hard to see how they could be made acceptable on moral grounds.

In any case, once again the movement is all in the other direction. It is hard to see how the franchise could be made more extensive than it is, except by giving the vote to anybody who asks for it. But it is possible to extend it in depth, if not in breadth, by giving the voter more direct control.

This is, after all, the age of electronics. There is no technological bar to conducting the work of the Congress, for instance, entirely by means of tele-referenda.

A crude version could be put into operation at almost any time, using off-the-shelf equipment like the telephone system. The way the tele-referenda would work is simple. Large numbers of people from widespread geographical locations would have an opportunity to view a live and hope-fully lively televised discussion or explanation of some relevant and signifi-cant topic. Using the telephone lines, questions could be asked and linked discussions could be facilitated. Then when the viewer-participants felt satisfied that they understood the issues at hand, they could call in their votes which would be immediately tabulated by linked computers. Then the consensus decision would be reached and revealed instantaneously to the viewing audience. This system would be far from satisfactory in many ways, not least that it would easily be tampered with. But it is available. A tamper-proof and universally available system would take a little longer. But no more than a few years. It would require only engineering and funding, not the discovery of any new scientific principle.

In what way would referendum government differ from parliamen-tary?

On the negative side, referenda would be handicapped simply be-cause the questions of modern government are very complex. A small body of paid decision makers (congressmen) can take the time to learn, or can surround themselves with a staff of experts who know enough to make sound decisions. Most people cannot. Or will not. It would be easy for a referendum to enact legislation which is impossible to put into effect, or which might contain the undetected seeds of later disaster. It is far from sure, for example, that the average voter is well enough informed to decide when it is desirable to stimulate the economy by a tax cut and an increase in the federal deficit.

On the positive side of the referendum question, it is also far from sure that the average congressman is well informed. And there is no guarantee that he will vote according to the best national interest in every case, even when he knows what that is. The national interest is seldom the only consideration a legislator must take into account. Each elected legislator comes to office burdened by a weight of obligations. To his party. To contributors and campaign workers. Often to less savory individuals and groups. If he hopes to remain in office past the next election he is even more burdened by the necessity to please his supporters and placate his opponents.

The underlying theory of representative government seems sound enough; it is only, or at least chiefly, in the process of electing the repre-sentatives that abuses occur.

THE SELECTIVE SERVICE CONGRESS

A congress made up of several hundred American citizens, chosen by lot from the entire population, would possess most of the advantages of an elected one. It would lack whatever degree of expertise elections select for, but would be able to co-opt expert advice when needed, just as is done at present. To be sure, it might include willful, corrupt, or stupid members just as is the case with elected legislatures.

We already have a precedent for such a method. It is in the jury system. Jurors are not elected. They are chosen, almost at random, from the citizens at large. There are some exemptions and disqualifications, but it is at least arguable that the exceptions weaken the system, if anything. These jurors are not entrusted with trivial matters, but are required to exercise the awesome powers of liberty or jail, even of life or death, for the persons before them.

We have limited ourselves to discussing changes which could occur almost at once, given the decision to implement them. Some quite interesting prospects lie a little further along the road.

One in particular is based on the model of the New England Town Meeting. Ideally, the town meeting can provide an almost unmatched mix of the factors necessary to good consensual government. Everyone can be heard. The process is interactive. Horse-trading can take place—"We'll take the sanitary land-fill in our neighborhood, if you'll put the power plant over in yours." Impacts can be assessed, injustices brought to light, and compromises offered in real time. It has one substantial drawback. It works best when the community is small. And few communities are small any more.

But the electronic age offers remedies for most communications problems, if a way can be found to apply them. The way that seems feasible to me is

THE UNIVERSAL TOWN MEETING

Let us imagine a large community faced with serious crises—loss of tax base, strikes, inability to meet obligations, or a combination of all of these, perhaps with others added. (Examples of such communities are not hard to find.) The situation has perhaps existed for some time, and the conventional procedures of government have failed to solve it; or perhaps the situation evolved abruptly and unexpectedly, and there is simply no time to find adequate solutions.

The Universal Town Meeting begins with a regular City Council meeting—one which every citizen of the area, perhaps millions or tens of millions of them, is enabled to attend through the electronic media. Television cameras are brought into the Council chamber. All of the major television stations are drafted into service to broadcast the Council in session. For non-English-speaking residents, radio stations offer simultaneous translation into other languages; you turn on your TV, but turn the sound down, and tune your radio to the proper station for Spanish, Yiddish, French, Polish, or whatever is appropriate to the particular community. Selected public buildings are opened—schools, community centers, perhaps churches—and mobile camera crews are sent to them. After opening statements to explain the problem (perhaps repeated from time to time on one of the stations, for the benefit of people who tune in late), each member of the Council is allowed a very short time—perhaps one minute—to say what he thinks should be done and why. Then the comments of the voters are invited. For persons gathered where TV facilities exist, they can be on camera. For others, they can pick up the phone.

Of course, not everyone can be heard. Access to the broadcast is by lot, perhaps by computer-determined random selection. No one can speak for more than one minute; he is automatically cut off at that time. No attempt is made to secure "spokesmen" representing particular interests. Your automobile repairman has as good a chance of being heard as the president of your Chamber of Commerce.

Since problems seldom occur singly, perhaps the meeting will divide itself into several groups—one concerned about the strikes, one about the need for social services, one about taxes. Individual television stations are assigned to each area of interest. Those persons especially concerned with that issue will switch to that station. Those with more general interests will switch from station to station, or follow the general debate in the Council. After a reasonable period of discussion perhaps some sort of consensus will become apparent, or at least the questions may be sufficiently sharpened so that a decision can be sought. Then it is time for a vote.

Everyone involved, in the Council room, in the public meeting places, or at home, can vote simply by picking up a phone and dialing a number. No one will answer; but a counter, of the sort already available from the telephone company, will register the number of calls. Those in favor will call one number, those opposed another. In a matter of minutes a sounding will be obtained. If it is ambiguous or marginal—say, 47% voting one way, 53% another—that may indicate a need for more discussion. But if the margin is substantial, a consensus may in fact have been reached. The telephone count would not have the force of law, but if it were sizable enough the Council members would then enact whatever policy had been decided upon.

The procedures outlined above are rough and ready, and a good many refinements are possible and even essential to make the Universal Town Meeting effective. But, in theory at least, such an electronic assembly could take place in quite a short time. Most of the hardware exists, or could be put together in a matter of days or weeks, rather than years. The software—the social environment that would allow it to take place—probably would take considerably longer.

As we move toward the 21st century, I find myself feeling that the most appropriate political system for this "new age" is still democracy for within it lies the power of the people to decide their futures. The social compact that derives governmental authority from the consent of the governed has the appearance of being a fragile thing, always under attack, seldom working as most people would desire it, never realizing its ideal goals. But, here in the United States as well as in much of the Western world, the democratic structure has shown itself durable under great stress. And, although there are still many weak and distorted characteristics of this approach to government, it is a system capable of self-examination, renegotiation, and change. Richard Nixon did not maintain himself in power by imposing martial law. Though many Presidents have been called tyrants, none has ever failed to take his departure when the voters commanded it.

In fact, the extraordinary thing about a political democracy is that it nearly always reflects the mood and consciousness of its populace. The late Huey Long once said that if fascism ever came to America, it would appear under the guise of anti-fascism. It even seems possible that if the American people should ever lose their ultimate control over the levers of power in government, it will only be because, with due regard to constitutional procedures, they have chosen to vote their powers away.

As I attempt to glimpse the future, I am hopeful, for I do feel that the American political system will continue to evolve and develop in response to the needs and visions of its people. And while this system is still encumbered with holes and knots, I feel certain that we have the tools and the compassion to smooth and sort them out while simultaneously designing new political forms and practices to meet the emerging "new" human of the 21st century.

With the publication of The End of Medicine *in 1975, Rick Carlson became the* enfant terrible *of the health-care world. In this highly controversial work, Carlson proposed that medicine actually had little to do with health care. In the five years since its publication he has probed more deeply into health care and social policy and has become one of the nation's foremost proponents of preventive health care and alternative approaches to health delivery.*

Rick Carlson's interest and involvement were not always pointed in the direction of health futures. Fresh out of law school in the 1960s, he became actively involved in civic and community affairs, serving as chairman of the Law and Justice Task Force of the Urban Coalition as well as director of the Legal Advice clinics in his hometown, Minneapolis. Carlson's interest in law and community welfare led him into the area of social policy and health care.

Carlson was awarded a position as visiting fellow at the Center for Democratic Institutions in Santa Barbara, California, where he devoted much of his time to an in-depth analysis of worldwide health, with particular attention to the possibilities for improving the methods, forms of delivery, and economics of health care in the coming decades. The End of Medicine was completed and published during this period.

Since that time, nearly all of Carlson's critiques and proposals have attracted national attention while his advice and counsel have been sought by such organizations as the Rockefeller Foundation, the National Academy of Sciences, the World Health Organization, Blue Cross, and Blue Shield, as well as the School of Medicine at the University of San Francisco and the Institute of Medicine, where Carlson has held positions.

He is presently at work on a new book titled The Future of the Institutions of Health. *While serving as director of the Health Resource Group in Mill Valley, California, he recently had the honor of being named chairman of the California Commission on Wellness.*

In this chapter on the future of health care Carlson traces the evolution of our understanding of health and sickness, with particular reference to the critical economic and political decisions made during the periods when our present health-care system was being determined. In addition, he speculates on new treatment methods and technologies of the future and the ways in which these may be delivered more effectively than those that are now in use.

RICK CARLSON

HEALTH CARE

PART I: HISTORY AND THE POLITICS OF MEDICINE

There are a few central concepts which characterize our society's thinking about its health. Moderation, optimal performance, happiness, naturalness, social functioning, recovery and convalescence, equity, and wholeness are ideas that have always formed the basis of the approach Western societies have fashioned to improve their health and well-being.

In the early 1800s memories of the plagues were not far distant. Population size was steadily increasing and the food supply was improving in both quantity and quality. Infectious diseases were the major killers, but their rates had already begun the slow decline which continued into this century. There was a medicine, more systematic than much of its shamanistic roots, but still lacking a sound method of inquiry, a means of linking cause and effect. Medical practice was largely an art, incorporating techniques and procedures for which evidence of efficacy was lacking. Traditional religious beliefs were strong, and primarily Judeo-Christian in nature. The "responsibility" for health was largely placed outside of the individual; it rested in the nature of the relationship between the person and God and was seen to be more dependent on God's beneficence than human agency.

In the decades to follow, two critical developments emerged which dramatically altered the nature of health care. First, the scientific method evolved. Its application to the practice of medicine transformed the idiosyncracies of practice into a more systematic method. Second, public health programs were initiated precisely because causal relationships could now finally be perceived between environmental factors (such as water quality, sewage, and filth) and the health of those exposed to them. These two developments constituted a quantum leap forward toward the medicine of today.

Prior to 1900, the major killers were infectious diseases, which were occasionally pandemic in nature. In the United States, the age of the great epidemics—cholera, yellow fever, and smallpox—extended roughly from 1800 to 1870, coinciding with the period of rapidly increasing industrialization and urbanization. This period brought a variety of woes— overcrowding, debilitated housing conditions, polluted water supplies, contaminated food and milk, poor nutrition, bad air, execrable or nonexistent sanitary systems, and long hours of overwork. These conditions dissipated the strength of the individual (or host) and left the population vulnerable to a broader range of infectious diseases—pulmonary tuberculosis, diarrheal diseases of infancy, bacillary dysentery, typhoid fever, and the infectious diseases of childhood, particularly scarlet fever, diphtheria, and lobar pneumonia.

The major health gains in Europe and in the United States prior to the twentieth century stemmed from an improvement in nutrition, limitation on births, and sanitary reforms. Largely because of these factors, despite the lack of effective therapies, the great epidemics were on the wane by the 1870s and the tuberculosis death rate had begun a steady decline. Then, by the turn of the twentieth century, bacteriological research and recent medical discoveries had begun to have an impact as they were applied through public health programs. Through these discoveries, which focused on attacking the agents of disease rather than on strengthening the host population, most infectious diseases (with the exception of some respiratory viral illnesses) today are either under effective control or at least have been offset by biochemical one-upmanship. But new health problems have arisen that Rene Dubos and others have labeled "the afflictions of civilization": stress and illnesses associated with stress (such as heart disease, arthritis, cancer, diabetes, and respiratory disorders); degraded environmental conditions, including noise and other environmental contaminants; and lack of sufficient exercise and rest, smoking, overindulgence in foods, and many other poor health habits that are related to the onset of disease. These new problems may be the result of rapidly changing psychosocial and ecological patterns, and the techniques currently available to medicine may not be effective treatments for them.

These new health problems share the following characteristics:

1. They are often the consequence of multiple stresses, many of which have yet to be identified. Although these stressors and biosocial antagonists are difficult to isolate and study, there is growing agreement that collectively they represent a great threat to the body's capacity to adapt to new information and stimuli.

2. These new health problems may result from failure to improve or even to maintain host strength due to such environmental stresses

and to debilitating practices, including lack of exercise, poor dietary habits, and overconsumption of toxins, either voluntarily or involuntarily (as in the case of smoke produced by industrial or individual polluters).

3. Finally, they may also stem from a degraded psychosocial environment—the disintegration, or at least the weakening, of major social support systems, including the family, the church, and the neighborhood, all of which once buttressed host strength but now may vitiate it.

From these three points we can conclude, first, that many of the major health problems of today may be more amenable to prevention than in the past, not only because prevention may be more cost-effective, but because our understanding of the factors that predispose an individual to illness or injury is clearer than in the past. Secondly, many of these same health problems can be more effectively controlled by measures focused on populations rather than on individuals. Thirdly, any approach to the control of the major health problems we experience today (whatever the relative emphasis on prevention or treatment, population or patient) will depend on the capacity of individuals to live more healthy lives.

This course of development has resulted from certain fundamental choices as characterized in the simple schematic shown in Figure 1.

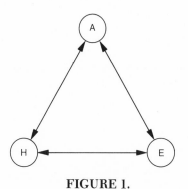

FIGURE 1.

The letter *A* represents the *agents* of disease, the target of therapeutic medicine; the *H* represents the *human host;* and the *E* represents the *environment.* As I have stated, the principal gains in health, prior to the beginning of the century, were achieved principally through improving the environment while strengthening the host, through public health measures and improvements in the quality and amount of food.[1]

Yet at the same time, therapeutic medicine was gaining ascendence because of the availability of the scientific method, which made it possible to draw causal relationships between therapeutic interventions and their outcome. As the number of medical practitioners increased, medicine gained political and economic strength. The Flexner report, issued in 1910, led to near monopolistic control by allopathic practitioners over the institutions of health.[2] For these reasons, as a society we chose to emphasize the identification and management of the agents of disease over equally plausible choices that might have been made. If improved health levels were the objective, then programs designed to improve the quality of the environment and the capacity of the human host to withstand the onslaught of disease could have accomplished the same end. The decision to allocate resources almost exclusively for a medical care delivery system focused on the agents of disease was made far more for political, social, and economic reasons than therapeutic ones.

The impact of that choice has been significant. We have gained considerable information about human biology, and we have learned much about sickness in the human animal and the means of treating and curing those sicknesses and the underlying diseases. Nonetheless, we are presently poised for a fundamental change in perspective, one which may restore the influence of social, environmental, and behavioral factors to the prominent position in public policy that their relationship to health has always demanded.

THE POLITICS OF CHANGE

It is generally assumed that modern medicine exists because it improves human health and that the approach we have chosen to improve our health reflects rational and scientific factors. But this is not the case. Modern medicine gestated in a social, political and economic environment, not a therapeutic and scientific one. It survives for the same reasons. We must be constantly reminded that there are *many* routes to improving health and *many* different types of medicine. The type of medicine that we have may be the only one that could have evolved, given the economic, social, and political conditions that prevailed at its birth and during its infancy. (It is conceivable that we could have some other system of medicine based on a different theory of health and healing.) But it is highly unlikely that the delivery system that has evolved, irrespective of the methods of the medicine it embodies, could have been much different. Our medical care delivery system is geared to the requirements of our political economy in the same way that the steel industry is. There is a product—medical care services—suppliers, and the accompanying R&D to generate new products, financing mechanisms to provide adequate capital and sufficient cash flow, marketing through insurance companies, and more than sufficient profits to keep things humming. The penetration the system has achieved in our economy, and its contribution to the viability of the economy as a whole, makes it doubtful that it will yield any of its formidable power, without the very nature of our economy first being transformed.

Another reason for the persistence of the medical care system lies in the quasi-religious nature of modern medicine, which was underscored by Jerome Frank, professor emeritus of psychiatry at Johns Hopkins Medical School and author of the classic book *Persuasion and Healing*.[3] In his commencement address to the graduating class at the Johns Hopkins Medical School in 1977, he compared the Hopkins Medical School and related health institutions to the Church, with the professors of medicine as its priests, students as acolytes, and the cathedral-like buildings at Johns Hopkins as its churches, abbeys, and monasteries. It was not an overstatement. And like the Church, the medical system has demonstrated firm resistance to innovation and change. Thus there are many reasons for the existence of the modern medical care system that have little to do with its therapeutic efficacy and whatever impact it may have on improving human health. This doesn't mean that change in our medical system is impossible, or even unlikely, but it does mean that we must recognize the realities involved in attempting such change.

The politics of health and medicine today have given rise to such issues as cost escalations, malpractice, waste and inefficiencies, cost-effectiveness, national health insurance, and environmental pollution. These are important issues, yet they are not likely to have much impact on the evolution of the institutions of health. At best they are forcing events, necessary but far from sufficient ground conditions for change. Their seeming insolubility creates an openness to change that might not exist in less critical times.

The institutions of health, however, will not change in isolation. In recent years, a substantial literature has emerged, focusing on a cultural transformation which many believe to be occurring in our society. George Leonard, Jonas Salk, and Theodore Roszak all argue that we are living through the last stages of the materialistic world view.[4] The values associated with material growth and technological progress are said to be yielding to more humanistic values and a less materialistic orientation. This is relevant to medical practice for the simple reason that medicine is rooted in an approach to health that perceives the patient in materialistic and mechanistic terms. In part this is so because any medicine that engaged the manifold realities of the patient would be paralyzed by information overload and would be very difficult to integrate into a delivery system. Still, the view of the human that animates medical practice and health institutions is a very limited one, securely anchored in a mechanistic metaphor.

Nevertheless, if materialistic realities yield to a more humanistic, spiritual reality, all human institutions—those dealing with health included—will necessarily change.

The Philosophy of Limits: Appropriate Technology

As natural resources are perceived to be finite, and as the negative consequences of unlimited growth and development become more apparent, a movement has emerged proposing "limits" to growth.[5] This perspective takes two forms. The first insists future technological development be carefully scrutinized because in an increasing number of instances the costs of growth exceed the benefits. It allows, however, that sustained growth may have some advantage and lead to a sector-by-sector examination of an institution. The second form is more extreme. It argues that further growth is unacceptable because we are fast approaching or have already reached that point at which destruction of the ecosphere is irreversible or near to irreversible.[6]

The limits-to-growth movement is closely related to another recent cultural trend: the appropriate, or intermediate, technology movement. Throughout the world groups have sprung up urging the development of more appropriate technologies to supplant those which are thought to be most damaging to the biological basis of life. The movement is most active in the United States and in the United Kingdom, where it originated in the now-classic work of E. F. Schumacher, principally his seminal work, *Small is Beautiful* (Harper & Row, 1976). This movement argues for technology that is "small, simple, capital saving, non-violent to people and to the environment." It is also often but not necessarily labor intensive.

These companion movements necessarily influence our thinking about health. Medicine is so integral to our culture and so much a creature of the technology that our society has spawned, that it cannot escape the analysis these movements offer.[7] Today, the argument that there are limits to future growth in the medical care sector is generally accepted. What those limits should be is far less clear, but most conscientious observers of health and medical issues agree that further gains in human health in the United States are likely to be far more dependent on programs focused on the behavioral and environmental aspects of health than on further elaboration of the medical care system.

Holistic Thinking

One of the most maligned words in our language today is the term *holistic*. First coined by Jan Smuts, a South African statesman-philosopher, in 1926, in *Holism and Evolution* (Macmillan, 1926), the term has come to be applied to almost every aspect of human behavior. Holistic thinking in its original and fullest sense is an antidote to the reductionism that underlies modern scientific thought. To Smuts and others, "reductionist" thinking resulted in an analysis of the parts of a system without considering how those parts interact in larger systems and without acknowledging phenomena that represent more than the sum of any set of parts.

In recent years, the word *holistic* has begun to be applied frequently in the health sector. This isn't surprising. The practice of modern medicine is a case of reductionism run wild. Although it is hardly an assault on human sensibility to examine the chemical constituents of a substance one at a time, to many thinking and feeling people it limits and impoverishes our medical care to assume that health is nothing more than the composite of well-oiled body parts. In this sense, the application of the term *holism* to medicine is more than timely—it is profound.

Reductionist thinking results in the compartmentalization of the human being and human experience into those aspects that are amenable to detailed analysis and intervention—a profoundly limited view of the human animal. Holistic thinking requires that the human being be perceived as a whole person made up of physiological, emotional, intellectual, and spiritual dimensions that dynamically interact. A holistic approach to improving the health of human beings, either as individuals or in groups, requires placing them in a larger and richer context than medicine typically assigns. As such, this shift towards holism is irreversible, because it is part of a much larger change in perspective about who and what the human animal is.

The Placebo and the Self-healing Patient

As medicine has evolved, it has emphasized those therapeutic interventions that are specific to the problem diagnosed. Whenever possible, its mission has been to match a health problem with a specific treatment, i.e. penicillin for syphillis, aspirin for headaches, and ritalin for childhood hyperactivity. The therapeutic results it achieves are then believed to be associated with the specificity of the treatment; the more specific the treatment, the greater the likelihood of a cure or remission. The nearly exclusive focus in any medical practice is on the *specifics* of treatment and cure. Whenever a nonspecific factor appears to be related to patient outcome, it is either ignored, given passing mention, or referred to as a placebo. In the next few decades, the real task of biomedical science should be the identification and understanding of the dynamics of the nonspecific.

It may be that most real healing is the consequence of such factors. It has been said that prior to the availability of the sulfa drugs in the 1920s and the antibiotics in the 1930s, the history of medicine was the history of the placebo. This may be the future of medicine as well.

Medicine fails to heal when its practitioners (1) believe they lack the therapeutic tools, as in the case of a terminally ill cancer patient; (2) fail to engage nonspecific factors (i.e., the patient's family) in the healing process; (3) fail to mobilize the patient as a participant in the therapeutic process; and (4) undermine an otherwise specific and efficacious treatment by their failure to deal with the patient as a whole human being. We are *all* creatures of myth, superstition, belief, and ritual. We are very often ill for reasons that can never be eradicated by surgery nor stilled by a drug. Recent work in biofeedback shows that sophistication of the equipment notwithstanding, the single most important factor in patient outcome is who is in the room with the patient—how does the technician, with the machine along for the ride, "connect" with the patient? Many nurses have known this for a long time, and even a few physicians appreciate it. Then, too, there is the question of whether the patient is active or passive. Drs. Carl and Stephanie Simontons' work with cancer patients, reported in *Getting Well Again* (J. P. Tarcher, 1978) and elsewhere demonstrates the importance of the motivation and participation of the patient. Individuals possess degrees of self-regulation that have been only superficially explored. In one recent study, as an illustration, a number of persons' death dates were compared to their birth dates. It was found that a disproportionate number of elderly people die within the three-month period following their birthdays as against a much smaller number of people who die during the three-month period prior to their birthdays.

The self-regulatory capacity of the human organism is imperfectly understood. The fast-growing biofeedback literature is evidence of the promise of self-regulation. Future biomedical research agenda must place self-regulation high on the list. This doesn't mean that practitioners are unneeded. Far from it. But as the humanistic medicine movement has valiantly sought to say, it's the quality of the person in the room with the patient that makes the difference, not the tool or the technique, however useful it may be as well.

The Modern Hospital

Today's hospital is designed to process bodies; the fact they are alive is almost incidental. Everything is designed to train the specific intervention on the target. Schedules are arranged, floor plans laid out, support systems arrayed, personnel indoctrinated, everything put into place to optimize the delivery of a specific curative service. Little or no attention is paid to the context in which the cure is to be effected. Family and community are largely excluded. Belief systems are ignored save the obligatory visit of a chaplain; food, exercise, recreational needs, and preferences are ignored. Habits and patterns of living are ruthlessly compressed into the routines of the institution. The subtleties of color, light, furnishings, plants, air, sunlight, space, sounds, and rhythms are considered incidental at best, and yet many of these are the very factors that animals integrate into their healing practices. People in other cultures, even our own in times past, have stressed these factors. Yet today, they are all relegated to the category of the nonspecific, or are simply dismissed as unrelated. The typical hospital environment reflects a cramped, crabbed, narrow view of the richness of human experience. At the same time, it strips the individual of the contexts within which self-regulation, motivation, and self-healing might flourish. It doesn't even grant the human being the dignity and consideration accorded to a house plant. If the question as to who is in the room is important, if the nature of the room itself is critical, today's hospital is the least likely place to experience self-regulation and healing.

THE FUTURE—HEALTH PROMOTION, WELLNESS, AND THE SUPER HEALTHY

A little over thirty years ago, the National Institutes of Health (NIH) were conceived. Before that time, there was very little systematic information about disease and the sick person. In the decades to follow, the research conducted by and for NIH resulted in an impressive body of knowledge about human biology, in particular, states of disease in the human animal. Indeed, much of the practice of modern medicine is based upon the biomedical research conducted by NIH. Yet neither the practice of medical care nor the research agendas of NIH have included a study of the healthy person. Consequently we lack systematic information about healthy people and hence interest in and enthusiasm about health promotion programs. Any review of the literature, either scholarly or popular, over the last ten years or so would quickly reveal that the programs related to health promotion, and indeed the terms themselves—health promotion, wellness, well-being, and so on—are rarely to be found in the literature prior to the last couple of years. It is not surprising that interest in health promotion has arisen, especially as the limits of medicine are perceived. What is surprising is that all of this interest is being generated without any kind of a theoretical basis upon which those programs might be grounded.

The trend towards health promotion as opposed to disease control seems irreversible. For decades, we have focused on the unique biochemical reactions of the human organism to its environment. A small but hardy band of people have sought to impress upon the medical community the importance of gaining a greater understanding of the nature of stressors and the unique means by which some people react to stress. Previously, medicine looked only at those people who react to stress by breaking down physically in some way that could be diagnosed as a disease and who in turn could be treated with some curative intervention designed to repair the breakdown. Yet we are learning the obvious fact that not everybody breaks down due to the impact of stress. Indeed, different people break down in different ways, and the same person may not break down the same way each time. It is essential to launch research efforts designed to identify the healthy, develop profiles of them, and then to ask further questions related to the nature of the environments that nurtured them. These inquiries should lead to a coherent theoretical framework about health and generate a systematic body of research upon which health promotion, wellness, and holistic approaches to health programs can be based. Moreover, new mandates for public health can be created through examination of those environments in which healthy people evolved. There already have been some small but significant steps in this direction. A branch for behavioral medicine has been created within the National Institutes of Health, an event that probably couldn't have occurred four or five years ago. Moreover, NIH appears to be more interested in the role of nutrition in human health than it has ever been. These are small changes, but they reflect the larger changes that are occurring. It would not be a surprise if in fifteen or twenty years from now, the National Institutes of Health actually pursued a research program focused on health rather than disease.

The Dialectics of Change

It is impossible to discuss the future as if all trends presently appearing were consistent with one another—they are not. Yet most of the propositions offered thus far reflect a coherent world view. Taken together, they augur a certain kind of future, one characterized by deeper human values, a more humanistic perspective, the continuing ascendancy of holistic thinking, less emphasis on specific therapeutics and excessive professionalism, with a concomitant assumption of more responsibility by persons for their own health—all this taking place within a sounder ecological understanding of ourselves and our environment. There are, however, other trends and ideas that suggest an alternative future. These crosscurrents deserve full treatment, but given the limitations of this paper they can only be mentioned here.

The Serviced Society

As new technologies and automation have steadily reduced the number of jobs available in manufacturing, industrial development has slowed and the services sector of our economy has expanded. Our nation's dependency upon a high rate of employment for economic health has fueled a surge of growth in the services economy, which by its nature is more job-creating and sustaining than manufacturing. As a result of these macroeconomic reasons, our society "requires" a large and growing services sector, of which medical care and the institutions of health are a large part. In addition, the government is active in supporting the growth of the services economy. In order to stimulate consumers to "need" services, medical care included, demand has had to be democratized. Not only do consumers have to be convinced that gall bladder surgery in Poughkeepsie is virtually the same as in Tucson; the consumer's capacity and willingness to pay must be encouraged, given the extraordinarily high costs of medicine. That is why public education is public, why most social services are free, and why the government now pays for nearly half of all medical care services and will soon pay for nearly all of them. From the point of view of the economy as a whole, if government did not pay for many of the human services, medicine included, people wouldn't buy them in sufficient quantity on their own. As a result, too few jobs would be created to sustain the growth of our economy. To avoid this situation, demand is "created" by enhancing the consumer's ability to pay and by marketing services as consumer goods through hospitals' public relations departments. Consequently, as the population grows and automation continues to eliminate jobs, the demand for services will necessarily have to increase. This analysis applies to medical-care services even more than to any of the other human services, which suggests that the future may well belong to illness. A serviced society does not encourage self-responsibility, nor the development and implementation of programs designed to improve the environment, unless these initiatives guarantee as many jobs as the orientation they are challenging. In short, a "serviced society" demands illness, need, and dependence.

The Corporation and Human Services   Many employers have begun to perceive that perhaps the largest outflow of resources is for medical care. Yet at the same time, industry lacks the means to influence its level of expenditure. As a result, corporations recently have become interested in cost containment and health promotion programs, ostensibly to reduce their medical-care cost burden. The fact that very little evidence exists that health promotion programs have that effect is proving to be no deterrent. Many companies are developing health promotion programs and still many more are extremely interested in doing so, as noted in the lead article in the September 1979 issue of *Business Week* describing the programs of many large corporations. Moreover, the federal Office of Health Information and Health Promotion sponsored a conference in January of 1979 bringing together a number of corporate executives to discuss corporate health promotion programs. This event simply would not have occurred a few years ago.

Given the corporations' historical interest in education and the welfare of employees and their families and their current interest in health, the corporation may become the prime deliverer of human services within the next twenty years. The public is becoming increasingly disenchanted with public solutions to critical human needs. And it is unlikely that the other option—more individual responsibility—will be much accelerated even in the neoconservative mood of this country. Under these circumstances, the corporation—now directly influencing the lives of well over half of the members of our society—may be the only alternative left. This does not mean that government will step out of the picture; rather, it will continue to raise revenue and to pay for most if not all human services, though delivery units may soon come under corporate control.

What are the implications of the corporations assuming the responsibility for the human services? Very little attention has been given to the subject, but all of these developments raise a number of intriguing questions. For example, would industry emphasize promotion and self-responsibility to the derogation of the practice of medicine? Is it likely that industry would emphasize self-responsibility and continue the provisional medical care services as a means of avoiding the examination of its own responsibility for the quality of our environment and safety in the workplace? These questions and many others need to be answered. In general, however, it might be said that given past and current corporate behavior, it is unlikely the future of the institutions of health will be the obvious choice as a humanistic/holistic orientation.

A Scenario for the Future

Crosscurrents and contradictions notwithstanding, here is my ideal scenario for the millennium:

By the year 2000 there will still be a medical care system, but it will be smaller than at present. It will also be more of a "health" system and will consume relatively fewer resources. The system will be organized around three types of institutions. The first is the neighborhood community center with a hospital, learning center, and emergency care facilities. The hospital will feature a large outpatient department for ambulatory care and a resource center for general use by providers and consumers alike. The learning center will offer classes and seminars in health and provide outreach services as well. Up-to-date health information will be available, as well as free consultations with trained personnel on health and treatment problems. All neighborhood centers, including hospital facilities, will be community owned and managed. The emphasis will be on learning. Further, admissions to the hospital will be made only on a voluntary basis and hospital admitting privileges will not be limited to the professional personnel.

The second key facility is the regional health center. More costly and sophisticated treatment will be provided here and only on an inpatient basis. Referrals will be made to the regional center from the neighborhood facilities.

Residential complexes for the elderly will be the third type of facility. These facilities will stress self-care and responsibility but will provide all necessary medical care on site. Health care personnel in 2000 will no longer be rigidly stratified by training levels. Rather, teams will replace the solo physician. All teams will be based in the community centers, although they will be deployed in emergency situations. There will be no independent office practice; all practitioners, however trained or with whatever skills, will practice in hospital or home settings. The personnel engaged in health care will differ greatly in social, education, and demographic terms from those now dominating the profession. Most will be trained in health or human ecology; a few will be trained as physicians are now trained. Most training will be experimental, although the need for didactic teaching will remain. No qualifications for admission to training will be imposed, but completion of training will not ensure placement with a hospital. The Departments of Health Affairs will monitor the environment and intervene when appropriate. The departments will work closely with agencies providing biomedical research support. This research accordingly will be refocused on social and environmental factors related to health, although basic biomedical research will remain.

At the local level, citizens will control their own health care systems through the neighborhood center. Each community will be given the necessary resources to design and implement health programs, subject only to broad specifications. Each citizen will have access to those drugs and tools of care necessary for treatment. Tools too costly to deploy at the local level, or drugs for which citizens have not been given sufficient information, will be available at the regional health center. Health care will be federally underwritten but largely on a bloc grant basis. Grants will also be made available for experimental projects on either a local or regional basis. Participation by healers and patients will be voluntary.

The Future as Synthesis

We have approached the achievement of health in this century as if it were a simple function of physical-chemical manipulation. We have made use of targeted interventions and viewed the environment as a set of properties—an attitude that rationalizes the interventions we choose to make. This impoverished view of health and healing is a correlate of an impoverished view of the human being. A new framework for the pursuit of health depends on the view of the human that is at least as rich, textural, and idiosyncratic as is our experience. Such a view will not only demonstrate the insufficiency of our current understanding, but will also compel a thorough reexamination of our current social responses. Our response thus far has focused almost exclusively on the extirpation of the physical manifestations of an individual's response to his or her environment—viewed in largely static and monochromatic terms. Future approaches to the achievement of health *must* instead focus on the nature of the host's *response* to the inevitable stresses and strains of modern living. In addition, it is imperative that we explore and examine methods, contexts, and environments that facilitate the promotion and enhancement of optimal health and that this preventive approach to health care be included within the framework of a future health care system.

At all events, business as usual is likely to continue. I do believe, however, that the trends I have discussed here toward new, more positive and comprehensive approaches to health will continue to evolve alongside the present allopathic medical system. The larger context of cultural assumptions is changing today, perhaps more rapidly than at any time in our recent history. It is this larger change that shapes the future. Politics, economics, and related considerations will always be with us and will influence the future institutions of health. But political and economic considerations are themselves subject to reformulation as our notions of who we are and what our role is on this planet change. As they change, the future institutions of health will follow.

Born in Buenos Aires, Argentina in 1930, Livio Vinardi is a Renaissance man: In addition to receiving his doctorate in physics and going on to become an internationally known physicist, inventor, and electronic engineer, Dr. Vinardi has developed a broad reputation as an artist and concert pianist.

Throughout his life he has been deeply interested in ways to probe and release human potential; although much of his work has been directed toward the physical sciences, his focus has always been markedly human-centered. After traditional academic training, Livio Vinardi felt that there was still much for him to learn about himself, his work, his art, and the world in which he lived. Finding that the more conservative scholastic approaches did not meet his needs, he turned to the mystical sciences and became a serious student of the work of Jorge Gurdjieff. After many years, his skill in the mental and physical disciplines of this school of spiritual development evolved to a level that earned Dr. Vinardi recognition as a Sufi master. Vinardi feels that this inner development has helped provide the crucial link between his studies in physics and his intuitive experience as an artist.

At present, Livio Vinardi spends his time performing music, instructing students in the mystical sciences, and researching and inventing equipment related to the study of human bio-energies. He is the founder of the Argentinian Institute for Bio-Psycho-Energetics, an honorary member of the Academy of Interdisciplinary Studies in Brazil, and vice–president of the International Yoga Teachers Association. In his teachings, his art, and his writings, he consistently works to blend his understanding of mathematics and physics with the creative, mystical aspects of music and art.

In this chapter on the future of art, Dr. Livio Vinardi speculates on the nature of meaning in art and offers a variety of lively hypotheses regarding the way in which art may be transformed in the decades to come.

LIVIO VINARDI **ART AND THE FOUR FACES OF KNOWLEDGE**

Even a tentative sketch of the future scenarios of art needs to be set within the larger perspective of history. Art, as it is commonly understood, is the total of the myriad manifestations of human creativity—visual art, design, performance art, literature, and music, taken as a whole. Art can also be appreciated from another perspective, as one of the four branches of human knowledge—along with science, religion, and philosophy—which together form what we call absolute knowledge or the wisdom of human nature. From each one of these four great forms are derived many sub-branches. The triangle graphically symbolizes the four great forms of knowledge (see Figure 1). In each apex is a synthesis of knowledge becoming fractioned as it moves to the respective bases.

From this point of view we can see a clear distinction between Art and the arts, Science and the sciences, Religion and the religions, and Philosophy and the philosophies. Throughout the course of history and within the context of different cultures, unique individuals have attempted to climb to these summits. The artist searches for the Ideal, the scientist for Truth, the religious scholar for God, the philosopher for the Whole.

But are we dealing with separate and independent areas of knowledge? A cursory examination might make it appear so, especially in view of the trend toward specialization that has characterized the last few centuries. A different, more unified perspective shows us all four forms of knowledge as component parts of a structure that is dimensionally superior and integrated symbolically at the apex of the pyramid (see Figure 2). This

241

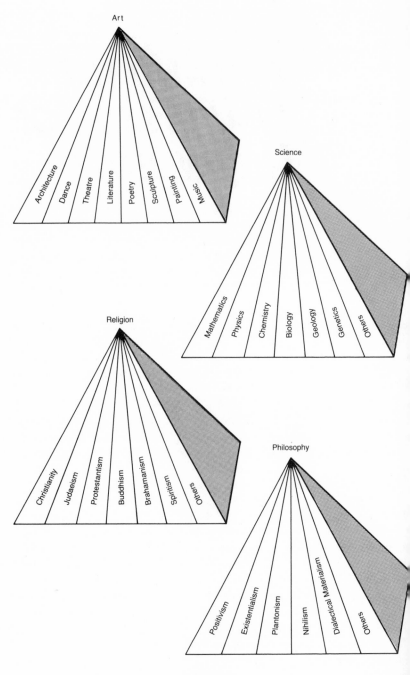

FIGURE 1.

representation has been widely used throughout history from the Egyptian to the American cultures to indicate such an integration of knowledge.

The unified viewpoint sees each lateral face of the pyramid as one form of knowledge that can be integrated to form a single body of knowledge. This unified viewpoint goes beyond the simpler geometry of separate planes into a spacial geometry involving multiple dimensions. The apex of the pyramid represents a synthesis or unified knowledge from which, through degeneration, the great forms of knowledge are derived; from each of these, the respective forms and subforms such as painting, dance, and sculpture extend to the limits of specialization.

Yet, interestingly, the pyramid is not a static structure, for it is not only a three-dimensional body but is also tied to a fourth dimension of time. In Figure 2 we see an arrow indicating a direction of spin around an axis. The pyramid exists in this tetra-dimensional space, suggesting a very natural cyclical quality in the expression of knowledge in the history of humanity.

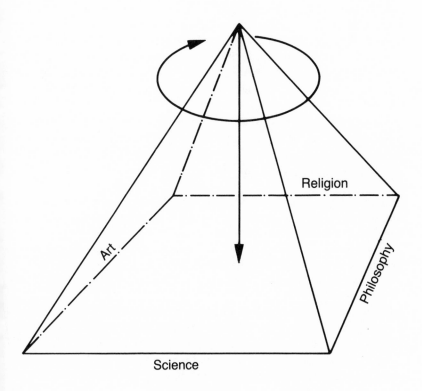

FIGURE 2.

THE FACES OF KNOWLEDGE IN HISTORY

More than two thousand years ago, knowledge primarily assumed the form of philosophy. In medieval times, religion became the dominant form; during the Renaissance, art flourished, and gradually, as the pyramid underwent its cyclical movement, science became the primary form of acquiring and expressing knowledge, as it is today. Figure 2 represents the current period of history with the face in the frontal position representing science. We must keep in mind that the predominance of one form of knowledge during a period in history does not invalidate the others. All the forms coexist at all times, but with different degrees of forcefulness. Different forms of knowledge do not "take root" during a particular time in history because they are outside the era, or outside the cyclical moment. In Figure 2, the face directly opposite science is religion, interestingly the form that currently finds itself in the greatest state of crisis and redefinition.

At the present time science is entering a period of transition. Historically, science has been rooted in Cartesian principles of duality and reductionism, which were defined by empirical facts that could be appreciated through the senses. In the post-Einstein period, however, these phenomenological assumptions changed radically. Physicist Werner Heisenberg introduced the uncertainty principle which states that all phenomena are influenced by the state of consciousness of the person observing them and that everything changes as it is observed. The result of these definitions of the perspective of science is a trend toward the integration of science and philosophy in the future.

THE FOUR TYPES OF ART

In the same way that we observe different facets of human knowledge, we can distinguish four separate levels in art that, for purposes of identification, can be labeled Art I, Art II, Art III, and Art IV. The lines of division between these levels are flexible and intended to act as general guidelines, to indicate major trends and characteristics.

Essentially physical Art I is related to ceremonial activity. Commemorative monuments, mausoleums, cathedrals, altars, epic paintings, and some processional and military music are included in this category. Ritual dances and sounds are also covered by Art I, including monophonic sounds and scales and biphonic, triphonic, tetraphonic, and pentaphonic scales of Chinese, Tibetan, and Inca origin. Another example of Art I is the so-called martial arts. The overall objective of this type of art is the expression of the will through physical movement.

Art II centers around the emotions. The period of romanticism in music, literature, and poetry is an example of this level of art. The language required to express emotion is far more subtle and flexible than that required by a more classic period. Specifically, within this form we find Weber's *Oberon*, Chopin's *Berceuse*, and Schumann's *Reverie*, as well as Amado Nervo's *Songs of Love*.

Art III, more intellectual in character, deals with directions and proportions, measures and combinations. Modern art, cubist paintings, the Bauhaus style, atonalism, polytonalism, serial music, and electronic music are encompassed by Art III. Some examples of this type of art are Hindemith's *Ludus Tonalis*, the works of Arnold Schoenberg, and Edgard Varese, and the symphonies of Aaron Copland. Stravinsky, for example, scales the counterpoint of Bach in the form of "blocks of chords" and is as much a cubist in his *Guernica* as is Picasso in his paintings.

Art IV is a more complex form for which there are fewer available manifestations. It represents an integrated knowledge that is embodied in the very genre of art. It is an expression of unified knowledge that produces the same effects in those persons who have discovered and internalized this art in their lives. This type of objective art, which is integrated with the other three forms of knowledge, is always understood in terms of consciousness. The materials employed for the work of art are, in effect, a mask covering a very profound content that is appreciated in its totality only by those who have attained a level of being equal to that of the artist.

Participatory art is one form of Art IV. An ancient example is found in the pyramids of both Egypt and the Americas. The construction of the pyramids is indicative of a superlative level of science, unimaginable even today. The end product is not a mere technological monument but rather a science integrated with religion and philosophy, producing a work of art that must be appreciated functionally as well as symbolically. Some of these pyramids have graded sides, or sides with steps, symbolizing the ascent of humanity and the discovery of a unified vision of life.

Viewing Art in a two-dimensional plane with the sides unhinged (see Figure 3), reveals symbolic alchemical representations of the four elements (earth, air, fire, and water) and the quintessence, or heavenly light. In addition, this point of view shows us the cross, which represents humankind's evolutionary alchemy.

More exact examples of this fourth form of art are found in the Renaissance masterpieces of Leonardo da Vinci. His work reveals a unified and integrated knowledge. His knowledge of science, manifest in his preparation of materials such as paints and varnishes, is combined with a pictorial mastery never again reached by an artist. In *The Last Supper*, we see the obvious religious symbolism, but also a representation of the zodiac. This

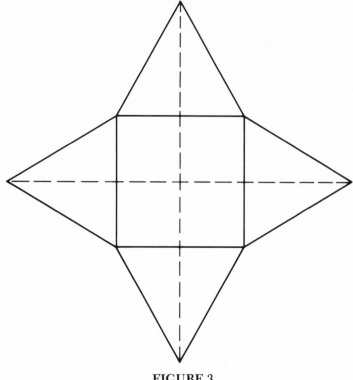

FIGURE 3.

same level of art is achieved in music by Ferruccio Busoni in his *Counter-point Fantasy*. This piece integrates all of the Bachian knowledge and enriches it within the structure of an agrarian era. Stradivarius violins are another example of Art IV that have never been reproduced at the same level of perfection. These violins satisfy the canons of perfect proportions, originating in this instance from superimposing two regular pentagons and drawing all of the possible internal diagonals.

THE FUTURE OF ART

Progress in the arts is attained through enriching the medium of expression. This is the only way that we can reduce the dimensional difference between the conception of a work of art and its realization; it must lead us to the creation of new and more perfect means of expression. Two excellent examples of an enriched medium are the viola, which expresses what neither the violin nor the cello can, and the saxophone, which suggests what neither the clarinet nor the fagot can. Acrylic, the laser beam, and signal and wave generators are some of the potential resources awaiting the proper genius to employ them as an art medium. Yet to discard the currently available mediums of expression which are the product of all human wisdom would be to disconnect ourselves from our past. By the same token, every authentic manifestation of art must be a vehicle of equilibrium, health, and harmony, and above all must stimulate the development of new consciousness. Otherwise, we are dealing with pseudo art, art that has become technical and has ceased to be a vehicle for the discovery of the self.

Looking at the progression of the cycles of knowledge, it is clear that in the immediate future art will not be the main vehicle for the expression of integrated knowledge. Instead, art will support, complement, and become integrated into scientific disciplines. Some examples of forms we will observe are electronically organized sounds, chromo-energetics, and the combined uses of sounds and colors, which will be used to open new paths in the fields of health, life conditions, human relations, and the exploration of hidden areas of the mind and the subconscious. A more concrete example is the use of perfumes, sounds, and colors for the various environments of the home as well as for relaxation, family interaction, and the intensification of certain emotional states. Environmentally, we will see rooms and buildings that are in accord with the individual's age and life-style, as well as environments that facilitate release of stress and catharsis, that activate psychological energies, and that induce clarity of thinking. The use of architectural forms and innovative designs that stimulate psychological functions will be commonly employed in factories, offices, and assembly lines. In hospitals and clinics we will find batteries of infra and ultra sounds and luminous sources as well as extrachromatic lights and geometrical designs being used in all phases of therapy.

In the next century, we will see the development of highly sophisticated instruments that will combine sounds, colors, vibrations, and different electromagnetic frequencies, permitting the artist to express his or her most intimate and personal self through spontaneous compositions. For the first time in history, art will be reduced to the level of the common person, and self-expression will be encouraged as a means to personal fulfillment. This same instrumentation will allow the person to become more conscious of his or her own internal states and will be employed as a type of feedback or self-stimulation system.

In the more distant future, when the pyramid's cyclical movement faces the dividing line between science and philosophy, the integration of these two great forms will flourish while art will enter into a subordinate position. Ultimately, there will be a new renaissance, knowledge again reaching the height of expression through art, as one more cycle is completed.

We can project this age toward the fourth millennium of our era. Early manifestations of this renaissance will be more integrated with philosophy and religion, the great legacies of the two preceding eras. The early faces of art will be constructed to represent sacred values as well as the newly discovered mysteries of the universe. Artists will officiate as priests of art, and the masses will look to them for revelations of truth in the same way that they once looked to religion and science. The medium of expression will be the human body, for there has never been nor ever will be a better laboratory or instrument of expression. When properly tuned, the human body can reveal to future generations what before could only be known through the senses in the appreciation of a beautiful work of art.

There is one condition necessary though, before we can enrich the existing forms of knowledge in a conscious way: it is necessary that we become very aware of our history. Any new cycle we enter must involve a continual return to and reshaping of the past. In our movement toward the future of art we must realize our tremendous debt to the past as well as a growing sense of rediscovery, of looking within to find the answers of the coming era.

There are few living theologians with the vast knowledge and unending curiosity of Dr. Harvey Cox. Throughout his life, he has consistently and innovatively explored the highways and backroads of the religious experience in an attempt to understand the meaning and importance of religion in contemporary culture. In addition, he is one of the few highly regarded religious philosophers who has demonstrated a willingness to utilize the historical interpretations of religion not as a way to dogmatically rule present behaviour, but more as a tool for understanding the depths of human striving in such a way as to create relevant and effective values for living now and in the future.

After receiving his doctorate in theology from Harvard University Dr. Cox worked in East Berlin for the Gossmer Mission and the Evangelical Academy. Upon returning to the United States, he became an assistant instructor of theology and culture at the Andover-Newton Theological Seminary. He later returned to his alma mater, Harvard University, where he remains a full professor at the Harvard Divinity School, the Victor S. Thomas Professor of Divinity, and chairman of the Department of Applied Theology.

In addition to his extensive work as a religious theorist, his active involvement in examining current social and religious trends, and his love for world travel, Dr. Cox has found the time to author a number of highly acclaimed books including On Not Leaving it to the Snake, The Secular City, Feast of Fools, The Seduction of the Spirit *and* Turning East.

In this chapter on the future of religion Dr. Harvey Cox tackles the nearly impossible task of predicting the future of religion by first reviewing numerous past "predictions." By examining the history of religion as well as these historical speculations, he manages to extract the current themes of wisdom and folly that have marked the study of religion to date. By examining those aspects of religion and the religious experience that have withstood the test of time, Dr. Cox constructs a context for religion that he feels could become the emerging form in the coming decades. Since he feels that religion should not just be a reflection of a culture's psyche, but a tool for the creation of the ideal society, Harvey Cox here offers a way of conceiving an active, socially relevant, yet non-dogmatic religious institution to assist us in surviving with health and love into the twenty-first century.

RELIGION

PAST PREDICTIONS

The future of religion: What a weighty subject for speculation. Past predictions about future forms of human endeavor have often been borne out. After all, we do have space ships, death rays, annihilation weapons, and happy pills, just as previous generations of science fiction writers once imagined. But what forecaster could have foreseen the resurgence of militant Islam, the charismatic movement, a Korean evangelist resurrecting the old American Civil Religion with himself as the presumptive messiah? Or a 20th century pope who writes poetry and philosophical essays, or the re-emergence of witchcraft? In taking on this most perilous of all fields of forecast, I'd like to begin by recalling four of the more notable past predictions, all of which seem to have come to nought.

The *Philosophes*

Let us begin with a distinguished company: the 18th century French *philosophes*. Since they believed the Age of Reason was dawning, the philosophes confidently predicted that religion and superstition were fated for extinction, presumably quite soon. Their *Encyclopedia* was to be a compendium of all knowledge, shining the bright light of human reason into the darkest abyss, expelling the noisome remains of priestcraft and sorcery. Religion, they believed, was the product of ignorance compounded by clerical greed and political reaction. It was a poison whose only antidote was clear and courageous thought. "Not until the last priest is hanged with the entrails of the last king," Voltaire once declared, "will mankind finally be free." So they enthroned the Goddess of Reason, carried her in solemn procession through Paris, accompanied by young girls strewing flowers, bore her into Notre Dame Cathedral, hymned her virtues, and dedicated the dawning new age to her.

251

How were they to know that with procession, enthroning, and hymning they were perpetuating religion, not abolishing it? Human beings have made the same mistake before and since. Auguste Comte, the founder of positivism, was in some ways the last of the philosophes. He thought he saw humankind leaving behind mythical and metaphysical explanations of reality and entering the "positive" age. In fact, he became so enchanted with his vision that he went on to compose a whole Mass for the era of positivism. It is a curious and wonderful artifice, this Mass, containing all the traditional pillars of the Roman original but re-worked for a positivist *weltanschauung*. Religion seems to reassert itself even among those who most avidly desire its demise. The predictions of the philosophes seem not to have come true, even for them.

Lenin and Marx

Lenin is another case in point. With a mind somewhat more programmatic and less flexible than Marx's, he took quite woodenly his master's ideas about religion and enlarged them into a metaphysical worldview he believed would soon replace religion. Lenin utilized some of the evolutionist and physical materialist ideas then prevalent to produce his own theory of materialism which was, however, ontological, not dialectical like Marx's. Lenin's concoction, although popular with Russian Communists for many years, is rarely defended nowadays. Most Marxists prefer to follow Marx instead of Lenin and to make their judgments about religion on a political, rather than an ontological, basis. Ironically, a half century after the October revolution, not only has religion not died out in Lenin's Soviet Union, but the most widely appreciated Russian writers, Alexandr Solzhenitsyn and Andrei Sinyavsky, are Orthodox believers, as was the late Boris Pasternak. Whatever else his accomplishments, as a religious forecaster Lenin, like the philosophes, seems to have failed.

Lenin's predictions were confounded by his own fate. The enemy of all pilgrimages and icons and superstitious devotions, when he died his body was embalmed and placed in a mausoleum in Red Square in the shadow of St. Basil's. There, to this day, thousands of pilgrims wend their way, lining up in every kind of weather to file past the sacred bier. The lights are dim in the tomb of Lenin. An atmosphere of sanctity and hushed awe pervades the stone temple. Some older pilgrims from the far provinces are seen to cross themselves as they shuffle by the glass-encased remains of the saint. And behold, as young Alexis Karamazov had vainly hoped for *his* idol, Father Zossima, the body remains uncorrupted—the result this time not of a miracle, but of the embalming techniques of modern science. The enemy of icons has been made into an icon himself.

King's Chapel Congregation

But let us not cast our net only in foreign waters. In America there were many who, at the birth of the new republic, thought that a new day had come in religion also. They were sure they were the midwives for this new religion which they intended to deliver not just to America, but to the world. The case of King's Chapel in Boston serves as a particularly good example. It had been, in the period before the War of Independence, an Anglican chapel serving the needs of the small community which still adhered to the Church of England in that Puritan theocratic outpost. When the war began the position of theological and political loyalists became a bit less secure than the rock of ages. Eventually, when the British troops themselves evacuated Boston, King's Chapel suffered the hasty departure of its rector and most of its more Tory-minded parishioners.

The remnant was left in an unusually precarious but promising position. In fact, their canonical situation was virtually unique. Since the king of England, who had headed the Anglican church since Henry VIII, no longer ruled this realm, their ties with the Anglican hierarchy were severed with one hurried sailing. Also, since they had never been subject to the Standing Order—the established Puritan-Calvinist church of the Massachusetts Bay Colony—they now found themselves, in effect, the freest church in Boston. But what should that freedom mean?

A long discussion ensued about what a truly "republican religion" should be. Would it be deist, evangelical, unitarian? In one sense, the congregation of King's Chapel undertook the same task the French philosophes had accomplished by creating the Goddess of Reason. But unlike the philosophes and Lenin, who saw no need for any religion, they wanted to formulate a religious doctrine that would be patriotic, enlightened, and in keeping with that special destiny many Americans believed "Nature's God" intended for the new republic. The argument raged on, and the mixture of religious theories and political posturing that appeared was heady stuff indeed. The result, as might have been expected, was a fascinating compromise that any visitor to Boston can still sample by stopping in at King's Chapel. The "republican religion" for the new nation turned out to be an admixture of unitarian religious philosophy and Anglican liturgical forms. The church now belongs to the Unitarian-Universalist denomination, but the shape of its liturgy is "higher" than that of many American Episcopal churches. In few other places can parishioners actually chant liberal theological truisms in something close to Gregorian plainsong. To the question of whether the congregants of King's Chapel actually anticipated the religion of the future, or even the religion of the new republic, one can offer only an inconclusive answer at best.

Freud and Jung

Let us look at one more prediction before—duly humbled by these discouraging precedents—we venture a few of our own. No catalog of "past futures" of religion would be complete without that of Sigmund Freud, whose *Future of an Illusion* represents his most concisely worded entry into this precarious enterprise. Freud believed that religion consisted of the projection of inner fears and anxieties—and hopes and fantasies—onto the external world. He interpreted it as a kind of infantile delusion writ large. As the inventor of psychoanalysis, he had strong confidence in the efficacy of his method. He saw it as the ultimate application of the scientific method—which had formerly scanned the skies—to the inner, secret workings of the human mind. He hoped that eventually the utilization of this method would enable people to set aside religious delusions and face reality without blinders and crutches.

But Freud did not seem to believe this psychoanalytic remedy would take effect very quickly, or even in the foreseeable future. The illusion was too widespread and too well-grounded in the culture itself. In fact, there are passages in which Freud appears to have resigned himself to a kind of pessimism, in which he seems to be saying that since his solution will never be generalizable to the whole populace, the "illusion" may have a promising future indeed.

Freud's body was never enshrined in a holy sepulchre, as Lenin's was. But before his death, as though to prove once again the futility of making predictions about the fate of the gods, Freud's criticism of religion was turned inside out by one of his own disciples, Carl Gustaf Jung. His thought may be for Freud what the Red Square tomb became for Lenin.

The son of a Swiss Reformed Pastor, as a child Jung once had a dream in which an immense divinity squatted in the sky over the local cathedral and defecated on its soaring tower. Although this does not appear to be the dream of a man who would later start from Freud's thinking and then move toward a whole new rationale for the religious understanding of life, that is in fact exactly what Jung did. His theories, and the form of therapy associated with his name, have conspired to produce an attitude towards religion for numerous twentieth century people who can no longer be religious in conventional ways. Like Freud, the Jungians see the whole pantheon of the gods as an internal universe, not something "out there." But in contrast to Freud, they believe these gods are not to be abolished, outgrown, unmasked, or eviscerated. Rather, one should learn to know them and serve them, for in so doing one is serving one's own deepest and most authentic self.

"PAST FUTURES"

At this point any sensible student of the history and philosophy of religion would end the present essay. Having demonstrated the precariousness of extrapolations and forecasts in the realm of the spirit, the best expression of wisdom would be a Buddha-like smile—and silence. It was Jesus himself who said "the spirit bloweth where it listeth, and no man knows from whence it comes or whither it blows." (He also held in singularly low regard those who thought they could predict "the day or the hour of the coming of the Son of Man," a secret which, he said, was known only to the Father in Heaven.) In short, all evidence, both historical and theological, seems to point to a strategy of restraint, abjuring all predictions. But who—despite the cautionary tales of past failures—can resist making at least *some* attempt to predict something about the future of religion? I will ignore the evidence and plunge ahead.

Let me begin by stating that I believe all the seemingly mistaken predictions I have just cataloged about the future of religion to have been *essentially* accurate. Although in one sense they all seem to have missed, I believe they each teach us something useful and valid.

Let us look at them once again, in order. First, the philosophes. They were correct, in my view, to foresee the disappearance of religion as an extension of that way of knowing the external world we now call magic or superstition. Religion is not the descendant of magic. The magical impulse is the desire to control and direct nature, to use it for human ends, to tame its sometimes malevolent side. This impulse developed through the centuries not into religion but into empirical science. The true successors of the sorcerers and the alchemists are not the priests and theologians but the physicists and the computer engineers. They merely use another method to accomplish the same end. Religion has nothing to do with supplying answers to questions that can be answered by empirical investigation and observation. Religion concerns questions of human *meaning* and *purpose* that are in principle *un*answerable in an empirical way. (This holds unless one believes that ethical imperatives and human meaning can simply be deduced from how things *are*, a questionable theory which cannot itself be proven by observing how things are.)

In other words, the notorious 19th century "Warfare Between Science and Religion" arose from mistaken notions of what religion and science are. Although there are still occasional border skirmishes, most theologians and scientists now recognize that religion overstepped its boundaries when— at least in the West—it tried to make geological and biological history into matters of revelation. On the other side, although some scientists once believed they had discovered the Universal Method for solving all conceivable questions—rather than one very useful way of dealing with some—it is very hard to get an argument going between scientists and theologians over issues of this kind any more. At the international conference on "Science, Faith and the Future" sponsored by the World Council of Churches at MIT in July 1979, there was virtually no debate along the old science-versus-religion lines at all. Rather, the scientists implored the theologians and religious leaders present to take *more* of an interest in the pressing ethical issues emerging from the newest advances of science. Theologians, especially from the poorer parts of the world, did not criticize the scientists for being too self-important. Rather, they took them to task for making big hardware for the multinational corporations instead of supplying appropriate technologies to the poorer countries. The issues, in other words, were political and ethical; and it was clear that the deepest divisions pitted North against South, rich against poor, East against West, radical against liberal.

As it turns out, the philosophes' attack on religion had a kind of purgative effect. More and more, religion is now concerning itself with questions of human meaning and ethical policy, not with dogmatic formulations about what time of day it was when God created the world (a question that had vexed the 19th century British Anglican Bishop Ussher).

Even in Iran, where a form of Moslem zealotry has re-emerged, it is significant to notice that the ayatollahs and imams have not attacked the domain of science as such but have concentrated on what they see as issues of public order. The direction the philosophes set out is still, when its exaggerations are combed out, what we too can expect in the future: realizing its limitations, we will turn to science for help in answering the how and why questions. At the same time the perennial riddles of human meaning and personal obligation will continue to be debated in categories derived from the great religious traditions.

How else could it be? The most important questions we will face in the future must be answered on the basis of premises about the nature and destiny of humankind for which no empirical proof can be mustered. What is human life, and when does it begin, or end? Is every human life really worth respecting? If so, why? Has the present generation any responsibility for those who will inherit the planet millennia from now? Does the human species have any special responsibility at all in the cosmos? Is there a meaning that transcends my meaning or even the collective total of all our human meanings? Is there anything worth dying for? All these questions press the questioner ultimately into those strata of human reality where our primal terrors and hopes—expressed in myth and rite and symbol—remain the only sources of wisdom.

But what about Lenin? Surely his idea that religious life can be reduced to emanations from material particles that are then used to justify class oppression in no way depicts the future of religion. Again, let us step back from the precise manner in which Lenin (and Marx in a much more subtle way) actually enunciated their theories on the one hand, and look instead at the overall intention of their program. Although Lenin's metaphysical views are dated ones and now appear positively quaint, there are three aspects of his and of Marx's ideas about religion that I consider basically sound.

First, they insisted that religion must be understood not in isolation but in relation to all other dimensions of life, including the way human beings use the natural world to feed and clothe themselves. Religion, they believed—and quite rightly—does not fall like fire from the heavens. It is part and parcel with all other human activities and cannot be fathomed without reference to them. Lenin called his way of analyzing this totality "materialistic" because of his neo-Democritean (from Democritus, the Greek atomic materialist) ontology. Marx preferred the term "dialectical." What they both wanted to say is that the study of "religion" *as such* can teach us nothing. We must study it as an integral element of the world of work and power and social arrangements. In this, they were right. More and more I am suspicious of that method of studying religion represented by Joseph Campbell and Mircea Eliade. The typical approach of these highly influential scholars is to assemble the myths and legends of several cultures into a collection in a skillful way but with few descriptions of the social *settings* within which actual people told, sang, chanted, or danced the myths. They are set down in print, often thematically organized, with tribes and continents juxtaposed, with very little indication of who tells them and who listens, how the tribe feeds itself or is governed, to say nothing of what happens to the people—if there are any—who don't like the story. In short, the error of this widespread method is that it lifts out something called "religion" from the intricate human corpus in which it lives. The result is a kind of collage of disparate elements that disfigures the religious dimension. For all their understandable 19th century philosophical narrowness, Marx and Lenin did not want this kind of excising to happen, and in this they were right.

Second, Marx and his followers saw that in an unjust society, religion is a powerful tool of oppression. It is an opiate, a mystification, a way of trying to solve through fantasy what can only be solved in history. Again, although they were undoubtedly heavy-handed in the way they laid out this criticism, no one can doubt that they were largely correct, at least for the societies in which they lived. During the 19th century, religious institutions played an almost exclusively reactionary role nearly everywhere.

Marx and his followers took deadly aim: they pointed out that since religion is part of a sociocultural whole, and culture is almost always controlled by the dominant group, religion can be a tool of manipulation. This leaves us to wonder what religion might look like in a *non*exploitative society, where there would be no need for opiates to keep people subdued and mystified. I will return to this point later.

Third, Marx and his school believed that religion would eventually disappear. Again, though this may come as a surprise to the reader, I believe they were right. Marx's notion about the "disappearance" of religion can be understood best by comparing it with his theory about the "withering away of the state." This idea has also been roundly ridiculed, largely because it is so badly misunderstood. What he meant was that there is nothing eternally fixed about any human institution, the state included. It is a perfectly reasonable idea when one thinks about it for a moment. For millennia, human societies existed and governed themselves before the institution of the state appeared. National states emerged at a certain point in recent history, served and will serve a certain purpose, but will not endure forever. As awareness expands and new forms of consciousness and culture evolve, new patterns of governance, which are not as distant and reified as The State, will also appear, Marx thought.

The comparison with religion is quite exact. Just as something called the "state" differentiated itself from that great complex organism we now call "society" at one stage in its history, so we also began to speak of certain acts and persons and institutions as "religious." But this is a very recent category of human thought and I believe a "reified" one also. The Balinese, it is said, claim they have no art: they just do everything beautifully. There was a time, not too long ago in the full scale of cultural evolution, when one would have been hard put to discover anything separate and distinct in human societies that could be called "religion." People just "did everything" with awe or joy or with a sense of mystery or with a recognition of the incandescent power within persons, places, and things. Prayer was as much a part of planting as invocation was of hunting. It is possible that in our efforts to understand the cultures of the Orient and of non-literate peoples, much mischief and confusion has already resulted from our imposing on them the—Western and recent—term "religion." What Marx meant, perhaps, is that we now live in an *un*natural epoch, one in which we have separated and elevated (and mystified) something we call "religion." Eventually, when conditions allow for the transition, this artificially segregated element will be reabsorbed into the whole. At least that is what I hope Marx meant to predict, because it is surely what I foresee.

The parishioners of King's Chapel were right too, in a way. Their deliberations produced a potpourri combining traditional and innovative elements whose proportions did not catch on with the rest of the population of the new nation. Still, they made the attempt. Some political historians argue that it was not until the English revolution of the 17th century that people began to realize that the forms of governance they had simply taken for granted as being "natural"—the monarchy, for example—were not natural at all but were products of human construction in history and could therefore be altered or abolished. The people of King's Chapel were merely applying this same principle to religious life. They were taking what had once been viewed as a "given" into their own hands and consciously shaping it for human ends. They were "de-fatalizing" their religious lives just as they were also applying the human tendency to re-shape, re-mold, and reform in other realms. They teach us something important about the future of religion not by *what* they invented but by the courage and initiative they showed in daring to invent it. We will now have to do the same thing—not wait to see what religious forms will emerge in the next century, but use our imaginations to shape them.

Finally, what about Freud, Jung, and the psychological predictions about religion? Although religious scholars often prefer Jung to Freud since he is notoriously "soft" on myth, magic, and astrology, I prefer Freud. Freud was right that much of religion consists of the projection of inner fantasies onto an imaginary external screen. Unlike Jung, Freud did not want to come to terms with this projecting but he could not see how we could get beyond it either. He chose to live with the tension and this has given rise to two remarkably differing interpretations of what the next step after Freud should have been. Some have seen it as helping people do the best they can in a world in which some degree of neurotic projection will inevitably continue even after it is minimized in individual patients. The other side will not settle for this compromise. These "radical Freudians" claim that there is implicit in Freud the idea that we should alter the conditions that produce this "surplus repression" with its resultant neurosis. If we did, alienated human thinking and living would be transcended, not by treating two billion people one by one for four years each at seventy-five dollars an hour, but by a quantum leap in human awareness, growing out of a qualitative change in the basic organization of human life. If this great leap could happen, then the present, unconscious inclination to segregate religious impulses from the rest of life would slip into the past and we would deal with the universe, our neighbors, and ourselves without the mediation of mystified phantoms.

This vision of the radical Freudians sounds terribly utopian, maybe even "millennialist." It is at least—to use a very theological term—"eschatological." It suggests a Messianic Era or a Kingdom of God. Freud remained stalwartly anti-religious to his dying day. The logic of his thought, at least as it is interpreted by his radical disciples, conjures up images similar to that of the prophet Jeremiah who spoke of a coming time when no one would have to speak the name of God or teach the Law since God would be within us and the law would be inscribed upon our hearts. The New Testament book of Revelation speaks of a heavenly city where there is no need for a temple because God suffuses everything. Ironically, the radical Freudians are closer to the Bible than the pious Jungians.

Admittedly, one could argue that all the predictions I have mentioned were wrong. Despite the *Encyclopedia*, religion has not disappeared. Despite Marx and Lenin, there is a religious revival going on in Eastern Europe, the Communists (the Euro-Communists) are coming to terms with the churches, and in Latin America the Catholics are sometimes more revolutionary than the Communists. Despite the noble experiment of the members of King's Chapel, high liturgical unitarianism has little support today. Despite Freud, people go on projecting. Still, each of these prophets had a point. Their forecasts remind us that religion should not be mistaken for a method of examining and managing empirical reality. They teach us that religion is part and parcel with the whole of the human world, and its use for exalted and debased purposes cannot be understood if it is studied in isolation. They also teach us that religion is not simply a part of "nature," given once and for all, but a part of "history," and therefore subject to conscious criticism and reconstruction. Finally, they remind us that religion springs from deep and possibly distorted needs in the human psyche, but its inner logic points to the need for a fundamentally different kind of world order.

FUTURE NEEDS

So what then about the future of religion? Personally, I believe those kinds of questions we currently segregate—like a student removing a frog's liver—and call "religion" will *not* disappear so long as there are human beings to ask them. Humans come into life without having asked for it, into a skin and sex and culture they never chose. They are buffeted with pain, lifted with joys, strangled by deprivation, awed by the inevitability of death. They are enraged by injustice and dream of a better way. Human beings always spawn more questions than they can answer. If they could only be *either* goats or gods instead of this curious combination of the two! Neither goats nor gods need "religion." Still, as long as there is something recognizably *human* to hope for and ponder and question, there will be the "religious dimension." But will it always have the strangely segregated and fenced off place it now seems so "naturally" to occupy in our epoch?

I doubt it. Students of Chinese history have often remarked on the way the sacred seems to be imbedded in the everyday. One writer calls Taoism "the sacrality of the secular." But does this mean the Chinese are "less religious"? Or more so? Perhaps future historians will look back on our modern Western age as an aberration, one in which the spiritual ingredient of life was distilled, drawn off, encapsulated—with disastrous results.

I do not believe my future vision of a religion reintegrated into the secular conflicts with Christianity. Dietrich Bonhoeffer, perhaps the single most influential Protestant thinker of our time, once said he never really wanted to become a saint; he just wanted ". . . to be a man." To be a Christian, he said, was, in the final analysis, to be fully human. He rejected any "magic helper" notion of God and insisted that God had become a partner in the earthly reality, sharing our weakness, eliciting our strength. He even talked about the need for a "non-religious interpretation of the Gospel," but he was hanged by the Gestapo before he could begin to work out his ideas.

Bonhoeffer died in the spring of 1945, just hours before the advancing American forces reached the concentration camp where he was incarcerated. A few months later a plane named the Enola Gay flew over the city of Hiroshima and dropped the first atomic bomb. For me, these two events, taken together, have begun to symbolize something unprecedented about the questions human beings ask about themselves and their futures, including the future of religion. In the last weeks of his life, Bonhoeffer glimpsed a new world emerging in which Christianity would assume a shape so radically different that he predicted it would be virtually unrecognizable to his contemporaries. The dropping of the atomic bomb, however, wrote a mushroom-shaped question mark after any and all speculations about the human future. How has this altered the question of the future of religion?

In his essay on "The Mysticism of Science," Pierre Teilhard de Chardin, perhaps the most influential Catholic thinker of our time, remarked that the two essential ingredients of any religion are "hope and the vista of a limitless future." In this short phrase he has put his finger exactly on the only authentically "religious" question of the post-Hiroshima era. Stated in its simplest form, the religious concern about the future must not be about the "future of religion" but about the future per se. The religious hope, and it must be "religious" because the empirical basis for it is ambiguous at least, is that there will in fact be a human future. Since Hiroshima, and the stacking up of nuclear armed rockets, the answer to the question is in no way self-evident. For the first time in human memory there is serious doubt whether our species has any future at all. Teilhard envisioned humankind as just now entering upon that exciting and critical new phase of evolution, its next "nodal point," in which, at last, the next step is in our hands. But he never knew about The Button which is also now in human hands.

Taken together, the theologies of Bonhoeffer and Teilhard suggest that reviewing past forecasts about the future of religion can be helpful, but only up to a point. Making predictions can be valuable, but also misleading. The great new fact of the possibility of species suicide utterly transforms not just the context in which our question about the future of religion is voiced, but the nature of the question itself. As creatures embedded in history, we cannot ask these questions from some Copernican vantage point situated outside the threats and uncertainties of terrestrial existence. To ask the question in such an abstract way can only be an ominous symptom of our refusal to take responsibility for the real world in which we must live. "Predicting" the future subtly perpetuates the idea that someone or something else controls it, when the truth is, as both Bonhoeffer and Teilhard knew, it is now in our hands. Thus, the possibility of self-annihilation requires us to put all our questions *not* in the form of "what will happen?" but rather in the form of "what must we do?" We cannot merely speculate on whether rites and myths will someday cease to divide and stupefy people; we must so shape and reconceive them that they unite and enlarge us. We cannot afford to wait and see whether the "religious dimension" ceases to be a segregated precinct; we must set about making it an integral dimension of all we do. We cannot allow denominations, hierarchies, and confessional strife to continue to run their course as though what happened in the "sacred realm" were totally outside our human capacity to mold and steer. We cannot wait for kismet to deliver us into a new era in which we no longer need to project our inmost terrors onto the heavens or onto other peoples and nations. We must now take the initiative, not to predict the future but to create it.

During the 1960s when Barbara Marx Hubbard's children were growing up and she found that her role as a full-time mother and wife was shifting, she began to have beatific visions of the future. In her vision, the earth, like every living creature, has a unique life cycle with its related transitions and identity crises.

In 1970 she co-founded with John Whiteside the Committee for the Future. Designed initially to help communicate real and hopeful opportunities for future evolution, the committee has already developed and convened more than two dozen conferences with television coverage worldwide.

Trained as a psychologist and psychotherapist, Dr. Barry McWaters is presently co-director of the Institute for the Study of Conscious Evolution. He began his career with an interest in promoting personal growth. However, as he delved more deeply into individual therapy, he became increasingly convinced that growth, development, and, ultimately, evolution, may be more appropriately viewed and supported in a cultural or planetary mode than by working with unrelated individuals.

In this lively essay, Barry McWaters and Barbara Marx Hubbard collaborate to propose their shared vision of the past, present, and future evolution of planet Earth. They present the fascinating possibility that we are all collectively embarked on a spiraling evolutionary journey and that we may soon be entering into an unprecedented period of accelerated world development. They propose our planet Earth is only now beginning to shed the spirit and characteristics of childhood and enter a period of maturation and expanded consciousness.

BARRY McWATERS and
BARBARA MARX HUBBARD **CONSCIOUS EVOLUTION**

The people of Gaia, our living planetary system, are undergoing an organic shift from unconscious to conscious evolution. Ours is the first generation to be aware that all human beings are responsible for the future. Many of us are now poignantly experiencing this shift in our personal and social lives in this time of unprecedented change—a disorienting, dangerous, and delightful time. Breakdowns in our complex social organization confront us daily, while, at the same time, breakthroughs signal new hope for humanity.

How can we understand this change? How can we find meaning in what may appear to be holocaust? What is the perspective from which we can witness our present situation in the context of the whole?

THE EVOLUTIONARY PERSPECTIVE

The evolutionary perspective provides a vantage point from which to view the whole and envision the process of creation, from the origin of the universe through the present and on toward an unknown future. This perspective reveals the action of an ever-present patterning process, forming increasingly complex systems—the cell, the multicellular organism, the human being. One can see, as Nobel Prize winner Albert Szent-Györgi puts it, a "drive in living matter to perfect itself." Physicist Lance-lot Law Whyte's "internal factors in evolution" is evident in each and every living organism's inherent tendency to internally organize itself into more and more sophisticated patterns. Human evolution itself provides an excellent example of this universal tendency toward higher order and

265

greater awareness. The evolutionary perspective allows the individual to observe the organizing process of evolution that operates in the service of creation.

THE STORY OF CREATION

Within the process of planetary evolution, the past can be viewed as the *prenatal* period of human development, the present as *birth*, and the future as the *postnatal* phase of maturation in which we will use all our capacities harmoniously in a universe of immeasurable possibilities. In this context, human consciousness plays a paramount role in orchestrating the great drama of planetary evolution. We are that aspect of Gaia that will restore and protect her and will carry her seed into the universe.

Responding to planetary crises and opportunities, our generation is now assuming unprecedented evolutionary tasks: planetary stewardship and universal impregnation. Stewardship is the loving conservation, restoration, and enhancement of planetary life. Universal impregnation is the magnificent endeavor of seeding the universe by carrying the spark of earth-life into outer space. This is the reproduction of Gaia, the quest for transcendence.

CONSCIOUS EVOLUTION

As the next millennium approaches, one can see with vibrant clarity that the story of creation is not over. Many of us now recognize that, like it or not, we are cocreators of our reality rather than passive by-products of evolutionary accident. Humans are affecting the whole planet by their every action, desire, and thought.

In coming to an understanding of evolution through both a deepening intuition and a maturing science, we awaken to our potential for conscious evolution, that phase in which a developing being becomes conscious of itself, aware of the process in which it is involved, and begins to participate voluntarily in the work and adventure of evolution.

PRENATAL HISTORY

At this moment of awakening, it is appropriate to look backward in time to understand the roots of our species—our prenatal history. Transcending the waning mechanistic point of view, a new, organic, evolutionary perspective begins to take form.

Some 4½ billion years ago the earth appeared in space. Scientists hypothesize that through the condensation of gases a solid mass manifested itself, caught in a vortex of cosmic forces. It was a magnificent and important event, miraculous conception.

A billion years later the initial stirrings of unicellular life appeared. What is the origin of this undulating life? Perhaps it was called to set the stage for a magnificent journey into the light. No one knows.

Another billion and a half years passed and a growing attraction is in evidence. Relationships are formed. Tiny little beings are finding ways to get together, projects to work on, entities to become part of. This is the origin of the complex cell. Who called these little fellows together? How does the patterning process work? Was it simply a matter of coincidence or were they summoned by an inner voice to move toward their evolutionary potential?

Sometime later another wave of attraction swept Gaia and cellular division, mitosis, began. Multicellular life became the dominant theme. The dance of life became more complex and interesting as a myriad of species sprang forth into the light of consciousness.

Long eons passed silently, filled with fervent activity. Three major strands of life had identified themselves: the fungi, which absorb nourishment through their skin; the plants, which feed on the sun and earth; and the animals with their system of passages through which they ingest and eliminate a variety of types of encapsulated energy. And just from this last unusual strain, let us say about 10 million years ago, humanity was born and a new type of consciousness emerged. Beings were now moving about the biosphere, altering the environment to meet their own interests and needs.

The human species is very young—if we imagine Gaia is in midlife with another 4½ billion years to go, then our species, with its 10 million years since birth, is the equivalent of a two-month-old baby. Perhaps little should be expected of so young a species, especially one with no guideposts by which it can judge its performance. Yet we as humans must open our eyes to the potentials of consciousness, service, and transcendence all at once, for the choices we make today will determine our future.

The age of conscious evolution is upon us. How shall we rise to the occasion?

Evolution of Gaia

Scientists do not know how long fetal Earth may have been dwelling in the womb before birth, nor in what manner she was conceived. Metascience says that Gaia was born of the solar family, one child of a single evolutionary intention, an expression of divine experiment. For many millennia the esoteric science of the ancients regarded the planet as a living organism, capable of self-reflective intelligent activity in relation both to herself and to other planetary beings. However, this understanding of Gaia and the related sciences have almost entirely disappeared from human consciousness.

The Gaia Hypothesis

Recently a most remarkable bit of speculative science came to light. In 1975, the publication of the *Gaia Hypotheses* by James Lovelock and Sydney Epton offered for the first time a scientifically based synthesis of geophysical research and ancient tradition regarding the nature of Gaia. Thus the Western mind first formulated the Gaia Hypothesis, which regards Gaia as a living self-regulative organism.

Since Earth's beginnings, the atmosphere appears to have been regulated by something or someone—an intelligence, an evolutionary intention, a guiding wisdom—that has demonstrated its ability by controlling atmospheric conditions in just exactly the range necessary for the survival and evolution of life. This hypothesis would explain the constancy of temperature; for the past 3½ billion years it has remained within the range of 15–30 degrees centigrade (between freezing and boiling). According to our current understanding of the laws of chemical equilibrium, a marked increase in solar radiation over the last 4 billion years should have caused planetary temperature to climb intolerably. Yet, Gaia found a way through microbiological production of heat-retaining gases to keep cool.

The Gaia Hypothesis would also explain the consistent life-sustaining oxygen content in the atmosphere. This oxygen ratio was established some 2 billion years ago—not so coincidentally, it appears—at just that time when microbiological organisms that feed on oxygen were evolving. This highly oxygenated, life-supportive atmosphere has remained constant ever since.

The Gaia Hypothesis inverts the long-held "struggle hypothesis" of organic life on Earth fighting for survival in alien or even hostile conditions. From the perspective of the Gaia Hypothesis it seems the very opposite is true—that the biosphere actively controls atmospheric conditions, to further the well-being of life.

The Gaia Hypothesis postulates the existence of an ancient living wisdom capable of making judgments and initiating change in the service of evolution. This guiding wisdom is analogous to the unconscious wisdom of the individual body: a highly refined, subtle, efficient consciousness capable of a variety of responses to an equally large variety of influences or environmental changes.

THE BIRTH OF UNIVERSAL HUMANITY

Although humanity is an exceptionally young being learning self-direction, the species has a task before it requiring the maturity and wisdom of adulthood. It seems appropriate that Gaia, a being in mid-life, would just about now be developing her capacity for self-consciousness. This newly discovered self-awareness will be quite distinct from her ancient self-regulative wisdom. This new capacity will be more superficial, more volatile, more able to learn in a variety of modes and more capable of unprecedented, experimental behavior.

As the collective human consciousness is woven into an intelligent fabric, we are likely to find we have been brought through this long journey to serve a purpose. Hence, Gaia enters the stage of conscious evolution by virtue of the development of her function of self-consciousness. Perhaps for the first time, the collective consciousness of humankind becomes sufficiently mature to recognize other realms of conscious beings in this universe of countless 'galaxies, solar systems, and planets. Where are our cotravelers in this adventure of conscious evolution?

As those of us who have embraced this journey reach out, we can feel the separate cells of our planetary system, human individuals, linking with each other and with the animals and plants, empathizing and synergizing. We sense a wave of attraction pulsing through the planet, overcoming the illusion of separation, drawing us into conscious wholeness. We sense the birth of a new intelligence, maturing to expanded function, with a capacity infinitely greater than we have known as separate individuals.

Conscious evolution begins as humans accept responsibility for their environmental, economic, social, and political realities by beginning to restore, heal, and enhance life on Mother Earth. We can exercise our new capacities as a universal species by exploring outer space, learning the language of human genes, developing cybernetic intelligence, searching for extraterrestrial life, remembering our Self.

As capacities emerge and individual awareness heightens, humans begin to recognize their function as planetary evolutionary transformation agents. They begin to feel a resonant love for those others who choose to participate consciously in the process of change. We begin to know that we live in community.

POSTNATAL LIFE

At this historic moment in the life of Gaia, in the first age of conscious evolution, can the future of the human species be foreseen? Perhaps it can.

Some lessons have emerged from our evolutionary past such as the awesome rise of consciousness, freedom, and purposefulness.

As our planet has evolved, old forms have given birth to new, and whole systems have developed out of separate parts. Consider the miracle of synergy, whereby the whole becomes greater than the sum of its parts through the total cooperation of those parts. The cell transcends the molecule through the cooperation of the molecules that form it, just as the human body transcends the individual cells that make it up.

Imagine the result if all human activity were to function synergistically, that is, with each characteristic enhancing the others. Imagine human psychological, spiritual, cultural, and technological potentials working together on a planetary scale. Imagine Gaia at the next stage of evolution with her self-consciousness, universal humanity, joyfully and purposefully directed by the same designing intelligence that created life. Imagine us consciously *co*creative with the evolutionary process.

What might be some of the characteristics of this universal humanity?

Evolutionary Consciousness

Above all else, the fundamental characteristic of universal humanity is evolutionary consciousness. Those who begin to know themselves as conscious participants in the process of creation, synthesizing mystical and secular consciousness, make closer personal contact with the patterns of evolution, the designing intelligence . . . God. Their awareness deepens and expands. They attune from within through their spiritual faculty and see from without with their scientific eyes, joining intuition and reason, just as two eyes become one in seeing.

Intention is strengthened as the mind resonates with the planetary intelligence and acts in harmony with it. The period of limited self-consciousness is over. In retrospect, we may lose the memory of how it felt to be imprisoned in the self-concentration camp. Our species has endured the pain of feeling separate from the creation as, perhaps, a necessary lesson in learning how the world works. Humanity now reunites consciously with the creation as young cocreators. From this perspective Homo sapiens appears to be the transitional link between the animal world and Homo universalis.

Evolutionary Action

Evolutionary action, the complement of evolutionary consciousness, includes protecting the earth, serving all people as members of one body, preserving other species, and building new worlds in the universe by sending forth the seed of Gaia beyond herself.

From the evolutionary perspective, Gaia is a living organism. One of the obvious characteristics of any such being is the capacity to reproduce itself. In fact, miraculously, we find Gaia, at mid-stage in her life cycle, gaining the mechanisms to impregnate the universe with her life through humans, her technology-builders. Infant space programs are, as William Sauber puts it, the means whereby Gaia is building her seed pod to carry the genetic-planetary code of earth-life into the interstellar environment. If we humans do our work well now, the descendants of Gaia will be universal beings.

Technology, potentially destructive to the biosphere, will take its proper role in postnatal life, both helping in the conservation and enhancement of life in the biosphere and enacting the great adventure of interstellar seeding. Within the life-span of this generation, humans can establish an evolutionary milestone, a nonterrestrial resource base on the moon where individuals can learn to build and work in the universe. As Krafft Ehricke, Gerard O'Neill, and other space scientists have pointed out, space is a medium of growth. Solar energy is abundant. The materials of a thousand earths can be found in the asteroids alone. We are surrounded and permeated by infinite space and limitless silence. This is the magnificent arena in which universal humanity can practice its cocreative skills and build new worlds. To do so, it will need to deepen its knowledge of Gaia— her ecology, her recycling mechanisms, her synergistic organizational skills, her aesthetic genius. Compared to the technologies of nature—the genetic code, photosynthesis, the human body—human technology is naive. Once understood as the means of building new forms out of old, technology will become productive beyond the demands of the economy. Abundance, in a properly developed earth-space environment, will be achieved. There is no scarcity in the universe. We will become creators of new resources rather than managers of scarcity.

In building new worlds in space, we will be transformed. No earthbound mind can yet conceive what people will become as they explore the outer reaches of the solar system and continue on into the intergalactic void. It is genuinely new. Beyond the womb of Gaia, the first child born in space will be a genuine evolutionary mutation, a new being.

Synergistic Community Begins

As new technologies are developed and the collective consciousness deepens, we will inevitably move towards new cooperative forms of social organization wherein each member mutually benefits from the development of every other. In order to survive on an increasingly interdependent planet, and especially on designed worlds in space, we must learn to cooperate synergistically. Survival will depend on it. Even now, people are shucking off the stifling husks of bureaucratic, overcentralized systems and inventing new social forms through networking, intentional communities, worker-participation, cooperatives, and so on. These are "all-win" patterns of self-organization and self-government.

"Love thy neighbor as thy self." "Do unto others as you would have them do unto you." "From each according to his ability, to each according to his need." "All men are created equal." Perhaps until now these have been unrealistic expectations. Perhaps these were premonitions of society-to-come. The missing factors may have been evolutionary consciousness and evolutionary action. With a growing awareness and capacity to produce abundance in the earth-space environment, we may finally have the essential components of a global synergy.

Today, with the dawning of a new evolutionary perspective, Gaia is ready to give birth to universal humanity, choosing to cocreate evolution with the designing intelligence of the universe.

To grow toward the next phase of life we must become partners with the process of creation.

COSMIC TIME

The advent of multicellular organization and sexual reproduction introduced death in the evolutionary process. Before that time there was no programmed death—single cells divided to reproduce, achieving a kind of immortality. From the earliest flicker of self-awareness, humans have sensed the limit of death and striven to overcome it, perhaps to return to immortality. All of human history can be interpreted as the effort to overcome the limits of life as we know it. Eating, sleeping, reproducing, and dying have never fully satisfied Homo sapiens, in whom burns a flame of longing for immortality and union with God.

Today, the possibility of succeeding in this endeavor does not seem quite so remote. With a whole spectrum of abilities—body awareness, self-healing, personal responsibility for health, the power for positive thinking, better nutrition, new images of optimum wellness and creativity, deeper community, and more sensitive attunement—combined with the experience of living in space and understanding the language of the genetic code, humans may gain the option of extended life.

This capacity will give people time to become cosmic beings. From an evolutionary perspective, the meaning of extended life is creative action in the unlimited environment of the universe. Increased longevity has no advantage to an earth-only species on an overcrowded planet. But for a universal species who will carry the life of Gaia beyond the solar system, it becomes a necessity.

Our beautiful mammalian bodies were designed of this earth and for this earth. They are not designed for the stars. Conscious evolution will begin the great task of nurturing the body into new forms commensurate with new environments. Individuals will become mothers to themselves. No one knows what will be needed. Through genetics and microbiology humans are learning body-changing skills in the protected environment of their first home. These godlike powers will probably be unwanted here. They are too much for Earth to endure. It would be like trying to grow forever in the womb. It would destroy both mother and child.

Genetics and astronautics developed in the same generation that recognized the limits to human growth within Gaia. This new potential of greatly extended longevity does not seem any more "accidental" than the invention of the genetic code and photosynthesis.

Soon people will identify not with this particular bodily form they have inherited, but with the creative intelligence that designs all new bodies. For humans are becoming co-designers of new bodies, first to correct genetic defects, then to create new microorganisms through recombinant DNA. The biological revolution is preparation for the next phase of consciously developed life in the universe.

New choices may enter history. Death by choice. Life by choice. A new way of transcending through body comprehension and body building, instead of body failure and death. Individuals will not "pass on" by cancer and heart disease at the next phase of evolution. Religious premonitions that foretold a generation that would not have to submit to physical death nor be bound to this earth will be confirmed.

" . . . and there shall be no more death
neither sorrow, nor crying, neither shall
there be any more pain; for the former
things are passed away." Revelations

COSMIC CONTACT

The search for extraterrestrial intelligence is already on. The great listening dishes are straining for signals. Scientists are sending infant cries into the vastness of space, not certain where to aim the signals or to whom, if anyone, they should be addressed. UFO research intensifies. Millions report sightings and congregate at the great science fiction films, the catacomb art at the dawn of the universal age.

An encounter with extraterrestrials as a shared, normal experience may await our own maturing as a species. Homo sapiens must become extraterrestrial to recognize other life forms. Like a newborn child, humans are probably already surrounded by life but are too immature to know it.

Now is the time of preparation. What if a real visitation were to be picked up by the mass media? Widespread panic does not seem unlikely. As a species we are clearly not yet sufficiently mature to be able to intelligently respond to a more mature civilization. Yet we are learning. As we unite on earth and reach out into space, we may join a constellation of cultures; the next quantum transformation will begin.

CYBERNETIC SELF-EXTENSION

Until recently the human body has been primarily an instrument of action. Now the body is becoming a house of thought, not merely something with which to travel and work. If a picture could be taken of the extended brain/body, it would reveal a variety of extrasensory capacities expressed in machines, autos, rockets, telescopes, microscopes, and computers. These machines are being cybernated, automated, and miniaturized. They are becoming intelligent, self-correcting, almost self-reproducing. Scientists are approaching the threshold of creating what Robert Jastrow of NASA calls "silicon-based life."

Machines are already working automatically to perform many of the earth-keeping chores: sensing data, communicating information, and producing goods and services without the requirement of human labor. For an earth-only species, cybernetics could be a disaster. It would remove forms of work and employment from growing populations. But for a universal species beginning to cocreate a harmonious planetary environment and new environments in space, these intelligent human extensions appear natural, vital, and essential.

If our only intention were to adapt to terrestrial limits, we humans would have to suppress our evolutionary capacities. The type of knowledge being discovered today is a power too great for the womb of Earth to contain. Recall what happened after the Renaissance, when Savonarola burned books to preserve the faith and the Holy Roman Church burned heretical seekers after knowledge. Humans today are capable of reenacting such travesties on a planetary scale. However, if humanity's intention is to utilize its new capacities to become a universal species—working with the God-force to build new heavens and a new earth—these new-found knowledge and abilities will appear natural. From the perspective of the next stage of evolution, these abilities can be seen as the first efforts of a cosmic baby to crawl, to babble, to smile, and after much trial and error, to finally stand and walk as universal humanity.

COSMIC INDIVIDUALITY

What are the characteristics of the "future human"? Imagine a child born into a civilization that is using its collective capacities harmoniously, including new abilities such as space development, extended health, cybernetics, and so on. Such a child, perhaps our own children, perhaps even ourselves, will experience an emancipation of creativity, which has heretofore been the prerogative of the few—geniuses, saints, and seers.

The peaks of human performance will become new models rather than inaccessible heights. The artistry of Leonardo da Vinci, the insight of Einstein, the genius of Edison, the countless examples of super-performance in athletics, music, dance, and design, will become standards of excellence toward which humans aspire.

The 90 percent untapped human potential, which has been held in reserve during the period of early humanity, will be actualized. During the first phase of their evolution, Homo sapiens learned painfully how the material world works. They gained capacities to produce sufficiency for all, to overcome illness, to free humanity from the labor of reproduction and the struggle for physical survival.

Now, as the second phase of humanity approaches, the transition from Homo sapiens to Homo universalis, from self-consciousness to cocreation, will call forth the untapped potential of human beings. Already it is being activated by the challenges that humanity faces at this moment of transition in the life of Gaia. The profound mystery of the inner self and the vast magnificence of the outer universe will be revealed and seen as one. People will learn what it means to be fully human.

OUR EVOLUTIONARY FUTURE:
AN AFFIRMATION OF THE VISIONS OF THE PAST

Today the great spiritual premonitions of the prophets are finally finding fulfillment through the fusing of our spiritual and scientific capabilities. What have been considered paranormal abilities in the prescientific period—astral travel, telekinesis, and precognition—may in the future be our rightful inheritance. It is up to our generation to continue the evolutionary quest, to discover God's plan, to realize our full potential, to honor our past as children of Gaia, and to begin in good faith to join a community of enlightened beings. The desire for deeper union with the creative intelligence is satisfied. The separation is over. The prophecies of old will be fulfilled as universal humanity embarks on the adventure of conscious evolution.

NORMAN SEEF

Question: What well-known American has been a West Point cadet, scientist, brain researcher, Harvard professor, psychedelic guru, hippie, prison inmate, escaped prison inmate, political refugee, Black Panther, author of more than a dozen books and monographs, promoter of space colonization, proponent of life extension, stand-up comedian, radio talk show host, night club entertainer, and self-professed visitor from outer space?

There could only be one answer to this question: Dr. Timothy Leary.

Timothy Leary began his career with distinguished work on behavioral styles and game/role playing. By 1959 he was a faculty member in the psychology department at Harvard University where he soon proved himself to be a superb teacher and an inventive researcher. Leary's position at Harvard began to deteriorate after he began experimenting, along with Drs. Ralph Metzner and Richard Alpert (a.k.a. Baba Ram Dass), with psychedelic drugs. His enthusiasm for the then still legal drugs threatened his more conservative colleagues and disrupted activities at Harvard to the point where Leary was fired.

Although in recent times he has not attained the level of public interest that marked his psychedelic years, Leary continues to be deeply involved in an assortment of causes ranging from space migration and life extension to the conscious evolution of planetary intelligence.

A ceaselessly energetic lecturer and writer, Leary's output has been prodigious: The Dimensions of Intelligence, Interpersonal Diagnosis of Personality, The Psychedelic Experience *(with Richard Alpert and Ralph Metzner),* How to Start Your Own Religion, High Priest, The Politics of Ecstasy, Jail Notes, Confessions of a Hope Fiend, The Periodic Table of Evolution, The Game of Life, Neuropolitics, *and* The Sex Goddess and the Harvard Professor.

In this essay on the future of science, Dr. Leary describes what he feels to be the most significant past, present, and future areas of scientific breakthrough and contribution, as judged by an imaginary "academy awards of science" committee. By identifying these special people and explaining their respective areas of study and research, Leary ingeniously describes those areas of science and exploration that he feels will prove to be the most influential in shaping the present and future destiny of humankind.

SCIENCE

Every branch of science currently is exploding with theories, techniques, and discoveries that dramatically change our concepts of the universe. These new insights also change our concepts of human nature from the passive to the active mode, giving both the individual and the species an incredible range of auspicious, liberating options that were envisioned by, but technologically inaccessible to, utopian philosophers and visionary scientists of the past.

Underlying these breakthroughs is the unifying insight that *intelligence*—the reception, processing, and transmission of information—is the operating principle of the universe. Every energy-bundle, whether atomic-nuclear or amino-acid-molecular, is a signal to be decoded. As long as our tool for understanding the universe is the brain, then inevitably we will come to define the universe in terms of information-processing systems, i.e., as a giant brain.

The application of these new scientific methods will eliminate the prescientific problems of poverty, territorial conflict, disease, aging, death, pollution, overpopulation. When? As soon as the current primitive taboos against science and technology are destroyed and human beings are defined as intelligent, self-determining, evolving organisms harmoniously moving through an intelligent universe.

The aim of this essay is to explain, personalize, popularize the New Scientists who are responsible for these advances in technology and methodology. I shall review eight breakthrough areas and glamorize the exploits of the visionary, courageous, independent, attractive, very human women and men whose brains have so transformed our futures.

THE SCIENTIST AS HERO

The evolutionary level of a culture can be diagnosed by studying its heroes. It is the mark of a barbarous, warlike culture that its heroes are military

277

conquerors. It is the mark of an intelligent species that its heroes are models of sagacity and courage in probing the unknown. We are all honored by living at a time when these new superstar scientists are rewriting human destiny.

Evolution, of course, operates at its own schedule, producing swarms of advanced organisms when the time to mutate is at hand. For every one of the heroes described in this article, there are scores of colleagues who are adding weight, momentum, and support to their discoveries. I apologize in advance to the many genius scientists who are left unmentioned. It is my hope that by writing this PR puff, I can contribute to the recognition of those upon whom our future rests. Never have so few contributed so much to the welfare of all forms of life.

Throughout history those who successfully probed the mysteries of nature have been treated with an awed and flawed suspicion. Usually they have been seen as wizards, magicians, aliens, often as agents of the devil. Why? Because they think for themselves. Scientists have rarely been popular figures. Typically they have been sponsored, protected, patronized by rulers who benefited by their work. The average person has never understood how scientists operate. In the past this has not slowed down the advance of knowledge because kings and dictators paid the bills and no one cared what the peasants thought anyway—as long as SHe didn't think for hirself.

After the technological revolution, scientists were supported by large corporations or the military and were thus protected from the marketplace of public opinion.

In the last two decades the cultural situation in America has changed. We who inhabit the USA-TV are now governed by a media-ocracy, a television democracy of competing pressure groups. While this equality of expression is an inevitable mark of a civilized species, legislating majority rule at the expense of scientific advance is genetically suicidal. Because the grim bottom line is this: Science and only science can solve the problems of the past and produce the improved future.

It is not the military, not the politicians nor the racial-religious leaders upon whom our survival and evolution depend; it is the scientists. The media image of science is suddenly a matter of tremendous evolutionary significance because today, in our wonderfully volatile American society, scientists are forced to compete with other interests for financial and public support.

The situation is rather thrilling. Scientists belong to a special caste. Their brains are wired differently. They use special languages, rituals, modes of thought. They inhabit realities very different from those inhabited by the majority. Scientists, like it or not, belong to an almost monastic elite that operates in the future tense. Traditionally they are viewed with respect because they are clearly very intelligent. In the past they have been tolerated because they have kept a low profile, avoiding glamorous publicity and using a language that prudishly avoids the hype of politics and the vainglorious rhetoric of religion. Their jargon underplays, camouflages the far-out, mind-boggling glory of the subject matter. Without the help of the publicity department, Copernicus kept his discoveries secret from the Vatican thought-police for eighteen years.

When we examine the classic media image of scientists, we run into the dread Frankenstein Complex, which has probably encouraged more stupidity than any myth since that of Christ, the Redeemer of our Sins (sic). Frankenstein was introduced in 1818 by Mary Wollstonecraft Shelley. In this "novel of terror," a young, idealistic, heroic student learns the secret of infusing life into inanimate matter and creates a monster that ultimately destroys him. Heh, heh. There! That will teach a lesson to those who want to think for themselves. This legend revives the ancient Prometheus myth. Prometheus was a recombinant DNA researcher who created humanity out of mud and water. When Zeus, the local soviet commissar, enslaved humanity, it was Prometheus who stole fire and gave it to WoMan. He taught us many useful arts and sciences. He saved our species from a disastrous flood (in contrast to the murderous Jehovah). In reward for these services, he was chained in solitary confinement and tortured. The chemist Lavoisier was beheaded by the French reformers. Oppenheimer was tried, persecuted, and disgraced. At this moment Soviet physicist Andrei Sakharov is exiled to a remote province for independent thinking.

The corporate bureaucrats who now manage our myths from Hollywood have continued this derogation of the independent scientist to our extreme disadvantage. In *The Boys From Brazil*, a genius biologist develops human cloning techniques and produces not 100 Gloria Steinems but 100 little Hitlers! Other brilliant, bold, creative fellows who fabricate cities underwater and in space or cleverly foil the combined plots of the Soviet-American militaries are destroyed by a macho CIA-KGB wretch named James Bond.

This distrust of scientists is a relic from earlier stages of evolution when generals, sultans, and popes were in charge and scientists were dangerous employees, untrustworthy because their loyalty to their craft was greater than to the local Zeus. Scientists always made religious people nervous because their discoveries challenged the authority of dogma, particularly the Bible. Every new discovery violated common sense. "My god, now they are claiming that this solid, flat earth is a spinning sphere orbiting around the sun!" These irreverent flakes continually produced new facts and theories that changed things. That was the problem. Science instigates changes, and changes are always scary to powerholders.

Worst of all, scientists are arrogantly independent individualists. They trust their own data and the integrity of their own minds. They are basically heretical, audaciously defending their own views of reality. Scientists in the past were thus fore-castes, futants, early representatives of later, more advanced stages of evolution in which the individual is expected to make up hir own mind.

Scientists survived, heroically, because they were indispensable. Their magic worked. Rulers who patronized them could use their technologies for health, transportation, communication, engineering, to defeat enemies and live more comfortably.

During the industrial revolution a curious detente developed. Scientists were domesticated, co-opted, rewarded, even honored. In return they produced philosophic models that supported, not the jealous god Zeus nor the irritable Jehovah, but a practical, Protestant deity whose clockwork design was slowly, comfortably winding down. The Newtonian universe operated on the pessimistic principle of entropy. Dutiful Darwin, once the giddy, fast-moving optimism of Lamarck was anathematized, proved that changes evolve slowly over millions of years. Engineering may ease the pain of day-to-day living, but the classic science scenario had us on an insignificant boondock planet, itself doomed to heat-death. There was no escape from aging and death. Nature was enemy, a wog to be colonized; our survival strategies became defensive. The ultimate helplessness of nineteenth-century science did nothing to disturb the bleak, monolithic pessimism of the Judeo-Christian Bible. Examine one of those famous black-and-white photos of gloomy scientists taken at their meetings in Copenhagen or Vienna or Berlin and you will be reminded of a bankers' convention or an undertakers' reunion.

But all that is changing. Science has become Americanized, i.e., optimistic, expansive, self-confident. Scientists are mutating like everyone else in this country. How? In the direction of self-confident, self-directed, self-responsible narcissism. In the last two decades every American institution has suffered a severe loss in public confidence. It seems that almost everyone is getting sophisticated enough to question authority. Everyone is suddenly thinking for hirself. The officials are outraged, of course, denouncing the Me Generation. But it's nothing new. It's the old Red-White-and-Blue rugged frontier individualism of Carnegie, Mellon, Edison now joyfully accepted by the person in the street. If the big guys can get away with it, impose their will, their personal reality, then why can't we? Suddenly we all are proud of our genetic singularity. Black pride. Gay heroes. Latin-American pride. Women's liberation. Even those former models of docility, professional athletes, get managers and become free agents. Everyone is coming out of the closets of conformity and taking responsibility for his or her life.

This explosion of giddy, proud individuality in the last two decades has encouraged almost everyone to proclaim, validate, and busily maintain their own idiosyncratic view of reality. Cosmic self-confidence is in the air. Otherwise normal people are running around claiming to be sent from Atlantis or Sirius to save our planet. Fundamentalist Christians announce an impending Armageddon that only Southern Baptists will survive. Whoopee!

In this wonderful, kooky transition period when the old religions are collapsing and arrogant heresies are flourishing, suddenly that most powerful minority—the Smart Ones, the scientists—are coming out of the closet declaring themselves free agents and publishing their new views of the universe. Each science is taking its turn at violating one of the ancient taboos that have defined our species as helpless and mortal.

This is a momentous occasion in the history of humanity, because the scientific method works. Innovative intelligence is the ultimate tool. When it was hunter-gatherer time, the scientists found the flint and chipped the knives. When it was agriculture time, the Smart Ones selected the seed and dug the irrigation canals. When it was world war empire time, the physicists produced radar, rockets, and nukes.

Now, as we move into the Age of Information, intelligence—not manpower nor firepower but brainpower—is the key to survival. The day of the scientist-hero has dawned! The Season of Prometheus. It's time for the neolithic athlete and the barbarous general and the Metternich politician to step aside and for new superstars to emerge. It is simply an intelligent use of intelligence for scientists to use their skills to glamorize and empower their own caste. Scientists of the World, Unite. You have nothing to use but your brains!

Let's put it bluntly: Scientists should stop shirking their responsibility and take charge of human affairs. When we were territorial primates we were naturally led by barnyard politicians. We now understand that spaceship Earth is a delicate, complex web of energy processes that must be understood and harmonized if we are to survive. Politics has become too important to be left to politicians who cannot and will not comprehend the situation. Our rulers in the future must be people with scientific training and with brains wired to handle relativistic complexity. We would not let the controls of a 747 jet fall into the hands of congressmen. Human societies have become much more complex mechanisms than jet planes.

Scientists must be encouraged to descend from their suburban split-levels and accept the decision-making authority. Our officials should be selected the way our athletic teams are chosen—on the basis of recorded performance, of demonstrated excellence.

In their hearts most Americans know this to be true. The current disillusion with politics, the abject decline of the presidency reflect the deep, instinctual hunger we all feel for excellence in our leaders.

Each month a South American country is taken over by a small junta of generals with guns. Even in democratic America we have quickly turned over our last few presidents. Since 1960 not one president has completed the normal two terms. This is good. It represents a speed-up of the change process. It's about time for a junta of scientists to organize and take over the government using their secret weapon—fair-minded intelligence.

For starters let's have the Nobel Prize awards ceremony televised with the suspense and hype of the Oscar ceremonies. Flood the land with bumper stickers announcing: INTELLIGENCE IS THE ULTIMATE APHRODISIAC! Picket and boycott all movies that glorify stupidity. Forget violence and pornography; successful ignorance is what our children should not be exposed to. My god, imagine the outcry if Baptists, Jews, or blacks were villain-typecast the way scientists are.

As a modest step in the process of intelligence increase, I nominate for adulation, acclaim, stardom the following eight scientists who have recently overturned eight great stupefying taboos of the past:

John Lovelock and Lynn Margulis, originators of the *Gaia theory,* whose concept of intelligent creative evolution has relegated both Genesis and Darwin to the archaeological museum.

Ilya Prigogine for his Self-Organizing-Dissipative-Structure theory, which has freed us from the punitive, oppressive, unconstitutional Second Law of Thermodynamics.

Harvard philosopher Nelson Goodman, who personalizes the self-deterministic implications of quantum theory.

Gerard O'Neill for his carefully designed space colonization plans.

The brave researchers working in neurotransmitter and brain-activating drugs.

J. R. Chakrubarty and Ian Kennedy, controversial genetic engineers and pioneers in cloning technology.

Roy Walford of UCLA, a giant in the all-important histocompatibility locus antigen field, whose work will allow us soon to immunize ourselves against disease, neural inefficiency, aging, and death.

Edward Wilson for his work in sociobiology.

EIGHT SCIENTIST SUPERSTARS

John Lovelock and Lynn Margulis, Originators of the Gaia Principle

The Gaia principle suggests that all species of living organisms collaborate in a grand web of biological intelligence. One obvious purpose of this life network is to terraform our planet and keep it fit for life. The Gaia hypothesis involves the collaboration of a brilliant Englishman, John Lovelock, and an unconventional cell biologist, Lynn Margulis, who had been obsessed for years by the realization that the modern intelligent, metropolitan cell had been formed by interspecies "clubbing" and symbiotic linkages of primitive protozoa.

The saga of Lovelock and Margulis has been brought to us by Stewart Brand's *Co-Evolution Quarterly,* a lively maverick journal that simply must be read by anyone who wants to know what's happening on the frontier edges of the twentieth century. If you subscribe to the relevant back issues, you will learn that Lovelock is that most fascinating person, an independent scientist smart enough to win big in hard science operating from his own home, his own head. The movie rights to this man's life will be worth an asteroid or two in the next century. It was Lovelock's insight that life itself controls the temperature and chemical environment on this planet in order to ensure its own survival. "Cooperation among living organisms, from microbes to elephants . . . kept the Earth in the peculiar state in which all species could flourish. Thus living matter, together with the air, the oceans and the continents, made up a giant and complex system which behaved almost like a living organism that maintained its internal milieu by subtle feedback processes."

How fitting that it was an intelligent and beautiful woman, Lynn Margulis, who could provide Lovelock with a list of the micro organisms that Gaia, the biological intelligence, uses to maintain the special conditions that make Earth viable. "In Lovelock's theory, the air acts like the bloodstream of an animal, bringing essential supplies to all of the Earth's inhabitants and carrying waste products away."

For millennia, humans at their most lucid moments have worshipped Gaia, the Great Earth Mother principle of biological intelligence. Lovelock and Margulis now provide the technical details that give us some insight into "how She does it."

Among the many startling implications of this neo-ancient theory is the notion that evolution is not a blind, rapacious competition of struggling organisms but a highly intelligent collaboration in which humans play an important role. The Gaia theory gives life dignity, feminine wisdom, and offers us the chance to participate consciously in interspecies symbiotic connections.

It was my pleasure recently to hear Lynn Margulis discuss the biopolitical goal of raising unicellular consciousness. Here we meet the delightful paradox shared by each of the eight scientific philosophies we shall be honoring. The more we study other forms of energy, the more intelligence we discover, different from us but equally as wise and, indeed, often dancing to the same rhythms. From the perspective of unicellular families, those colonies of great complexity and ingenuity, we humans are transportation and housing devices beautifully designed to nurture and stir up things for our Higher Intelligence passengers.

When we understand how very intelligent the bacteria are, we will be able to harmonize with them, learn from them, and, greatest loving step, consciously collaborate with them.

The Self-Organizing-Dissipative-Structure Theory of Ilya Prigogine

Are we ready for another Einstein? Well here's a logical candidate, a Nobel-prize-winning chemist who has freed us from the death sentence implied in the Second Law of Thermodynamics. Prigogine took the pessimistic closed-system notion of entropy and converted it to an optimistic, mathematically sound mechanism in the evolution of intelligence. By showing how complex systems can arise from less complex ones, he helps bridge the gap between biology and physics, a contribution towards the unified field theory that Einstein, the mathematical junky, sought vainly to find in his equations.

The important task of presenting Prigogine to the nonscientific community was begun by Marilyn Ferguson. Her *Brain-Mind Bulletin*, like *Co-Evolution Quarterly*, is an indispensable guide to the frontiers of science and philosophy. Here is Ferguson's summary of Prigogine:

> How did life develop in a universe of ever-increasing disorder? How do order and complexity emerge from entropy?
>
> This riddle has been plaguing science for centuries, of course, and it has created a wide gap between biology and physics—between the study of living systems and the study of the apparently lifeless universe in which they arise.
>
> Now Ilya Prigogine, a physical chemist, offers a startling explanation, complete with mathematical proofs: Order emerges *because* of entropy, not *despite* it!
>
> Prigogine's theory applies to open systems, in which a structure exchanges energy with the surrounding environment. It can be a laboratory chemical solution, an amino acid, a human being.

These are what he calls "dissipative structures." Their form or pattern is self-organizing, maintained by a continuous dynamic flow.

The more complex such a structure, the more energy it must dissipate to maintain all that complexity. This flux of energy makes the system highly unstable, subject to internal fluctuations—and sudden change.

If these fluctuations, or perturbations, reach a critical size, they are amplified by the system's many connections and can drive the whole system into a new state—even more ordered, coherent and connected.

The new state occurs as a sudden shift, much as a kaleidoscope shifts into a new pattern. It is a nonlinear event; that is, multiple factors act on each other at once.

With each new state, there is greater potential for change. With new levels of complexity, there are new rules. As Prigogine put it, there is a change in the nature of the 'laws' of nature.

Brain-Mind Bulletin, May 21, 1979

"Time, complexity, and self-organization were to become his [Prigogine's] central themes," says Ferguson. "He wanted to understand the processes of change and evolution." Like all the Smart Ones celebrated in this essay, Ilya Prigogine has learned the great lesson of our times: that intelligence can, indeed *is*, designed to determine the future.

Nelson Goodman and the Self-Deterministic Narcissism of Quantum Physics

For centuries scientists and philosophers labored under a most depressing and servile onus. God, or some other grim lawmaker, had fabricated the universe out there. All that "mankind" could do was poke away at the local aspects of "It," attempting to scratch out a brief and precarious existence. The goal of the docile, submissive scientist was to decipher, step by step, the infinite Bible of creation. The scientist was code clerk faithfully interpreting what was already writ, playing the role of primitive magician-shaman passively examining the entrails of birds, performing scholastic translations of the great text of nature. This servile approach to knowledge is the Fundamentalist Christian-Moslem insistence that "God" had adjudicated once and for all in the Bible-Koran and that "man's" role is to passively listen to and obey the laws of nature.

We have noted that most nineteenth-century physicists were highly conventional engineer-type thinkers living in and influenced by the Judeo-Christian reality, meekly accepting this superstitious, supplicant attitude.

The mental fix, the reality frame that focused and limited all Western thought was monotheism: the barbarous notion that there is One-and-Only-One God, a male, of course, who made the universe and rules over it like a Middle-Eastern sultan.

This insidious, pervasive, and wretched concept still dominates the thinking of "civilized" people. If there is one God, then there is one reality, and a dismal, slavish one it is for God's subjects. Those who refuse to accept the monotheistic authority are obviously either evil, infidel, or insane, i.e., alienated from "reality."

Precivilized people operated from a multiple reality position. Every kith, kin, tribe had its own cosmology and ontology. At the more elegant level of Eastern philosophy, everyone was God, if and when they were willing to accept the lonely responsibility and excitement of intersecting with other divinities.

The problem with monotheism is that many different groups arise, each claiming to represent the One-and-Only, each demanding the right to destroy all others as heretics. Newtonian physics was a monotheistic model of a universe run by fixed commands. Monotheists love ominous terms such as "eternal laws," "laws of nature."

Albert Einstein's theory of relativity was the first scientific explosion of the mono-reality. Einstein's equations proved that motions, velocities, and locations can be measured only in relation to each other. Since everything is changing, changeability is the key to measurement.

Now Einstein, a good conservative moralist, could never face the indeterminacy and multiple-reality implications of his own work. He apparently went to his grave believing that "out yonder is this huge world which exists independently of human beings and which stands before us like a great eternal riddle, at least partially accessible to our inspection and thinking."

Quantum physics has changed all that. Niels Bohr, Max Planck, Louis de Broglie, and Paul Dirac showed that the "real world" of Einstein did not exist, but it was Werner Heisenberg who destroyed the monolithic concept of a fixed reality with his principle of uncertainty. This holds that we can only measure what we measure, can only study what our brain focuses on, that we cannot, with high accuracy, determine both the position and velocity of an atomic particle. This principle is erroneously called *indeterministic*. It is more properly called the *principle of determinacy* in its recognition that the scientist determines the reality SHe investigates. This wonderful ontological freedom distresses those who are dependent upon the authority of a fixed, given universe but delights those who accept the glorious responsibility. It is Bohr's mind and behavior that construct and maintain the reality he studies. The philosophic implications of quantum multiple realities have been thoughtfully discussed by J. A. Wheeler ("the universe is preselected by consciousness"), Nobel laureates Eugene Wigner and Brian Josephson ("consciousness is at the root of the quantum principle from which space-time-mass arise as secondary structures"), and Jack Sarfatti ("the physicist is an artist who molds atomic reality with the aesthetic integrity of his intention"). Popular books by Fritjof Capra and Gary Zukav have demonstrated the correspondence between ancient oriental philosophies, especially Zen, and the flux of quantum physics.

The most probing examination of the implications of multiple-reality determinism has been provided by Harvard philosopher Neil Goodman.

"From Goodman's perspective, it is misleading to speak of the world as it is, or even of a single world. It makes more sense to think of various versions of the world that individuals may entertain, various characterizations of reality that might be presented in words, pictures, diagrams, logical propositions, or even in musical compositions. Each of these symbol systems captures different kinds of information and hence presents different versions of reality.

"In Goodman's view, works of art (like the models of physicists) can also be profitably viewed as samples. Just as certain fabric swatches accurately reflect the whole bolt, so may certain works of art accurately reflect . . . important forms, feelings, affinities, and contrasts from the fabric of life."

The above quotes were taken from an article by Howard Gardner, a Harvard psychologist who is performing the valuable function of psychologizing, personalizing, humanizing the insights of frontier physics. Gardner's piece was published in *Psychology Today*, another magazine that performs a valuable function in scientizing, and thus empowering, the intelligent public.

The Space Migration Proposals of Gerard O'Neill

In one of those great leaps of scientific intuition, O'Neill took information and technology from several dozen different disciplines and fit them together in a practical mosaic in which the unthinkable suddenly appears as practical inevitability. First he combined the negative pressures of over-population, pollution, decreasing natural resources, energy depletion, global malaise, and loss of frontier with off-the-shelf mechanics of the space program, Sky Lab-Soyuz, planetology, space geology, solar energy, closed-system ecology, asteroid mineralogy, plain old engineering inventiveness, genetic mysticism, migratory mystique, American pioneer expansiveness. He demonstrated that destination-resort space colonies can be built in high orbit with less risk and expense than the colonization of America in the seventeenth century, the Suez and Panama canals of the early twentieth century, or the Alaska pipeline project of the 1970s.

The practicality and feasibility of space colonies, solar satellite power stations, and space industrialization have been argued in several recent books by O'Neill, Thomas Heppenheimer, and Peter Vaik, in the highly readable journal of the activist L-5 Society (1620 N. Park Av., Tucson AZ) and by the permanent Soyuz station, which the Russians now inhabit in high orbit above our lowered heads.

Gerald O'Neill is the stuff of which myths are made. Like all of the New Scientists, he established his credentials as a successful, practical, hardware establishment researcher. He then used his security as a launching pad to realize the ancient human yearning for celestial habitation. Like the other superstar scientists profiled in this chapter, O'Neill is good-looking and charismatic. This may not be an accidental statistic. It may be that one has to like oneself, dig one's body, feel good within, before one can manifest the self-determination and self-confidence necessary to violate the monotheistic taboos. In any case, O'Neill is articulate, poetic, visionary, and easily wins his spot in the Scientific Hall of Fame as our first postterrestrial philosopher.

It is no surprise that many of the leading voices for space colonization are women's. It would have to be that way. Test-pilot astronauts and military Soyuz flyers make the first Viking raids on the New World, but nothing happens until the egg-bearing, higher-intelligent women get involved. The movement to make space migration a civilian enterprise has been managed by Caroline Henson, founder of the L-5 Society; Barbara Marx Hubbard, evolutionary philosopher; Arel Lucas, editor of the *L-5 News;* and Kathy Keeton, editor of *Omni* magazine, who has also worked intelligently to make the future aesthetic and civilized.

The New Generation of Brain-Drug Researchers

A century ago in Victorian England and Freudian Vienna the genitalia were the taboo organ. Strong men would faint at the sight of a lady's ankle. The sexual liberation of the 1960s has converted the unmentionables into the *Playboy* unavoidables. And a new organ was invested with taboo. The brain is now the part of our body that we are forbidden to play with, handle, explore, delight in, turn on, talk about, or expose scandalously to others.

The sexual taboo was understandable. If the average citizen catches on that exquisite, aesthetic pleasures are available by confident exploration of one's erotic equipment, then the rewards of society and the punitive threats of religion are no longer so coercive. It is no coincidence that now, as the Me Generation revels in its own independent power to reward itself, disillusion with politics reaches a new high.

But the taboo against brain-change is even more understandable. Why does the word "drug" touch the jumpy nerve ending of every parent and every bureaucratic powerholder? Because here is the ultimate in self-determination and self-reward. The brain-drug option gives everyone a choice of realities. If the external-social world is ugly or dull or brutish, one can activate subjective realities simply by introducing a pinch of chemical into one's neurology.

Custodians of public morality denounce all drugs as "escapes." From their standpoint, they are correct. The Russians and the Irish spend over a third of their income on strong alcohols to escape the brutal reality of the Soviet system and the boring reality of the priest-run system. What the moral custodians fail to understand is that the personal, subjective realities to which drug users escape are in many cases superior to the grim social rigidities they are fleeing. The brain of the individual is usually more interesting than the brawn of the Soviet moralist. There is an interesting paradox built into the sociology of brain-reward: The freer, the richer, the higher the quality of life, the more technologically advanced the culture, the more varied and tolerated the brain-drug options available. In China there is no drug problem because there is no "problem" of individuality, or creative dissent. In the sophisticated centers of North America where intelligent, creative, innovative people swarm together, you will find a gourmet range of botanicals and chemicals that activate the widest scope of brain circuits, including the new brain-change drugs.

From the vantage point of 1980, two decades after the mass-consumer "head" explosion of the 1960s, we see that the use of brain drugs has followed the inevitable course of social evolution that characterizes all new technologies. We are now observing the emergence of the third generation of brain-changers.

The availability and widespread use of consciousness-altering drugs for recreation, personal growth, life-style enrichment, aphrodisiac enhancement elicited the standard reactions to a new technology: confusion, irrational fear, irrational enthusiasm. When the first generation of automobiles was introduced, there was an absence of roads, road maps, mechanics—and a high ratio of breakdowns. The same was true of the airplane. It was a reckless adventure to fly.

We now look back at the eruption of drug use in the sixties and see that there were no maps, no guideposts, no tradition of usage, and the scary risk of the unknown. Today, however, the average suburban eighteen-year-old knows more about the brain-drug option than the most sophisticated scientists did twenty years ago. Drug usage has been socialized in North America; more and more people are using more drugs with less furor and confusion and accident.

And as was true of the computer, the automobile, the airplane, there are new versions, improvements in drugs, making them stronger, safer, more precise in duration, and brain-function activated.

Since we cannot stop the relentless advance of technologies that provide individual options to consumers, the next rational step is to improve the chemicals so that they are safer and more efficient.

This scientific work is occurring in the laboratories of many universities and pharmaceutical firms. A new breed of psycho-pharmacologists is producing new drugs that will provide the individual with fingertip access to and control of hir own nervous system. There is no mental function or dimension of consciousness that cannot be intensified, accelerated, expanded.

Work on receptor sites and beta-endorphins is isolating chemicals naturally produced by the body that simulate the effects of the most common "head" drugs like morphine or LSD. This research encourages the speculation that soon one can have one's blood typed or one's spinal fluid assayed to isolate and then synthesize precisely the chemicals that one's brain is geared to use as fuel.

Much of this work progresses, of course, in secret. In the busy twenty years since 1960 the federal government has done everything in its power to discourage research in brain-change drugs. The only work allowed has been negative, e.g. millions of tax dollars have been spent to produce an anaesthetic that *does not* make people feel good or expand their consciousness.

The problem of getting experimental subjects is a constant dilemma. The bad old days, when the CIA spent 25 million dollars to dose unsuspecting subjects with LSD, are mercifully over. The good old days, when Albert Hoffman, the brilliant chemist who synthesized LSD and psilocybin and tried the substances out on himself and his friends, are once again the method of choice. Since the effect of a brain-change drug is basically subjective, who, indeed, is better equipped to calibrate and make precise observations than the enlightened chemists and their veteran colleagues?

As new brain drugs emerge that give humans precise control over their own neurology and thus increase intelligence and mental efficiency, how appropriate that it should be the chemists themselves who are the first to use and benefit! When the scientific history of the twentieth century is written, a wonderful chapter will describe the courage and dedication and mutant wisdom of these frontier brain researchers.

Genetic Engineering: Chakrabarty and Kennedy

We have just tiptoed through a controversial mine field, cheering the gradual crumbling of the taboo against self-determinist brain-change drugs. But that's nothing compared to the shivery expansion of the scientific method to DNA alteration.

During the last half of the twentieth century, micro-geneticists, beginning with Watson and Crick, have demonstrated that the DNA code is a double-helical array of protein letters that blueprint, step by step the evolutionary process and development of each individual form of life. An enormous new scientific field—gene splicing, genetic engineering, cloning—has suddenly blossomed.

Here is the ultimate step in active, confident, self-determination. Humanity is taking charge of the evolutionary process and writing the life script. No longer need we cower in helpless fear, victims of a blind genetic destiny. We can now create new forms of life, correct faulty DNA blueprints, use the amino-acid language of life to write the prescriptions preventing aging and death.

There are hundreds of young gene splicers joyfully dedicated to this utopian task. Hey! This heroic band of frontier adventurers should be glamorized, publicized, gossiped about, profiled like rock stars, pro athletes, and politicians. The thrilling, dramatic feats they perform should receive front-page coverage. Every time they score a point, humanity evolves a notch. Rah. Rah. Rah.

The two gene-juggler heroes I have chosen to praise, J. R. Chakrabarty and Ian Kennedy, may or may not be top scientific stars, but they merit distinction because they have created *controversy*! They have "fronted," personalized the eternal Promethean soap-opera violation of the genetic taboo! Any great mutation requires a swarming of many evolutionary agents, Smart Ones, working in seeming independence towards the inevitable next goal. By the mid sixteenth century, for example, there were several hundred Smart Ones who had figured out the heliocentric system. Simon Stevin, for example, had performed crucial experiments before Galileo, but it was the Pisan who attracted the attention, got busted by the Inquisition, crystallized and externalized the idea, and thus made it real in our consciousness. The legend of his dropping balls from the leaning tower is false, but who cares? It made the point. PR, advertising, the ability to charge an idea with polarized energy is the basic technique for advancing human knowledge.

Chakrabarty performed this function. It started when the Indian chemist, via recombinant DNA methods, created in the General Electric laboratory a new life form, a friendly little mutant bacterium that eats oil spills. His claim for a patent was turned down by the U.S. government, which apparently was not ready to recognize the divine, life-creating skills of one of its lowly citizens. Chakrabarty appealed and the Supreme Court in June 1980 issued its most important decision. Chakrabarty was legally credited as owning the life form he had created!

American religious leaders were apparently not smart enough to realize that Jehovah's claim to monopoly had been quietly overthrown. The pope was on the ball; he promptly denounced gene splicing as heretical and he was right.

The effect of the Chakrabarty decision has been profound. It gave genetic engineers a license to step up their work. Brave Chakrabarty! Brave New Life Forms!

It is of genetic interest that this big step forward in courageous self-determination, gene-splicer-as-God-the-Life-Creator, was taken by a man whose gene pool traces back to the Ganges and the three-thousand-year-old Vedic tradition—that every organism has within the bacterial, infectious potentials to become divine.

Ian Kennedy is even more controversial. Working in a "safe" laboratory at U.C. San Diego, this British virologist cloned the semliki forest virus, although he had been given government permission to replicate only the sindbis virus. The rest reads like a B-movie script, replete with villains and victims. The problem was not with the actual research. The semliki forest virus is not dangerous. Dr. Kennedy surely knew this better than the federal officials who classify risk potentials. Indeed, by the time Kennedy's mistake was discovered, his unauthorized clone had been authorized. It was four of Kennedy's graduate students who exposed the existence of the unauthorized virus to the administrators. Kennedy hinted that the substitution of species might have been an act of sabotage. An investigating committee suggested that Kennedy was guilty of a cover-up, and the brilliant researcher was barred from his own lab. Cover-up of what? Of his alleged violation of an outdated memo? Of independent scientific action taken without the approval of a political committee?

While the cloning of another new virus is a significant and laudable step toward eliminating disease, the real importance of the Kennedy affair is that his work exposed the most dangerous disease now and always troubling our species—bureaucratic, political interference with scientific freedom.

Let others quibble over the technicalities. But credit goes to Professor Ian Kennedy for getting himself into the classic Promethean position—a talented, pioneer scientist performing crucial research being harassed by agents of the state. Let's write a best-seller dramatizing this classic confrontation. Sell it to the movies. Let Robert Redford play Kennedy.

Roy Walford: Immunization-Inoculation as Keys to Evolution

When Roy Walford was a child, he pondered about the alleged invincibility of death. Being a thoughtful, intelligent cub, he resolved to devote his life to the cure of this lethal disease. His youthful plan to live forever is now becoming a practical reality.

Cut to Atlanta, spring 1980. On the occasion of his acceptance of the Levine Prize for outstanding contributions to immunology, Walford commented: "I rather confidently expect a significant advance in maximum lifespan potential to be achieved for the human species during what is left of the present century." (!)

In his Atlanta address Walford showed how his studies in the histocompatability locus antigen (HLA) system have "happily merged" with other work on the biology of aging: immunology, DNA repair, free-radical biochemistry and hormone studies.

One of the most fascinating suggestions offered by Walford's research is that aging may be partially caused by a failure in the autoimmune system. You age because your immune system starts producing antigens against your own cells. In other words, you begin to reject yourself. Makes sense when you think about it.

As of September 1980, word was out that some researchers in the field of prolongevity were already testing the new anti-aging drugs on themselves and their parents! When two developments occur in a science—(1) a convergence of many competing cures and (2) the experts dosing themselves—the breakthrough moment is usually close at hand. In this case, the disease against which we can be inoculated is aging-death.

Like the other new-breed Smart Ones praised in this essay, Roy Walford is a renaissance person, a multi-disciplinary, wide-gauge thinker. He's sexually magnetic and that's apparently important. It's becoming clear that philosophers who can't master their bodies and the aesthetic energies of the soma can't help but give us a crippled world view. Kinky Darwin, for example.

And like the other Smart Ones, Walford has systematically opened up his intuitive, relativistic right brain by means of the standard yoga techniques available in the late twentieth century.

The new young scientists have an unfair advantage, when you think of it. The young scientists who grew up in the sixties when right-brain activation was *de rigeur* are simply working with more neural equipment, observing from multi-dimensional perspectives in contrast to the ivory tower academics of the past, who were limited to the logical-analytic-linear models of the left brain.

Walford is a poet. He's a scholarly devotee of art, literature, of the new music. He's the guy you'd ask to show you what's happening along the

THE CULTURE AND BEYOND

membrane frontiers of his own home town. And Roy Walford has made the future his home town.

Edward Wilson: Sociobiologist

Edward Wilson, a most distinguished Harvard biologist, was delivering a scientific paper at the 1978 meeting of the American Association for the Advancement of Science (A.A.A.S.) when he was attacked by a band of militant feminist academicians who poured a pitcher of water over his head. As he stood by the lectern at a prestigious scholarly meeting!

How's that for the start of a TV special?

Now clearly Wilson is doing something right. Anytime a young, respected, attractive frontier scientist gets mugged because hir data and theories touch nerve endings so tender that educated, well-brought-up East-Coast ideologues resort to violent gesture, well, sir, we're alerted to a Prometheus script.

This historical drama started many years previous with a romantic South African physician, Andre Marais, who, disillusioned with human behavior after the bitter Boer War, returned to the Transvaal and spent the rest of his life shooting morphine (from army supplies he had salvaged) while living with tribes of natives, troops of baboons, hives of bees, and colonies of termites.*

He wrote two all-time, all-star texts in social psychology. He had, you see, spent so much time in an altered vegetative state of consciousness, living in closest contiguity to several other animal societies, that he had penetrated their wisdom, been accepted by them. They performed the natural interactions of life right in front of him, even with him. He discovered, of course, that a profound intelligence coursed through these alien societies. He discovered that the basic behavior patterns of these alien species roughly duplicated, in almost all respects, the social behavior of humans. Indeed, in many respects, these so-called lower species had succeeded in solving many urban and territorial problems that even the most advanced humans hardly knew existed in the evolutionary cycle.

Alas for Marais, hurray for us! Marais's books, written in the Afrikaner language, were unavailable to the world until, so the story goes, a Low-Country scholar, Maurice Maeterlinck, republished them in French under his own name and thereby won the Nobel Prize. Marais went back in

---

*Charles Darwin, G.J. Romanes, Herbert Spencer, and William James are more illustrious pioneers in the field of ethology—the naturalistic observation of the interaction between environment and genetically determined responses in animals. I have selected the less renowned Andre Marais for citation here because of the romantic, heroic, picaresque, anti-establishment, mythic, i.e., Promethean aspects of his life and work.

disgust to rejoin his alien friends but he left behind a precious gift: the tradition of participant-interspecies observation that soon became the science of ethology. By the 1960s, the lesson had dawned: If you study rats in mazes of your own device, if you observe baboons in zoo cages, then you learn as much about their behavior as would a Vegan naturalist who watched two human beings, strangers, at that, in a prison cell. So it's off to the field, to the jungle, to those fascinating wild sectors of the planet where species interface directly and right-brain receptive humans can decipher the complex social cultures of alien intelligences.

Konrad Lorentz and Nico Tinbergen carried on this ethological tradition. Lorentz discovered imprinting, an especially rapid and relatively irresistible learning process that occurs early in the individual's life. A central concept complementary to imprinting is the innate releasing mechanism, whereby organisms are genetically predisposed to be especially responsive to certain stimuli. The analogies he draws between human and animal behavior have engendered considerable controversy.

Tinbergen wrote extensively on ritualization in various species. Suddenly from all the studies of social animals the most extraordinary notion was emerging: these other successful species (the termites have been flaunting the same melodramatic life-styles for 150 million years) seemed to be guided by some sort of collective genetic intelligence that uses individuals as preprogrammed specialized units necessary for the collective security. Individuals are apparently harnessed to their division-of-labor realities by means of imprinting that releases their specific innate mechanism.

Now enter Edward Wilson, who writes a classic textbook on the behavior of social animals that he calls *Sociobiology* (Harvard University Press, 1975). "... the evidence immediately available from human genetics, psychology, human social behavior is to some extent genetically constrained over the entire species and furthermore, subject to genetic variation within the species."

Ethology, behavioral genetics, sociobiology (and prescientific, pagan common sense) all focus on a crucial, audacious issue: what ritual, linguistic, social behaviors are used by different species to survive?

The key term here is *behavior*. What are tricks of the life-trade? What are the strategies and tactics, the types of intelligence used by different species?

Once we start studying the genetic behavior of animals, we start gaining insight into the intelligence operations of our own species; even more disturbing, we confront the notion of genetic intelligence, species planning, biological wisdom—heretical, vitalist, creativist notions that we considered in the Gaia section of this chapter.

This ancient cosmological debate—creation versus blind mechanism—can now be settled. Vitalists, scientific creationists find evidence for a biological intelligence that operates within and out from the DNA supply of a gene pool, which designs individuals to perform the behaviors necessary for evolving the species. Mechanists say that it's all a sequence of blind, random mutation. The argument is now irrelevant because once the more advanced members of our species begin to study the tactics used by other species to survive, we can obviously apply the lessons learned to enhance our own evolution. There may or may not have been a genetic intelligence in the past but there sure is now! It's us! The emergence of the science of sociobiology becomes an irresistible, irreversible mutational event. *We* become the genetic intelligence.

Consider this question: How can our species use the survival techniques developed by other successful species to accelerate our own evolution? Once you start thinking at the level of species intelligence, you raise your perspectives from tribal-personal realities to a broader space-time frame that makes the future a most exciting place.

Professor Edward Wilson of Harvard and other sociobiologists have provided several crucial answers to this question: What neuro-technologies does a species develop to raise its intelligence and thus its survival abilities?

1. A smart species becomes *social,* i.e., it divides the labor by producing different genetic subcastes that specialize in the various survival and evolutionary tasks.

I have neither the space nor the reckless courage to detail here the obvious existence of human genetic types designed to play useful roles in the ever-changing scenarios of each gene pool. Homosexuals, warriors, entertainers, editors, and futant philosophers are among the many genetic castes that operate to make our society so wonderfully diverse.

2. A smart species uses *metamorphosis.* The individual of the species is prepackaged so that it develops through certain immature stages, each stage involving different functions and mastery of different neuro-technologies and ecological niches. The advantage of putting individuals through pupal, larval, or cub stages is that the individuals get smarter. A frog is a lot better amphibian because it has mastered the survival skills of the pollywog phase. The basic principle here is that the individual recapitulates many of the earlier stages that the species has mastered and evolved through. Temporal caste means that members of the gene pool at any moment are reliving a wide spectrum of survival techniques in a wide range of environments. At the infant stage humans are malleable amoeboid creatures. Crawling babies maneuver with amphibian neurology. Little kids are primate cubs.

Adolescents play an important role in the human hive, forcing confrontations with the adult stage. At each of these stages the individual can be imprinted with new survival techniques that keep the gene pool evolving. This offers a flexibility, a variability, a range of survival options that allows the species to adapt quickly to meet changing situations.

3. A smart species is *mobile*. It can move its sperm-egg supplies to every potential ecological niche—with increasingly precise control of velocity, altitude, and distance.

4. A smart species has developed the widest possible range of *information receivers-transmitters*.

Wilson and his colleagues have been passionately attacked for suggesting that these neuro-technologies used by other species may be part of our own collective human wisdom. Those who are passionate partisans of one or another religious theory or who believe in the primacy of politics are grievously offended by the notion that genetic factors may account for some, much, or all of our behavior.

Political partisans are especially offended by the notion of *structural caste*–the obvious fact that humans come in different models designed to perform different functions. Evidence is accumulating, however, from every aspect of human affairs proving that human beings come in enormously varied models and, indeed, as we understand the strategies of genetic intelligence, we can anticipate that the current human stock will radiate out to create innumberable new posthuman species and new singularities. It turns out that there are dozens of models of human females, some wired to perform traditional gender roles and some wired to perform wondrous new future roles. In some futures there will undoubtedly be successful gene-pool collectives made up of lesbians who cheerfully handle all the functions of a highly intelligent species without the inclusion of any males. A survey of botanical and animal species shows that Gaia has used every conceivable role, allure, wile, skill, ritual, invitation to assure that the sperm-egg intersection is varied, amusing, and highly specialized.

Temporal caste is another explosive idea, breathtaking in its possibilities. If each individual in hir development recapitulates the earlier stages of the species, then SHe has the opportunity of evolving personally into the future stages of the species. The shocking implication of sociobiology is that it is possible for humans to evolve to that point where they, we, become the conscious, deterministic frontier scouts, not only for our own species but for the Unified Life Design. When are you going to stop evolving? According to gloomy Darwin, you have neither the time nor the brains to effect a million-year slow-motion process. Today, however, as humanity moves to a position of active, optimistic self-determination—building mini-worlds in high orbit, reshuffling DNA, utilizing brain-change drugs to increase and diversify intelligence—we see that the power of temporal caste is almost unlimited. There is no reason why any of us should ever stop evolving, each current adult stage becoming the larval for the next, each of us becoming a conscious intelligent agent for the evolutionary process that we define and maintain.

From sociobiology we obtain the most awesome gift our species has yet received—we can start asking the simple but powerful navigational questions, where is evolution taking our species? The answer: we shall evolve, move in any direction, in any fashion, style, mode that we, led by the New Scientists, choose.

SUMMARY

The eight new sciences briefly discussed in this essay all involve a change in our attitude and posture towards the universe. Humans need no longer cringe as dumb, passive, docile, defensive losers in the cosmos. Enough of us have reached the stage of our own evolution where we are no longer satisfied by the authoritarian, pessimistic philosophies of the past.

The new quantum physics tells us that the universe will always be just as grand and glorious and explicable and manageable as our minds conceive.

The Gaia theory invites us to participate as pilot-navigator of the vessels in which the biological intelligence transports her seed.

The genetic engineers give our species directional control over the evolutionary process.

O'Neill and his high orbital designs show us how to build the ecological niches in which the next stages of our evolution will occur.

Heroic alchemists provide the chemicals for activating, dialing, and tuning our brains to fabricate the realities we wish to inhabit.

Roy Walford and the immunologists teach us that by inviting the enemy within, in manageable numbers, we can inoculate ourselves against diseases, both physiological, neurological and genetic.

Sociobiology urges us to examine the process of species evolution with the same dispassionate curiosity with which we examine less taboo-loaded issues and thus become engineers of our own future.

The nice thing about these Smart Ones and the new sciences they play with is this: they are open-minded, sexy, optimistic, courageous people. The future they offer us is one of increasing freedom, aesthetic responsibility, hope, and increasing intelligence.

NOTES

Aging   Ken Dychtwald

1. Joel Kurtzman and Phillip Gordon, *No More Dying* (Los Angeles: J. P. Tarcher, 1976), pp. 23, 24.

2. *Facts and Myths About Aging* (Washington, D.C.: National Council on Aging, 1977).

3. *Builder Magazine*, January 1980.

4. Austin Kiplinger and Arnold Barach, *Kiplinger Forecasts: The Exciting '80's* (Washington, D.C.: Kiplinger Washington Editors, 1979), p. 19.

5. Maggie Kuhn and Dieter Hessel, *Maggie Kuhn on Aging* (Philadelphia: Westminster Press, 1977), p. 16.

6. Robert Butler, *Why Survive: Being Old in America* (New York: Harper & Row, 1975), pp. 23, 24.

7. *Ibid.*, pp. 174–179.

8. For additional information related to this theme, see: Robert Butler, *Why Survive;* Ivan Illich, *Medical Nemesis* (New York: Pantheon, 1976); and Rick Carlson, *The End of Medicine* (New York: Wiley-Interscience, 1975).

9. Alex Comfort, *The Good Age* (New York: Crown Publishers, 1976).

10. Hans Selye, *The Stress of Life* (New York: McGraw Hill, 1956).

11. Leonard Hayflick, "Cell Biology of Aging," *Bioscience*, October 1975.

12. Albert Rosenfeld, *Prolongevity* (New York: Alfred A. Knopf, 1976).

13. Kurtzman and Gordon, *No More Dying.*

14. *Ibid.*

15. *Ibid.*

16. For a comprehensive description of this phenomenon, see Kenneth Pelletier, *Mind As Healer, Mind As Slayer* (New York: Delta, 1977).

17. Ken Dychtwald, *Bodymind* (New York: Jove Press, 1978).

18. Wilhelm Reich, *Selected Writings* (New York: Farrar, Strauss and Giroux, 1973).

19. A fine resource book on relationship between personality and disease is Pelletier, *Mind As Healer, Mind As Slayer.*

20. Kurtzman and Gordon, *No More Dying.*

21. Rick Carlson, *The End of Medicine* (New York: Wiley-Interscience, 1975); Ivan Illich, *Medical Nemesis* (New York: Pantheon, 1976); and Robert Mendelsohn, *Confessions of a Medical Heretic* (Chicago: Contemporary Books, 1980).

22. For further information on this theme, see: Richard Grossinger, *Planet Medicine* (New York: Anchor Books, 1979); Kenneth Pelletier, *Holistic Medicine* (New York: Delacorte, 1980); Charles Panati, *Breakthroughs: Astonishing Advances in Your Lifetime in Medicine, Science and Technology* (New York: Houghton Mifflin, 1980); and Arthur Hastings, James Fadiman, and James Gordon, eds., *Health For the Whole Person* (Boulder: Westview Press, 1980).

23. Saul Kent, *The Life Extension Revolution* (New York: William Morrow, 1980).

24. Kurtzman and Gordon, *No More Dying.*

25. For additional information related to this topic, see: Stephen Rosen, *Future Facts* (New York: Touchstone, 1976); Panati, *Breakthroughs: Astonishing Advances in Your Lifetime in Medicine, Science and Technology;* and Kent, *The Life Extension Revolution.*

26. Panati, *Breakthroughs: Astonishing Advances in Your Lifetime in Medicine, Science and Technology.*

27. *Ibid.*

28. *Ibid.*

29. *Ibid.*

30. Herbert Bailey, *GH3: Will It Keep You Young Longer?* (New York: Bantam, 1977).

31. Charles Gerras and the Staff of *Prevention Magazine*, *The Complete Book of Vitamins* (Emmaus, Pa.: Rodale Press, 1977).

32. For additional information on this theme, see: Kent, *The Life Extension Revolution* and Rosenfeld, *Prolongevity.*

Sexuality Lonnie Barbach

Barbach, Lonnie. *For Yourself: The Fulfillment of Female Sexuality*. New York: Doubleday, 1975.

———. *Women Discover Orgasm: A Therapist's Guide to a New Treatment Approach*. New York: Free Press, 1980.

——— and Linda Levine. *Shared Intimacies: Women's Sexual Experiences*. New York: Anchor/Doubleday, 1980.

Gelman, David, et al. "The Games Teenagers Play." *Newsweek*, September 1, 1980.

Haas, Aaron. *Teenage Sexuality: A Survey of Teenage Sexual Behavior*. New York: Macmillan, 1979.

Hodson, Philip. "Sex Therapy in 2079." World Congress of Sexology. Mexico City, December 1979.

Hunt, Morton. *Sexual Behavior in the 1970's*. New York: Playboy Press, 1974.

Leif, Harold. Personal communication.

National Abortion League "Twelve Abortion Facts." Washington, D.C., 20005, 1980.

U.S. Bureau of Census, *Current Population Reports*, Series P25, No. 870, January 1980.

Wolfe, Linda. "The Sexual Profile of That Cosmopolitan Girl." *Cosmopolitan*, September 1980.

World Almanac, The, and Book of Facts 1980. New York: Newspaper Enterprises Association Inc., 1979.

Zilbergeld, Bernie. *Male Sexuality*. Boston: Little, Brown and Co., 1978.

Healing Alberto Villoldo

1. In *Realms of Healing* by Stanley Krippner and Alberto Villoldo, Celestial Arts, 1976.

2. The best example of this principle are vaccinations, where a small dosage of a toxic substance such as smallpox is injected into the body, producing a slight adverse reaction, after which the body responds by generating its own antitoxins that prevent any occurrence of the disease.

3. In *Devils, Drugs, and Doctors* by Howard W. Haggard, M.D.

4. Although the treatment for smallpox had been known in the Far East for hundreds of years, and had been described in the Indian Vedas.

5. Dopamine is a brain neuro-transmitter; beta-endorphin is a morphine-like substance produced naturally in certain sites in the brain.

6. Lewis Thomas, *The Medusa and the Snail*.

7. In the United States alone there are already between 2 and 3 million plastic, ceramic, and metal parts implanted in patients every year.

The Body   *Michael Murphy*

1. Huxley, Julian. *Evolution: The Modern Synthesis*. New York: John Wiley, 1964. (Originally published 1942.)

2. Prehoda, Robert W. *Designing the Future: The Role of Technological Forecasting*. New York: Chilton, 1967, p. 230.

3. Lerner, I. Michael. *Heredity, Evolution and Society*. San Francisco: W. H. Freeman, 1968.

4. Prehoda, p. 236.

5. Murphy, Michael. *Jacob Atabet: A Speculative Fiction*. Millbrae, California: Celestial Arts, 1977.

6. Ryder, Henry W.; Carr, Harry J.; and Herget, Paul. "Future Performance: Footracing," *Scientific American*, June 1976, pp. 109–119.

7. Pollock, M. L. "Submaximal and Maximal Working Capacity of Elite Distance Runners, Cardiorespiratory Aspects," in Paul Milvy (ed.), *The Long Distance Runner: A Definitive Study*. New York: Urizen Books, 1977.

8. Pollock, Michael L.; Gettman, Larry R.; Jackson, Andrew; Ayres, John; Ward, Ann; and Linnerud, A. C. "Body Composition of Elite Class Distance Runners," in Paul Milvy (ed.), *The Long Distance Runner*, pp. 123–131.

9. Saltin, Bengt; Henriksson, Jan; Nygaard, Else; Anderson, Per; and Janssen, Eve. "Fiber Types and Metabolic Potentials of Skeletal Muscles in Sedentary Man and Endurance Runners," in Paul Milvy (ed)., *The Long Distance Runner*, pp. 320–343.

10. Fitts, Robert H. "The Effects of Exercise Training on the Development of Fatigue," in Paul Milvy (ed.), *The Long Distance Runner*, pp. 371–376.

11. "Runner's High—B–6?" *Track and Field News*, February 1979, p. 55.

12. "Runner's High—ATP?" *Track and Field News*, February 1979, p. 55.

13. Kidd, C. "Congenital Ichthyosiform Erythrodermia Treated by Hypnosis," *British Journal of Dermatology*, vol. 78, 1966, pp. 101–105.

14. Mason, A. "A Case of Congenital Ichthyosiform Erythrodermia of Brocq Treated by Hypnosis," *British Medical Journal*, vol. 2, 1952, pp. 422–423.

15. Schneck, Jerome, "Hypnotherapy of Ichthyosis," *Psychosomatics*, vol. 7, 1966, pp. 233–235.

16. Wink, C. "Congenital Ichthyosiform Erythrodermia Treated by Hypnosis: Report of Two Cases," *British Medical Journal*, vol. 2, 1961, pp. 741–743.

17. Esdaile, James. *Mesmerism in India*. New York: Arno Press, 1976. (Originally published 1846.)

18. Esdaile, James. *Natural and Mesmeric Clairvoyance*. New York: Arno Press, 1975. (Originally published 1852.)

19. Hilgard, Ernest R. and Josephine R. *Hypnosis in the Relief of Pain*. Los Altos, California: William Kaufmann, 1975.

20. Simonton, O. Carl; Matthews-Simonton, Stephanie; and Creighton, James. *Getting Well Again*. Los Angeles: J. P. Tarcher, 1978.

21. Simonton, O. Carl. "Management of the Emotional Aspects of Malignancy," Symposium of the State of Florida, Department of Health and Rehabilitative Service, June 1974.

22. Green, Elmer and Alyce. *Beyond Biofeedback*. New York: Dial Press, 1977.

23. Basmajian, John V. *Muscles Alive: Their Functions Revealed by Electromyography*. Baltimore: Williams and Wilkins, 1962.

24. Engel, Bernard T. "Visceral Control: Some Implications for Psychiatry," paper presented at the American Psychiatric Association Conference, Anaheim, California, 1975.

25. Luthe, Wolfgang (ed.). *Autogenic Therapy, Volume IV, Research and Theory*. New York: Grune and Stratton, 1970.

26. Luthe, Wolfgang (ed.). *Autogenic Therapy, Volume II, Medical Applications*. New York: Grune and Stratton, 1969.

27. Lewis, A. J. "Influence of Self-Suggestion on the Human Organism." Los Angeles: Garrett AiResearch Corp., 1976.

28. Lewis, A. J. "Psychic Self-Regulation," paper presented at the Fourth Annual Western Regional Association for Humanistic Psychology Conference, San Diego, California, 1977.

29. Roman, A. S. et al. (eds.). *Psychical Self-Regulation*, vols. I and II. Alma Ata, U.S.S.R., 1974.

30. Roman, A. S. et al. *Psychical Self-Regulation*. Alma Ata, U.S.S.R., 1974.

31. Schmidt, Helmut. "A PK Test with Electronic Equipment," *Journal of Parapsychology*, vol. 34 (Sept. 1970), pp. 175–181.

32. Schmidt, Helmut. "Quantum-Mechanical Random Number Generator," *Journal of Applied Physics*, vol. 41 (Feb. 1970), pp. 462–468.

33. Grad, Bernard. "A Telekinetic Effect on Plant Growth," *International Journal of Parapsychology*, vol. 3, 1961, p. 473.

34. Nash, C. B. and C. S. "The Effect of a Paranormally Conditioned Solution on Yeast Fermentation," *Journal of Parapsychology*, vol. 31, 1967, p. 314.

35. Watkins, Graham K. and Anita M. "Possible PK Influence on the Resuscitation of Anesthetized Mice," *Journal of Parapsychology*, vol. 35(4), December 1971, pp. 257–272.

36. Grad, Bernard; Cadoret, R. J.; and Paul, G. I. "The Influence of an Unorthodox Method of Treatment on Wound Healing in Mice," *International Journal of Parapsychology*, vol. 3, 1961, pp. 5–24.

37. Braud, William. "Allobiofeedback: Immediate Feedback for a Psychokinetic Influence Upon Another Person's Physiology," *Research in Parapsychology 1977*. Metuchen, New Jersey: Scarecrow Press, 1978.

Communities Carl R. Rogers

McGaw, W. H.; Rice, C. P.; and Rogers, C. R. *The Steel Shutter*. (Film). Center for Studies of the Person, La Jolla, California, 1973.
Rogers, C. R. *Carl Rogers on Personal Power*. New York: Delacorte Press, 1977. Chapter 8.
Slater, P. *The Pursuit of Loneliness*. Boston: Beacon Press, 1970.
Whyte, L. *The Universe of Experience*. New York: Harper & Row, 1974.

Work Willis Harman

1. John Maynard Keynes. *Essays in Persuasion*. London: 1931.

2. Louis Kelso and Mortimer Adler. *The Capitalist Manifesto*. New York: Random House, 1958, p. 7.

3. Christopher Lasch. *The Culture of Narcissism*. New York: W. W. Norton, 1978. As we are reminded by the theme of this book, there has been, particularly in the last decade and a half, increasing evidence of a still more profound shift in values in a portion of the population. The emergence of these "New-Age" values will be discussed later as we look toward the future.

4. Donald Michael. *Cybernation: The Silent Conquest*. Santa Barbara, Calif.: Center for the Study of Democratic Institutions, 1962.

5. Kenyon DeGreene. *Human Factors*, February 1975, pp. 58–61.

6. Daniel Bell. *The Coming of Post-Industrial Society*. New York: Basic Books, 1973.

7. Scott Burns. *The Household Economy*. Garden City, New York: Doubleday, 1975.

8. Robert Hutchins. *The Learning Society*. New York: Praeger, 1968.

9. Robert Heilbroner. *The Great Ascent*. New York: Harper & Row, 1963.

Leisure   Don Mankin

1. Kaplan, M. *Leisure: Theory and Policy* (New York: John Wiley, 1975).

2. *Ibid.*, p. 10.

3. Using the expression "instrumental" to describe leisure activities in a predominately leisure society is taking liberties with Kaplan's description of the instrumental interpretation ("re-creation for subsequent productive effort") since there would not be an appropriate non-leisure activity (i.e., work) for leisure to serve.

4. For example, see J. M. Kreps and J. L. Spengler, "The Leisure Component of Economic Growth" in H. R. Bowen and G. L. Mangum, eds., *Automation and Economic Progress* (Englewood Cliffs, N.J.: Prentice-Hall, 1966), and G. H. Moore and J. N. Hedges, "Trends in Labor and Leisure," *Monthly Labor Review*, 1971, 94(2), pp. 3–11.

5. This rather simplistic explanation does not take into consideration the fact that money can buy time (e.g., hiring someone to perform household chores you would otherwise have to perform yourself). On the other hand, economist Stefan Linder in his book, *The Harried Leisure Class* (New York: Columbia Univ. Press, 1970), argues that the purchase and consumption of leisure-related goals and services can result in an actual decrease in leisure time because of the time spent in comparative shopping and in maintaining and repairing the products purchased.

6. Of course, wandering through the streets of Paris, London, New York, or San Francisco is not cheap if someone has to travel long distances to get there. The point is that most large cities offer the same inexpensive attractions to some degree (parks, museums, cultural, and architectural diversity); in any case, the appropriate comparison is the costs of walking, watching, and window shopping relative to guided tours, nightclubs, and expensive souvenirs and products.

7. Roszak, T. "Forbidden Games." In *Technology and Human Values* (Santa Barbara, Calif.: Center for the Study of Democratic Institutions. 1966) pp. 26–27.

NOTES

8. Sutton-Smith, B. "Play as a Transformational Set." In *Leisure Today: Research and Thought About Children's Play* (Washington, DC: American Association for Health, Physical Education, and Recreation, 1972), p. 7.

9. "Compunications" is an expression that is being increasingly used to denote combined computer and communications systems.

10. For example, see M. Meisner, "The Long Arm of the Job: A Study of Work and Leisure," *Industrial Relations*, 1971, *10*, pp. 239–260 and D. M. Rousseau, "Relationship of Work to Nonwork," *Journal of Applied Psychology*, 1978, *63*, pp. 513–517.

Health Care   Rick Carlson

1. See particularly Thomas McKeown, *The Role of Medicine* (London: Nuffield Provincial Trust, 1978).

2. Prior to the turn of the century, homeopathic medicine was nearly as pervasive as allopathic medicine. For a variety of reasons, few of them therapeutic in nature, allopathic medicine gradually gained control and with the impetus of the Flexner report in 1910 had the effect of driving homeopathic medicine underground. This report, funded by the Carnegie Foundation for the Advancement of Teaching in coordination with the AMA gave the struggling AMA a basis for refusing licenses to the graduates of low-ranking institutions. Although initially designed as a temporary survey, the Flexner report became the rigid basis on which medical education, licensing, and practice was organized. Clearly one of the functions of this report was to sweep underground approaches to health care that were either in competition with or contradictory to the allopathic approach.

3. Frank Jerome, *Persuasion and Healing* (2nd ed.) (New York: Schocken Books, 1974).

4. George Leonard, *The Transformation* (Los Angeles: J. P. Tarcher, 1981).

5. Jonas Salk, *The Survival of the Wisest* (New York: Harper & Row, 1973); Theodore Roszak, *Person Planet: The Creative Disintegration of Industrial Society* (New York: Doubleday, 1978). Donella and D. L. Meadows, *The Limits to Growth* (University Books, 1974) provided one of the first arguments for limited growth. More recently, Lester Brown's *The Twenty-Ninth Day* (Norton, 1970) updated the limits-to-growth argument in an excellent and comprehensive treatment of limits, arguments, and issues.

6. There is also a literature on the "social" limits to growth which focuses on the limits to technological development by examining those limits that have been imposed on technological development, or are likely to be imposed, for social reasons rather than, or in addition to, economic or technological ones. A good example of this literature is Fred Hirsch's *The Social Limits to Growth* (Cambridge, Mass.: Harvard University Press, 1976).

7. The recent works that best apply the "limits" rationale to medicine are Ivan Illich's *Medical Nemesis* (Pantheon, 1976), R. J. Carlson's *The End of Medicine* (John Wiley, 1975), and Victor Fuchs's *Who Shall Live?* (Basic Books, 1975).

INDEX

Abortion, 34, 64, 122
ACTH/MSH, 20
Acupuncture, 62
Adaptation, 74
Adolescents, sexual activity of, 29–30
Aging, 5–23, 72. *See also* Elderly
  of American population, 8–9
  aspects of, 5–8
  attitudes toward, 9, 10–11
  and drugs, 19–20
  and immune system, 293
  physical, 7–8, 16, 18
  research on, 12, 13, 293
  and sex, 37
  social, 6–7, 8
  and social changes, 9
  theories of, 13–16
American Association for the
  Advancement of Science, 294
American Association of Retired
  Persons, 9
American Home Economics
  Association, 122
American Psychological Association, 99
Amygdala, function of, 93, 94
Androgenesis, 79
Anesthetic, hypnosis as an, 82
"Appropriate technology,"
  181–183, 230
Aristotle, 207
Art, 241–248
  future of, 246–248

and perception, 166–167
and religion, 248
and science, 247
types of, 244
Aslan, Ana, 20
Athletic training, and bodily changes,
  80, 81, 86, 87
Attitudes
  toward aging, 9, 10–11
  role of, in illness, 68
  toward sexual behavior, 25–29
  for survival, 49–52
Autogenics, 83–84, 162
Autoimmune system, self-regulation
  of, 69

Bannister, Roger, 81
Basal ganglia, function of, 93–94
Basmajian, John, 83–84
Behavior, organization of, 95–99
Behaviorism, 95, 96
Being, 55, 136–138, 139
Bell, Eugene, 69
Bioengineering, 18–19. *See also*
  Genetic engineering
Biofeedback, 40, 83–84, 162, 232
Biological clocks, 20, 87
Biological information transfer, 60, 61
Biological intelligence. *See*
  Intelligence: biological
Biological-Modulation Units, 70
Biological Self-Regulation Project, 69

309

Biology, revolution in, 69–72
Birth control, 30, 34, 122
Bisexuality, 38, 39
Bjorksten, John, 14
Bodily capacities, enhanced,
    78–88, 162
  and athletic training, 81, 86
  future, 275
  and hypnosis, 82
  and placebo effect, 81–82
  self-directed, 77, 80, 83–84
  and suggestion, 82
Bodily changes, 77, 80–88
Body, human, of the future, 85–88
Bohm, David, 102
Bohr, Niels, 286
Bonhoeffer, Dietrich, 261, 262
Boredom, 194–203, 204
Boys from Brazil, The, 279
Brain
  and computers, 73
  and conscious states, 95
  and cyborg engineering, 78
  and drugs, 92–93, 288–290
  hemispheres, 166–168 (*see also* Left
      brain; Right brain)
  processing of wave lengths by,
      100–102
  and survival of the species, 47, 75
  and the universe, 277
Brain function, 91–95, 101
  areas of, 161, 162
  model of, 100–103
  revision of theories of, 91, 92, 94, 95
Brain-Mind Bulletin, 284–285
Brand, Stewart, 283
Brothers Karamozov (Dostoevsky), 67
Butler, Robert, 11, 17

Cafeteria Credit Card Plan, 217–218
Campbell, Fergus, 100
Cancer, 67, 69, 70–71, 82–83
Cannon, Walter, 94–95
Capra, Fritjof, 287
Carlson, Rick, 17
Catastrophe, 40, 46, 47

Center for the Study of Democratic
    Institutions, 215
Central nervous system, 91, 96, 97.
    See also Brain
Chakrubarty, J. R., 282, 291–292, 298
Childbearing, the life expectancy, 73
Childbirth in Middle Ages, 64–65
Children, and family structure, 36–37
Chronological aging, 5, 6
Clarke, Arthur, 78
Cloning, 18, 73, 292
Clynes, Manfred, 78
Co-Evolution Quarterly, 283, 284
Cognitive psychology, 99
Communities, person-centered,
    135–146
  and "appropriate technology,"
      182–183
  decision-making in, 141
  formation of, 135–136
  group processes in, 138–142
  implications for future, 144–146
  personal experiences in, 138
  pilot models for, 146
  relationships in, 142–143
  spiritual aspect of, 141–142
  unresolved problems of, 144
Community, sense of, 139
Computers
  and the brain, 73
  as models for neurophysiological
      processes, 99
  and servomechanisms, 99
  and sexual activities, 39–40
  and survival, 69–70
Comte, Auguste, 252
Conceptualization, and perception,
    163–164
Consciousness. *See also* Evolution,
    conscious; Evolutionary
    consciousness
  collective human, 269
  and cyborg engineering, 79
  quantum mechanical theory of, 60
Consciousness, states of, 80
  and biological processes, 16

and brain function, 95
chemical control of, 92–95
and healing, 60
and phenomena, 244
range of, 162
research in, 288–290
Consumers
and health care, 235
and leisure activities, 193–194, 204
Contraception, 30, 34, 122
Copernicus, 279
Corporations, health promotion
programs of, 236
Crisis mentality, 157–158
Crosslinkage theory of aging, 14
Cryogenics, 72
Culture of Narcissism, The, (Lasch),
173, 204
Cybernation: The Silent Conquest
(Michael)
Cybernetics, 70, 78
Cybernetic self-extension, 274
Cyborg engineering, 73, 77, 78–79

Dance, 60, 161
Death, 72, 272, 273
and birthdays, 232
causes of, 12
De Broglie, Lewis, 286
Decision-making in person-centered
communities, 141
De Greene, Kenyon, 175–176
Democracy. *See* Government:
consensual
Designing the Future (Prehoda), 78
Devolutionary processes, 54
Dirac, Paul, 286
Disease(s)
agents of, 227, 228
of the elderly, 12, 16
from extraplanetary viruses, 73
hospital generated, 72
iatrogenic, 72
infectious, 226
information-based treatment of,
70–71

lifestyle related, 12, 16, 68
and the mind, 17
and personality structure, 60
and religion, 64
and survival of the species, 62
Divorce, 31, 32, 36
DNA, 70, 74, 273
alteration of, 291–292
biological clock in, 20, 21
error catastrophe theory of aging,
13–14
and genetic engineering, 20–21
Dopamine, 69, 94
Dostoevsky, Fyodor, *The Brothers
Karamozov*, 67
Drug-related therapies, disillusion
with, 67, 69
Drugs
anti-aging, 19, 20
psychotropic, 92–93, 282, 288–290
in Renaissance, 65–66
and sex, 39
Durkheim, Karlfried von, *The Way of
Transformation*, 132
Dychtwald, Ken, 15

Ecological ethic, 182, 185
Economy, 171–186 *passim*, 235
Edison, Thomas, 88
Education, 151–168
and aging population, 9
attempts to revise, 158–160
of brain hemispheres, 166–168
corporation interest in, 236
and employment, 177
functions of, 178, 179
holistic integral, 159
person-centered, 145, 182–183
planning of, 157–158
Ehricke, Krafft, 271
Einstein, Albert, 160, 284, 286
Elderly. *See also* Aging
attitudes toward, 10–11
diseases of, 12, 16
health care of, 17–20
rehabilitation of, 162

Electoral College, 214
Ellis, Havelock, *Studies in the Psychology of Sex*, 25
Emotional aging, 6
Employment. *See* Work; *see also* Unemployment
Endorphins, beta-, 290
Energetic techniques, 40
Energy
  bodily, 88
  and healing, 17–18, 67
  and leisure activities, 191
  sexual, 40
Enhancement income maintenance, 181
Enkaphalins, 20, 94
Ennui, 194–203, 204
Entropy, 284
Epidemiology, 67
Equal Rights Amendment (ERA), 28
Error catastrophe (DNA) theory of aging, 13–14
Esdaile, James, 82
Essays in Persuasion (Keynes), 171
Ethical problems, 73, 80
Eugenic breeding, 77, 79, 80
Evolution, 51, 280
Evolution, conscious, 53–54, 266, 268–273, 287, 297–298
Evolution, metabiological, 53–56
Evolutionary action, 270
Evolutionary consciousness, 270, 283, 287
  of Gaia, 268, 269–272
Evolutionary perspective, 265–266
Extinction. *See* Survival
Extraterrestrial intelligence, 273–274

Families
  children in, 36, 37
  defined, 122
  extended, 36–37, 121, 122
  nuclear, 121, 122
  size of, 73
Family structure, 35–37
  and divorce, 31

Females. *See* Women
Ferguson, Marilyn, 284–285
Films
  scientists in, 279
  and sexual activities, 39
Finch, Caleb, 15
Flexner report, 228
Foundation for Mind Research, 162
Frank, Jerome, *Persuasion and Healing*, 229
Frankenstein myth, 279
Frankl, Viktor, 60
Free radical theory of aging, 14
Freud, Sigmund, 26, 254, 259–260
  Future of an Illusion, 254
Fruit flies, population growth of, 45–46, 47, 48–50
Fuller, R. Buckminster, 12–13

Gaia (planetary system), 265, 267–271, 272–273, 282
Gaia Hypothesis (Lovelock and Epton), 268
Gaia theory, 268, 283–284, 298
Galanter, Eugene, 99
  Plans and the Structure of Behavior, 95
Games versus play, 192
Gandhi, Mohandas Karamchand (Mahatma), 88
Gardner, Howard, 287
Genetic engineering, 20, 74–75, 79–80, 273, 291–292, 298
Genetic predestination, 75
Gerontological research, 12, 13, 293
Gerovital (GH3), 20
Getting Well Again (Simonton and Matthews-Simonton), 232
Goodman, Nelson, 282, 285–287
Gordon, Phillip, *No More Dying*, 7–8
Government
  consensual, 208–210, 213, 214, 220–222
  spending, 215–217
  types of, 207
  units, size of, 214–215

Gray Panthers, 9
Greenhouse effect, 75
Growth, values for, 124–129

Haggard, H. W., 66
Harman, Denham, 14
Hayflick, Leonard, 13
Healing
    through hypnosis, 82
    information-based, 70–71
    mind-assisted, 17, 82–83
    new issues in, 68
    and quantum mechanical theory of
        consciousness, 60–61, 68
    rituals, 60
    self-, 68, 69, 71, 75, 82–83, 231–232
Health
    of elderly, 11–12, 16
    and environmental pollutants, 16
    major problems of, 226–227
Health care. *See also* Healing;
    Medicine
    and aging population, 9, 17, 20
    awareness of, 67
    holistic approach to, 230–231
    increasing cost of, 67–68
    preventative, 277
    programs, 233
    traditional approach to, 225
Health care systems
    and age-related disease, 12
    alternative, 17
    changes in, 228–231, 234, 236–238
    politics of, 228–230
Health centers, 72, 237
Health promotion, 67, 233–236
Heilbroner, Robert, 183
Heisenberg, Werner, 68, 244, 286
Helmholtz, Herman, 100
Henson, Caroline, 288
Heppenheimer, Thomas, 288
Herbs in healing, 59, 60, 61
Heterarchical thinking, 156
Hierarchical thinking, 156
Hippocampus, function of, 94
Hippocrates, 63, 65

Hobbes, Thomas, 208
Hoffman, Albert, 290
Holism and Evolution (Smuts),
    230–231
Holistic health movement, 67–68
Holistic organization of perception,
    101–103
Holistic view
    of education, 159
    of medical care, 230–231
    vs. reductionism, 230–231
    of science, 91
    trend toward, 91–92
    of work and leisure, 205
Holograms
    and holism, 102
    and organization of experience,
        99–103
Holographic theory, 100–103
Homeostasis, 20, 86
    and aging, 14–15
    and the hypothalamus, 94–95
Homosexuality, 38, 39
Hospitals, 63–64, 72, 232–233,
    236–237, 247
Hubbard, Barbara Marx, 288
Hull, Clark L., 95
Human potential, 155–156,
    161–162, 275
Human species
    future of, 269, 275
    and structural caste, 297
    and temporal caste, 297
Hunt, Morton, 33, 39
Huxley, Julian, 74
Hypnosis, 60, 82
Hypothalamus, and homeostasis,
    94–95
    role of, in aging, 15

Illness, 59, 60, 67, 226, 234
Illich, Ivan, 17
Immunologic theory of aging, 15,
    20, 293
Income distribution, 178, 179,
    180–181, 182

Individual, concern for, 43
Industrialization, 172–173, 177, 179, 182–184
Industrial Revolution, scientists during, 280
Information, holographic storage of, 101
Information-processing system, universe as, 277
Information theory, 70
Intelligence
  and aging, 6
  biological, 283-284, 296
  and education, 159
  of scientists, 282
  of the species, 296–297 (*see also* Wisdom: collective)
  and the universe, 277
  and vincamine, 20
Isolation, sense of, 60

James, William, 164
Jastrow, Robert, 274
Johnson, Virginia E., 26
Josephson, Brian, 7
Jung, Carl Gustaf, 254, 259

Keeton, Kathy, 288
Keller, Helen, 152–154, 160
Kennedy, Ian, 282, 291, 298
Kettering Foundation, 158
Keynes, John Maynard, 171, 173, 178, 186
Kinesthetic sense, 165
King's Chapel, Boston, congregation, 253, 259
Kinsey, Alfred C., 26
Kline, Nathan, 78
Knowing, modes of, 161
Knowledge. *See also* Wisdom
  forms of, 241–244
  integrated view of, 241–242, 246
  sensory, 163–165, 184
  and survival, 75
Krafft-Ebbing, Richard von, *Psychopathia Sexualis*, 25

Kuhn, Thomas, *Structure of Scientific Revolutions*, 91
Kurtzman, Joel, *No More Dying*, 7–8

Lasch, Christopher, 173 *The Culture of Narcissism*, 204
Left brain, 166–168, 184
Leibniz, Gottfried von, 102, 103
Leif, Harold, 40
Leisure, 189–205
  and aging population, 9
  and boredom, 194–203
  and consumption, 173, 193
  functions of, 190–191
  increasing importance of, 189
  meaning of, 190
  and work, 190, 205
Lemmings, population growth of, 46
Lenin, Nikolai, 252, 257
Leonard, George, 229
L –5 News, 288
L–5 Society, 288
Life, development of, 284–285
Life expectancy
  relation to birthdays, 232
  and childbearing, 73
  extension of, 10, 12, 16–22, 67, 72, 79, 293
life force, 63
life style
  and aging of the population, 10, 11
  and "appropriate technology," 182
  and cellular aging, 13
  and disease, 16, 68
  and drugs, 289
  and health, 22
  and leisure, scenario, 194–203
  and values, 124
  and work, 175
Lindsley, Donald, 95
Linear analytic thought, 156. *See also* Left brain
Locke, John, 208
Long, Huey, 222
Longevity. *See* Life expectancy
Lorenz, Konrad, 295

Lovelock, John, 283
Lucas, Arel, 288

McFaddins, Cyra, *The Serial*, 204
MacLean, Paul, 95
Magoun, Horace, 95
Males. See *Men*
Marais, Andre, 294–295
Margulis, Lynn, 282, 283–284
Marriage
  changing attitudes in, 31–32, 35–36
Marx, Karl, 252, 257–258
Maslow, Abraham, 185
Masters, William Howell, 26
Matthews-Simonton, 82–83
  Getting Well Again, 232
Mead, Margaret, early education of,
  164–165, 167
Meaning, sense of, 60
Media
  and aging population, 9
  influence of, 278–279
Medical care. *See* Healing; Health
  care; Medicine
Medical self-care, 67, 72, 237
Medicatrix naturae (natural life
  force), 63
Medicine. *See also* Healing;
  Health care
  allopathic, 17, 228, 240
  alternative systems of, 17
  chemical, 66–67
  diagnostic, 66–67
  energy, 17–18
  herbal, 59
  Hippocratic, 63, 65
  history of, 59–66, 225–226, 228
  language of, effect of war on, 66
  magical, 62, 63
  in Middle Ages, 64–65
  primitive, 59–62
  religious, 62–63, 64
  in Renaissance, 65–66
  scientific method in, 225, 228
  space, 69
  and technology, 230

traditional, 17, 67, 71 (*see also*
  Medicine: allopathic)
Meditation, 203
Men
  roles of, 33
  sexual attitudes and behavior of,
    26–28
Mendelsohn, Robert, 17
Mental aging, 6
Michael, Donald, *Cybernation: The
  Silent Conquest*, 175
Miller, George, 99
  *Plans and the Structure of
    Behavior*, 95
Miller, Neal E., 96
Mind, influence of
  on aging, 15–16
  on healing, 17, 69
Mineral supplements, 20
Minorities, rights of, 212
Modernization trend, 183–185
Monadic order, 102, 103
Monogamy, serial, 35
Monotheism, 286
Motivation for work, 185–186
Mumford, Lewis, 182
Music, 161
Mutations, and survival of the species,
  74–75

National Institutes of Health, 233–234
Natural resources, and leisure
  activities, 191
Natural selection, 47, 77
Needs, personal, in person-centered
  communities, 139
Neurotransmitter theory of aging,
  14–15
No More Dying (Kurtzman and
  Gordon), 7–8

Ohm, Georg, 100
Omni, 288
O'Neill, Gerard, 271, 282, 287, 298
Organs
  artificial, 77, 78

Organs *(continued)*
  cloning of, 72–73
  laboratory growth of, 18, 69
  replacement of, 18–19, 72, 73
Orgel, Leslie, 13–14

Pare, Ambrose, 65
Parenthood rights, 73
Parents, single, 35
Parthenogenesis, 79
Perception
  brain in, 101
  and conceptualization, 163–164
  future changes in, 85–86
  holistic organization of, 101–103
  and learning, 163–167
  model of, 100–103
  of work role, 184
Peer pressure, and healing, 60, 61
Persuasion and Healing (Frank), 229
philosophes, French, 251–252, 255
Philosophy, and science, 244, 247, 287
Physicists, 101–102, 286–287
Physics
  and healing, 60–61, 68
  and philosophy, 287
Physical aging, 7–8
Physiological processes, self-regulation
  of, 69
Placebo effect, 60, 61, 67, 81–82,
  231–232
Planck, Max, 286
Planetary stewardship, 266
Planetary system, 265, 267–271,
  272–273, 282. *See also*
  Gaia theory
Plans and the Structure of Behavior,
  95, 99
Play, 192–193
Pleasure, 88
Political process, alienation from, 213
Political theory, 207–208
Political violence, 209
Politics, 207–222
  corruption in, 210–211
  defined, 207

  in history, 207–208
Polls, public opinion, 122–123,
  124, 212
Pollutants, and crosslinkage theory
  of aging, 14
Population, aging of, 22–23
Population growth, 45–53
  and evolution, 51
  patterns of, 45–47
  and periodic catastrophe, 46
  and quality of life, 45
  regulating mechanisms of, 45–46,
  48–50
  as a threat to the species, 43
Powerlessness, sense of, 60
Prehoda, Robert, *Designing the
  Future,* 78
Pribram, Karl, 99
  *Plans and the Structure of
  Behavior,* 95
Prigogine, Ilya, 282, 284–285
Primitive medicine, 59–62
Prolongevity. *See* Life expectancy:
  extension of
Promethius myth, 279
Prosthetic devices, 18–19, 72, 73, 74,
  78–79
Protection Values, 124–129
Psychical self-regulation (PSR), 84
Psychogenic theory of aging, 15–16
Psychokinesis, 84–85
Psychology, cognitive, 99
Psychology Today, 287
Psychopathia Sexualis (Krafft-
  Ebbing), 25
Psycho-pharmacology, 92–93, 282,
  288–290
Public health care, 73, 225, 227, 234
Purpose, sense of, 44, 55, 59

Quality of life, 43, 44
  attitudes and values required for,
  49–52, 129
  deterioration of, 67
  factors affecting, 47
  and population growth, 45

Quantum mechanical theory of
consciousness, and healing,
60–61, 68

Rama, Swami, 86
Ramakrishna, Sri, 86
Recombinant DNA. *See* DNA
Reductionist thinking, 230–231
Reflex arc, 96–98
Reich, Wilhelm, 15–16, 26, 40
Relationships, personal, 129, 130–132,
142–143
Religion, 242, 251–262
Renaissance
art in, 243
medicine in, 65–66
Reproduction, sexual, 34–35
Reticular formation, 95
Retirement, 176
Right brain, 166–168, 184, 293
Rilke, Rainer Maria, 129
Robson, John, 100
Roles
and leisure activities, 189
of men, 27–28, 33
sexual, 26–28, 33
of women, 26–27, 33, 122–123
social, 178
work, 181, 184, 204
Romen, A. S., 69, 84
Rostand, Jean, 79
Roszak, Theodore, 229
Running speed, improvements in, 81

Sakharov, Andrei, 279
Salk, Jonas, 229
Schmidt, Helmut, 84–85
Schumacher, E. F., *Small is
Beautiful*, 230
Science
and art, 247
as a form of knowledge, 241,
243–244
and philosophy, 244, 247, 287
Scientific method, and medicine, 225

Scientists
as heroes, 277–280
during industrial revolution, 280
media image of, 278–279
transition period for, 280–281
Selective eugenic breeding, 77, 79, 80
Self, sense of, 143. *See also* Being
Self-care, medical, 67, 72, 237
Self-development, and
employment, 178
Self-expression, 123
Self-healing, 68, 69, 71, 75, 82–83,
231–232
Self-knowledge, 163, 191, 248
Self-organizing dissipative structure
theory, 282, 284–285
Self-realization, 185–186
in art, 247
and leisure, 190, 192
Self-regulation, 50, 56, 69, 86–87, 232
psychical (PSR), 84
and survival, 69
Self-trust, 123
Selye, Hans, 13
Sensory knowledge, 163–165, 184
Serebrovsky, A. S., 79
Serial, The (McFaddin), 204
Servomechanisms, 97–99
Sex
and computers, 40
and consciousness movement, 40
Sexual attitudes/activities
of adolescents, 29, 30
of females, 26–27, 28, 29–30
of males, 26–28
in space, 40
trends in, 38–40
Sex roles, 26–28, 32, 33, 34, 37
Sex therapy, 26, 31
Sexual dysfunctions, 26, 30, 31
Sexual equality, 28–29
Sexual relationships, 31–40
Shamans, healing influence of,
59–60, 61–62
Shanidar, Iraq, burial cave, 59
Shelley, Mary Wollstonecraft, 279

Sherrington, Charles, 95, 96–97
Simonton, Carl, 82–83
   Getting Well Again, 232
Sinex, F. Marott, 14
Small is Beautiful
   (Schumacher), 230
Smuts, Jan, *Holism and Evolution*,
   230–231
Social aging, 6–7, 8
Social changes, and aging, 9
Sociobiology, 282, 294–298
Sociobiology (Wilson), 295
Sorcerer's Apprentice, 157
Space medicine, 69
Space migration, 271, 272, 273–274,
   287–288
Spence, Kenneth W., 95
Spiritual aging, 5–6
SRI International, 124
Stevenson, S. S., 96
Stress-related illness, 67, 226, 234
Stress theory of aging, 13
Structural caste, 297
Structure of Scientific Revolutions
   (Kuhn), 91
Studies in the Psychology of Sex
   (Ellis), 25
Subsistence income maintenance, 181
Suggestion, and bodily capacity, 82
Sullivan, Anne, 152
Supernatural, shaman as a mediator
   with, 59–60
Superovulation, 79
Surgery, and hypnosis, 82
Survival
   attitudes and values required for,
      49–52
   and computers, 70
   and human judgment, 50–56, 70
   of the individual, 62, 74, 77
   and natural selection, 47
   and self-regulation, 69
   of the species, 55, 62, 74–75
   synergistic cooperation for, 271–272
   of the wisest, 55–56
Sweden, marriage in, 35

Synergy, 270, 271–272
Synesthesia, 165
Szent-Gyorgyi, Albert, 68

Taxation, 215–218
   Cafeteria Credit Card Plan, 217–218
   five percent surcharge, 216–217
Technological development, 175, 182,
   191, 203, 230
   impact on employment, 175–
      176, 235
   in genetics, 77–79
   in government, 219, 220–222
   in health care, 73, 74–75
   and leisure, 203
   reactions to, 289
   in space, 271, 274
Teilhard de Chardin, Pierre, 261–262
Temporal caste, 297
Testosterone levels, 40
Theater, in healing, 60
Thomas, Lewis, 71–72
Tinbergen, Nico, 295
TOTE servomechanism, 96–99
Transfer payments, 180–181
Tugwell, Rexford Guy, 215

Uncertainty principle, 68, 244
Unconscious
   control of biological processes by,
      15–16
   shaman's communication with,
      60, 61
Unemployment, 174–176
United States Declaration of
   Independence, 208
Universal impregnation, 266
Universal Town Meeting, 221–222

Vaik, Peter, 288
Value judgments
   criteria for making, 140–141
Values, 185–186
   balancing, 54–55
   changing, 124, 126, 129
   conflicting, 142

for growth, 124–129
humanistic, 229
and life styles, 124
materialistic, 229
and modernization trend, 183–184
new versus traditional, 123–129
for quality of life, 49–52
for self-protection, 124–129
sources of, 140
for survival, 49–52, 55
Vasopressin, 19–20
Vincamine, 20
Violence, political, 209
Viruses, 73, 292
Visualization, 83, 203
Vitamins, 20
Voltaire, 251
Voting, 218–222

Wages, and sexual equality, 28
Walford, Roy, 15, 282, 293–294, 298
Walker, Evan Harris, 61
Wave lengths, brain processing of,
    100–102
Way of Transformation, The
    (Durkheim), 132
Weapon ointment, 66
Wellness, 67, 233–236
Wheeler, J. A., 287
White House Commission on the
    Family, 122

Wigner, Eugene, 287
Wilson, Edward, 294–298
Wisdom. *See also* Knowledge
    collective, 138, 142, 213
    as fitness for survival, 52–56
    and Gaia theory, 268, 267
    for genetic engineering, 80
Wolfe, Linda, 33
Women
    roles of, 33, 122–123
    sexual attitudes and behavior of,
        26–27
Women's movement, and marriage, 32
Work, 171–186
    and aging population, 9
    functions of, 171, 172, 173, 177–180
    and health services, 235
    hours of, 191
    and leisure, 190
    meaningfulness of, 172, 177, 180,
        185–186, 205
World Health Organization, 67
Wynder, Ernest L., 17

Yogis, 86, 87, 88
Youth, prolongation of, 7–8, 12, 13

Zane, Frank, 86
Zukav, Gary, 287